Mapping the Megalopolis

Mapping the Megalopolis

Order and Disorder in Mexico City

Edited by
Glen David Kuecker and Alejandro Puga

LEXINGTON BOOKS
Lanham • Boulder • New York • London

Published by Lexington Books
An imprint of The Rowman & Littlefield Publishing Group, Inc.
4501 Forbes Boulevard, Suite 200, Lanham, Maryland 20706
www.rowman.com

Unit A, Whitacre Mews, 26-34 Stannary Street, London SE11 4AB

British Library Cataloguing in Publication Information Available

Library of Congress Cataloging-in-Publication Data

Names: Kuecker, Glen David, editor. | Puga, Alejandro, editor.
Title: Mapping the megalopolis : order and disorder in Mexico City / edited
  by Glen David Kuecker and Alejandro Puga.
Description: Lanham : Lexington Books, 2018. | Includes bibliographical
  references and index.
Identifiers: LCCN 2017044496 | ISBN 9781498559782 (cloth : alk. paper)
Subjects: LCSH: Mexico City (Mexico)
Classification: LCC F1386 .M34 2018 | DDC 972/.53—dc23
LC record available at https://lccn.loc.gov/2017044496

Printed in the United States of America

Contents

Introduction

Mapping the Megalopolis

Glen David Kuecker and Alejandro Puga

TWO PROFESSORS WALK A GREAT CITY

This collection of essays came into formation one fine Saturday afternoon in Mexico City. It was in 2014 when Alejandro Puga was in the city working on his sabbatical project, variations of the *flâneur* in *el Defe*, a term derived from *Distrito Federal* or Federal District, the formal name of Mexico City that became renamed as CDMX, the Spanish abbreviation for *Ciudad de México*, in January 2016. Glen Kuecker found a quick airfare and headed to *la capital*, yet another avatar of this perplexing space, for a weekend of absorbing the inevitable and welcomed contrasts that the city has to offer any professor laboring at a small liberal arts college in Indiana. Our main agenda was to have a deep conversation about the city we research and teach, something we were unable to do during the semester at DePauw University. We decided that the best way to have the conversation was in the style of Walter Benjamin's *flâneur*, the wandering urban explorer of nineteenth-century Paris. We set out one morning to walk the city. We took a particularly bourgeois, if not snobbishly elite route, from Condesa to *Nuevo Polanco*, ending at the *Plaza Carso*, the city's most recent attempt at pitching itself as world city. Along the way we talked, and the conversation was enriched with requisite stops at cafes and *taquerías*. Only knowing where we were going in the broadest sense of conversation and urban navigating, we got lost in talk and the city several times. But, the exercise of being lost was part of the endeavor, a key to the logic of the conversation. That logic aimed to bring together the perspective of the literary studies and history professor, to have the conversation that does not happen on campus, despite the purported interdisciplinary dialogues available a liberal arts college. The fusion of intellectual projects—Puga an expert on the Mexico City novel and Kuecker an expert on Porfirian Mexico and twenty-first century urbanism—and their fusion with the emergent property of the *flâneur* exploring the city generated the seeds for our grant project, "Mapping the Megalopolis."

Serendipitously, Puga and Kuecker's Mexico City walk corresponded with the Andrew W. Mellon Foundation's decision to undertake a second round of significant faculty development funding for the institutions of the Great Lakes Colleges Association (GLCA), which became the Expanding Collaboration Initiative. The grant's main objective is to provide funding for liberal arts faculty to undertake collaborative research. As the call for proposals states, the grant "seeks to foster and sustain communities of practice that extend beyond the perimeters of individual campuses and enhance the vitality of the liberal arts." Puga and Kuecker knew the grant offered the opportunity to pursue the ideas stirred up by their Saturday walk in the megalopolis. We put forward a proposal and were awarded funding for a project entitled "Mapping the Megalopolis: Making an Urban Atlas of Mexico City."

The grant began a wonderful collaboration involving ten faculty members from seven schools. With good fortune we ended up with an even number of faculty from literary studies and the social sciences. From literary studies we have Alejandro Puga from DePauw University, Patty Tovar and Patrick O'Connor from Oberlin College, Marta Sierra from Kenyon, Dan Rogers from Wabash College, and María Claudia André from Hope College. From the social sciences, we have Glen Kuecker (History) from DePauw University, Shannan Mattiace from Allegheny College (Political Science), Jennifer Johnson from Kenyon College (Sociology), Karen Velasquez from University of Dayton (Anthropology), and Charlotte Blair from American University (Anthropology). Our diverse group boasted a wide range of talent, experience, and knowledge. Some had collaborated before and knew each other's work well, while others were entirely new to this type of teamwork. We are united in our intellectual love for Mexico City, one inspired by the strange attraction of wanting to understand a place that defies capacity to ever truly know it.

Our work together involved a robust combination of planning meetings, extensive online conversations, the development of a project webpage (http://gkuecker.wixsite.com/mappingmegalopolis), a scaling of the ArcGIS Story Maps and Google Maps learning curve, weeks of field research in Mexico City, mentoring student research collaborators, processing the research, creating maps, drafting essays, holding mini-cluster meetings, a mapping workshop, a writing workshop, presentations at the American Comparative Literature Association and the Latin American Studies Association Congress, and the publication of our research findings in this collection of essays. Through the process we learned the value of research and teaching in collaboration, not as a happy accident of shared interest, but as a vital means of challenging known methods and rhetorics that are specific to our fields. The new insights rendered by these encounters were only enriched by the participation of outstanding student researchers.

IDEAS IN CONVERGENCE

While Puga and Kuecker walked Mexico City in 2014, they discussed different authors who influenced their thinking about Mexico City and the urban form. Benjamin's *flâneur,* the casual people watcher turned social actor, held center stage. But, so did other great city thinkers. Ángel Rama ([1984] 1996) and his *The Lettered City,* Henri LeFebvre ([1970] 2003 and [1974] 1991) and David Harvey's (2012 and 2008) "right to the city" wove in and out of the chatter. Where exactly it happened is lost to the streets of la capital, but along the route Kuecker brought up Rebecca Solnit's (2012) brilliant urban atlas of San Francisco, *Infinite City*. It gained traction in the conversation, as Puga was an enthusiast of Solnit's (2001) also brilliant *Wanderlust: A History of Walking*, which served as a post-Benjamin inspiration for Puga's interest in the *flâneur*. It was *Infinite City*, however, with its direct engagement of the city as a space to be known through embodiment within it that became the inspiration for *Mapping the Megalopolis*.

In Solnit we found a companion for those who are driven by the intellectual fool's errand of attempting to know something grander than what the capacity of field-specific lines of inquiry and discrete analysis could capture. The introduction to Solnit's *Infinite City* embraces this gambit within urban studies, especially within its literary form, as well as certain social science trends within post-modern pokings at the universal narrative of the modern urban form. Maps, after all, are social-cultural constructions of a complex reality that generate fictions, simulacra, and mythical representations of the *real* constitution of urban space. The authors in this collection find one passage from Solnit's introduction particularly valuable. She (2012) states, "An atlas is a collection of versions of a place, a compendium of perspectives, a snatching out of the infinite ether of potential versions a few that will be made concrete and visible" (vii). This principle of seeking multiple and idiosyncratically rendered narratives of the convergence known as the city has guided our work from that first walk from Condesa to Plaza Carso, and it has rendered the present volume.

Solnit's *Infinite City* presents readers with a wide diversity of maps that represent San Francisco. The atlas's maps are presented in color and with high artistic flair, and are accompanied by essays that offer interpretations of San Francisco. The reader is drawn into the text through its creative force.

For Solnit an urban form like San Francisco is a dynamic space, one that has multiple realities that are imagined in infinite ways by its inhabitants and those who represent it. This infinite quality of the urban form challenges the humanities and social sciences to make the city knowable, especially when the urban form is Mexico City, a megalopolis of 25 million people. As suggested by Solnit's book title, the abstractions of space can be articulated in the visual display of a map in seemingly endless ways where each map stands as a paradox of being a realistic representation of a slice of the city, and an artificial construction of the urban form.

IMAGINING THE UNIMAGINABLE
AS A (DIS)ORDERING ACT

When Solnit invites us to consider an atlas to be "versions of a place," although a potentially futile effort to make it "concrete and visible," she is joining a conversation known to those who study Mexico City. We can, for example, turn to Rubén Gallo's (2004) introduction to the *Mexico City Reader*, which he chooses to title, "Delirious Mexico City." Indeed, he claims Mexico City maybe the most delirious city in the world (3). Confirming Puga and Kuecker's strategy of walking the city, Gallo writes: "Strolling through the streets remains the best strategy for understanding the cultural complexities of Mexico City: its delirious nature, its endless contradictions (it is a place of extreme poverty and extreme wealth), its surreal images (André Breton famously called it the most surreal place on earth), and its jumbling of historical periods (modernist high-rises next to eighteenth-century palaces are a common sight)" (3–4). Acknowledging the challenge, Solnit reminds us that an atlas only captures part of the infinite city, offering us a hopeful glimpse into understanding its magic.

Gallo's choice of delirious as the word to capture the reality of Mexico City carries two meanings. The first is a disturbed state of mind that produces incoherence. The second conveys the emotional experience of wild excitement, even ecstasy. The delirious city suggests to us the Mexican notion of *desmadre*, literally "de-mothering," but meaning a situation defined by a loss of order, or chaos that results in an upset state of affairs and inescapably negative outcomes (Zolov 1999). Delirious for us calls our attention to an important theme in urban studies, which is the mutually constitutive interplay between order and disorder. In part, Solnit's *Infinite City* plays with this theme. For a city to be ordered it needs to be something that can have an imaginary, a normative vision for what kind of city is desirable. An infinite city, however, is very hard to imagine. It's an exercise that leaves the mind in a disturbed state, Gallo's delirious city.

Building from Solnit and Gallo's invitation, *Mapping the Megalopolis* provokes consideration of several lines of inquiry about Mexico City and the urban form. Our intellectual engagements with Mexico City share a singular purpose that is best phrased in Spanish as *abarcar lo inabarcable*, a phrase that awkwardly translates into English as "imagining the unimaginable." This purpose is widely shared by the many scholars, poets, cinematographers, and chroniclers, many of them represented in *The Mexico City Reader*, who have been spellbound by the struggle to render Mexico City knowable.

Understanding that our atlas would necessarily be an incomplete representation of Mexico City, and wrestling with bringing the humanities and social sciences into a productive conversation, we determined to anchor our approach with two major propositions about the urban form. From the humanities we turn to Rama's ([1984] 1996) *Lettered City* as our frame for understanding how elites mold Mexico City into a particular urban form through their written discourses. The GIS Story Maps that serve as the foundation for the chapters in this volume aim to illustrate how urban ordering can be revealed through novels, poems, short stories, song, theater, movies, and public demonstrations, and how those revelations can be visualized by mapping the imaginary of their authors. The second major theme comes from Henri Lefebvre's ([1970] 2003 and [1974] 1991) "right to the city," especially David Harvey's (2008 and 2012) development of the idea. It is the dual right of every urban dweller to transform the city, and to be transformed by it. Our collective goal is to bring the lettered city and the right to the city together in an analytical and interpretative synthesis that generates our attempt at imagining this unimaginable megalopolis.

The chapters presented in *Mapping the Megalopolis* take the challenge of understanding the mutually constitutive relationship between order and disorder as its central question. This line of inquiry is one of general value within urban studies, while also being pertinent to the attempt to comprehend Mexico City. By "order" we mean the disposition of people or things in a particular fashion, as well as a condition in which everything is in an appropriate place. Ordering has an association with spatial arrangements, both abstract and material, that pertains to the social, political, economic, and cultural processes of place making. An ordering's disposition of people or things necessitates or implies an actual, perceived, or potential disordering. We find that the urban form seeks ordering as it reproduces itself, but the reproduction generates an unstable fluidity, a disordering that necessitates disposition. Order and disorder are fundamental to the deeper logic of the city: the higher the urban ordering, the greater the city's propensity to disorder, explained literally and metaphorically by the laws of thermodynamics, especially entropy. When the mutually constitutive relationship between order and disorder operates at the scale of the megalopolis, their interplay takes on characteristics of Solnit's infinite city as well as Gallo's delirious urbanism. We engage the notion of *abarcar lo inabarcable* in the exploration of order and disorder.

In mapping Mexico City from the perspective of order and disorder and the attempt to imagine the unimaginable, the chapters in this volume explore multiple themes common to urban studies. The right to the city finds a central place in our work, especially because it provides a valuable line of inquiry and analysis for thinking about several other key themes, such as the privatization of public space and how urban spaces are contested. Contestations over who imagines the city and how it is imagined raise questions about urban ordering, its reproduction, and why it does not collapse from its instability. Given the unstable nature of megalopolis's reproduction, one that generates a culture of ephemerality in time and place, we see linkages between the right to the city and questions of how people make meaning of the places and spaces they inhabit and navigate while in the megalopolis. Associated with the problem of how Mexico City's residents make meaning amid an unimaginable city— which is perhaps a deeper meaning of right to the city—we are interested in how people find security by creating order. At the same time, the security/ order question invites us to consider how people make meaning of insecurity and disorder. Wandering among these themes, and most often producing the urban realities that give rise to the themes we use in this book, we have millions upon millions of city dwellers navigating the city, acting as *flâneurs* who question the order and disorder of the megalopolis.

While not necessarily novel attempts at understanding the city, our core research questions about order and disorder bring a couple of new twists. First, the collaboration between literary studies and social sciences brings different—sometimes sharply so—perspectives on the theoretical frames underlying our lines of inquiry. The construction of space in literary studies, for example, tends to emphasize constructs such as the *flâneur* and the textual palimpsest, or layering of registers, while in the social sciences the focus on capitalist reproduction is often paramount. Second, our method of making maps as part of the writing process brings different insights into established ways of disciplinary thinking about key concepts in urban analysis. For example, can the *flâneur* move beyond a position of male privilege and become a social actor of varied gender and class? Is the right to the city guaranteed or derailed by private investment in public space? Do mappings that address such issues serve as addenda to critical writing, or are they essays in their own right?

Questions about how power is asserted and contested within the unstable reproduction of urban order inform our writing collective's embrace of Edward Soja's (2010) notion of spatial justice. We find value in his "consequential geography" concept, which is derived from critical theory's concern for power and social justice that is fundamental to the "spatial turn" in geography and rests at the base of critical urbanism. In building the consequential geography idea, Soja takes from Erik Swyngedouw, who states, "Questions of justice cannot be seen independently from the urban condition, not only because most of the world's population lives in cities, but above all because the city condenses the manifold tensions and contradictions that infuse modern life" (Swyngedouw quoted in Soja 2010, 1). Soja also takes from Edward Said, "just as none of us is beyond geography, none of us is completely free from the struggle over geography. That struggle is complex and interesting because it is not only about soldiers and cannons but also about ideas, about forms, about images and imaginings" (Said quoted in Soja 2010, 1). A consequential geography is the process and outcomes of the struggle for and about space that results from the tensions and contradictions of urban life. Soja states, "This definitive struggle over geography can best be understood from an assertive spatial perspective, one that emphasizes what can be described as the explanatory power of the consequential geographies of justice" (2). Our collection of essays is a modest example of this "explanatory power," because we share Soja's embrace of the right to the city. Soja explains, "Lefebvre's original concept was packed with powerful ideas about the consequential geography of urban life and the need for those most negatively affected by the urban condition to take greater control over the social production of urbanized space" (6). Left unstated in Soja are the ways that the ordering of elite projects produce consequential geographies and are often informed, if not constituted by the disordering of their order by resistances.

Our engagement with Mexico City is not the first attempt to understand the megalopolis by using visual representations such as maps. Felipe Correa and Carlos Garciavelez Alfaro's *Mexico City: Between Geography and Geometry* (2014), for example, uses maps and design sketches to explore the "constant struggle between the geometries of urbanization and the lacustrine landscape that resists the strictures of a city grid" (13). Their probe of the intersection between urban mobilities and design reaches the conclusion that Mexico City "is perhaps more knowable, predictable and operable than many might expect or believe" (6). Likewise, architect Fernando Romero's *ZMVM* (2000) brings the perspective of an architect's design lab to the challenge of mapping the megalopolis. He accomplishes this feat by mapping an array of statistics that reveals the quotidian inner logic of the city's urban form. The book offers no essay to accompany the visuals, as Romero is content to let the statistics and maps represent the city. While not an atlas, the collection of thirty short essays accompanied by provocative photographic interventions in *Citámbulos Mexico City: Journey to the Mexican Megalopolis*, embrace the concept of journey, in this case riding the Mexico City metro, to explore the megalopolis. The editors conclude, "looking closer, however, we see there is order within the chaos" (25). Distinct from these positivist knowledge claims,

Mapping the Megalopolis positions itself with the delirious city. We offer our essays as humble attempts as interpretations of an unknowable city.

VERSIONS OF A PLACE: AN OVERVIEW OF THE CHAPTERS THAT OFFER OUR MAPPING OF THE MEGALOPOLIS

Marta Sierra opens *Mapping the Megalopolis* with a consideration of two intertextually related novels dealing with prostitution in the city of Mexico during the regime of Porfirio Díaz (1876–1911), *Santa* ([1903] 2013) by Federico Gamboa and *Nadie me verá llorar* (*No One Will See Me Cry*) ([1999] 2014) by Cristina Rivera Garza. Sierra explores how the debate on prostitution became central in Mexico with the increasing urbanization following Porfirio Díaz's rise to power. City and body became synonyms, the symbols of a paradoxical Mexican modernity seeking to cultivate the body, and yet fearful of its diseases. Sierra demonstrates how in both works, the city is represented as a dichotomic space, in which two parallel worlds coexist almost without touching each other. But whereas *Santa* depicts the abstract or conceptualized space of urbanism, what Henri Lefebvre ([1974] 1991, 38) calls the "conceived" space, *Nadie me verá llorar* focuses on the city as a spatial practice that is constantly modified through dialectical interactions. Chapter 1 (Sierra's chapter) highlights how the Mexico of Porfirio Díaz embodies urban designs to create what Rama ([1984] 1996) styles the "lettered city," a city of symbols modeled after the European ideals of nineteenth-century modernity. The city of the *Porfiriato* (the reign of Porfirio Díaz) was conceived as a way to control illness and social chaos, to classify social and ethnic groups, to control and regulate sexual desire. Studies about this historical period in Mexico underline the obsession of the ruling classes to control bodies, languages, and identities, through an urban model reflecting a sanitized version of modernity. And the city was the place to imagine a modern way of fighting the war against disease, as theories on *higienismo* (hygienism) took over the political imagination of Porfirio Diaz's regime.

Transitioning from Sierra's presentation of Porfirian modernizers' concerns for social order in the urban form, chapter 2 (Glen Kuecker's chapter) explores a contemporary articulation of the Porfirian urban imaginary by looking at a project of one of the richest persons in the world, Carlos Slim. Kuecker aims to understand how Slim orders the disorder of Mexico City through analysis of one of his most important urban projects, Plaza Carso, which is the largest mixed use development project in Latin America. The plaza features *Museo Soumaya*, Slim's tribute to his deceased wife. The Museum is an act of philanthropy, as it makes Slim's private art collection accessible to the public. Plaza Carso's office towers host Slim's business empire, *Grupo Carso*. The residential buildings offer luxury living that boosts security and easy access to work and entertainment. In exploring what Plaza Carso might tell us about Mexico City, Kuecker uses the notion of privatization of public space to evaluate the multiple ways Slim's urban imaginary can be located in a variety of spaces: within circuits of global capitalism, within the circulation of globally significant iconic architecture, within Mexico City, as well as within the challenges of twenty-first century urbanism. The chapter also considers the centrality of consumption in Slim's attempt at place making by exploring the spaces within Plaza Carso's upscale shopping mall. It concludes with evaluation of Slim's urban imaginary from the perspective of Lefebvre's ([1970] 2003 and [1974] 1991) "right to the city," which invites consideration of contestations to Slim's ordering of Mexico City.

From Plaza Carso, chapter 3 (Daniel Rogers's chapter) takes the reader back to the streets of Mexico City as seen from the ordering lens of the city's golden age of film. Rogers focuses on the urban imaginary of Luis Buñuel's cinematic output in Mexico, during his exile from Spain beginning in the late 1940s. Of the twenty-one films he made during this period, one in particular foregrounds the geography of Mexico City. *Los olvidados* (1950) maps out sections of the megalopolis that, to use urban planner and theorist Kevin Lynch's (1960, 6) words, define the boundary between the imaginable and the unimaginable, the coherent and the chaotic. In an effort to explicate not just the cinematic text, Rogers uses contemporary photographs and movie stills to locate the neighborhoods and streets that Buñuel used as exterior locations in *Los olvidados*. In his analysis of these locations, and the changes that have occurred over the last half-century, Rogers pays particular attention to what Mexican theorist Carlos Garrocho (2011, 160) categorizes as the "sociospacial" (*socio-spatial*). In *Los olvidados*, urban space produces and encourages certain social relationships at the same time that it discourages and impedes others. These relationships leave historical "marks" that remain as physical and discursive imprints on, in the case of Buñuel's films, members of Mexico City's working classes.

In their chapter (chapter 4), "Novelistic Cartographies," a consideration of *flânerie* and monumental city space, Alejandro Puga and Patricia Tovar draw from the context of Mexico City in the late twentieth century, which marks the beginning of a movement to make the city's monumental presence more accessible and desirable to its residents and visitors, culminating in the problematic ordering gestures of the bicentennial celebrations of 2010 and, more currently, its new designation as CDMX, a purportedly more user-friendly term than the long-standing *Distrito Federal*. In the first part of the chapter, Puga and Tovar examine the self-guided downtown tour taken by retired professor Juan Manuel Barrientos, the main character in Gonzalo Celorio's second novel, *Y retiemble en sus centros la tierra* (1999). In the second part, the authors analyze the case of Soledad, the invisible protagonist in Ana Clavel's first novel, *Los deseos y su sombra* (2000), who promenades through *Paseo de la Reforma* in her search to resolve issues of gender, access, and self-determination. Both protagonists begin their urban wandering as a recuperative act in which the cultural patrimony available to them on the street serves as a backdrop for the exercise of memory and identity construction. Through their engagement of monuments and monumental gestures, each has struggled with self and city, either by claiming a right to the city through consecrated or self-styled cultural patrimony, or through the awareness of the disorder brought on by lost social positioning. Their varied approximations present a deviation from the traditional *flânerie* that makes privileged constructs of both the *flâneur* and the city. Ultimately, in both novels, the articulation of acts of *flânerie* and the identification of the street as a contested space transform this rarified pastime into a new form of social action.

Transitioning from Puga and Tovar's invitation to consider the marginalized or disjointed voices within the elite orderings of Mexico City's monumental spaces, chapter 5 (Shannan Mattiace and Jennifer Johnson's chapter) on Santa Fe, an area on the extreme western fringe of Mexico City proper, provides us with a study of spatial and socioeconomic contrasts. New Santa Fe is one of the newest and wealthiest residential and commercial districts of the city and represents the vision of an elite class in terms of residential preferences and lifestyles. One of its most prevalent features is a closing off and privatization of residential spaces known as "gating." In the shadow of New Santa Fe is the historic Pueblo Santa Fe. Old Santa Fe, founded in the sixteenth century, is a working class neighborhood known for its marginality and crime. In the first section of the chapter, Mattiace and Johnson examine the contrasting utopic visions of elites who designed and built Old and New Santa Fe, drawing on the work of Rama's *Lettered City* ([1984] 1996). The essay's second section focuses on global capital, examining the industries at the center of both areas' development in the twentieth century. Santa Fe housed one of Mexico City's largest open-air garbage dumps from the 1950s to the mid-1980s when it was closed and filled in. Symbolically, perhaps, New Santa Fe was built on top of these garbage dumps in an effort to showcase Mexico's turn toward neoliberal economic development. In the third and final section of the essay, the focus is on citizen resistance and rights. Drawing on David Harvey's work on citizens' struggles to shape the quality of urban life, Mattiace and Johnson look at how residents of both New and Old Santa Fe are responding to one of Mexico City's most pressing contemporary problems, that of security and crime. New Santa Fe's nouveau riche have privatized most security functions whereas in Old Santa Fe neighbors rely on small improvement projects from the city government to improve lighting and public spaces, funding from philanthropic organizations, as well as borough monies.

From elite attempts at ordering insecurity in Santa Fe, Chapter 6 (María Claudia André's chapter), brings the reader to Mexico City's muralist movement (1920–1950) to illustrate the interplay between arts and place making in constituting the ordering of the urban imaginary within the swirl of modernizing chaos. It endorses Néstor García Canclini's ([1996] 2015: 22) opinion that postmodern movements in Latin America are relevant and interesting as "they prepare the ground for a rethinking of the links between tradition, modernity and postmodernity" (22). André's essay focuses first on the role of muralism and museum building in Mexico City as instrumental devices set in place by the state and the elites to modernize the country and consolidate the ideals of the Mexican revolution (1910–1920). The chapter next moves to consideration of the significant role of urban artwork and graffiti as counter-culture strategies to question obsolete power structures and contribute to social change. André contends that the muralist movement, infused by the capital modernization of the state, aimed to erase social and racial divisions by fusing European aesthetics with vernacular Mexican arts and crafts. Nonetheless, she demonstrates how the dominance of politics over art as well as the emphasis on dogmatic realism hindered the movement's dynamism and dissolved its original agenda. Challenging the progressive mindset of modernism, contemporary graffiti and urban artists seek to reformulate the political scenario through the implementation of ingenious cultural practices centered on the construction of collective identities. Within the frame of the Mexican megalopolis, these artists are taking the streets to reach vast audiences beyond the restraints of museum or art gallery walls. This social frame of protest allows them to produce experimental artwork that expresses strong aesthetic values without sacrificing the underlying social or political message.

From the muralists' urban imaginary of post-revolutionary Mexico City, Jennifer Johnson and Shannan Mattiace introduce us to a very different urban imaginary reflected in one of Mexico City's *colonias populares* (working class or poor people's neighborhood) located in Iztapalapa. In this chapter, they explore citizen responses to insecurity through a case study of a leftist housing cooperative, the *Unidad Habitacional La Polvorilla-Acapatzingo*. Johnson and Mattiace bring focus to how the interplay between utopic visions, global capital, and resistance shapes urban space. Located on the eastern flank of the metropolis, Iztapalapa constitutes the youngest and most populated borough in Mexico City, and one of its poorest and highest crime areas as well. The central paradox they address is one of "walled resistance," that is, how and why the working poor deploy spatial forms that mimic the enclosure or gating of neighborhoods so prevalent in wealthier parts of the city such as New Santa Fe. The first part of the chapter traces the origins of this cooperative and its leaders' radical vision of autonomy to the Mexico City urban popular movement that gained momentum following the 1985 earthquake and, later, to the Zapatista movement for indigenous self-governance in Chiapas. The second section outlines the history of land use in *La Polvorilla*, highlighting how urbanization in this part of the city occurred in the 1980s and 1990s largely in the absence of capital, that is, significant public or private investment in decent and affordable housing for workers in Mexico City's booming service sector. It attributes the cooperative's success to the militant occupations and squats it spearheaded to obtain *de facto* control over land for 600 families, but also to its ability to take advantage of the privatization of Mexico's land rights regime in order to secure legal title to this property. In the final section, the authors draw on David Harvey's (2008 and 2012) notion of the right to the city to examine La Polvorilla's attempts to insulate members from the disorder of their surroundings by controlling access to their community through walls, gates, and the self-help provision of policing. Johnson and Mattiace bring us to consider, is this what Harvey has in mind when he exhorts urban denizens to reclaim their right to the city?

La Polvorilla's bold assertion to the right to the city takes a different form in Charlotte Blair's consideration of community contestations of elite ordering in her chapter, "Porous Urbanism: Order and Disorder in Colonia Santo Domingo." Blair focuses on elite ordering in *Colonia Santo Domingo* and the subsequent pushback to such ordering by members of the politically radical neighborhood group, *Pedregales en Resistencia*. Practically overnight on September 2nd, 1971, Santo Domingo was part of one of Mexico City's largest land grab. After President Luis Echeverria (1970–1976) announced that the land would be given to families who were willing to settle it, thousands of people from as far away as the southern states of Oaxaca and Chiapas "grabbed" the land; they built makeshift homes and worked collectively to establish permanent dwellings. In 2015, Colonia Santo Domingo's neighborhood group Pedregales en Resistencia drew from their collective experience as a self-built, squatter's settlement in order to defy current elite ordering. Such ordering, Blair argues, has taken the shape of public-private development initiatives that are imposed on the neighborhood by external, profit-driven actors. Many of those living in Colonia Santo Domingo in 2015 believed that this urban reordering would lead to a major increase in the cost-of-living followed by wide-scale displacement. Members of Pedregales en Resistencia were neither silent nor complacent toward elite-ordering projects, however. Rather, they used collective memory, art, and play in order to protest profit-driven megaprojects and forge a sense of belonging amidst burgeoning uncertainty.

While memory, art, and play are central to the interplay between order and disorder in Colonia Santo Domingo, chapter 9 (Karen Velasquez's chapter) focuses on the tension between linguistic order and disorder in the Mexico City megalopolis, through an analysis of Korean business signs in Pequeño Seúl (Koreatown), which is located in the *Zona Rosa* neighborhood of *Colonia Juárez*. Velasquez analyzes a collection of these signs to explore their characteristics and the ways they communicate their messages to diverse audiences in the megalopolis. Signs in Pequeño Seúl reflect a unique mosaic of linguistic features that are simultaneously Korean, Mexican, and transnational. Many of these signs are multimodal; they incorporate Chinese, English, and Romanized Korean; they contain pictures of food and quaint characters, and they appeal to both tourists and locals. The chapter offers a guide to reading familiar and unfamiliar signs in Pequeño Seúl, and brings features of the urban landscape into focus. These signs show how the Korean community has become an established part of Zona Rosa; it also shows how the Korean language exists alongside several other languages in the neighborhood. A linguistic analysis of the neighborhood highlights how Mexico City has been home to diverse languages and cultures for many centuries. More than ever before, it is a globalized, internationalized, and super diverse city where people from around the world pursue their dreams of finding economic and educational opportunities.

In the final chapter, Patrick O'Connor brings the reader back to the *flâneur* as a figure ordered by gender through examination of the first three books—one essay collection, two novels—by the young literary phenomenon Valeria Luiselli (b. 1983). Mexican by birth and cosmopolitan by upbringing, Luiselli puts forward the idea that the best way to wander the streets of a city nowadays is on a bicycle, which suggests that her gender prevents her from imitating more fully the ideas on the *flâneur* or urban stroller as put forward by male writers such as Walter Benjamin. Luiselli then gives an example of her belief by narrating her thoughts during a bike trip she takes through Mexico City's Colonia Roma (*Dos calles y una banqueta* [Alternative routes]), in which each brief section is keyed to one of the streets she travels along. One can map this bicycle trip, only to find that the trip is slightly different in the English translation; so are the essayistic reflections in the English translation. Curiously, then, an essay that takes as its topic the Portuguese topic of *saudade* and melancholy feels less solitary in the English version; one feels that the collaborative effort of translating her piece with Christina MacSweeney has brought about the change. Indeed, Luiselli doesn't like to travel the streets of Mexico City alone, unlike her self-presentation in her first novel *Los ingrávidos* (*Faces in the Crowd*) (2011), where the character based on her wanders the streets of New York by herself (but is seen later as a wife and mother in Mexico City who can't or won't leave the house). In her next novel, *La historia de mis dientes* (*The Story of My Teeth*) (2012), her picaresque protagonist has the full "right of the city," but he is a man, and now

Luiselli's collaboration is even greater: she wrote the first draft of the novel in installments with the workers of a juice factory in Mexico City's far northeast, Ecatepec, who gave her feedback and suggestions; the juice factory was also the preliminary site of the art gallery *Galería Jumex*. Luiselli and her translator, Christina MacSweeney, pile comic ironies into that novel's last section as her protagonist chases his son by bicycle through the streets of Ecatepec. In a final irony beyond the novel, Mexico City's first massive women's march *Vivas Nos Queremos* (We Want Them Back Alive) in April 2016 connected distant Ecatepec to the city center, demanding the right not just to ride, but to walk the streets of México City, *solidaridad* to accompany or counteract *saudade*.

For this volume's conclusion, Puga and Kuecker summarize our effort at making the unknowable city knowable by considering the megalopolis's transition from DF to CDMX, a name transition that we suggest reflects deeper transformations within the logic of Mexico City's experience with order and disorder. We explore the fate of the *novela defeña* and the possibilities for the *novela sedemequis*, which provides the basis for exploring the latter's implications for social science analysis of Mexico City's uncertain future within a crises driven twenty-first century. We hint at these themes in the next section of this introduction.

THE *DESMADRE* OF MAPPING

Contemporary Mexico City finds itself in its newest crisis of representation. As many of our contributors will bring to bear, it has always been a global city, and yet it seeks that status as such in an interesting parallel with the movement during the *sexenio* (six-year presidential term) of Mexican President Miguel Alemán (1946–1952) to make of La Capital a cosmopolitan destination. Most recently, the city has witnessed the removal of its longstanding identification of Distrito Federal—or Defe, to those who would claim intimate pertinence to such a staunch ordering—to CDMX, which manifests itself throughout the city in giant letters readymade for photo opportunities. This certainly more approachable term still raises questions about the right to the city and what exactly makes it global. Are access and globalization to be found in magnanimous gestures that distract residents and visitors from the challenges and contradictions of the megalopolis, or is a truly more inclusive merging of people and city space at hand? As ever-morphing visualizations of the city, maps can begin to engage this dilemma. We have seen how this seemingly unbiased activity, mapping, has challenged the limits of our fields of study and made us question how we do our work. Literary criticism takes on the nomenclature like urban studies, while the account of a social movement begins to assume a novelistic arc. We have returned to Mexico City many times since that first walk, and it is we who are contaminated by new forms of inquiry. In this way, the ordering supposed by the cartographic act is set adrift. By merging our attempts to plot the dynamics of the street as we understand it, we demonstrate that the street cannot be contained, and so the interplay of ordering and disordering, the desmadre of the city, finds itself among our meticulous trajectories and plotted points.

In his introduction to *Hybrid Cultures,* Néstor García Canclini (2005) muses, "Maybe this text can be used like a city, which one enters via the path of the cultured, of the popular, or of the massified. On the inside, everything gets mixed together; every chapter refers to all the others and thus it is not important to know the approach by which one arrived" (4). García Canclini goes on to speculate on what kind entrance or exit to the city a representative of a given field might select. While we may disagree with García Canclini that "an anthropologist enters the city by foot" or a "sociologist by car on a main highway," thinking about how we enter and leave the desmadre of the delirious city serves us well. From the now mythical experience of watching the clouds part to reveal the endless city, to the contestations of traffic that defy the promise of an easy Google Map itinerary, strategies for entering and exiting Mexico City as both place and representational image, or even spectacle, are easily assumed but never clearly delineated. Still, we offer these readings of the megalopolis as a companion to the forces that draw us and tear us away from CDMX, *el Defe, la capital, la región más transparente, la ciudad más pinche,* the unimaginable place, knowing full well that we have yet to know it.

For this volume, the authors and editors provide translations for the original Spanish language texts. We provide the English language in the main text and offer the original Spanish in endnotes. Shorter passages have both English and Spanish provided in the main text.

WORKS CITED

Álvarez, Ana, and Förderverein Deutsches Architektur Zentrum, eds. 2008. *Citámbulos Mexico City: Journey to the Mexican Megalopolis = Viaje a La Megalópolis Mexicana = Reise in Die Mexikanische Magalopole.* Berlin: Jovis.

Buñuel, Luis, director. 1950. *Los Olvidados.* Film. Directed by Luis Buñuel. Mexico City: Ultramar Films.

Celorio, Gonzalo. 1999. *Y retiemble en sus centros la tierra.* México: Tusquets.

Clavel, Ana. 2000. *Los deseos y su sombra.* México: Editorial Alfaguara.

Correa, Felipe, and Carlos Garciavelez Alfaro. 2014. *Mexico City: Between Geography and Geometry.* San Francisco: Applied Research + Design Publishing.

García Canclini, Néstor. (1996) 2005. *Hybrid Cultures: Strategies for Entering and Leaving Modernity*. Translated by Christopher L. Chiappari and Silvia L. Lopez. Minneapolis: University of Minnesota Press.

Gallo, Rubén. 2004. "Delirious Mexico City." In *The Mexico City Reader*, edited by Rubén Gallo and Lorna Scott Fox, 3–29. Madison: University of Wisconsin Press.

Gallo, Rubén, and Lorna Scott Fox, eds. 2004. *The Mexico City Reader*. Madison: University of Wisconsin Press.

Gamboa, Federico. (1903) 2013. *Santa*. Madrid: Drácena.

Garrocho, Carlos. 2011. "Pobreza urbana en asentamientos irregulars: La trampa de la localización periférica." In *Ciudades mexicanas: Desafíos en concierto*, edited by Enrique Cabrero Mendoza, 159–209. Mexico City: Fondo de Cultura Económica.

Harvey, David. 2008. "Right to the City." *New Left Review* 53 (October): 23–40.

———. 2012. *Rebel Cities: From the Right to the City to the Urban Revolution*. New York: Verso.

Lefebvre, Henri. (1970) 2003. *The Urban Revolution*. Translated by Robert Bononno. Minneapolis: University of Minnesota Press.

———. (1974) 1991. *The Production of Space*. Translated by Donald Nicholson-Smith. Cambridge, MA: Blackwell.

Luiselli, Valeria. 2011. *Los ingrávidos*. México D.F., México: Editorial Sexto Piso.

———. 2012. *La historia de mis dientes*. México D.F., México: Editorial Sexto Piso.

Lynch, Kevin. 1960. *The Image of the City*. Cambridge, MA: MIT Press.

Rama, Ángel. (1984) 1996. *The Lettered City*. Post-Contemporary Interventions. Translated by John Charles Chasteen. Durham, NC: Duke University Press.

Rivera Garza, Cristina. (1999) 2014. *Nadie me verá llorar*. Barcelona: Tusquets. 4ª edición.

Romero, Fernando, and Pablo León de la Barra. 2000. *ZMVM*. México, D.F.: LCM/ Fernando Romero.

Soja, Edward W. 2010. *Seeking Spatial Justice*. Minneapolis: University of Minnesota Press.

Solnit, Rebecca. 2001. *Wanderlust: A History of Walking*. New York: Penguin Books.

———. 2010. *Infinite City: A San Francisco Atlas*. Berkeley: University of California Press.

Zolov, Eric. 1999. *Refried Elvis: The Rise of the Mexican Counterculture*. Berkeley: University of California Press.

Chapter 1

Mapping Subjectivities

The Body-City of Porfirian *Mexico City*

Marta Sierra

BODIES-CITIES: MAPPING DESIRE, MAPPING MODERNITY

In *Invisible Cities*, Italo Calvino (1978) describes the city of Zobeide as a woman whom men of different nationalities chase unsuccessfully. Their dreams of possession lead them to build Zobeide: "In laying out the streets, each followed the course of his pursuit; at the spot where they had lost the fugitive's trail, they arranged spaces and walls differently from the dream, so she would be unable to escape again" (45). Zobeide is a city made of ghostly itineraries, each representing a different cartographer's desire. Many implications follow Calvino's illustration. Zobeide poses the question of how space is both an imagined and a material reality. In other words, does desire have a materiality that we can map? Where do we locate the place of our imagination and our dreams? And further, how do maps represent our physical and emotional space? As Calvino well describes, desire is a fugitive force, difficult to be mapped. The city of Zobeide embodies urbanism's impossible dream of order by regulating desire. In many theories of the city we perceive the tension between such dreams and the undeniable reality that space results in material social constructions, ever changing, unstable, disordered and never fully regulated. Ángel Rama ([1984] 1996) describes such tensions between dreams and reality through his concept of the "lettered city," a city that orders the urban imaginary of the modern nation-state, a city that creates a ring of protection for the *letrados*, a city that erects the walls of writing and urbanism, and yet, a city that fails to represent the many thousands left out of them.

Similar to other Latin American cities of the turn of the nineteenth century, the Mexico of Porfirio Díaz (1876–1911) embodies urban designs intended to create a lettered city, modeled after European ideals of nineteenth-century modernity. The Porfirian city was conceived as a way to control illness and

1

social chaos, to classify social and ethnic groups, and to control and regulate
sexual desire. Studies about this historical period in Mexico underline the
obsession of the ruling classes to order the city by controlling bodies, languages, and identities, through an urban model reflecting a sanitized version
of modernity. And the city was the place to imagine a modern way to fight
the war against disease, as theories on *higienismo* (hygienism) took over the
political imagination of Porfirio Díaz's regime. In this chapter, I explore the
interplay between urban order and disorder by focusing on one aspect of Porfirian urbanism, the development of a spatial structure that sought to regulate
what was considered the disease of prostitution. I analyze two novels dealing with prostitution in Porfirian Mexico City, *Santa* by Federico Gamboa
([1903] 2013) and *Nadie me verá llorar* by Cristina Rivera Garza ([1999]
2014).

There is the real city, and the city of symbols, Ángel Rama states in *La
ciudad letrada*. The debate on prostitution in Mexico embodies ideas about
how desire would affect both representations of the city, and it became
central in Mexico with the increased urbanization that marked Díaz's rise
to power (Bliss 2010). City and body became synonyms, the symbols of a
paradoxical Mexican modernity seeking to cultivate the body, and yet, fearful of its diseases. Gamboa published his novel *Santa* in 1903, as an army of
urbanists beautified the city of Mexico in preparation for the 1910 centenary
celebrations of Mexican Independence. As the city increasingly emulated
the European urban ideals of the time, Gamboa wrote a novel whose main
character, a prostitute named Santa, was also a European creation modeled
after the French naturalism of Emile Zola and Gustave Flaubert. But whereas
the City of Mexico was a celebration of the dreams of modern order, *Santa*
showed the dark face of modernity: a disordered, unseen city that, like a
sick body lying under the pristine buildings and avenues, warned us of what
can go wrong when modernity is not properly regulated. *Santa* conflates the
prostitute's body and the city, while it fleshes out the perils of unorganized,
disordered society ruled by unregulated pleasure. Gamboa writes through
the voice and perspective of his third person narrator, an alter ego of the
city planner who outlines the map of what is outside the confines of a city of
decay that he seeks to redeem through his tale. Written from the perspective
of a prostitute secluded in the mental hospital La Castañeda, Rivera Garza's
Nadie me verá llorar also exposes the impossibilities of Porfirian dreams of
modern order. Contrary to *Santa*, *Nadie me verá llorar* gives a voice to the
prostitute and places the perspective of an outcast living outside the boundaries of the "ideal city" of Porfirio Díaz. In both works, the city is represented
as a dichotomic space, in which two parallel worlds of order and disorder
coexist almost without touching each other. But whereas *Santa* depicts the
abstract or conceptualized space of urbanism, what Henri Lefebvre calls

the "conceived" space, *Nadie me verá llorar* focuses on the city as a spatial practice that is constantly modified through dialectical interactions (Lefebvre [1974] 1991, 38).

Here I intend to first trace the map of Porfirio Díaz's modern city by using historical studies to outline both novels. In seeking to establish the traces of the metropolis, I build a map of the internal borders that separate the Por-firian's ideal city from what was left out: the city of decay as represented in the body of the prostitute. Second, I establish a parallel between urbanism and literary representation. I argue that as architects designed streets, monuments, and parks in México City, the writer also "establishes an order" in the raw material of fiction. He or she designs, as in Calvino's Zobeide, imaginary itineraries of subjectivities, a literary spatiality that translates unheard voices in the incomplete narratives of Mexican history. It is in fiction where the real space of the city collapses to give way to the symbolic city, a city made of disparities, a dystopian city of contradictions and disillusionment. As the state "writes" a city, the writer "writes" the body of the prostitute, a fugitive subjectivity that, like Zobeide, seems difficult to capture.

THE SCIENTIFIC CITY: MEXICO IMAGINES ITS MODERNITY

The Mexico of Porfirio Díaz was characterized by modern European influences, the desire to turn the autochthonous into the cosmopolitan, the Baroque into Modernism, the Spanish influence into the French. Order and progress were predominant ideas of the positivist ideology that many of Díaz's advisers, *los científicos*, deemed as necessary to complete the project of modernization they had in mind. The main changes the city experienced happened at the turn of the twentieth century, as the City of Mexico was transformed into a modern metropolis for the celebrations of the centenary. Electric lighting, the first line of electric streetcars, the introduction of the telephone and telegraphs, were luxuries that became widely available in preparation for the 1900 universal exhibition. Under the close supervision of Díaz, architects designed commercial centers, avenues, and buildings, seeking to transform Mexico into the new Paris. All those transformations paved the way to the unprecedented 1910 celebrations of the centenary of Mexican Independence. Mexico received the praise of foreign delegations that visited the country and donated statues and monuments to decorate the new urban landscape (Tenorio-Trillo 1996, 85).

At the time, the City of Mexico was divided into two areas: the West with the newly developed Colonias Juárez, Cuauhtémoc, Roma and Condesa, as well as two huge projects for the middle classes, the Colonias San Rafael and Limantour. The western area was connected to the traditional city through the Paseo de la Reforma and Avenida Juárez. Juxtaposed to the Porfirian imaginary's urban order, the East was the poor area that lacked public services, suffered constant flooding, and where trash piled up on the streets. As depicted well by *Santa*, this area had the reputation as a zone of vice and criminality, the area where unregulated prostitution took place. As Mauricio Tenorio-Trillo (1996) states, the city of the centenary was a city that pushed Indian communities to the edges along with other populations affected by poverty; the project of a modern Mexico City was a "frontier expansion" that displaced the limits of the traditional city to the South (90). Institutions such as the mental hospital La Castañeda—opened in 1910—and the national penitentiary—inaugurated in 1908—were built outside the limits of what the *ciudadanos de bien* (elite class) could see. As Tenorio-Trillo explains, the city borders separated sickness and health—following the ideals of hygienist theories—and wealth and poverty, while they established notions of racial supremacy (91). Considering that the ideal city embedded ideals of nationality and citizenship, only those living within its borders were considered true citizens of the modern nation.

Santa narrates the story of a young woman who moves from the countryside in search of a better fortune. Gamboa contrasts the space of the country—an unpolluted site that the novel associates to Catholic ideals of chastity—with that of the East side of the City of Mexico where the majority of the action takes place. As Rivera Garza (2014, 53) notes, Gamboa sets his novel primarily on the East side to show the debilitating impact of corruption and illness on its inhabitants. Santa arrives to work in a brothel in one of the neighborhoods of this nether region, filled with small shops and businesses that otherwise do not seem acquainted with the illegal activities going on in the brothel. The narrator's eye provides a panoptic view of the area, but centers his description on the meat shop, La Giralda, as an anticipation of the scenes that will take place in the brothel:

> La Giralda stands out, a butcher shop in the modern style, with three doors, an artificial wood floor, a marble and iron countertop, with very thin supports so that the air ventilates everything freely; with huge scales that shine with pure cleanliness, with a metallic semicircular rack, from whose thick hooks hang immense decapitated beef carcasses, cut down the middle, displaying the dirty whites of their ribs and the repulsive bloody red from the fresh and recently slaughtered flesh; with clouds of fidgeting voracious flies, and one or two corpulent street mastiffs with tough, prickly hair, lying about on the sidewalk.[1] (Gamboa [1903] 2013, 14)

Following this passage, the narrator describes the brothel comparing it to the meat shop: ". . . within the brothel that fed her; a brothel that in a very short time would devour that beauty and that young flesh that was surely unaware of all the horrors that awaited it"[2] (Gamboa [1974] 1991, 17).

As Debra Castillo (1998, 53) explains, the comparison of human beings and meat for consumption is a sustained metaphor throughout the book, at times even in cannibalistic compositions. The city of the edges is a filthy body for, as Mauricio Tenorio-Trillo (1996) states, "the Mexican elite shared with their European and North American counterparts a belief in the evil and degenerating characteristics of cities. Agglomeration, pollution, lack of nature, and industrialization led to corruption, laziness and degeneration of races, as crystallized in Federico Gamboa's myth of *Santa*" (88). As with the brothel, La Giralda embodies such fears of urban degeneration; the city acquires traits of a brutal animal haunting the powerless, whose bodies possess little or no agency to oppose the inescapable forces of an omnipotent modernity.

In such circumstances, the novel narrates the downward path of Santa through corruption. The maladies of the city spread into Santa's immaculate body. Her reproductive organs become ill as if the novel itself also victimizes a woman's body and its capacity to give life. Nothing can live in this city, Gamboa seems to state, especially those who are too vulnerable to fight the threats of disease. Described as an ill body, the east side contrasts with the Zócalo. Gamboa sets a few scenes there to show the contrast. The sequence I comment below takes place during the celebration of Mexican Independence. The narrator describes Santa circulating in her carriage through majestic avenues where all signs of a sumptuous and ordered modernity are on display: monuments, streetcars, and electricity. The description of the Plaza de Armas acquires almost a filmic quality; the omniscient perspective of the narration gives the passage to an impersonal tone, the narrator transformed in a colossal eye seeing everything and everybody. The narrative voice changes from the third person to the first person plural many times, as if he were speaking to an implied audience of fellow citizens, sharing with them the patriotic enthusiasm of the celebration:

A dense rain of gold falls from the cathedral, its bells toll rapidly. Thousands of rockets thunder in the skies, the bands strike up our hymn, the national anthem. In the faraway Citadel, the canons fire off an honor salute; the stars in the heavens look down on the earth and blink, as if they were going to shed sidereal tears, moved by the spectacle of a people delirious with love for its homeland, which one night out of each year grows in itself, and remembers that it is sovereign and strong.[3] (Gamboa [1903] 2013, 90)

The cathedral and the Palacio de la Constitución are the two focal points of the narration. They locate the center of this urban order in the figure of the president as the divine ruler of the state, an impersonal figure who disappears behind the monumentality of the Palacio. City and nation conflate in this description, a "lettered city" ruled by the president, and transmitted by the narrator, thus embodying symbolic and absolute power. The monumentality of this public site is a powerful reminder of another body that emerges in the novel, the city-body of the nation, a body that is clean, ordered, approaching disembodiment. As the ceremony celebrates the city as the embodiment of the nation, the narrator's panoptic view builds a city of patriotic pride for the reader to identify. In his seminal work *The Production of Space* ([1974] 1991), Henri Lefebvre describes in detail the abstract qualities of the space of the state as described in Gamboa's novel. Lefebvre describes this space as "conceived," an ideal city that hides its ideological purposes but that also implies a political use of knowledge. Designed as a "technological utopia," it evidences the projects of architecture, urbanism, or social planning (9). It is a "transparent," abstract space: "What we seem to have, is an apparent subject, an impersonal pseudo-subject, the abstract 'one' of modern social space, and—hidden within it, concealed by its illusory transparency—the real 'subject' namely state (political) power" (51).

Many implications emerge from this description of the Zócalo in *Santa*. The first one is that the panoptic view of the narration corresponds to the transparent space of modernity as designed by the architects of Porfirio Díaz's project. Contrary to the sections taking place in the disorder of the brothels where Santa works, the Zócalo is a space that the narrator experiences as his own, as expressed by the use of the first person plural. It is a patriotic space, a place of collective pride, a site of the political power of the state. Designed as "transparent" and planned around the Paseo de la Reforma, the ideal city that extended to the Southwest in Colonias of wealth such as Juárez, Cuahtémoc, Roma and Condesa, also connected to the city center through fashionable streets. As Tenorio-Trillo (1996) analyzes, the Porfirians intended the new urban developments to be a patriotic spectacle: "Therefore, the Zócalo remained the central point of departure, but the Paseo de la Reforma became the path of power, the representation of the course of the nation toward supreme order and progress: from la Plaza de la Reforma (with the statue of Carlos IV, *El Caballito*) to Columbus's monument, past Cuauhtémoc and the monument of independence, arriving, finally, at the Castillo de Chapultepec (the Presidential residence)" (86–87). The city is here a grid of political meaning and power, which are complicit in the control and manipulation of simultaneously real and metaphorical space. The body of the president embodies in this representation the powers of such spatial ordering, located at the center, and echoing the alliance between a phallic space and abstract (capitalist, modernist) power relations, as Steven Pile (1996, 214) reminds us.

Santa, however, remains expelled from this symbolic center. She can visit the Zócalo, but she has to admit her condition as an outcast, for her only homeland is that of the brothel. At the end of the chapter she tells El Jarameño, a bullfighter and one of her clients: "You told us that your home-land was a window with geraniums and carnations, right? Well you are happier than I, who finding myself in mine, I can't even call it that . . . My homeland, at the moment, is Elvira's house, tomorrow it will be another, who knows? And I . . . will always be a . . . And she spelled out the horrible word, the stigma, in the little carriage window, outwardly, as if she spit out something that would harm her"[4] (Gamboa [1903] 2013, 91). Whereas Santa's body houses the vices of modernity, the masculine body of Díaz establishes itself as a nationalist remedy to cure them.

The Porfiriato's ordering of the city-body served to limit spatial access to its promises of wealth and citizenship. As Tenorio-Trillo (1996) explains, those limits were clearly outlined: "This ideal encompassed the Zócalo and its surroundings, ran west to the Alameda and then along the Paseo de la Reforma as far as Chapultepec. On the South side of Reforma, the ideal city ended at the Río de la Piedad, and the border went from there to Niño Perdido and back to downtown. On the north side, the city blurred into haciendas and countryside (especially Anzures and Los Morales)" (85). Protected and immaculate, the ideal city erected imaginary walls to order space by regulating the threatening variables of disorder presented by race, gender, and social class. According to Rivera Garza (2014), positivism was the ideology that sustained such spatial divisions. And, contrary to ideals of progress embedded in positivism, Díaz's regime was based on a number of fears about the disorder of violence, disease, gender and class clashes that the theories of the científicos sought to contain: "As selective as they were enthusiastic, the Porfirians chose to preserve and cultivate a social and moral order that would support the existing classes and ethnic hierarchies, the patriarchy, and the nuclear family. They planned to achieve it by designing a series of legal initiatives to regulate public life, urban spaces, and even human bodies"[5] (51).

Although *Santa* stresses the spatial, medical, and social regulations experienced by the prostitute, the novel's ultimate message is that such control and order is not fully possible. In fact, the ill body of the prostitute embodies the threat of contagion that emerges as a circular motif in the narrative. The scenes of the Carnival describe a destabilizing moment of disorder when the prostitute can circulate disguised on the streets. Thus Santa periodically circulates around the city in her carriage that opens or closes according to the time of day:

They always sent her a car; covered at midday, when they invited her to drink an *aperitif* in some cantina of high lineage that nonetheless admits women to its discreet interiors. In the evening, [it was] an open car, a two-seater with a blue flag, on whose Moroccan leather back she would ride, reclined indifferently, to Chapultepec to breathe fresh air, with little more tyranny than to pass by the doors of the club and smile from her jogging carriage at the cluster of members, who with wise stoicism exchanged with each other their grimaces and winks, and in rigorous successive order, one by one stayed up all night with her in an erotic battle.[6] (Gamboa [1903] 2013, 99)

However, full transgression is never possible for Santa, for the message in Gamboa's novel is that illness can be contained, territorialized, and expelled outside the walls of the city. Although the danger is always there—flowing through the city as in Santa's carriage—it is possible to contain it if the right urban policies and order are set in place. As Pile (1996) states, "The body-ego-space is territorialised, deterritorialised and reterritorialised—by modalities of identification, by psychic defense mechanisms, by internalised authorities, by intense feelings, by flows of power and meaning. Bodies are made within particular constellations of object relations—the family, the army, the state, the movies, the nation, and so on" (209). The novel describes such processes of deterritorialization and reterretorialization of the prostitute's body, a body that internalizes flows of power and meaning, a body that ultimately dies due to the internalization of disease.

As he does with the city, Gamboa builds an ideal representation of the prostitute. Although her body ultimately corrupts and dies, Gamboa's narrator transforms his subject into an aesthetic object of cult, this being the most controversial ethical position of Gamboa around his narrative subject. The religious ideology of martyrdom is at the base of many of the novel's descriptions, the lacerations and pains experienced by Santa's body as ominous warnings against the illicit practice of prostitution. But further, Gamboa's skillful narrator combines religious underpinnings with the aesthetic practice of naturalism. He is a tourist experiencing the city off limits with the curiosity of an expert voyeur, seeing Santa almost as an object of cult. However, the narrator's curiosity is veiled through a series of narrative devices, such as the character of Hipólito, a blind pianist obsessed with Santa. Gamboa only accesses the forbidden—the body of Santa—through a series of mediations to overcome Hipólito's blindness, the most evident, Jenaro, Hipólito's young assistant. In one scene, Jenaro describes Santa's body to Hipólito with a lowered voice in an extended metaphor of her bosom as "two hatched doves" attempting to break free of her dress (Gamboa [1903] 2013, 131). And, in another scene, the narrator uses Hipólito's imagination to see her body: "And with his imagination, his blind eyes closed shut, he saw it all, when Santa got naked while changing her blouse, one for indoors and another to go out to the street, made of silk, too, that revealed its quality by its friction against her clean and firm flesh."[7]

Through these eroticizations, Gamboa's voyeuristic perspective applies not only to the forbidden zones of the city, but also to those of the prostitute's body. The narrator maintains an ambivalent approach to this body through the trope of blindness. Experienced first as an aesthetic object, Santa's body also represents the fears of contagion. In Debra Castillo's (1998) words: "The import of Santa's transformation from an object of innocent aesthetic appreciation to a vulgarly usable body moves in two distinct directions. She is reinvented, first, as an aesthetic object, eroticized in the traditional sense as the seductive work of art that becomes Santa; second, she is re-created as a deaestheticized commodity, a common whore (. . .)" (44). The voyeuristic perspective on Santa's body reinforces its quality as an object, turning the prostitute into a subjectivity without a voice, a visual token within Mexico's patriarchal model of social order. As with the Porfirian ordering of city, she a is matter to be sculpted, and yet, an imperfect vision that cannot be fully seen, as Margo Glantz (1983) explains: "The characterization of Santa, about whom the author says, 'Santa was not a woman, no, she was a . . . .' And with that ellipsis, he silences the term 'loathsome one,' making the prostitute an ambiguous being; neither a woman nor a pronounced word, the whore as a marginalized although public animal; feminine, although denied femininity, barely terrestrial: only a body"[8] (42).

"Only a body" states Glantz, a body reduced to artistic matter to be sculpted, erected as a monument for the public contemplation of the reader. In that, Gamboa seeks to transform us into accomplices of his visions, turning us into a set of eyes participating in his desire, raising questions about the ethical dimensions of his novel. Are we to participate in the voyeuristic contemplation of disease? Are we going to visit with him the forbidden boroughs of the city? This dimension questions our role as readers, as it establishes gender implications of who is in charge of modeling the matter of fiction. As with Calvino's Zobeide, the city is a woman, and the architect, a man dreaming to find her in the hidden itineraries of the city. Also as in Zobeide, Gamboa's ordering gets lost in itineraries of desire that he cannot fully map.

NADIE ME VERÁ LLORAR: AT THE EDGES OF MODERNITY

Nadie me verá llorar brings to the fore the contradictions in Porfirio Díaz's project of modernity as the perspective shifts to that of the city's outcasts. The novel is located primarily in La Castañeda, a mental hospital that opened in 1910 in the outskirts of the City of Mexico. La Castañeda embodied the modernization project of Díaz; it was the production center of scientific knowledge that sought to regulate and explain the order of social hierarchies. Built with the goals of preventing the biological and moral contagion and disorder of Mexico's citizens, La Castañeda would guarantee the project of Mexican modernity's order and progress. In this section, I would like to focus on how La Castañeda corresponds to the spatial construction of what Michel Foucault (1984) defines as "heterotopia." Contrary to a utopia—a site with no real place—heteropias are "real places, places that do exist and that are formed in the very founding of society, which are something like counter-sites, a kind of effectively enacted utopia in which the real sites, all the other real sites that can be found within the culture, are simultaneously represented, contested, and inverted" (3). Foucault employs the figure of the mirror to further explain how heterotopias work in society:

> But it is also a heterotopia in so far as the mirror does exist in reality, where it exerts a sort of counteraction on the position that I occupy. From the standpoint of the mirror I discover my absence from the place where I am since I see myself over there. Starting from this gaze that is, as it were, directed toward me, from the ground of this virtual space that is on the other side of the glass, I come back toward myself; I begin again to direct my eyes toward myself and to reconstitute myself there where I am. The mirror functions as a heterotopia in this respect: it makes this place that I occupy at the moment when I look at myself in the glass at once absolutely real, connected with all the space that surrounds it, and absolutely unreal, since in order to be perceived it has to pass through this virtual point which is over there (4).

In her study of La Castañeda, Rivera Garza (2014) explains that the mental hospital was a detailed reflection of the external social order. Built as a mirror of Porfirio Díaz's society, it transformed its image into what Foucault calls the "heterotopia of deviation," a place where individuals whose behavior is deviant in relation to the required norm are located. One of the most important models for La Castañeda was that of Georges-Eugène Haussmann, who not only transformed mid-nineteenth-century Paris, but also designed a number of psychiatric institutions in Seine (Rivera Garza 2014, 58). Conceived as a city in miniature, La Castañeda had—besides the sections for residents and medical observation—a pharmacy, kitchen, laundry area, bakery, workshop, a farming colony, and a funeral home. The buildings established divisions of gender and social class, with a wing reserved for distinguished residents. Because of the ambitious characteristics of the project, La Castañeda became a monumental and onerous state business. As a small city, it mirrored the class and gender order of Porfirian society: "In brief, the project of Echagary and De la Barra's proposed a geographic distribution of pavillions that, while it reflected the latest development in the construction of psychiatric hospitals, also revealed the Porfirian ideas of a heirarchical social order in which men and women, rich and poor, occupied unequal positions"[9] (Rivera Garza 2014, 48).[10]

As a mirror, the novel distorts and reflects both the space and the language constructed by the Porfirio Díaz regime. The narrative is a diglossia—or a heteroglossia as Rivera Garza states, split into two languages: one scientific—represented in the medical discourse of Eduardo Oligochea—and one artistic—brought to life in the images of the photographer, Joaquín Buitrago. The third central character, Matilda Burgos, is the prostitute challenging Eduardo and Joaquín's attempts to define her. Thus the title of the novel, "no one will see me cry," a phrase that refers to her refusal to be portrayed as a "victim," and that can also be interpreted as the narrator's impossibility to fully "represent"—or "see"—her fluctuating subjectivity. At the center of the novel is Rivera Garza's questioning of historical narratives as mechanisms to deal with marginal subjectivities such as the insane, a topic that the author has further explored in her doctoral thesis in the field of history about La Castañeda.[11]

Before being confined to La Castañeda, Matilda worked at a brothel called La Modernidad (Modernity), a place run by a cross dresser, la Madame Porfiria. In La Modernidad, Matilda engages in erotic performances with another prostitute, Ligia, each of them a parody of different aspects of Porfirian society, the most famous one being a parody of *Santa*. Rivera Garza establishes the brothel as an inverted reflection of a society that seeks order by regulating and controlling women's sexuality as other titles of Matilda and Ligia's performances make also evident—*Enfermedad, Cárcel, Hospital, Neurastenia*, and *Reglamento* ("Illness," "Prison," "Hospital," "Nervous Exhaustion," and "Regulation"). Rivera Garza splits her narrative voice into two as well: one that focuses on fiction, and another that writes from the perspective of the historian, as in sections that provide historical background or citations of texts from the period of Federico Gamboa's *Santa*. There is lengthy reflection, for instance, about the role of the prostitute in the period: "Of all the obsessions that emerged at the end of the century, only prostitutes reached the status of legend. Poets pitied and celebrated them equally. Sculptors carved marble and wood with them in mind. Painters immortalized them. Physicians and lawyers created the first prostitution regulation to defend themselves from their risk and establish rules for playing with bodies"[12] (Rivera Garza [1999] 2014, 160). These meta-texts offer feminist perspectives about the situation of the prostitute at that time, and contrary to the naturalist narrative of *Santa*, present the issue as a layered, complex problem in Mexican society seen from the perspective of the victims.

The role of performance in the novel is central. Along with the direct performances by Matilda, Rivera Garza's seeks to breach the gap between voice and vision, by creating a "visual" proximity to the past. Modernist in tone, the novel questions the role of modernity in shaping the subjectivities of those on the margins of Porfirian society, such as prostitutes and the insane.

The novel is thus a counter-memory, an alternative narrative of the Porfirian years, conceived from a feminist perspective. Central in the historical reconstruction of the novel is the question of how women are erased images, the omitted voices in the ordering created by the historical narrative of Mexican modernity. Perceived as a source of social disorder, women were at the center of inquiry of Porfirian statesmen, intellectuals, and doctors. Because Porfirians believed women to hold the future of the nation, their bodies were examined, measured, photographed and turned into objects of inquiry. As a counter-memory, *Nadie me verá llorar* turns women into the performers of an alternative modernity.

This alternative modernity is particularly significant in how women walk the city and in how they perform space to create spatial relations with others. Gillian Rose (1993) states that discourse, fantasy, and the body are three critical elements in the thinking of space, "because each participates in the relation between self and other" (247). This "relationality" of space is "performed," "constituted through iteration rather than through essence," Rose explains following Judith Butler's discussions of gender as performance. Space also enables the playful repetition through mimesis of the role a woman occupies in a discourse (Rose 1993, 253). Fantasy is crucial in the formation of spatial difference and desire by women as it creates an "imaginary space" that is the *mise-en-scène* of desire; "they are the scenarios, the settings, the articulations of desire," Rose states, following De Laureti's notions of sexual difference; such space is permeable, is "doubling and splitting" (257) and acts as a mirror of certain gender roles and expectations embedded in spatial locations.

In her walks in the city, Matilda deconstructs the solemnity of streets and monuments, creating a "sentimental map" of the city, a description that contrasts with the ordering imagined by the Porfirian urban project. In her itinerary, Matilda creates what Michel de Certeau (1988) defines as a "linguistic and pedestrian enunciation" where location "has the function of introducing an other in relation to this 'I' and thus establishing a conjunctive and disjunctive articulation of places" (99). Matilda's walking selects (orders) and fragments (disorders) the space traversed, it skips over links and also names aspects that are only present in her memory:

> This is the fountain where Matilda heard the voice of her destiny for the first time. There is the morgue where Joaquín undertook the [photographic] developing of the first faces of death. Matilda lived in that festoon-adorned house under the rules of a man she never knew and a woman whose name she doesn't remember. May they rest in peace. There is the Parisian. That place that is now called Progress once went by the name of Modernity. In the sentimental map of the city the monuments are transparent and the scale is uneven. Matilda and Joaquín don't like to cry.[13] (Rivera Garza [1999] 2014, 213)

Through her walking, Matilda rewrites and reorders space in a playful repetition of her biography; she reenacts sites of her memory transforming the given meaning. She builds a "sentimental city where the monuments are transparent and the scale, asymmetrical." But most importantly, her walking stresses an emotional, experiential connection with space that transforms Matilda into an active subject who refuses to be placed or secluded into a document, a category or a photo, like the ones Joaquín takes at La Castañeda, photographs seeking to measure the inmates' bodies, seeking to determine their deformities. In creating an emotional map of the city, Matilda refuses to be mapped, located, named, or ordered. Contrary to Santa's strolls through the city, Matilda acts as a protagonist of her walk; she is not simply the tourist hiding in a carriage. Matilda appropriates space making it her own. She is not a passive streetwalker, but rather a joyful, participative walker: "Once over the benches, however, her eyes become anxious. In disorder, with the voracity of the self-taught, her eyes open more to take it all in. Every window, every cornice, every cloud, all the colors, every man and every woman who passes by her side leaves indelible footprints in her memory"[14] (Rivera Garza [1999] 2014, 121). Matilda devours the city, thus not allowing others to devour her.

Rivera Garza establishes the walk in the city as a way in which historical subjects articulate their inner stories, "a method without doors," as she names it: "They both walked on the edges of history, always about to slip and fall out of their spell and still always within it. Very within it"[15] (Rivera Garza [1999] 2014, 212). This quote is particularly significant for the importance of the minor stories within the narrative of the Porfirian years. Those minor stories are mobilized in the act of performing their roles within the landscape of history in subverted ways. As De Certeau (1988) explains in "Walking in the City," the act of walking in the streets mobilizes other subtle, stubborn, embodied, and resistant meanings. The "proper spaces" created for the city by the ordering of the lettered class are interrupted, disordered, and re-signified by the everyday practices of moving on foot (93).

Photography has a central role in the novel at two levels. As archives, photographs serve as companion pieces to interview documents. More specifically, photographs of the insane reveal an underlying discourse on how art transforms its subjects, namely prostitutes and the insane. This novel is about conducting an impossible interview with one of the many prostitutes documented in Rivera Garza's research. Joaquín Buitrago acts as Rivera Garza's alter ego, carrying on an aesthetic project of reconstructing Matilda's subjectivity. Given the importance it had at the height of *higienismo* in México, it is not surprising that vision is a predominant ordering strategy in this novel. Photography played a central role in the modern objectification of the female body. Framed according to visual codes that John Tagg

(1988) describes as guided by the "burden of frontality," the photographs of prostitutes, along with those of criminals and the insane, signify a bluntness and naturalness that present women as objects of supervision or reform (36–37). However, Rivera Garza manipulates such a visual archive following a tradition of Avant-gardist experimentation. Spacing is one of the main strategies to break this illusion of visual objectification of the female body in photography. Referring to the Surrealists, Rosalind E. Krauss (1996) states, "the photographic image, thus 'spaced' is deprived of one of the most powerful of photography's many illusions: it is robbed of a sense of presence. It is the image of simultaneity. It is spacing that makes clear that we are not looking at reality, but at the world infested by interpretation or signification" (107).

This spacing constitutes another performative practice in the novel. The spacing to which Krauss refers is produced in the novel by juxtaposing Matilda's voice against the photographical record. As a performative subject, she situates herself outside of the visual archive, in an imaginary narrative flux that rewrites her position in hegemonic historical narratives. Her dissonant voice contests a set of discourses that seek to regulate women's subjectivity, as represented by Joaquín and Eduardo, the voices of art and science. The polyphonic quality of the narrative parallels the walking itineraries previously described, as historical subjects construct and deconstruct the discourse of history. As Laura M. Kanost (2008) states, "these multiple narrative strategies point to and reinforce a central preoccupation at work on many levels in the novel: the ethical problem of how one person can access and represent another individual's private history and perspective" (303). Key in this polyphony of voices is the use of parody and intertextuality as previously mentioned.

Nadie me verá llorar thus explores the possibilities and challenges of women's writing through the image of the "performing woman." This recurrent image at the beginning of the twentieth century contrasts with the woman as object of contemplation or inspiration as present in Spanish American *Modernismo*: "Much as the classical muses synthesized the capacity for inspiration with their own artistic talent, the performing woman as portrayed in Latin American literary culture of the time offered a bridge from representations of women as art objects or catalysts to their conception as cultural actors" (Unruh 2006, 6). In so doing, performance becomes a way of constructing what Edward Soja (1999) defines as the "third space," a space of resistance, or a "critical thirding-as-Othering": "This Othering does not derive simply and sequentially from the original binary opposition and/or contradiction, but seeks instead to disorder, deconstruct and tentatively reconstitute in a different form the entire dialectical sequence and logic" (269). Such "Othering" as this section demonstrates adopts both a spatial and linguistic characteristic, by which the figure of the prostitute gains an agency as the maker of her own historical narrative, the city being the locus of her enunciation.

POSTCARDS OF THE URBAN IMAGINATION

I would like to return here to the question that opened these reflections on spatial ordering and subjectivity. How does one reconstruct itineraries of desire? Is it possible to map the subjectivities that desire and that are desired? As J. B. Harley (1989) has extensively studied, maps are objects culturally situated revealing certain rules of ethnocentricity and social order. Operating behind the mask of a seemingly neutral science, a map "hides and denies its social dimensions at the same time as it legitimates"(8). Harley further explains, "maps are a cultural text. By accepting their textuality we are able to embrace a number of different interpretative possibilities" (9). As such, a map shows the experiential dimension of social relationships, their instability, and potential disorder: what I map is always something that I want to establish in relation to an "other."

I have discussed two types of maps in this chapter. The first one shows the reinforcement of a social order, a way of establishing boundaries between the ideal city of the Porfirian imaginary and what was left out. These boundaries are a form of ordering as they are ways of containing desire, regulating its flows, and determining possible directions for a collective imagination of place determined by what is inside and outside of the map. Although no physical borders were marked in this map, its imaginary walls are built by the discourse of modernity that is at the base of the Porfiriato. This map establishes a positionality for bodies: it locates them into a geographical and social grid. However, as seen in *Santa*, the efforts of mapping are always threatened by desire's disorder, making the map an impossible object. The second map is Rivera Garza's novel. It is experiential, the spaces of the disorder imagined by the Porfirian order, a "map of contingent identities and circumstantial memories" as the one drafted by Solnit and Gómez-Peña (2010) in *Infinite City*. This second map establishes openness instead of the closing of modern order, a radical openness that locates the space of the other at its center. As I attempted to demonstrate for the case of Rivera Garza's novel, this experiential map does not locate desire, but rather it shows its imaginary flows through the textuality of social life. This map of flowing desire is then the map of a "mobile city" as De Certeau (1988) calls this type of representation: "A migrational, or metaphorical, city thus slips into the clear text of the planned and readable city" (93). Whereas Gamboa establishes representation as the erotic and regulatory construction of a body-city, Rivera Garza opens up the endless possibilities of the disordered margin, of bodies-cities that resist location, migrational bodies that choose the margin as a site of resistance. In bell hooks's (2000) words, "I am located in the margin. I make a definite distinction between that marginality which is imposed by oppressive structures and that marginality one chooses as a site of resistance—as location of radical openness and possibility. . . . We are transformed, individually, collectively, as we make radical creative space which affirms and sustains our subjectivity, which gives us a new location from which to articulate our sense of the world" (209). As two postcards of the Porfirian imaginary, the novels by Gamboa and Rivera Garza open new possibilities for the understanding of space in the construction and deconstruction of a social order.

NOTES

1. . . . *destácase La Giralda, carnicería a la moderna, de tres puertas, piso de piedra artificial, mostrador de mármol y hierro, con pilares muy delgados para que el aire lo ventile todo libremente; con grandes balanzas que deslumbran de puro limpias; con su percha metálica, en semicírculo, de cuyos gruesos garfios penden las reses descabezadas, inmensas, abiertas por el medio, luciendo el blanco sucio de sus costillas y el asqueroso rojo sanguinolento de carne fresca y recién muerta; con nubes de moscas inquietas, voraces y uno o dos mastines callejeros, corpulentos, de pelo erizo y fuerte, echados sobre la acera. . .*

2. . . . *dentro del antro que a ella le daba de comer; antro que en cortísimo tiempo devoraría aquella hermosura y aquella carne joven que ignoraba seguramente todos los horrores que le esperaban.*

3. *Cae de catedral tupida lluvia de oro, sus campanas replican a vuelo. Atruenan los aires millares de cohetes, las bandas ejecutan nuestro himno, el canto nacional; en la lejana Ciudadela, disparan los cañones la salva de honor; los astros en el cielo, miran a la tierra y parpadean, cual si fuesen a verter lágrimas siderales, conmovidos ante el espectáculo de un pueblo delirante de amor a su terruño, que una noche en cada año crece en sí, recuerda que es soberano y es fuerte.*

4. *Usted nos dijo que era su patria una ventana con geranios y claveles, ¿verdad. . .? Pues usted es más feliz que yo, que hallándome en la mía, ni siquiera debo llamarla . . . Mi patria, hoy por hoy, es la casa de Elvira, mañana será otra, ¿quién lo sabe? . . . Y yo . . . seré siempre una . . . Y la palabra horrenda, el estigma, la deletreó en la ventanilla de la calandria, hacia fuera, como si escupiese algo que le hiciera daño.*

5. *Tan selectivos como entusiastas, los porfirianos luchaban por preservar y cultivar un orden social y moral que apoyara a las clases existentes y a las jerarquías étnicas, al patriarcado y a la familia nuclear. Planearon lograrlo al diseñar una serie de iniciativas legales para regular la vida pública, los espacios urbanos e incluso los cuerpos humanos.*

6. *Mandábanle siempre coche; cerrado al mediodía, cuando la citaban a beber el aperitivo en alguna cantina de prosapia y que ello no obstante, admiten mujeres*

en sus discretos interiores. A la tarde, coche abierto, una victoria de bandera azul en cuyo respaldar de tafilete, indolentemente reclinada, íbase al bosque de Chapultepec a respirar aire puro, sin más tiranía que pasar por las puertas del club y sonreír desde el fondo de su victoria al trote, al racimo de socios en sus redes cautivos, los que, con sabio estoicismo, juntos se disputaban sus muecas y guiños y por riguroso orden sucesivo, a noche por barba, con ella se desvelaban en erótica lid.

7. *Y con el pensamiento, muy cerrados los ojos ciegos, lo presenció todo, cuando Santa quedó desnuda, al mudar de camisa, la de casa por una de la calle y de seda también, que acusó su calidad en el frote contra la carne limpia y dura.*

8. *La caracterización de Santa, de quien dice su autor: 'Santa no era mujer, no; era una . . .' Y con estos puntos suspensivos calla la palabra 'nefanda,' haciendo de la prostituta un ser equívoco; ni mujer ni palabra pronunciada, la puta como animal marginado, aunque público; femenino, aunque negado a la feminidad, terrestre apenas: un cuerpo solamente.*

9. *En suma, el proyecto de Echegaray y De la Barra proponía una distribución geográfica de pabellones que, al tiempo que reflejaba el último desarrollo en construcción de hospitales psiquiátricos, también ponía de manifiesto las ideas porfirianas de un orden jerárquico social en el cual hombres y mujeres, ricos y pobres, ocupaban sitios desiguales.*

10. As the novel (Rivera Garza [1999] 2014) describes: "The asylum has twenty-five buildings spread out over 141,662 square meters. Inside, protected by high walls and iron fences, the patients and the employees project their shadows over places set aside from time. The asylum is a toy city. It has sentries, streets, infirmaries, jails, and dwellings. There are workshops where men assemble coffins and carpets without piercing their hands with nails and without slitting their wrists. They don't receive payment. The women clean the blue uniforms until they have left them faded and in the sewing workshops, they make shawls and raps, they mend shirts [and] frayed sheets. There are poets writing letters to God; mechanics, pharmacists, policemen, thieves, anarchists who have given up violence. Love stories happen. Silenced melancholy. Social classes. Despair that is expressed vociferously. The pain never ends." "*El manicomio tiene veinticinco edificios diseminados en 141.662 metros cuadrados. Dentro, protegidos por altos muros y rejas de hierro, los locos y los castaños proyectan sus sombras sobre lugares apartados del tiempo. El manicomio es una ciudad de juguete. Tiene garitas, calles, enfermerías, cárceles, viviendas. Hay bullicio y riñas, tráfico de cigarrillos y estupefacientes, intentos de suicidio. Hay talleres donde los hombres fabrican ataúdes y alfombras sin agujerearse las manos con clavos y sin cortarse las venas. No reciben sueldo. Las mujeres lavan los uniformes azules hasta dejarlos desteñidos y, en los talleres de costura, hacen rebosos y sarapes, remiendan camisas, sábanas raídas. Hay poetas escribiéndole cartas a Dios; mecánicos, farmacéuticos, policías, ladrones, anarquistas que han renunciado a la violencia. Ocurren historias de amor. Melancolía callada. Clases sociales. Desesperación que se expresa a gritos. El dolor nunca se acaba*" (37–38).

11. "Among the historiographical debates that typically emphasize the processes of State construction, reconstruction, or centralization, the polysemic narratives of mental sufferings vividly recall destruction, dismantling and dispersion; in other

words, the centrifugal forces that Bakhtin associated with heteroglossia." *"En medio de los debates historiográficos que por lo regular enfatizan los procesos de construcción, reconstrucción o centralización del Estado, las narrativas polisémicas de los padecimientos mentales recuerdan de manera vívida la destrucción, el desmantelamiento y la dispersión; es decir, las fuerzas centrífugas que Bakhtin asoció con la heteroglosia"* (Rivera Garza 2014, 31).

12. *De todas las obsesiones que emergieron a finales del siglo, sólo las prostitutas alcanzaron la calidad de leyenda. Los poetas las compadecieron y las celebraron por igual. Los escultores tallaron el mármol y la madera con ellas en mente. Los pintores las inmortalizaron. Los médicos y los licenciados crearon el primer reglamento de prostitución para defenderse de su peligro y establecer las reglas del juego de los cuerpos.*

13. *Ésta es la fuente donde Matilda oyó la voz de su destino por primera vez. Ahí estaba la morgue donde Joaquín se encargó de develar los primeros rostros de la muerte. En esa casa adornada con un festón Matilda vivió siete años bajo las reglas de un hombre al que jamás conoció y una mujer cuyo nombre no recuerda. Descansen en paz. Aquí está la Parisina. Ese lugar que ahora se llama Progreso alguna vez llevó el nombre de La Modernidad. En el mapa de su ciudad sentimental los monumentos son transparentes y la escala desigual. A Matilda y a Joaquín no les gusta llorar.*

14. *Una vez sobre las banquetas, sin embargo, sus ojos se vuelven ansiosos. En desorden, con la voracidad de los autodidactas, sus ojos se abren más para captarlo todo. Cada ventana, cada cornisa, cada nube, todos los colores, cada hombre y cada mujer que pasa a su lado dejan huellas indelebles en su memoria.*

15. *Los dos anduvieron siempre en las orillas de la historia, siempre a punto de resbalar y caer fuera de su embrujo y siempre, sin embargo, dentro. Muy dentro.*

WORKS CITED

Bliss, Katherine. 2010. *Compromised Positions: Prostitution, Public Health, and Gender Politics in Revolutionary Mexico*. University Park, PA: Penn State University Press.

Calvino, Italo. 1978. *Invisible Cities*. Translated by William Weaver. New York: Harcourt Brace Jovanovich.

Castillo, Debra. 1998. *Easy Women: Sex and Gender in Modern Mexican Fiction*. Minneapolis: University of Minnesota Press.

De Certeau, Michelle. 1988. *The Practice of Everyday Life*. Translated by Steven Randall. Berkeley: University of California Press.

Foucault, Michel. 1984. "Of Other Spaces: Utopias and Heterotopias." Translated by Jay Miskowiec. *Architecture/Mouvement/Continité*. October: 1–9.

Gamboa, Federico. (1903) 2013. *Santa*. Madrid: Drácena.

Glantz, Margo. 1983. *La lengua en la mano*. México City: Premiá.

Harley, J. B. 1989. "Deconstructing the Map." *Cartographica* 26 (2): 1–20.

hooks, bell. 2000. "Choosing the Margin as a Space of Radical Openness." In *Gender, Space, Architecture. An Interdisciplinary Introduction*, edited by Jane Rendell, Barbara Penner, Iain Borden, 203–309. New York: Routledge.

Kanost, Laura M. 2008. "Pasillos sin luz: Reading the Asylum in *Nadie me verá llorar.*" *Hispanic Review* 76 (3): 299–316.

Krauss, Rosalind E. 1996. *The Originality of the Avant-Garde and Other Modernist Myths.* Cambridge, MA: MIT Press.

Lefebvre, Henri. (1974) 1991. *The Production of Space.* Translated by Donald Nicholson-Smith. Cambridge, MA: Blackwell.

Pile, Steve. 1996. *The Body and the City: Psychoanalysis, Space and Subjectivity.* New York: Routledge.

Rama, Ángel. (1984) 1996. *The Lettered City: Post-Contemporary Interventions.* Translated by John Charles Chasteen. Durham, NC: Duke University Press.

Rivera Garza, Cristina. (1999) 2014. *Nadie me verá llorar.* Barcelona: Tusquets. 4a edición.

———. 2014. *La Castañeda. Narrativas dolientes desde el Manicomio General.* México: Maxi-Tusquets. 4a edición.

Rose, Gillian. 1993. *Feminism and Geography. The Limits of Geographical Knowledge.* Minneapolis, MN: University of Minnesota Press.

Soja, Edward. 1999. "Thirdspace: Expanding the Scope of the Geographical Imagination." In *Human Geography Today*, edited by Doreen Massey, John Allen and Philip Sarre, 260–278. Cambridge: Polity Press.

Solnit, Rebecca. 2010. *Infinite City. A San Francisco Atlas.* Berkeley: University of California Press.

Tagg, John. 1988. *The Burden of Representation.* Amherst: University of Massachusetts Press.

Tenorio-Trillo, Mauricio. 1996. "1910 Mexico City: Space and Nation in the City of the Centenario." *Journal of Latin American Studies* 28 (1): 75–104.

Unruh, Vicky. 2006. *Performing Women and Modern Literary Culture in Latin America.* Austin: University of Texas Press.

Chapter 2

Carlos Slim's Urban Imaginary

Plaza Carso and the Privatization of Public Space

Glen David Kuecker

PLAZA CARSO AND THE DELIRIOUS CITY

Those who encounter Mexico City's Plaza Carso are confronted with a jarring spatial experience. Its location—an intervention, if not invasion, into a de-industrialized neighborhood that is undergoing an intensive and extensive urban renewal defined by a gated community, an elite sensibility—throws the visitor off balance. Its disorientating location is matched by an oddly nonsensical mish-mash of architectural design that throws sharply contrary horizontal and vertical lines into conflicting angles, split levels, and otherwise incongruent geometric configurations. The space is a *non sequitur* urban form within a megalopolis flooded with spatial contradictions.

To make some sense of it all, the Plaza Carso visitor would be well advised to read Rubén Gallo's (2004) introduction to *The Mexico City Reader*. He attempts to capture the essence of Mexico City with the adjective "delirious." It is a place "where one's five senses are constantly bombarded by the cultural contradictions that make life in the capital unpredictable" (3). Gallo describes the "complexities of Mexico City" as having a "delirious nature" defined by "endless contradictions (it is a place of extreme poverty and extreme wealth), its surreal images (André Breton famously called it the most surreal place on earth), and its jumbling of historical periods (modernist high-rises next to eighteenth-century palaces are a common sight)" The city is "a vast stage for unpredictable everyday dramas: a chaotic, vibrant, delirious city" (3). The adjective "delirious" is potent enough to give meaning to the reality of the megalopolis that others have deployed it to make meaning of the city. Daniel Hernández (2011), for example, uses it in his edgy chronicle, *Down and Delirious in Mexico City*.

The Oxford English Dictionary defines "delirious" as "an acutely disturbed state of mind resulting from illness or intoxication and characterized by restlessness, illusions, and incoherence of thought and speech." Carrying emotional and mental meanings, these are fascinating words for describing the 20–25 million souls that constitute Mexico City. They suggest many things to us, among them the tension between order and disorder within the urban form that is a central concern of this chapter's exploration of Mexico City through a case study of Plaza Carso, one of its newest spaces.

The restlessness, illusions, and incoherence of the megalopolis call for ordering, and Plaza Carso is one of the ways the city has recently become ordered. Situated in *Nuevo Polanco*, in what once was an industrial neighborhood, Plaza Carso is Latin America's largest mixed-use building complex (http://www.plazacarso.com.mx/historia.php). It consists of residential and office towers, an upscale shopping mall, two art museums, a theater, and recreational facilities. The *Wall Street Journal*, in 2011, estimated its value to be USD800 million, while another observer (Bird Pico 2011) marked it at USD1.4 billion. Construction started in 2008 and finished, for the most part, in 2011. The *Wall Street Journal* (Whelan 2014) reports that Plaza Carso has 980 apartments, more than 1.9 million square feet of offices, stores, and a hotel. This chapter's consideration of urban order and disorder focuses on the urban imaginary revealed by the Plaza Carso project, especially how the twenty-first century articulation of Rama's lettered city is knowable by exploring the different ways we can locate Plaza Carso within Mexico City.

THE URBAN IMAGINARY AND PRIVATELY OWNED PUBLIC SPACE

The way a mega-project brings order to a delirious city can be understood from the perspective of the urban imaginary. Jean-Paul Sartre was one of the first to deploy the "imaginary" to critique society. He wrote (1940), "Imaginaries are historical constructions defined by the interactions of subjects in society . . . and the set of values, institutions, laws and symbols that are common to a particular social group." As an urban imaginary, Plazo Carso is a material articulation of the social construction of values and symbols conveyed by a group of elites, in this case the mega-project's intellectual author, Carlos Slim and his son-in-law, Fernando Romero, who is the project's architect. Charles Taylor (2004), in his *Modern Social Imaginaries,* invites us to understand imaginaries to be "the ways people imagine their social existence, how they fit together with each other, how things go on between them and their fellows, the expectations that are normally met, and the deeper normative notions and images that underline these expectations" (23). As an urban imaginary, spaces like Plaza Carso provide the structures that order daily life, which generate the ways people mentally map their place within society. Full of symbolic meanings, the structures of the built environment provide a schemata for people to perform the ideologies and norms sought after by architects and designers. These hegemonic projects, of course, are never quite so complete, as people construct contested meanings of the spaces and often produce uses alternative to the architect and designer's intent.

Building from Taylor, Columbia University's The Urban Imaginary Project (2014), invites us to consider: "Yet if we talk about *Urban Imaginaries* [original italics] we could say that they are the construction of the chosen idea of cities that their inhabitants intentionally produce, a system conformed by social relations, architectural operations, urban policies and the ideology behind them." Plaza Carso projects a "chosen idea" of the city that is Carlos Slim's urban imaginary. With his billions of dollars, Slim has the capacity to build spaces and define the urban form. Slim's urban imaginary is a combination of four key elements. First, it is defined by his business empire, *Grupo Carso*. Plaza Carso's office towers host Slim's empire. Second, his urban imaginary is defined by Slim's philanthropy that comes in the form of *Museo Soumaya*, which serves as the venue for the richest man in the world to share his private art collection with the public. Third, Plaza Carso's shopping mall manifests an urban imaginary defined by capitalist consumption. Fourth, it is defined by private residences that take the form of gated-communities for the elite. These four elements come together through Slim's embrace of neoliberalism, a political and economic ideology that promotes the private sector over the public.

The spatial turn in critical theory, led by urban geographers like Edward Soja (2010), can help us to think through how Slim's urban imaginary is rooted in privately owned public space. Soja's (2010, 44–46) consideration of "spatial justice" posits that all urban space has been reduced to three bounded forms: property held individually, property held by corporations, and property held by the state. The name "Plaza Carso" reveals how this works. In Latin America, "plaza" takes special meaning as a public space available for all to use. The plaza, as a commons, is often bounded by buildings that represent other spaces: the cathedral, governing palaces, merchant houses, and private residences. While those spaces often carry immense power within the urban form they yield to the public on the plaza itself. With neoliberalism, and the urban imaginary of elites like Slim, an enclosure of the commons has taken place as the "plaza" is now owned privately. The world "Carso" represents both the corporatization and individualization of space. The word is derived from Slim's first name, Carlos, and his deceased wife's first name, Soumaya. The individual family name is constituted within the corporate conglomerate,

Grupo Carso. With Slim's urban imaginary, the city's public space becomes enclosed by his private ownership and corporate identity.

Fernando Romero, Plaza Carso's architect, stated the following about Museo Soumaya, which is the architectural centerpiece of Plaza Carso (Butler 2010):

> The Soumaya Museum is located on a former industrial zone dating from the 1940s which today presents a very high commercial potential. The Soumaya Museum plays a key role in the reconversion of the area: as a preeminent cultural program, it acts as an initiator in the transformation of the urban perception. Moreover, its institutional status activates the public space with functionalities other than commercial and grants the new neighborhood the urban intensity it required. In order to create a new identity for the site, the building needed to acquire a strong urban presence. Thus, the Soumaya Museum was conceived as a sculptural building that is both unique and contemporary. Its avant-garde morphology and typology define a new paradigm in the history of Mexican and international architecture.

LOCATING PLAZA CARSO IN THE DELIRIOUS CITY

The *Oxford English Dictionary* defines "locating" as: "The action of placing; the fact or condition of being placed; settlement in a place." At first a simple exercise in geography, location and locating can take on layers of meaning that merit reflection for locating Plaza Carso in the delirious city. Location is one of the ways the mind makes sense of the intersection between abstract and fixed space that enables us to understand the world we inhabit (Gregory 1994; Hägerstrand 1975; and Haggett 1965). Locating is one of the ways people order cities and it is integral to the urban imaginary. Location is both an intellectual abstraction—we can "locate" Shanghai even if we are (a) not there, or (b) have never directly experienced it—and the fixed, material space defined by the "fact" of physical location. Shanghai exists in a specific, fixed, physical space that is about as close to being a fact as we can get in this postmodern age. The tension between abstract and fixed space is suggested by the *Oxford English Dictionary* definition, "condition of being placed." The passive voice raises the question of agency, the "who" or "what" does the placing, as well as those who are the objects of the placing.

In the case of Plaza Carso, "the condition of being placed," is an ordering proposition, the putting of things in their place, or what Ángel Rama ([1984] 1996) calls the "harmonious disposition of things" (4). Location brings order to disordered urban spaces. It helps to frame, stabilize, and fix the fluidity of the urban form, especially as it experiences the constant and necessarily turbulent process of urban reproduction that comes with capitalism's "creative destruction" (Schumpeter [1942] 1994) and Marx's notion of "all that is solid melts into the air" (see Berman 1988). The *Oxford English Dictionary*'s definition, "settlement in a place" further suggests the "harmonious disposition of things," although we know from the history of colonialism that "settlement" is often accomplished with displacement, removal, dispossession that suggests the "location" of Plaza Carso is closely associated with the problem of capitalist reproduction in the urban form, what David Harvey (2004) calls "accumulation through dispossession." We are mindful here that Plaza Carso brings the upscale *Polanco* neighborhood of Mexico City to a de-industrialized space: an area where glass was once made in a factory is now a prime location for Saks Fifth Avenue.

Answering the question of agency, the central protagonist in the story of Plaza Carso's location is Carlos Slim, who is, after all, the intellectual author of the development project. Fernando Romero, the architect, plays an equally important role, as he is the agent translating Slim's urban imaginary into the reality of the built space, the person who orchestrates the act of placing. Understanding "location" as the "act of being placed" suggests a subject-object relationship. The protagonists are acting upon an object or objects in their act of placing, resulting in an objectification of space. As signifiers, Slim and Romero not only create the sign of Plaza Carso, but also locate it, giving a particular meaning to a fixed space within the space of Mexico City. Location as the act of signifying generates a new meaning for the city, while displacing and erasing the previous location, what was the before the act of settlement takes place with location. Also, location as signification, blocks, prevents, or denies potential "locations" from happening, especially those seen as undesirable by those ordering the city.

LOCATING PLAZA CARSO WITHIN MEXICO

In a conventional way we understand Plaza Carso to be located in a neighborhood called Nuevo Polanco, which in turn is located in Mexico City, the capital of Mexico. While these are physical locations in fixed spaces, they are also socially, politically, economically, and culturally constructed abstractions that help us to make spatial sense of the world we live in.

If we start with saying that Plaza Carso is located in Mexico, that statement appears obvious enough. Benedict Anderson's (1991) *Imagined Communities*, however, suggests otherwise. A location like Mexico is the product of deep historical processes involving multiple, often conflicting understandings of Mexico and *mexicanidad* (Mexican-ness), what Mexicans call *lo mexicano*. Guillermo Bonfil Batalla's *México Profundo* (1996), informs us that often the project of imagining the nation-state, so essential to the process of making modern Mexico, is in tension with a "deep" Mexico contained within the survival of its Mesoamerican civilization. Locating Plaza Carso within Mexico is necessarily entangled within the larger narrative of Mexico's national identity. Suddenly, we become newly delirious as order gives way to disorder. We might go so far as to say that Plaza Carso is Carlos Slim's attempted ordering of the disorder, his urban imaginary of what it means to be Mexican, as well as his normative vision of what Mexico should be.

Locating Plaza Carso within the Mexican nation invites us to ask how people in Mexico City know that the city is a significant articulation of lo mexicano, and if Plaza Carso meets the metric. It is the experience of everyday life that helps to locate city residents in Mexico, especially the sensory encounters, the smells, tastes, noises, and the physical contact. These rest at the core of the city dwellers' *habitus*, the routines of life as citizens navigate urban space in set patterns that come to constitute behavior that scales up to the national identity. But, it is the iconic places that locate Mexico City in Mexico. A picture of the *Zócalo* immediately locates the image in Mexico City, but also the nation. A drunk evening with friends in *Plaza Garibaldi* only happens in Mexico and only in Mexico City. An afternoon on the lawn in the commons at *UNAM* with the great, multi-story mural on the *Biblioteca Central* firmly locates us in Mexico and Mexico City. A celebration at night after the victory of the national fútbol team at the base of *El Ángel*, the Monument to Independence, locates firmly in the national narrative no matter how turbulent that narrative might be. Likewise, the *Torre Latinoamericana*, once the tallest building in Latin America, locates the viewer in Mexico, but also Mexico City.

Plaza Carso is still too new to become an iconic space that locates those who experience it within Mexico and Mexico City. Prospects are good, however, that with time it will become an iconic place, especially with the distinctive architectural design of Museo Soumaya, the rising star of its architect, and the prominence of its patron as one of the world's richest men. The interesting thing, however, is the lack of lo mexicano in Plaza Carso. There is little reference to Mexico within this space. The Mexican flag does not fly as it proudly does in the Zócalo. Instead, Slim's corporate logos dominate the plaza's signs: Telcel and Sanborns circulate freely in this space. Indeed, this corporate presence may well be the only signification that Plaza Carso is in Mexico. The iconic building, Museo Soumaya, may even be understood as a blatant rejection of Mexico's iconic structure, the pyramid.

LOCATING PLAZA CARSO WITHIN GLOBAL CAPITALISM

We might have better luck finding the logic of Plaza Carso's location within the circuits of neoliberal globalization, especially given the importance of privately owned public space within Slim's urban imaginary. Carlos Slim's ability to locate Plaza Carso, to generate Rama's "harmonious disposition of things," rests within his USD70 billion in accumulated capital. His emergence as one of the richest men in the world is the story of Mexico's economic transformation of the 1980s and 1990s, the time when structural adjustment policies shifted Mexico from a statist to neoliberal economy. The neoliberal transformation, following arguments advanced by scholars like William Robinson (2008), subordinated Mexico to a triad of transnational forces—a global elite class, corporations, and institutions—that transcended previous restraints on power rooted in the sovereign nation-state. Robinson argues that Slim belongs to the "polyarchy," which is a new political and economic group in Latin America that has unprecedented power in society due to their ability to subordinate the state to their agendas. From this perspective, we can see Plaza Carso's location as a form of polyarchic urbanism.

Polyarchic urbanism derives from the logic of neoliberal globalization's freeing of global networks of capital that permitted the unrestrained pursuit of profit. The forces of neoliberal restructuring generated much of the reworking of Mexico City's urban form that constitutes polyarchic urbanism. The building of a strip of corporate office buildings along the highway to Toluca and on the fringes of the impoverished Santa Fe neighborhood during the 1990s, as presented in chapter 5 of this volume, was one of the early manifestations of the neoliberal restructuring of Mexico City. The massive urban renewal project in Centro Histórico, another Carlos Slim project, is another example, as well as the pre-Plaza Carso development of Nuevo Polanco.

From the perspective of global circuits of capital, Plaza Carso is best located with other urban development projects that feature mix use buildings catering to an elite class. These include the shopping mall complexes of Singapore, urban development in the United Arab Emirates, gated-communities in Chinese cities, or boutique cities built from scratch like South Korea's New Songdo City (Kuecker 2013 and 2015). Among these, Plaza Carso shares many common features with the "instant cities," such as New Songdo City. Each has provocatively designed office towers for the local branches of transnational corporations and their national partners. Each has luxury condo/apartment units with all the amenities: spa services, fitness centers, tennis courts, social spaces for entertainment, valet parking, and high levels of security. Each has a shopping mall featuring the highest of high-end stores that mark social status through conspicuous consumption. Amenities like upscale fitness centers, cinemas with VIP seating, beauty salons, and health spas further mark how places like Plaza Carso are located within the habitus of the transnational elite.

Following Rama, neoliberal globalization's "harmonious ordering of things" is reminiscent of David Korten's (2001) "cloud minder" metaphor for the transnational elite class. He is borrowing from a *Star Trek* episode in which the elite lived in luxury comfortably distant from the masses, so much so they were detached from basic reality of human existence. Plaza Carso is located in this detached "cloud minder" world, separate and distant from the daily realities experienced by millions upon millions of Mexico City's citizens. Slim's "harmonious ordering of things" thus takes on the disturbing resemblance of the growing global urban apartheid of the world city, a point discussed in this volume's conclusion.

LOCATING PLAZA CARSO WITHIN MEXICO CITY'S SPLINTERED URBAN IMAGINARY

As a "settlement within a place," Plaza Carso is located within Mexico City, a place whose delirious nature has defied attempts at explanation, interpretation, and analysis. Working through his architect, Fernando Romero, Slim attempts to "imagine the unimaginable" with Plaza Carso. Slim joins a deep history of urban elites who have sought a harmonious disposition of the city. While Plaza Carso is not the equivalent of the pyramids at Teotihuacan, or the arches built by colonial elites to welcome and honor new viceroys (Curcio-Nagy 2004), it does constitute a continuation of elite attempts at imagining the unimaginable.

Slim's urban imaginary is most reminiscent of the age of Porfirio Díaz (1876–1910), discussed in the previous chapter, when a group of elites sought to build a modern city using Paris as their inspiration. Grand boulevards, elaborate buildings, monuments, parks, and gardens, recast the urban form under their tutelage, as well as modern infrastructure such as urban trams, electricity, potable water, and sewers (Johns 1997). Department stores also brought the spectacle of consumerism to the city (Bunker 2014), which invited new adventures for the city dweller. The Porfirian project formally took the label "order and progress," a testament to the boldness of their desire to order the city. As the city and nation gave way to revolution in 1910, it was all too clear the "harmonious disposition of things" was beyond the limits of Porfirian power. The disorder of the Mexican Revolution haunts all subsequent orderings of Mexico City.

Plaza Carso settled within a particular geographic location in Mexico City. Prior to its construction, Plaza Carso was a post-industrial landscape of vacated factories and expanding brownfields that symbolized the end of post-revolutionary Mexico's economic miracle. Under statist economic policies, Mexico City experienced industrialization, a growing middle class, and a degree of prosperity that suggested the nation was realizing the promises of modernity (Davis 1994). In its glory day, the place that was before Plaza

Carso boasted factories that produced working class jobs and products for consumers. General Motors made cars there. The Vitro Glass factory rested directly where Plaza Carso now does. The Modelo brewery is the only contemporary survivor. When the economic miracle gave way to economic crises with the Mexican default in 1982, the structural adjustment policies designed by the neoliberals displaced the production facilities in the global race to the bottom. Urban decay set in, which created the opportunity for capitalism's magic act, "creative destruction," the process in which capital escapes its crises of accumulation by destroying the old in order to build the new. Ripe for urban renewal, in the 2000s a wave of capitalist property speculation began the process of building Nuevo Polanco from the ruins of post-revolutionary Mexico. The same process enabled Carlos Slim to earn his USD70 billion and undertake his iteration of elite imaginings of and order for the unimaginable, delirious city.

The post-revolutionary ordering of Mexico City was defined by what some critical urbanists call "inclusive urbanism" (Swilling 2013). It strove to overcome the ills created by nineteenth-century urban modernization by attending to the needs of urban citizens. At the forefront was the attempt to order the city around public infrastructure, which intended to generate a more equal and fair city. An urban public would permit for what Lefebvre ([1970] 2003) calls the "right to the city," which is each citizen's dual right to be transformed by the city, as well as to transform the city. Neoliberal reordering transformed the public into the private, which incrementally erased progressive steps toward the right to the city. Inclusive urbanism gave way to what Stephen Graham and Simon Marvin (2001) call "splintered urbanism," which is defined by the privatization of the urban public sector and the deeper integration of the city into flows of globalized capital. Gone is the high modernist dream of equity and equality through urban planning. A splintered urban imaginary is defined by privately owned public space, privileged access to urban services, and a sharper demarcation of social and economic space. Plaza Carso is an example of splintered urbanism ordering of Mexico City.

The only poor who enter the space of Plaza Carso are service sector workers, hardly the poorest of the poor among Mexico City's 20–25 million people. Within the tucked away spaces of this "orderly disposition of things," you will not find homeless Mexicans sleeping on the cement, as you will find along the sidewalks of *Calle Florencia* in *Zona Rosa*. We can only speculate how many millions of the 20–25 million will find their way to see Slim's public display of privately owned art, but we can safely estimate that the soft mechanisms of urban apartheid will work to prevent *ciudadanos* (citizens) from enjoying this articulation of their right to the city. They are the casualties of splintered urbanism, purged from this particular location within the megalopolis. The cloud dwellers come and go as they please, it's their place, at least until the harmonious disposition of things is turned upside down in the next Mexican revolution.

LOCATING PLAZA CARSO WITHIN THE COMMODITY FETISH

Nested within Plaza Carso there is a shopping mall, the twenty-first century's articulation of the Parisian Arcades that so fascinated Walter Benjamin. It is phantasmagoria, a word that attempts to capture modernity's ontological tension between dream and reality that Benjamin found to be central to understanding the modern urban experience, and which echoes Rama's lettered city, as well as this collection's exploration of order and disorder. Located within the shopping mall, and defining its core meaning, is the commodity fetish and modernity's ordering logic, shopping.

The mall is located within the spatial center of the fragmented spaces of Plaza Carso, a centering that provides a familiar anchoring for people visiting the complex. It is flanked on two sides by the towers that house the varied offices of Grupo Carso. Within the mall are iconic stores that have meaning particular to Mexico, such as the upscale Sanborns on the first floor, and the more globalized icon of consumption, Saks Fifth Avenue. Plaza Carso's mall is a place for elite consumption: Saks Fifth Avenue defines this fruit of the culture-ideology of consumerism. At the center of the ground floor of Plaza Carso's shopping mall is Salvador Dali's *Bailarina Daliniana* (Dalian Dancer) (1979), one of the many surrealist pieces of art from Slim's collection on public display throughout Plaza Carso. It is grotesquely framed on both sides by a GMC sports utility vehicle and a Chevy of lesser status, icons of modern consumption and our planetary existential denial. They are distant competitors to Dali's art, but more at home in the shopping mall. The flow of people entering the mall fail to note the display of Dali's work, but stop to engage the automobiles, clearly revealing the disciplinary logic of the mall.

Slim's fetish for Dali is fitting on many levels. Dali's critics emphasized how his potential was undermined by showmanship, a relentless quest for self-promotion that approached a pompous arrogance necessary for iconic status. That Slim collects a pretender is revealing of Plaza Carso's logic, its attempt to be an iconic place that circulates in the Mexican imaginary without connection to lo mexicano while also circulating in the cultural capital of global architecture. The Dalian Dancer's display is also significant because it is surrealist art, which fittingly locates the center of the shopping mall within the deeper logic of commodity fetishism, especially the feisty territory of phantasmagoria.

It is hard for us to imagine what Walter Benjamin might make of Carlos Slim, what might be said if we could conjure up a conversation between them. Benjamin was part of the circle of Marxist scholars, mostly Jewish and German, who came together prior to the rise of the Nazis to form the Institute for Social Research that became known as the "Frankfurt School." They aimed to develop theory into a critique of reality that would transform modern society from its dark side to modernity's promise of liberation from suffering, the perfection of the human condition. For Benjamin that project could only mean the city, and that city was Paris, which he saw as the "capital of the 19th century."

Benjamin's attention fell to the great urban *problematique*, the tension between the alienation of modern urban life and the city's capacity to liberate human potential. Never fully part of the Marxist thinking of the Frankfurt School, Benjamin retained a place for mysticism, especially as articulated in the surrealism of the early twentieth century, that great attempt at coming to terms with the ways World War I spawned disillusionment in the modern project. Charles Baudelaire's explorations of the great transformations in mid-nineteenth-century Paris, however, had the greatest impact on Benjamin. Baudelaire's *flâneur*, for example, was a central preoccupation for Benjamin, and served as one of the origins to Benjamin's ([1982] 1999) analysis of the Arcades, the precursor to the twentieth century shopping mall and its twenty-first century articulations, such as Slim's shopping mall in Plaza Carso.

Benjamin's entrance to the city was through the sociology of his early mentor, Georg Simmel. He attended Simmel's lectures that produced one of the foundational essays on urbanism, "The Metropolis and Mental Life" ([1903] 1950). It aimed to explain the impact of city life on the mind by exploring the dystopian realities of the modern city, especially the depths of alienation encountered by the individual in the urban form. But, Simmel also put forward a vision of the modern city as a force for liberation. Merrifield's *Metromarxism* (2002), which traces the centrality of commodities within Marxist urbanism, explains how Simmel understood money to be the core of the modern urban form. "Simmel," Merrifield states, "evokes money as a source of *Alienation* and the metropolis its devilish incarnation, someplace where people are atomized, bundled together in lonely crowds, where they're naked and vulnerable, and where everybody is weighing and calculating things, including each other" (52).

Simmel's description of urban alienation lurks within the halls of the modern shopping mall, where the lonely crowd meanders mindlessly through the wasteland of consumption. The vast majority of Plaza Carso's visitors are sojourners, passing through the shopping mall in a ritual performance of navigating urban space, conforming to the disciplinary logic of the mall. Few of the visitors make a purchase, not surprising given the expense of the commodities displayed in the retail stores. How many tour Plaza Carso with the aspiration of being more than Mexican middle class, to have the chance to consume conspicuously at Saks Fifth Avenue, and how many, walking with hands empty of the latest fashion, are wounded in their sense of inadequacy within consumption's host, the urban drama of the shopping mall? Are they somehow content in knowing their time spent in Slim's universe was not a Saturday afternoon spent in *Tepito*, the shopping mall of Mexico City's urban poor?

It was György Lukács take on Marx's commodity fetishism, in his *History and Class Consciousness*, that brought Benjamin to the Arcades. Lukács saw the commodity as a totalizing influence on society, especially due to the way the commodity fetish constituted false consciousness. Merrifield (2002) explains it best, "For Lukács, the commodity became 'crucial for the subjugation of men's consciousness . . . and for their attempts to comprehend the process or to rebel against its disastrous effects and liberate themselves from the servitude of the 'second nature.'" (57). The subjugation was rooted in the laws of capitalist production. "In order to produce commodities," Merrifield paraphrases Lukács:

> working people themselves become commodities. Both become abstractions somehow, both become things, one containing value, the other producing it. As commodities, both take on a nonhuman objectivity, are determined by 'natural' laws, normalized in everyday consciousness. People, as labor power, as peculiar commodities, become separated from their activity, from the product of that activity, from their fellow workers, and from themselves. Isolation, fragmentation and atomization ensue. Needless to say, the ruling class prospers from this reification, yet the proletariat become submissive, unable to grasp fully themselves and their real conditions of life. The world of things takes on a hallowed status. The split within the workers' labor power and their own personalities marks their metamorphosis into a thing, into an object for sale that produces another object for sale. Reification permeates all social life—it isn't just a workplace deal. It flourishes in politics and culture, is reinforced through media and ideology, through subtle messages and repressive force (57).

In a newspaper interview, George Grayson (Piore 2010), a political scientist with years of experience commenting on the Mexican reality, captured the totalizing meaning of commodity fetishism for a place like Plaza Carso. "Cradle to grave, in Mexico, you can spend your whole day—your whole life—in a Slim bubble. . . . From your first telephone call, to listening to radio stations owned by him, to eating his food products—to, yes, shopping in his malls." Plaza Carso's shopping mall is where people perform this disciplinary logic of capitalist consumption, where they become the objects of Slim's power, even if they walk out of the mall empty handed.

The social geography of Plaza Carso's shopping mall reflects Lukács' take on the commodity fetish. The mid-level management labors in the office towers of Slim's Grupo Carso, orchestrating the reification of twenty-first-century capitalist consumption, extracting value from the labor of others, while they themselves become objects of production, one more part to the machine that generates Slim's USD70 billion in profit. The calculating columns of the accountants are mirrored in the straight lines of the towers, modernist in form and function. At lunch hour the Grupo Carso white-collar, desk worker will eat at the food court, or, if upper management, in one of the shopping mall's upscale restaurants, perhaps at *Cantina La Imperial,* where the interior brings the consumer to a dining experience laden with Porfirian era nostalgia. Is that "Pepe," José Ives Limantour seated among the bankers and railroad magnates? Some partake in the paternalistic, "company town" gambit of purchasing a lunch ticket that is used in the outdoor dining space at the entrance to the *Teatro Cervantes,* under the plaza's pavilion. The processes of becoming "a thing"—one of Carlos Slim's things from cradle to grave—deepens as the food ticket provides a lunch from Sanborns.

Lukács teaches us that commodity fetishism masks the exploitation of the worker who makes the commodity, as well as the alienation experienced by both worker and consumer. Plaza Carso's shopping mall is a space where exploitation and alienation are hidden despite being in plain sight, especially within commodities on display. A space for the rich, Plaza Carso necessarily has an army of workers all laboring to make the experience happen. The bathroom attendant hands the patron a paper towel. A team of cooks, prep-cooks, dishwashers, and waiters provide the food. Service workers mop the floors after the patron spills, making it appear the clumsy incident never happened. The invisible working class reproduces Plaza Carso both in its material form and its fetish. The reproduction, however, blends into the background, or happens behind the physical walls, within the shopping mall's inner places, as well as the social-cultural walls represented by the commodity fetish. The drama of splintered urbanism is contained within the microcosm of Slim's shopping mall—the host, from cradle to grave.

While Benjamin's Marxism was shaped by Lukács, he found something more at play in modernity as evidenced by the Parisian Arcades. Benjamin rejected the totalizing vision of Lukács. Instead he advanced an open, fluid understanding of the commodity form that was suggested by the fetish. Merrifield (2002) explains Benjamin's encounter with the Arcades:

> Benjamin is fascinated by glass-roofed structures that house toyshops and perfume and liqueur-glass stores, and which "hold their own beside fairy-tale galleries." Day and night, these mighty pavilions "glow with the pale, aromatic juices that teach even the tongue what porosity can be" . . . these "fairy-tale galleries" were, to be sure, key arenas of the commodity fetish, new forms of urban life dedicated to servicing the commodity, prostrating itself to its needs.

At the same time, they were equally new forms of public space, ambiguous and dialectical, like modern life itself, blending together the outside public street with the interior, quasi-private store. Now, outside became inside, and inside outside, in dizzy, pleasurable ways; they were indeed places of pilgrimage to the fetish commodity. (59)

THE HOST IS A MARVELOUSLY COMPLICATED SPACE

The blurred geography of the Arcades was the fluidity of modernity, where order and disorder are mutually constitutive. Interior blended with exterior serves as an apt representation, a mapping of Plaza Carso, that brings together the architectural form with spaces of commodity fetishism. The sojourner's exterior entrance from the chaotic public of the Mexico City street flows into the shopping mall through a small, transitional space of the outdoor plaza. While the outdoor, exterior plaza has urban furniture, it is the type that invites a short rest before continuing the journey. There is one main entrance, a forced and claustrophobic conveyance to the mall-host, that shifts abruptly from the chaos of fragmented lines and inadequately counter-punctual curves that define the exterior of Plaza Carso, to the stable, well-proportioned geometry of the shopping mall's interior. It is a disciplinary space, where we know the script, how to behave, and we self-regulate, giving way to the order inherent with the mall design. The blurred exterior and interior spaces reflect the tension between Plaza Carso's public and private, where privately owned public space confuses the distinction between interior and exterior, a confusion that makes the exterior disorientating. Just off the street, the exterior plaza suggests public to its user, but the office towers and residential buildings assert the private, a disciplinary logic that is reinforced by their secure entrances. The gated community is present. The shopping mall contains the tension: the commodity is private property offered to the public, made possible by the transaction of the money fetish, which transfers the corporately held private property to the individual.

LOCATING PLAZA CARSO WITHIN THE CHALLENGES OF TWENTY-FIRST CENTURY URBANISM

Plaza Carso is also located within an urban infrastructure that miraculously sustains 20–25 million people. Microbus routes pass its entrance along an overly congested road system. They link passengers to the city's phenomenal subway. Cars circulate through the roadway arteries, entering into and leaving the complex's subterranean parking. For the true cloud minders, helicopters land on nearby buildings. Plaza Carso is connected to the electrical grid; its stores, restaurants, and theaters consume some of the more than 550 exajoules of energy annually consumed in the global economy (one exajoule is equivalent to 174 million barrels of oil). Water enters mostly clean and leaves significantly dirtier through its pipes that connect to the city's stressed hydraulic system. Trucks bring loads of food and commodities for the stores. Other trucks carry away the garbage. The skeletons, walls, windows, roofs, pipes, and wirings that forge the buildings were once minerals from the earth. The 16,000 hexagonal tiles that constitute Museo Soumaya's outer shell have an ecological footprint: they are built from aluminum that must be extracted from earth and processed with intense heat and chemical mixtures that consume materials and energy that generate pollution and contribute to Mexico City's share of gases that cause global warming.

Plaza Carso is located deep within the sinews of our "hydrocarbon civilization" (Yergin 2008). Hydrocarbons are everywhere in Carlos Slim's harmonious disposition of things. They are in the fuel for the cars and buses that carry people to and from Plaza Carso, and once burned, hydrocarbons are in the air breathed by cloud minder and service sector worker alike. They are used in the intensive, industrialized agriculture system that provisions Plaza Carso. The hydrocarbons are in the plastics that constitute many elements of its built environment, they are in the excessive packaging for consumer goods, and the commodities production process is significantly fueled by hydrocarbons. Slim's urban imaginary is entirely dependent on hydrocarbons, making it a highly unstable disposition of things.

Plaza Carso is located within Mexico City's urban metabolism, a beast that is perhaps the most unimaginable part of this place that defies the ordering of imagination. The urban metabolism locates Mexico City within a larger system of circulation, one defined by inflows and outflows of living beings and material properties. Plaza Carso is located within a nested system of systems revealed by multiple, overlapping geographies: local, regional, national, and global; urban and rural; and biospheres that are harder for the mind to map. Contemplating the scope and scale of its metabolism makes us delirious yet again.

Within its metabolism a range of micro to macro ecosystems exists. Despite the artificial, built landscape of Plaza Carso, it still has microorganisms, the trillions of bacteria that circulate unseen to the cloud minder and cleansed by the service workers, and from it a food chain of being scales up. Plaza Carso is part of the megalopolis' urban metabolism, and its location fits within the inflow of materials and outflow of garbage. The urban metabolism is nothing more than the laws of thermodynamics, which ultimately place Plaza Carso within the grander scale of energy in the universe and the unavoidable "arrow of time" where the urban metabolism churns away in the cosmic process of putting energy's potential to work (the inflow) and generating waste (the out-flow), which is energy's spent potential for work (Clark 2002). Carlos Slim's attempt at the harmonious disposition of things is located in entropy (Rifkin 1980). Not far from this temple of entropy, masked by the ideologies of capitalist consumption that premise an infinite universe, a previous civilization had its temples, places where priests attempted the harmonious disposition of things by sacrificing humans to feed the gods and ensure the sun did not die. They assumed the universe was finite and built a great city, *Tenochtitlán*, on that premise.

Thermodynamics teaches us that entropy is the tendency of an ordered system, what we call "complexity," to move to disorder, what we call "simplicity." To keep order the system uses the potential of energy for work, which results in waste. The more order the more waste. To counter a system's disordering propensity, more ordering is needed and more energy is spent. The arrow of time drives the system to its collapse, as eventually the system cannot sustain its complexity. Mexico City is a stunningly complex system, a highly ordered metabolism that requires phenomenal levels of energy to reproduce itself day in and day out. It is highly unstable, oscillating between moments of reproduction and collapse and on the edge of chaos, where disorder overtakes order and the system passes a critical threshold and tips into a new system either through collapse or by means of a collapse-less transition driven by emergent properties liberated from within the system by being in the moment of chaos. Slim's urban imaginary is in defiant denial of the physical laws of the universe, and Plaza Carso, Slim's attempt at the harmonious disposition of things, is located at this edge of chaos, the critical threshold to modernity's tipping point.

We can locate Plaza Carso within C. S. "Buzz" Holling's (Gunderson and Holling 2002) notion of "panarchy," which maps the behavior of complex systems like the urban form as they move through a cycle of ordering and disordering. Holling's panarchy loop has four phases: reorganization (the state of disorganization and simplicity), exploitation (when interacting parts of the emerging system start to form patterns that lead to rule-sets), conservation (the relentless pursuit of rule-set efficiency), and release (when ordering tips to disordering and the system collapses). Plaza Carso is located somewhere between the late conservation phase and the early release phase. The hegemony of the conservation phase rule-set can sustain it within a trajectory of continued growth well past the threshold of sustainability, which places the system in a precarious state of overshoot. It is a place of business as usual at the offices of Grupo Carso, as well as a place of overabundant consumption and waste. The key variable for the transition between conservation and release phases is how extensive the loss of complexity will be within the extremes of hard and soft collapse. The deeper and further we drive the system in overshoot, the greater the prospects for a species threatening collapse. Slim's urban imaginary is not designed to survive collapse.

Carlos Slim's harmonious disposition of things operates within the hegemonic rule-set of the late conservation phase. Plaza Carso symbolizes the predicaments humanity faces. We are increasingly aware of the release phase, yet unable to break free from the conservation phase rule-set. Facing collapse, we build monumental spaces that celebrate the triumph of the system that is headed toward a species threatening collapse.

CONCLUSION: LOCATING PLAZA CARSO WITHIN THE URBAN REVOLUTION

David Harvey's *Rebel Cities* (2012) advances the provocative thesis that it is the city not the proletariat that has the revolutionary potential in the twenty-first century. From this perspective Plaza Carso is located within the theoretical and practical problem of who or what will serve as capitalism's gravedigger. Plaza Carso looks to be the twenty-first century version of the *Casa de los Azulejos*, the "House of Tiles," the Porfirian era Jockey Club, which was the location in Mexico City where those who ordered the city went for food and entertainment, but also went to see and be seen (Beezley 1987). Today it houses one of the fancier Sanborns that is part of Slim's empire. Yet, it is unclear from the example of Plaza Carso if the moment for the gravedigger is upon us. While we know that the elite class' ordering of the city is never complete, and we recognize the potential for alternative urban imaginaries rests within the contradictions of Slim's attempt at ordering Mexico City, it also appears to be that the power of the commodity fetish, the daily struggle for survival in the megalopolis, and the deeper pathologies of late modernity keep the grave from being dug. For elites like Slim, alternative urban imaginaries constitute a disordering that the ruling class, in collusion with the political class, continue to contain, negate, and neutralize. Lacking a viable alternative imaginary for the urban revolutionary, the most likely twenty-first century gravedigger is capitalism's ecocide.[1]

NOTE

1. This chapter was originally presented at the Latin American Studies Association Congress in New York City, May 27, 2016. Thank you to Alejandro Puga for introducing me to Plaza Carso, Leopoldo Burguete for helping me to unpack the space, and Dan Rogers for his pictures and analysis.

WORKS CITED

Anderson, Benedict. 1991. *Imagined Communities: Reflections on the Origin and Spread of Nationalism.* New York: Verso.

Beezley, William. 1987. *Judas at the Jockey Club and Other Episodes of Porfirian Mexico.* Lincoln: University of Nebraska Press.

Benjamin, Walter. (1982) 1999. *The Arcades Project.* Translated by Howard Eilin and Kevin McLaughlin. Prepared on the basis of the German text by Rolf Teidemann. Cambridge, MA: Belknap Press of Harvard University.

Berman, Marshall. 1988. *All That Is Solid Melts into Air: The Experience of Modernity.* New York: Viking Penguin.

Bird Pico, Maria. 2011. "How Antara Polanco Revived a Corner of Mexico City." February 1. Accessed June 16, 2017. http://www.thecenterofshopping.com/blog/how-antara-polanco-revived-a-corner-of-mexico-city

Bonfil Batalla, Guillermo, and Philip Adams Dennis. 1996. *México Profundo: Reclaiming a Civilization.* Translated by Philip A. Dennis. Austin: University of Texas Press.

Bunker, Steven. 2014. *Creating Mexican Consumer Culture in the Age of Porfirio Díaz.* Albuquerque: University of New Mexico Press.

Butler, Andy. 2010. "Soumaya Museum by Fernando Romero Architects." October 8. Accessed June 16, 2017. http://www.designboom.com/architecture/soumaya-museum-by-fernando-romero-architects/

Casey, Nicholas. 2011. "Emperor's New Museum." *The Wall Street Journal*, March 3. Accessed June 16, 2017. http://www.wsj.com/articles/SB100014240527487033 00904576178381398949942

Clark, Robert. 2002. *Global Awareness: Thinking Systematically about the World.* Lanham, Md: Rowman & Littlefield Publishers.

Columbia University. 2014. *The Urban Imaginary Project, Barcelona's Moveable Feast: a Post-Crash Urban Imaginary.* Columbia University GSAPP, Advance Studio. Accessed June 16, 2017. http://www.columbia.edu/cu/arch/courses/syllabi/20143/A4105_008_2014_3_Goberna.pdf

Curcio-Nagy, Linda Ann. 2004. *The Great Festivals of Colonial Mexico City: Performing Power and Identity.* Albuquerque: University of New Mexico Press.

Davis, Diane. 1994. *Urban Leviathan: Mexico City in the Twentieth Century.* Philadelphia: Temple University Press.

Gallo, Rubén. 2004. "Delirious Mexico City." In *The Mexico City Reader*, edited by Rubén Gallo and Lorna Scott Fox, 3–29. Madison: University of Wisconsin Press.

Graham, Stephen, and Simon Marvin. 2001. *Splintering Urbanism: Networked Infrastructures, Techno- logical Mobilities and the Urban Condition.* London: Routledge.

Gregory, Derek. 1994. *Geographical Imaginations.* Cambridge, MA: Blackwell.

Gunderson, Lance H., and C. S. Holling, eds. 2002. *Panarchy: Understanding Transformations in Human and Natural Systems.* Washington, DC: Island Press.

Hägerstrand, Torsten. 1975. "Space, Time and Human Conditions." In *Dynamic Allocation of Urban Space*, edited by A. Karlqvist, 3–14. Farnborough: Saxon House.

Haggett, Peter. 1965. *Locational Analysis in Human Geography*. London: Edward Arnold.

Harvey, David. 2004. "The New Imperialism: Accumulation by Dispossession." *Socialist Register* Vol. 40. Accessed June 16, 2017. http://socialistregister.com/index.php/srv/article/view/5811/2707#.V0YKgVcVbts

Harvey, David. 2012. *Rebel Cities: From the Right to the City to the Urban Revolution*. New York: Verso.

Hernández, Daniel. 2011. *Down and Delirious in Mexico City: The Aztec Metropolis in the Twenty-First Century*. New York: Scribner.

"Human Energy Consumption Moves Beyond 500 Exajoules." 2012. *Business Insider*, February 17. Accessed June 16, 2017. http://www.businessinsider.com/human-energy-consumption-moves-beyond-500-exajoules-2012-2?utm_source=readme

Johns, Michael. 1997. *The City of Mexico in the Age of Díaz*. Austin: University of Texas Press.

Korten, David C. 2001. *When Corporations Rule the World*. San Francisco, CA; Bloomfield, CT: Berrett-Koehler Publishers; Kumarian Press.

Kuecker, Glen David. 2011. "Book Review Essay: Understanding Latin America in The Era Of Globalization." Review of *Latin America and Global Capitalism: A Critical Globalization Perspective*, by William Robinson. *Journal of World-Systems Research* 17 (1): 236–243. Accessed June 16, 2017. http://www.jwsr.org/wp-content/uploads/2013/02/Kuecker-vol17n1.pdf

———. 2013. "South Korea's New Songdo City: From Neo-liberal Globalisation to the Twenty-first Century Green Economy." *Papers of the British Association for Korean Studies* 15: 20–36.

———. 2015. "New Songdo City: A Case Study in Complexity Thinking and Ubiquitous Urban Design." In *Complexity And Digitalisation Of Cities—Challenges For Urban Planning And Design*, edited by Jenni Partanen, 188–226.

Kunstler, James Howard. 1994. *The Geography of Nowhere: The Rise and Decline of America's Man-Made Landscape*. New York: Simon & Schuster.

Lefebvre, Henri. (1970) 2003. *The Urban Revolution*. Translated by Robert Bononno. Minneapolis: University of Minnesota Press.

Lukács, György. 1971. *History and Class Consciousness; Studies in Marxist Dialectics*. Cambridge, MA: MIT Press.

Merrifield, Andy. 2002. *Metromarxism: A Marxist Tale of the City*. New York: Routledge.

Piore, Adam. 2010. "Carlos Slim's Bulging Portfolio." *The Read Deal*, October 1. Accessed July 1, 2017. https://therealdeal.com/2010/10/01/carlos-slim-s-bulging-portfolio-1/

Plaza Carso. N/D. Accessed June 16, 2017. http://www.plazacarso.com.mx.

Rama, Ángel. (1984) 1996. *The Lettered City. Post-Contemporary Interventions*. Translated by John Charles Chasteen. Durham, NC: Duke University Press.

Rifkin, Jeremy. 1980. *Entropy: A New World View*. New York: Viking Press.

Robinson, William. 2008. *Latin America and Global Capitalism: A Critical Globalization Perspective*. Baltimore: Johns Hopkins University Press.

Sartre, Jean-Paul. 1940. *L'Imaginaire: Psychologie Phénoménologique de l'Imagination*. Paris: Gallimard.

Schumpeter, Joseph. (1942) 1994. *Capitalism, Socialism and Democracy*. New York: Routledge.

Simmel, Georg. (1903) 1950. "The Metropolis and Mental Life." In *The Sociology of Georg Simmel,* edited and translated by Kurt H. Wolff, 409–426. New York: Free Press.

Soja, Edward. 2010. *Postmodern Geographies: The Reassertion of Space in Critical Social Theory*. New York: Verso.

———. 2010. *Seeking Spatial Justice*. Minneapolis: University of Minnesota Press.

Swilling, Mark. 2013. "Contesting Inclusive Urbanism in a Divided City: The Limits to the Neoliberalisation of Cape Town's Energy System." *Urban Studies* 51 (15) (September): 3180–3197.

Taylor, Charles. 2004. *Modern Social Imaginaries*. Durham: Duke University Press.

Whelan, Robbie. 2014. "Tony Mexico City Neighborhood Becomes a Cautionary Tale." *The Wall Street Journal*, June 3. Accessed June 16, 2017. http://www.wsj.com/articles/tony-mexico-city-neighborhood-becomes-a-cautionary-tale-1401838409

Yergin, Daniel. 2008. *The Prize: The Epic Quest for Oil, Money & Power*. New York: Free Press.

Chapter 3

Luis Buñuel's Fictional Geographies

V. Daniel Rogers

In 1950, Luis Buñuel released *Los olvidados*, a film that would redefine Mexican cinema and firmly establish his own reputation as an internationally recognized director and auteur. Emilio García Riera (1970), an actor and prolific critic of Mexican film captured the importance of *Los olvidados* in his multivolume study when he wrote: "*Los Olvidados* was the first Mexican film that transcended the values of *costumbrismo* (defined in the next paragraph), of populist instincts, or of good folk art. It was the first work from an auteur of consequence, and in its tenderness and intelligence, humor and indignation, was the first authentic work of genius that was produced in the framework of Mexican national cinema" (192).[1] García Riera recognized that *Los olvidados* didn't just overturn or refute the cinematic values and esthetic modes dominant in Mexico's mid-century film industry. Buñuel's film gestures toward those values, and then transforms them into something that represented (for García Riera and many other critics) the turning point of twentieth-century Mexican cinema. *Los olvidados* adopts costumbrista tropes from earlier films and texts, divests them of any lingering essentialism or nostalgia, and deploys them to explode the "dream of an order" (Rama [1984] 1996) within the facile nationalism of post-revolutionary cinematic discourse. Mapping the historic locations in the film and examining their symbolic role in the growth of twentieth-century Mexico City's esperpentic urban landscapes flesh out the theoretical work that García Riera and many others have laid out in previous decades. The mapping brings forward a palimpsest of order and disorder, whose temporal layering is mirrored in the Buñuel's use of consequential geographies that juxtapose the post-revolutionary bourgeois "dream of an order" against the peripheral spaces of disorder represented by poverty and delinquency.

41

Sometimes infelicitously anglicized as "costumbrism," *costumbrismo* in Spain and Latin America, a literary movement first and foremost, emerged from the romantic realism of the nineteenth century as an effort to activate an emerging middle class readership through texts that focused on the minutia and "colorful" details of folk tradition and customs. Developing hand-in-hand with the nineteenth-century newspaper industry, costumbrism articulated a new bourgeois subjectivity and ordering through sentimental and often mawkish descriptions of regional communities and mores (Kirkpatrick 1978, 28–29). Benedict Anderson ([1983] 1991) famously takes up this thread in *Imagined Communities*. His examination of the growth of the newspaper industry and its involvement in the development of late nineteenth and early twentieth-century nationalism is required reading for anyone interested in the relationship between national consciousness and the commodification of indigenous cultures (36). Helpful in a discussion of *Los olvidados*, Anderson points out that the ideological underpinnings of these new national identities relied on the Enlightenment's "fatal distinction between metropolitans and creoles" (60).

For enlightened elites, "it was only too easy from there to make the convenient, vulgar deduction that creoles, born in a savage hemisphere, were by nature different from, and inferior to, the metropolitans" (Anderson [1983] 1991, 60). Even while nineteenth-century costumbrism sought to "rescue" indigenous culture and folk identity that was declining in the face of growing metropoles, it cast these folkloric details through a lens of sentimentality and nostalgia that inadvertently (in the best cases) reinforced a fundamental asymmetry between rural landscapes and urban spaces. Costumbrism provided bourgeois ideology with the ability to layer modernity onto the past while distributing that order in the increasingly distinct geographies of urban and rural society. Anderson adds this critical piece of the puzzle to this bourgeois ordering: geographical hierarchies undergird the alliance between industrial capitalism and the most destructive forms of nationalism. The geographical differences between regional and urban identities don't just run in tandem with the ideological divide between the two, the different physical spaces help constitute and produce those differences. Unlike earlier films[2] that uncritically adopted a sentimental and nostalgic view of Mexico's rural culture and peoples, Buñuel's *Los olvidados* both acknowledges the ordering of these preexisting hierarchies and works to disorder and undo them as it peels away the layers and subverts the older costumbrista ordered binary of rural subjectivity against cosmopolitan identity. In this fashion, *Los olvidados* was an affront to post-revolutionary Mexico's bourgeois "dream of an order."

Many scholars have worked to unpack the subversive nature of Buñuel's film. One of the most famous recent treatments is Ernesto Acevedo Muñoz's (2003) comprehensive study, *Buñuel and Mexico: The Crisis of National*

Cinema. For Acevedo Muñoz, the destabilizing work of the film begins with the fact that Buñuel grounded it in a mid-century current of intellectual thought that critiqued the ordering of official narratives regarding the outcomes of the Mexican Revolution. In this assessment, *Los olvidados* reiterated a new school of thought (articulated by Daniel Cosío Villegas three years previous to its release) that was becoming more and more aware of the Mexican Revolution's failure to achieve its "utopian goals"—its "dream of an order"—to significantly "improve the conditions of the masses" (58). He also explores the way the film deploys costumbrism to engage in a moral analysis of the plight of the urban working poor, rather than engage in populist nostalgia and sentimentalism (63). However, the role of geography in this "moral analysis" deserves further exploration. Acevedo Muñoz, echoing other significant scholars of the film, carefully points out that the "physical reality" present in almost every scene is central to its critique of modern urban realities in Mexico City. The significant theoretical work provided by Acevedo Muñoz and others benefits from a deeper exploration of the particular urban spaces, what Edward Soja (2010) calls "consequential geographies"—or the ways contradictions and tensions of modernity find particular expressions in particular locations and the contestation over their potential meanings—Buñuel exhibits in the film. In other words, a systematic mapping of the "physical reality" that has been effectively theorized in previous studies helps locate the ordering hierarchies and asymmetries implicit in the tension between the "metropolitans and creoles" that is so central to Benedict Anderson's account of the production of nationalism.

Los olvidados is a film that starts as a pseudo-documentary and ends as tragedy. After the opening credits, Buñuel presents us with a blunt title card that blurs the line between representation and reality: "This movie is based comprehensively in real life facts and all its characters are authentic."[3] To underscore this true-to-life gesture, the film opens with aerial views of several twentieth-century metropoles (New York, Paris, London, and finally the *Centro Histórico* of Mexico City) as a narrator reminds us that these newly modernized and technologically magnificent urban spaces hide within them disenfranchised youth who suffer the effects of debilitating poverty. The voiceover closes with the promise that the film we are about to see will present a pessimistic view of society's efforts to ameliorate juvenile delinquency. These generic second unit shots are replaced with the image of the film's principal antagonist, Jaibo (played by a young Roberto Cobo) who has just been released from juvenile detention and walks jauntily down *Avenida San Juan Letrán* (now *Eje Central Lázaro Cárdenas*).

Jaibo quickly meets up with the members of his gang and promises to teach them all of the new skills for living on the street that he has picked up from his time in jail. The gang, including the film's protagonist, Pedro, follows

Jaibo's lead as they attempt to steal and defraud various people with limited success. One of their early victims is a blind street musician played by the most famous actor in the film, Miguel Inclán. The various encounters and characters the gang interacts with call to mind both the folkloric realism of costumbrista narratives as well as the street-smart, picaresque archetype from the Spanish Golden age, Lazarillo de Tormes. These brief encounters present us with generic street scenes populated with the urban poor and remind us that the order of an apparently modern cityscape hides an apparently chaotic and marginalized underclass.

After the gang's limited success, Jaibo convinces Pedro to help him confront another youth named Julián. Julián is a slightly older boy who has decided to leave the gang and finds a job on a construction crew. The new, mid-century modern metropolis is rising quickly around them and it demands a workforce that the urban poor can provide. Julián exchanges his labor for low pay, but a chance to perhaps work his way out of poverty, and at the same time participate in the utopian goal of transforming post-revolutionary Mexico City into the post-revolutionary elite's "dream of an order," the modern landscape the equal of any other major national capital. Determined to take revenge for sending him to jail, Jaibo lures Julián to an abandoned lot near the construction site where he works, and there, with only Pedro as a witness, Jaibo kills him and hides his body. Jail has taught Jaibo that respect on the streets is a product of violence, and warns Pedro that if he tells anyone, he will suffer the same fate.

As Pedro's connection to Jaibo deepens, his relationship with his mother (brilliantly played by the award-winning Stela Inda) deteriorates. His involvement with the murder forces Pedro to spend longer periods of time away from home to avoid the police. Increasingly disillusioned with Jaibo, Pedro decides to emulate Julián and takes on a series of humiliating odd jobs in an effort to survive on his own. In one crucial moment, the film even suggests that Pedro considers prostituting himself to older men, a stunningly subversive moment in the normally sanitized and "family friendly" films of the 1940s and 1950s. Pedro's narrative constitutes a sharp, destabilizing questioning of the patriarchal ordering of the metaphorical family of the post-revolutionary order where the disciplinary power of the male head of the family degenerates to the social chaos termed *"desmadre"* in Mexican society (see Eric Zolov [1999] for the concept of post-revolutionary family and the desmadre concept).

Pedro eventually catches a lucky break and lands a job as an apprentice at a blacksmith shop. But as the film moves toward its tragic end, Jaibo finds him and threatens him to keep him quiet. Unfortunately for Pedro, when no one is looking, Jaibo steals one of the knives laying around the shop. When the blacksmith returns, he discovers that the knife is missing and calls the police, blaming Pedro for the theft. When the police arrive at his home, Pedro's mother (with whom Jaibo has begun a sexual relationship) refuses to believe her son and with Jaibo looking on, commits him to reform school. Several scenes of the film take place inside this juvenile detention facility, a place of ordered discipline. After a difficult period of adjustment, Pedro seems about to turn a corner when the director of the reform school trusts him enough to send him to a nearby store with a significant sum of money. The director tells Pedro that he knows he could run away and return to his gang and old ways, but explains that he has confidence that he will return after running the appointed errand. At this critical moment, Jaibo reappears and ambushes him a few blocks from the school, stealing the director's money. Unable to return to the farm school, Pedro heads back to the city center in search of Jaibo. When he finds him, Pedro fights Jaibo and reveals his crime to the gang and others in the neighborhood. By the end of the film, Jaibo has destroyed every opportunity that Pedro had to escape the desmadre of his impoverished condition, and has even displaced him within his own family in a particularly disturbing oedipal twist that suggests the latent but real disorder within the patriarchic order of the post-revolutionary family implicit in the discourse of Mexican nationalism.

In a final confrontation, Jaibo who is older and stronger, murders Pedro. Already sought by the police for the murder of Julián, Jaibo is gunned down in an abandoned lot. The last scene of the film is gut wrenching. Neighbors find Pedro and, afraid that the police will blame them, cover him in a tarp, load him on a mule, and dump the body in an enormous trash heap. In the original ending, Buñuel creates a consequential geography through his rigorous use of physical space to constitute the subjectivity of his characters, and this means that Pedro's body can't receive a proper burial. Pedro's grave is, literally, an area that serves as the *cloaca* (sewer) for the insatiate, modern megalopolis that Mexico City is becoming. The camera is unflinching as it subverts the post-revolutionary bourgeois' "dream of an order" by following the tumbling corpse to its final resting place at the bottom of a trash-strewn ravine. The quiet and stasis that mark the scene serve as a profound contrast to the peripatetic movement and anxious journeys that Pedro endures throughout the film.

It shouldn't come as a surprise that Luis Buñuel's *Los olvidados* is populated with characters who move in and out of neighborhoods and street corners in a series of restless peregrinations that destabilize the post-revolutionary spatial order. Buñuel and his famous cinematographer, Gabriel Figueroa, shot in locations throughout Mexico City as they move the film's characters in and out bourgeois neighborhoods and business districts in ways that showcase their *otredad* or "otherness." Throughout the film, characters travel in and through areas of the city that compete to construct different subjectivities with divergent political objectives. This chaotic movement of subjects through the consequential geographies of urban landscapes is perhaps clearest in scenes showing Pedro's home life in the shantytowns northwest of the city's center. *Nonoalco*, the crowded collection of shacks and hovels that frame several scenes with Pedro, Jaibo, and other outcasts whose activities propel the plot, will become the *Tlatelolco* housing project in the 1960s. Like a palimpsest, the historical traces of Nonalco live on in the footprint of the 1960s high modernist architecture and their proximity to the Buenavista train station.

Luis Buñuel was a consummate outsider himself. Exiled from Franco's Spain after the Civil War (1936–39), he wandered between Mexico, the United States, and France in subsequent decades. Peter William Evans (1995), in his important study, *The Films of Luis Buñuel*, links the director's nomadic life in exile to his construction of fictional landscapes and geographies. "Though admittedly not bereft, like other exiles, of his own language [during his long stay in Mexico], he was nevertheless severed from roots and customs, habits of mind and pleasure, making films in which the recurrent and related motifs of journeys and various forms of confinement express the inner loneliness of someone destined for many years to play out in his mind the memories of what eventually becomes a fantasy homeland" (6). Buñuel's "fantasy homeland" is a sort of doubled vision in which the reality of Mexico City's post-revolutionary geography informs a cinematic imaginary of Buñuel's own work. The diegesis of these films, as characters move from one location to another, articulates a plan of the city—the "dream of an order— that sits uneasily beside the actual Mexico City streets, buildings, and neighborhoods that function as referents for the cinematic text. The tensions arise both from the contrast between the squalor of Buñuel's Tlatelolco shanty-towns, *La Romita, Tlalpan*, and the stock bourgeois characters and locations that protagonists encounter. Whether it is productive to implicate Buñuel's own biography in the construction of a "fantasy homeland" (as Evans does) is another question. However, his description is useful as a marker for the exilic peregrinations of characters in many of his films. The gang of juvenile delinquents in *Los olvidados*—as do the tram driver ("Caireles") and his sidekick ("Tarrajas") in *La ilusión viaja en tranvía* (1953)—spend most of their time wandering through the streets and neighborhoods of Buñuel's version of an apparently mimetic, but ultimately aestheticized geography of Mexico City.

Mario Bassols Ricardez, a social scientist at the Universidad Autónoma Metropolitana and prolific theorist who examines urbanism and the particular features and history of Mexico City's built environment, provides a useful framework for understanding the relationship between urban geography and identity. His perspective is particularly important as a scholar who is a resident of the city he theorizes. Although less interested in literary and cinematic texts that imagine Mexico City's geography, his scholarship (elaborated from the perspective of a citizen of the DF) provides substantial purchase in an analysis of Buñuel's films set in the city. In his essay, "*México: la marca de sus ciudades*," Bassols Ricardez (2011) pushes against the notion that the form and *ordering* structures of urban spaces are the unique purview of social elites. Although elites dominate, he concedes, in particular times and places through their cooptation of political mechanisms and social institutions writ large, urban spaces (in Mexico in particular) are the product of what Raymond Williams called emergent and residual ideological moments. Echoing Bassols Ricardez in broader terms (and more specifically addressing the issue of literary texts), Williams writes in his magnum opus, *Marxism and Literature* (1977): "The social location of the residual is always easier to understand, since a large part of it . . . relates to earlier social formations and phases of the cultural process, in which real meanings and values are generated" (123). These residual cultural processes, mostly marginal and often rural, palimpsestically find avenues of survival in the midst of dominant, majoritarian expressions of the political and cultural elite. In Mexico, Guillermo Bonfil Batalla ([1987] 1996) might have called Williams' "residual" cultural moments an illustration of his trope, *México profundo*, that is, marginalized *mestizo* communities and the urban poor in Mexico City who resist their status as colonized subjects.

Focusing more particularly on Mexico's urban geography, Bassols Ricardez describes a heterogeneous landscape that is the product of conflict and negotiation between political and social classes: "It is also clear that other emergent or marginal ways to organize space coexist contemporaneously in their historical development. In this sense, the urban form of a city is the product of multiple factors: topographic, legal, economic and cultural that are at times linked to a conception of society or territory more less well defined" (20).[4] Bassols Ricardez's important insight is that these urban spaces aren't just the product of multiple agents serving a variety of ideological ends, it's that these conflicts and negotiations happen in the lived history of the city and leave their marks on it layered through time. From this perspective, the urban settings of Buñuel's *Los olvidados* are a palimpsest of the negotiations, tensions, and accommodations that are lived out in a historical process that leaves its marks on people and places: "it's constituted, in a way, of an urban fabric constructed over centuries, that presents itself to us today as urban disarray"[5] (Cabrero Mendoza 2011,13). *Los olvidados* is a film that is both informed by these traces that constitute consequential geographies and sets a temporal baseline (1950) for identifying others whose space and meaning have survived the sixty odd years since its filming. The architecture and street scenes visible in the film reveal the historical traces that shaped them (from Haussmann-inspired transformations in the nineteenth century to the growth

of high modernism at mid-twentieth century) at the same time that they establish a kind of baseline for changes that would occur in the late twentieth and
early twenty-first centuries.

My research included visiting and photographing every location from *Los
olvidados* that can be clearly identified and recognized today. The scale of
change in the last fifty years is obvious to any serious student of Mexico
City, but side-by-side comparisons of specific locations provide a real metric for the enormity of those transformations. Finding most of these places
requires the patience and facility to read the palimpsest and see beyond the
surfaces and edges of present-day buildings and city blocks to the deeper
skeleton underneath. In most cases, the architecture of Mexico City in the
second decade of the twenty-first century is a chaotic mixture of new and
old, especially in neighborhoods affected by the 1985 earthquake. But even
those older buildings that survived the ravages of earthquakes (or developers)
often present themselves as a motley agglutination of new elements obscuring
older layers underneath. Locating the sites that Buñuel and his extraordinary
cinematographer Gabriel Figueroa chose for *Los olvidados* demands a sort of
visual archeology to sort through the extraneous markings of the present to
older strata that are sometimes only barely visible.

One clear example of this visual archeology occurs near the beginning
of the film as we see Jaibo sauntering down a crowded, modern boulevard.
Buñuel and Figueroa set up this shot on a major thoroughfare near center of
the city called *San Juan Letrán*. Now known as *Avenida Lázaro Cárdenas*
or *Eje Central*, Buñuel's choice of location was significant. The street was
known colloquially among *defeños* (Mexico City residents) as *"Niño Perdido,"* or "Lost Child." The same area is also the location of the controversial
scene showing an older, upper-middle-class gentleman propositioning Pedro.
"Niño Perdido" was also the name of the neighborhood centered around
La Iglesia de Nuestra Señora de Guadalupe el Buen Tono a few blocks to
the west. In his fascinating book, *The Imagined Underworld*, James Garza
(2007) reminds us that prior to mid-twentieth-century modernization: "Contemporaries described the neighborhood as beset by 'pestilent miasmas' that
produced an 'asphyxiating' atmosphere. Tenement housing was common.
Observers, fascinated with the lives of the poor, described the tenements in
sad but exotic terms, with families living in close, crowded conditions and
naked children running around" (22). If Luis Buñuel didn't know the history of the neighborhood, his experienced cinematographer certainly did.
Figueroa was often frustrated with Buñuel's decision to show urban blight
rather than more audience-pleasing cityscapes (Jones 2005, 24). Today, a
photo taken from approximately the same angle is only barely recognizable.
Many of the same structures are still in place, but modern signage, street-
face, and superficial changes make them difficult to recognize. The changes

evident in the modern photo, taken on July 19, 2015, show a section of the city where consumer capitalism and the frenetic work of modern marketing is drowning the original art deco structures.

The scene, quite early in the film, also alerts viewers to the visual play and inside references that will continue throughout. Buñuel has positioned his actor almost directly underneath the marquee for one of Mexico City's most iconic movie theaters of the period, *El Cine Teresa* (Martínez Assad 2004, 32). But as iconic as the marquee may have been for audiences in the 1950s, the same scene today would be dominated by the *Torre Latinoamericana*, completed only six years after the film. The curious choice of location (beyond the colloquial name for San Juan Letrán and the kind metonymic resonance it has with the character on screen) slyly undermines the apparent objectivity of the documentary style of the film. Buñuel seems to be reminding his audience, by placing Roberto Cobo directly underneath the Cine Teresa marquee, that *Los olvidados* is a film: a product of his own aesthetic sensibilities and not the unvarnished reality of *cinéma vérité* that the opening promises.

If the first audiences of the film had been more attentive to its geography, it might not have caused such a scandal. *Los olvidados* famously lasted only three days in the theater (Buñuel would erroneously remember four) before closing due to public outrage. Buñuel himself, in a 1982 memoire, describes the furor over the film in stark and somewhat humorous terms:

> Premiering quite disappointingly in Mexico, the film only lasted four days on screen and it caused, in the process, violent reactions. . . . The sparse audience left the theater as if from a funeral. At the end of a private showing, while Lupe, the wife of the painter Diego Rivera looked arrogant and disdainful, without saying a word, another woman, Berta, married to the Spanish poet Luis Felipe, came at me, wild with indignation, her fingernails aimed at my face, shouting that I had just committed defamation, a horror against Mexico[6] (1982, 172).

In the film, Mexican audiences saw the city as it was, not as they imagined it to be. And even worse, Mexico City's warts had been revealed by a foreigner, and a Spaniard at that.

In fact, Buñuel was a severe critic of nationalisms. A survivor and refugee who fled Francisco Franco's fascist government in Spain, he had little patience for national chauvinism in his new home: "one of Mexico's greatest problems, today as in the past, is nationalism carried to extremes"[7] (Buñuel 1982, 172). Nationalist sensibilities are located in the human psyche somewhere between fantasy and madness, so the film's metafictional elements and symbolic use of geography may not have mattered to early audiences even if they had been noticed.

In a now famous moment that saved the film, Mexican poet and leading public intellectual of the 1950s, Octavio Paz, came to Buñuel's defense in 1951 in France at the Cannes film festival. Standing at the door of the theater where *Los olvidados* was to be screened, Paz handed out a mimeographed article he'd written for the audience as they entered. For Paz, Buñuel's film was, first and foremost, a work of art rather than propaganda or committed social realism. The title of the essay is a thesis statement in three words, "El poeta Buñuel." While Paz doesn't mention geography in his analysis, he states unequivocally that "*Los olvidados* no es un filme documental" (*Los olvidados* is not a documentary film) (2000, 34). For Paz (and presented in admittedly hyperbolic terms), the film is an evocation of the picaresque and he places Buñuel alongside Spain's greatest literary figures: Quevedo, Cervantes, and Galdós. Without using the term *costumbrismo*, Paz insists that Buñuel's film is art because it melds an archetypically Spanish literary trope with a distinctly Mexican mythology, "archetypal images for the Mexican people, *Coatlicue* [the monstrous mother-goddess] and sacrifice"[8] (35). "Coatlicue" and notions of sacrifice are intimately connected in western reconstructions of Aztec mythology (Keen 1990) and Paz employs a kind of doubled reference here. On the one hand, he is alluding to the troubling conclusion of the film that requires the "sacrifice" of Pedro, the film's protagonist, and the ignominious disposal of his body in a city trash heap—an ending that so disturbed Mexican bourgeois audiences that Buñuel was forced to film an alternate version. On the other, Paz is connecting the apparently mundane anonymity of the film's twentieth-century street urchins to his notion of Mexican identity as a contradictory attempt to recognize the past, assimilate it and use it to reconcile Mexican history and identity. Paz's cooptation of the Coatlicue myth to elevate Buñuel from documentarian to poet relies on an articulation of identity that links history and geography. After all, his estranged disciple Carlos Fuentes ([1992] 1999) calls Coatlicue, "the central figure in [the Aztec] pantheon," a "mother goddess" of terrifying aspect who gives birth to the principal deities in pre-colonial Mexico City ritual (102).

Her most famous incarnation, a nearly nine-foot granite statue that terrified the creole population of Mexico City, was discovered in the late eighteenth century near the even more famous Sun Calendar in the *Templo Mayor* precinct at the geographic and symbolic center of *Tenochtitlán*. One of Mexico's first students of pre-colonial archeology, Antonio León y Gama ([1792] 2006), described the discovery in monograph published in 1792:

> On the occasion, then, of the government having ordered that the plaza mayor [the Zócalo] be leveled and paved, and that sewers be laid to conduct water in subterranean canals: as they excavated in the month of August in the year before 1790, they found, not very far from the surface of the earth, a curiously wrought

stone statue, of a shocking size, that represented one of the idols the Indians worshiped in pagan times.[9] (2–3)

León y Gama was particularly aware of the significance of the location of his finds. He begins his description and analysis of these early discoveries by underscoring the centrality of their physical position relative to the city center: "I always had had the thought that in the principal plaza of the city, and in the neighborhood of Santiago Tlatelolco there were to be found many precious monuments from Mexican ancient past"[10] (1). Like León y Gama, geography, both as mechanism for ordering concrete facts and representations of political and symbolic power, was never far from Paz's mind. And his proselytizing at Cannes worked. Buñuel won Best Director and the film returned to Mexico with its newly won European accolades for a successful two-month run.

The particular geography of *Los olvidados* moves the audience from city center to periphery along a roughly north-south axis. Buñuel and Figueroa used locations as far north as the west side of Nonoalco near what would become *Estación de Ferrocarriles Buenavista* (Quirarte 2014). Just a decade after the movie was shot, famed Mexican architect Mario Pani, who promoted the post-revolutionary high modernist "dream of an order," transformed Nonoalco into a kind of Le Corbusier, high-density residency project called, *Conjunto Urbano Nonoalco Tlatelolco*. When Buñuel used the area as the location for the slums that housed the families of many of the adolescents in the film, Nonoalco was peripheral to the bourgeois ordering of Mexico City in both the literal and figurative sense of the word. Soon after its completion, an article in the *North American Review* interviewed Pani and his staff: "Pani hoped to rehouse the 100,000 people then living in this deteriorated zone" (Woods 1971, 4). Unfortunately, the real-life families on whom Pedro, his mother, and siblings are modeled didn't fare much better than the characters in the film. Pani's staff admitted to the interviewer that, "some of the very poor [were] uprooted by the project" and ultimately, "the poor cannot afford the rents at Tlatelolco [in 1971]" (4).

The small municipality of Tlalpan, twelve plus miles south of present-day Tlatelolco marks the southern extent of the film's locations. In some of the most famous series of scenes from the movie, Pedro is framed by Jaibo, arrested for a theft he didn't commit, and sentenced to the *Tlalpan Escuela Agraria*, a reform school for juvenile delinquents, and one of the film's most consequential geographies. A product of "modern penal" theory and criminology popular within the elite "dream of an order" in the first decades of the twentieth century, reform schools that used farms, fresh air, and hard work were seen as the answer for boys and young men whose criminality was the product of disordered, blighted urban spaces such as Nonoalco. The

institution was predicated on the elite's belief that taking troubled youth out
of the urban chaos and housing them in a rural setting where they could work
fields and raise livestock would break the cycle of delinquency and disorderly
conduct. This theory of juvenile reform depended on a symbolic categoriza-
tion and ordering of space that privileged the rural as a more moral place and
the city as a kind of dangerous machine that turns the young urban poor into
criminals.[11] A book review article in the 1918 *Journal of the American Medical Association* provides a useful summary of the practice from a contempo-
raneous perspective. "Penal institutions will still, however, have to conform
to about four types: industrial reform schools and reformatories; industrial
farm colonies; asylums for the insane, the feebleminded and the inebriates,
and penitentiaries for the incorrigible. Release and after-care are important
in the scheme, as are substitutes for imprisonment, such as labor on roads,
farms, etc." (218). The fact that articles on penal theory and criminology are
appearing in medical journals in the first decades of the twentieth century
demonstrates the curious and problematic relationship between medicine,
penitentiaries, and power (see Sierra in this volume for more on this topic).
In this iteration of the post-revolutionary "dream of an order," young ado-
lescent boys work off their sentences in fields and orchards that turn them
into apparently productive subjects and also allow guards and directors a
panopticon-like view of the prisoners. While not as harsh as Lecumberri, the
Benthamite, Porfirian era prison near the city center that boasted a true pan-
opticon arrangement, the *escuelas granjas* permitted nearly constant surveillance of the incarcerated subject. Buñuel famously recreates the dynamic of
this ordering surveillance, turning it on the audience, in one of the most meta-
cinematic moments of the film. As the camera follows Pedro, dressed now in
overalls that mark him both as laborer and prisoner, we see him stealing eggs,
puncturing them with a nail, and sucking out the contents. Pedro crouches on
a crate as he avoids the gaze of the other inmates and the adult guards, but the
audience can still see him. Pedro suddenly turns his eyes toward the audience
and seems to return our gaze just as he throws one of the eggs directly at the
camera and, by extension, the bourgeois audience surveilling him with their
bankrupt post-revolutionary "dream of an order."

  The Escuela Granja of Tlalpan, used for many scenes in the film, was
located due south of what is now University City and the UNAM, Mexico's
National Autonomous University, between *Calle Moneda* and *Ignacio
Allende* and the corresponding area across from what is now *Insurgentes
Sur* near the Metrobus stop "*Fuentes Brotantes*." Today, the terrain once
occupied by the Escuela Granja was developed into a youth sports complex
(*Deportivo Vivanco*, see Figure 3.1) on one side of the current location of
Insurgentes Sur and the enormous *Instituto Nacional de Neurología y Neuro-
cirugía* (National Institute for Neurology and Neurosurgery, see Figure 3.2).

Figure 3.1 Deportivo Vivanco. *Source*: This view recapitulates the shot from Los olvidados. Author's photo.

Figure 3.2 The National Institute of Neurology and Neurosurgery Located on the Old Grounds of the Escuela Granaja. *Source*: Author's photo.

Buñuel would have certainly appreciated the irony. The barracks, open fields, and livestock pens that in the 1950s comprised a juvenile penal institution championing the most modern and "enlightened" combination of punishment and treatment for troubled adolescents (a treatment regime that blended hard work and rural values) is today, a massive hospital complex providing the latest medical therapies for young patients with mental and nervous pathologies. This particular example of a palimpsest in transformation, as the mid-twentieth-century Escuela Granja Tlalpan evolved into today's sports complex for youth and hospital for neurological disorders, could have been a case study from Michel Foucault's *The Birth of the Clinic* ([1963] 1973).

The old dialectic of evil against virtue, embodied in the farm school/ juvenile detention center and characterized by the topographical binary of urban decay and disorder versus rural morality and order, is medicalized and updated in the second half of the twentieth century as criminality comes to be seen as a disease rather than sin. Foucault ([1963] 1973) describes this transformation (captured by Buñuel in his portrayal of Pedro's ill-fated journey) and notes the important moment of rupture when, "disease breaks away from the metaphysic of evil, to which it had been related for centuries" (196). If disease and criminality are the afflictions of newly medicalized subjects (and more specifically, as bodies that belong to the state) in Mexico's mid-twentieth century modernizing ideological gesture, the Escuela Granja de Tlalpan is the appropriate, consequential geography for Pedro and other street children to be interpolated as new subjects of a rational, ordered, post-Revolutionary Mexico. By the early 1970s the old Escuela *Granja* had morphed into the *Hospital Granja Bernardino Álvarez*, an intermediate step before becoming the Instituto Nacional de Neurología y Neurocirugía that retained the notion of *granja* or "farm." ("*Granja*" in Spanish comes from the old French "*grange*," which gives us "grange" in English.) The last step in the palimpsest's ordering conversion, the literal "birth of the clinic" moment in the history of the Escuela Granja de Tlalpan, happened when a social worker named María Louisa Flores saw it as a potential location for the mentally infirm (Rodríguez de Romo and Castañeda-López 2013). A recent article in the *Archivos de Neurociencia* (Jiménez-López, Rodríguez De Romo, and Castañeda-López 2014) describes both the history of the location and the ideological presuppositions, the "dream of an order" that inform its practice:

> There is a reference to the Hospital Granja Bernardino Álvarez, located on the terrain of the INNN [Instituto Nacional de Neurología y Neurocirugía] and that around that date was under consideration for replacement, which finally happened in 1972. On that same site once stood the Escuela Granja of the same name. . . . Maria Luisa Flores visited the Hospital Granja to look into the possibility of creating in its place a "custodial workshop" for the learning disabled,

a project that never came to pass. These workshops were created so that the patient could work and return to being a productive member of society; in these places the activities of the mentally ill could be supervised by technical personnel, specialists in their particular ailment, receive a salary, take their medicine, and enjoy the therapeutic benefits of manual labor.[12] (67–68)

Apparently unaware of the famous movie shot on location there, Jiménez-López underscores the length of time (nearly a century) that this particular parcel of land south of Mexico City has been a site for reordering and rationalizing subjects of the state's medical-penal complex. *"Los débiles mentales"* (feeble minded) are supervised by a technologically proficient medical staff who help them return to productive roles in society through therapy and hard work. In *Los olvidados*, the therapeutic reconstruction of Pedro's pathology (the product of careless and disordered urban development) can only happen on the outskirts of Mexico City in a penal institution that combines the bucolic, sentimentalized, and romantic elements of Mexico's rural past ("México profundo") with the demystified, post-metaphysical rhetoric of the institutionalized Revolution.

But Buñuel wasn't making a documentary about Mexican penal institutions. He was creating a film that used real world geographical referents when useful, and transformed others to fit the aesthetic logic of the project. Tlalpan may be the location of one of the most enduring historical "marks" in the sense that Bassols Ricardez theorized, but it was also the site of one of the most interesting "geographical substitutions" that Buñuel and Figueroa managed to pull off. In a critical scene in the film, the director of the Escuela Granja lets Pedro walk freely out the front gate of the institution (see Figure 3.3). The director demonstrates his faith in Pedro by giving him 50 pesos and asking him to go outside to purchase a packet of cigarettes. Pedro walks through the gate with the wad of money and toward the possibility of a "therapeutically positive" outcome. Of course, Buñuel won't let his bourgeois audience off the hook so easily. Pedro leaves, we assume, with every intention of returning with both the cigarettes and absurdly large quantity of change, but he runs into Jaibo lurking outside the walls of the reform school. Jaibo beats him, takes the money, and with it any possibility of redemption.

The gate then, represents a whole series of transitions and orderings in the film. Not only does it mark the boundary between incarceration and freedom, it also delineates the moment beyond which any possibility of Pedro's reemergence as a newly healed and reordered subject of the state becomes impossible. One side marks the post-revolutionary family's protective space of a rational, paternal, and orderly remedial organ of the state. The other marks the desmadre of a chaotic, disturbed urban landscape that devours children and blights their futures.

Figure 3.3   Pedro Runs through the Front Gate of the Escuela Granja (*Los olvidados*).

Buñuel and Figueroa must have been unsatisfied with the actual gate of the Escuela Granja Tlalpan because they pressed another architectural feature of the town into service—the front gate of the nineteenth-century mansion near the center of the town that would become President Adolfo López Mateos' residence in 1964 (see Figure 3.4). López Mateos, President of Mexico from 1958 to 1964, purchased a Porfirian era mansion known as the *Casa Frissac*—an important example of Second Republic French architectural influence that reached even the periphery of Mexico City (*Reforma* 9). The imposing brick and mortar structure is a reproduction of one of Paris's most famous monuments, the Carrousel Arch (1806), down to its triple arch-way structure and circular motifs on top. The substitution that Buñuel and Figueroa made in using the Casa Frissac arch rather than the actual entrance generates a powerful visual metaphor in the scene where Pedro, dressed in his farm school uniform, is framed against the majestic and very European-looking structure. The contrast emphasizes both Pedro's powerlessness and the profound gulf between Mexico's moneyed and working classes. The director and cinematographer also have Pedro approaching the gate from the west with the afternoon sun behind the main archway. The timing and natural lighting put Pedro in deep shade cast by the tall gate, the shadows and after-noon sun providing stark contrasts and borders that restate the liminal status of the protagonist in purely visual terms. The architectural legacy of the gate

Figure 3.4 The Casa Frissac Gate in Central Tlalpan that becomes Front Gate of the Escuela Granja in *Los olvidados*. *Source*: Author's photo.

is, ultimately, Constantine's triumphal arch in Rome, and here it serves as a sharp and bitter irony for an audience conscious of geography.

After his fateful encounter with Jaibo, Pedro returns to the small plaza that serves as the gathering place and home base for his gang, his only real family in the film (see Figure 3.5). Buñuel chose *Plaza Romita* on the northeast side of *Colonia Roma* as headquarters for the gang. The church that can be seen in the background, *San Francisco Xavier*, is one of the oldest in the area and Plaza Romita has a sense of identity and character that find roots in the earliest years of the colonial period. Before the arrival of the Spaniards, the area was an islet named *Atzacoalco* (place of the herons) on the edge of Lake Texcoco near the terminus of the canals leading south out of Tenochtitlán (Mundy 2014). The area was known for banditry from early times as the marginalized peoples stole from the wealthy in the city center and then

Figure 3.5   Plaza Romita with Pedro's Gang in Front of San Francisco Xavier Church (Still from *Los olvidados*).

escaped to the relative safety of the labyrinthine streets around the small plaza and church. Surrounded by giant cypress trees, legend has it that thieves were routinely hung from their branches when caught.

In a curious moment of intertextuality, the plaza also serves an important function in José Emilio Pacheco's (1981) *Las batallas en el desierto*. In the novel, the long history of the plaza maintains extraordinary potency in the protagonist's present, the 1950s.

> Romita was a world apart. The *Hombre del Costal* lurks there. The terrible Child-Thief. If you go to Romita, boy, they kidnap you, pluck out your eyes, cut off your hands and tongue, and force you to beg for money, and the *Hombre del Costal* [the Man with a Sack] takes everything you get. By day he's a beggar; by night an elegant millionaire thanks to the exploitation of his victims. The fear of being near Romita. The fear of riding the streetcar over the Coyoacán Avenue bridge: nothing but rails and track; and below the dirty Piedad River that sometimes overflows when it rains.[13] (14)

In Pacheco's novel, the neighborhood retains the threatening sense of marginalization and disorder that made it such an appropriate place for Buñuel's

Figure 3.6 Plaza Romita Today. Compare the Left-Hand Pilaster in the Church Facade with Figure 3.6. *Source*: Author's photo.

characters. The Hombre del Costal, a kind of mash up of the bogey man and a mob boss, presides over a criminal syndicate that entraps the young. Today, the plaza is undergoing the same relentless gentrification that characterizes most of the rest of Colonia Roma (see Figure 3.6). The difference between the plaza as Buñuel found it in 1950 and the present is enormous. Trees, gardens, and pavers have replaced the uneven sidewalks and unpaved streets bringing gentrified order to the rough edges and chaos of its previous incarnation.

From Nonoalco Tlatelolco in the north along an axis that passes along San Juan Letrán, through Plaza Romita and Doctores, and ends in Tlalpan on its southern periphery, *Los olvidados* maps a geography of Mexico City that underscores the marginalized status of its characters. In this mapping, the film isn't exactly alone. From Antonio Moreno's *Santa* (1932), Ismael Rodríguez's *Nosotros los pobres* (1947), and Alejandro González Iñarritu's *Amores Perros* (2000) and beyond, film makers have used Mexico City's urban disorder to underscore the otherness of its working class and the profound disparities in wealth it generates. But *Los olvidados* does so in ways that articulate the architectural traces that mark the particular history of alienation its protagonists embody. In visual terms, Buñuel orders the cinematic geography of the city to show his audiences the violent negotiations required of his characters in their effort to survive in the peripheral spaces and neglected gaps of the city.

NOTES

1. *Los olvidados fue la primera película mexicana que trascendió los valores del costumbrismo, de la intuición popular o de la buena artesanía. Fue la primera obra de un autor consecuente con su ternura y su inteligencia, con su humor y su indignación, la primera auténtica obra de genio que se producía en el marco del cine nacional.*

2. Films such as Fernando de Fuentes' *Allá en el Rancho Grande* (1936), Emilio Fernández' *María Candelaria* (1944), and Ismael Rodriguez' *Nosotros los pobres* (1948).

3. *Esta película está basada integralmente en hechos de la vida real y todos sus personajes son auténticos.*

4. *También es cierto que coexisten otras formas emergentes o marginales de organizar el espacio, pero presentes en su devenir histórico. En tal sentido, la forma urbana de una ciudad es producto de múltiples factores: topográficos, legales, económicos o culturales que en ocasiones se ligan a una concepción de sociedad o territorio más o menos bien definida.*

5. *se trata, así, de un tejido urbano construido a través de los siglos, que hoy se nos presenta como desorden metropolitano.*

6. *Estrenada bastante lamentablemente en México, la película permaneció cuatro días en cartel y suscitó en el acto violentas reacciones. . . . Los raros espectadores salían de la sala como de un entierro. Al término de la proyección privada, mientras que Lupe, la mujer del pintor Diego Rivera, se mostraba altiva y desdeñosa, sin decirme una sola palabra, otra mujer, Berta, casada con el poeta español Luis Felipe, se precipitó sobre mí, loca de indignación, con las uñas tendidas hacia mi cara, gritando que yo acababa de cometer una infamia, un horror contra México.*

7. *uno de los grandes problemas de México, hoy como ayer, es un nacionalismo llevado hasta el extremo.*

8. *las imágenes arquetípicas del pueblo mexicano, Coatlicue y sacrificio.*

9. *Con ocasión, pues, de haberse mandado por el gobierno que se igualase y empedrase la plaza mayor, y que se hiciesen tarjeas [alcantarilla/sewers] para conducir las aguas por canales subterráneos; estando excavando para este fin el mes de agosto del año inmediato de 1790, se encontró, a muy corta distancia de la superficie de la tierra, una estatua curiosamente labrada en una piedra de extraña magnitud, que representa uno de los ídolos que adoraban los indios en tiempo de su gentilidad.*

10. *Siempre he tenido el pensamiento de que en la plaza principal de esta ciudad, y en la del barrio de Santiago Tlatelolco se habían de hallar muchos preciosos monumentos de la Antigüedad Mexicana.*

11. For an example of elite perceptions of the distinction between rural and urban spaces, and their concern for the moral degradation of urban space on the popular classes, see Emily Wakild's (2007) article on Porfirian era urban planners who built parks and gardens to cleanse the city.

12. *Se hace referencia al Hospital Granja Bernardino Álvarez, ubicado en terrenos del INNN y que por esa fecha ya se pensaba desplazar, lo que finalmente*

sucedió en 1972. El Hospital inició sus funciones en 1960. En el mismo sitio estaba la Escuela Granja de igual nombre . . . Ma. Luisa Flores visitó el Hospital Granja para ver la posibilidad de crear en su lugar un "Taller Protegido" para débiles mentales, proyecto que finalmente no cristalizó. Los talleres protegidos fueron creados con el fin de que el paciente pudiera trabajar y volviera a ser productivo para la sociedad; en estos lugares la actividad del enfermo estaría supervisada por personal técnico conocedor de su padecimiento, percibiría un sueldo, tomaría sus medicamentos y recibiría el beneficio terapéutico del trabajo.

13. *Romita era un pueblo aparte. Allí acecha el Hombre del Costal, el gran Robachicos. Si vas a Romita, niño, te secuestran, te sacan los ojos, te cortan las manos y la lengua, te ponen a pedir caridad y el Hombre del Costal se queda con todo. De día es un mendigo; de noche un millonario elegantísimo gracias a la explotación de sus víctimas. El miedo de estar cerca de Romita. El miedo de pasar en tranvía por el puente de avenida Coyoacán: sólo rieles y durmientes; abajo el río sucio de La Piedad que a veces con las lluvias se desborda.*

WORKS CITED

Acevedo-Muñoz, Ernesto. 2003. *Buñuel and Mexico: The Crisis of National Cinema.* Berkeley: University of California Press.

Anderson, Benedict. (1983) 1991. *Imagined Communities: Reflections on the Origin and Spread of Nationalism.* London: Verso, 1991.

Anonymous. 1918. Review of *Criminology* by Marurice Parmelee. *Journal of the American Medical Association* 71 (3): 218–219.

Bassols Ricardez, Mario. 2011. "México: la marca de sus ciudades." In *Ciudades mexicanas: desafíos en concierto*, edited by Enrique Cabrero Mendoza, 19–64. México, DF: Fondo de Cultura Económica.

Bonfil, Batalla Guillermo. (1987) 1996. *México Profundo: Reclaiming a Civilization.* Translated by Philip A. Dennis. Austin: University of Texas Press.

Buñuel, Luis, director. 1950. *Los Olvidados.* Ultramar Films.

———. 1953. *La ilusión viaja en tranvía.* Clasa Films Mundiales.

———. 1982. *Mi último suspiro.* Barcelona: Plaza & Janes.

Cabrero Mendoza, Enrique. 2011. "Introducción." In *Ciudades mexicanas: desafíos en concierto*, edited by Enrique Cabrero Mendoza, 9–18. México, DF: Fondo de Cultura Económica.

Evans, Peter William. 1995. *The Films of Luis Buñuel.* Oxford: Clarendon Press.

de Fuentes, Fernando. 1936. *Allá en el Rancho Grande.* Lombrado Films.

Fernández, Emilio. 1944. *María Candelaria.* Films Mundiales.

Foucault, Michel. (1963) 1973. *The Birth of the Clinic.* Translated by A. M. Sheridan. New York: Routledge.

Fuentes, Carlos. (1992) 1999. *The Buried Mirror: Reflections on Spain and the New World.* New York: Houghton Mifflin.

García Riera, Emilio. 1970. *Historia documental del cine mexicano: Época Sonora tomo 2.* México: Era.

Garza, James. 2007. *The Imagined Underworld: Sex, Crime, and Vice in Porfirian Mexico City*. Lincoln: University of Nebraska Press.

González Iñarritu, Alejandro, director. 2000. *Amores Perros*. Alta Vista Films.

Jiménez-López, Erandi, Ana Cecilia Rodríguez De Romo, and Gabriela Castañeda-López. 2014. "La Historia del Instituto Nacional de Neurología y Neurocirugía a Través de un Documento." *Archivos de Neurociencias* 19 (1): 67–70.

Jones, Julie. 2005. "Interpreting Reality: *Los Olvidados* and the Documentary Mode." *Journal of Film and Video* 57 (4): 18–31.

Keen, Benjamin. 1990. *The Aztec Image in Western Thought*. New Brunswick, NJ: Rutgers University Press.

Kirkpatrick, Susan. 1978. "The Ideology of Costumbrismo." *Ideologies and Literature: A Journal of Hispanic and Luso-Brazilian Studies* 2 (7): 28–44.

León y Gama, Antonio de. [1792] 2006. *Descripción Histórica Y Cronológica De Las Dos Piedras Que Con Ocasión Del Nuevo Empedrado Que Se Está Formando En La Plaza Principal De México, Se Hallaron En Ella El Año De 1790: Explícase El Sistema De Los Calendarios De Los Indios . . . Noticia . . . A Que Se Añaden Otras Curiosas . . . Sobre La Mitología De Los Mexicanos, Sobre Su Astronomía, Y Sobre Los Ritos Y Ceremonias . . . En Tiempo De Su Gentilidad.* México: Impr. de Don F. de Zúñiga y Ontiveros, 1792. Alicante, España: Biblioteca Virtual Miguel de Cervantes. Accessed June 30, 2017. http://www.cervantesvirtual.com/nd/ark:/59851/bmc1n7z8

Martínez Assad, Carlos. 2004. "La ciudad de México en el cine." *Chasqui* 33 (2): 27–40.

Moreno, Antonio, director. 1932. *Santa*. Compañía Nacional Productora de Películas.

Mundy, Barbara E. 2014. "Place-Names in Mexico-Tenochtitlan." *Ethnohistory* 61 (2): 329–355.

Pacheco, José Emilio. 1981. *Las batallas en el desierto*. México: Ediciones Era.

Paz, Octavio. 2000. *Luis Buñuel: el doble arco de la belleza y de la rebeldía*. Barcelona: Galaxia Gutenberg/Círculo de Lectores.

Rama, Ángel. (1984) 1996. *The Lettered City. Post-Contemporary Interventions.* Translated by John Charles Chasteen. Durham, NC: Duke University Press.

Rivera, Garza C. *Nadie Me Verá Llorar*. México: Tusquets, 1999.

Quirarte, Xavier. 2014. "Resumen la estética nacionalista de Gabriel Figueroa." *Milenio*, Noviembre 5. Accessed June 30, 2017. http://www.milenio.com/cultura/Resumen-estetica-nacionalista-Gabriel-Figueroa_0_296970340.html

Reforma. 2002. "Alberga cultura la Casa Frissac." *Reforma*, Febrero 25, 9.

Rodríguez, Ismael, director. 1947. *Nosotros los pobres*. Producciones Rodríguez Hermanos.

Rodríguez De Romo, Ana Cecilia, and Gabriela Castañeda-López. 2013. "El Hospital Granja y La Escuela Granja Bernardino Álvarez: Antecedentes del Instituto Nacional de Neurología y Neurocirugía." *Revista de Investigación Clínica* 65 (6): 524–36.

Soja, Edward W. 2010. *Seeking Spatial Justice*. Minneapolis: University of Minnesota Press.

Wakild, Emily. 2007. "Naturalizing Modernity: Urban Parks, Public Gardens and Drainage Projects in Porfirian Mexico City." *Mexican Studies/Estudios Mexicanos* 23 (1): 101–23.

Williams, Raymond. 1977. *Marxism and Literature.* Oxford: Oxford University Press.

Woods, William K. 1971. "American Eye: Cities of Mexico: Old, New, and Dreamt of." *The North American Review* 256 (2): 2–6.

Zolov, Eric. 1999. *Refried Elvis: The Rise of the Mexican Counterculture.* Berkeley: University of California Press.

Chapter 4

Novelistic Cartographies of the Mexico City *Flâneur*

Alejandro Puga and Carmen Patricia Tovar

WALKING THE "CITY OF PAPER"

In *La ciudad letrada* (*The Lettered City*) Ángel Rama (1984) marks a distinction between real or "empirical" urban space and one onto which the literate elite imagines and transposes an idealized territory. One of Rama's premises is that the intelligentsia projects its "dream of an order" onto the city, thereby forging pivotal urban transformations. In this manner, the city transforms over time, not according to societal needs and demands, but rather by the changing aspirations of the lettered class. Beyond tracing the modifications on the imagined social order, Rama focuses on how the lettered sphere managed to adapt to the many power disputes that emerged from the colony to the present era. In his last chapter on the "Revolutionary City," Rama discusses the transition from the intellectualization of the Mexican Revolution to the new industrial technocracy, a topic central to Carlos Fuentes' totalizing urban novel, *La región más transparente* (1958). *La región* monumentalizes the city during a re-ordering phase through an integration of multiple characters representing diverse but carefully hierarchized social strata. Old moneyed families, destabilized by the Revolution of 1910–1916, give way to the industrial technocrats who credited themselves with the "Mexican Miracle," an era of political stability and economic prosperity from 1940 to 1970. Alejandro Puga (2012) points to authors in the aftermath of this cultural shift, such as Fernardo del Paso, Cristina Rivera Garza, Bernardo Ruiz, Gustavo Sainz, and so many others[1] who offer an indistinct type of lettered character who problematizes the function, positionality, and vision of the writer. The urban novels that follow *La región* present variations on the novel of adolescence, the counter-cultural and psychedelic experience, a renewed novel of the borough, the queer novel, and other important reflections on the city that steer the urban

65

novel to the post-1968 Tlatelolco phase. These constant reevaluations of Mexico City's cultural representation require equally constant inquiries into its transformations. The more micro-narrative responses to Fuentes' "total" regard of Mexico City narrative have shifted the conversation from *novela de la ciudad* to *novelística de la ciudad*, that is, a movement away from emblematic visions of the city to an intertextual network of urban narratives.

Just as Rama (1984) traces the ideologically convenient phasing of the lettered class, the Mexican urban novel of the late twentieth century offers a palimpsestic layering that speaks to the ordering and re-ordering of the city as its image shifts from metropolis to megalopolis in the novelistic form, from the Mexican Miracle to the 1968 Tlatelolco Massacre, to the unsettling 1982 default of the peso, and the catastrophic earthquake of 1985 which has inspired narratives of disaster and has rendered fiction that imagines an apocalyptic or post-apocalyptic city.

Consider now the latest, and most controversial, transformation of the *Distrito Federal* (Federal District): the switch from its traditional designation, "DF" to the trendier CDMX—the abbreviation for *Ciudad de México* or Mexico City (see the "Introduction" and "Conclusion" to this volume)—which signals very explicit spatial strategies of purification and exclusion. The renaming of CDMX proposes a renewed cultural, political, and geographic demarcation that excludes the space of the megalopolis surrounding the city proper. The legislative approval of this acronym purports the transposition of an updated cosmopolitan identity. As a branding strategy, CDMX updates the encumbered Distrito Federal as a culinary, artistic, and architectural travel destination in an attempt to purge it from problems of over-urbanization and its violent reputation. Such maneuvering hearkens to Rama's chasm between the imagined social order and its reality, and it is, in fact, one of the questions Fuentes attempted to address in *La región*: how the elite maintain and/or protect their vision of a modern Mexico while dynamics such as overpopulation, ecosystem pressures, class divisions, and political corruption problematize what John Brushwood (1981) has called the "heroic" or "epic" vision of the city (51).

With the goal of engaging the ordering and re-ordering cycles that the contemporary Mexico City novel articulates, this chapter takes particular interest in how the figure of the *flâneur*, the seemingly casual urban wanderer, does or does not manage to traverse the contemporary "empirical" city, as Rama (1984) would have it, and to find in it the functional vestiges of the imagined (lettered) metropolis. *Flânerie*, the practice of the *flâneur*, strikes us as a particularly revealing focal point for the study of urban prose narrative, since *flâneurs* always teeter between an informed regard of the cityscape and a predilection for street level, chance encounters. The intellectual and biographical (personal memory) baggage that *flâneurs* take with them to the street participates in their signification of the city, and the signification that the city would project onto them. In the works to be discussed here, the *flâneur* will occupy, often uncomfortably, the space of disorder that results from the re-ordering process described above.

As a literary construct, the *flâneur* was imported from French poetry and essay, particularly from the work of Charles Baudelaire, whom Walter Benjamin's (2006) essays epitomize as the *flâneur par excellence*. In Mexico, the *flâneur* begins as an emulation of the francophile tradition in the wake of the Napoleonic occupation (1864–1867), from which the modernist writer Francisco Zarco (1829–1869), who self-identifies as a *flâneur*, posits himself as a roving street persona charged with the task of witnessing and cataloging a paradigmatic urban landscape—that is, its monumental structures—with a syntagmatic, street-level gaze. In this way, the *flâneur* is thought to engage the phenomenology of the cityscape, wherein he seeks a schema for it while maintaining the immediate, contingent experience as his main mode of inquiry. Through his social codification of passersby, he exercises a right to gaze and makes logical sense of the urban dynamic that might otherwise be disordered. Undoubtedly, Zarco's *flânerie* is a privilege of his race, gender, and class position. As contingent as it is purported to be, his wandering gaze regulates as much as it discovers. In brief, the street in early Mexican *flânerie* is a space to be ordered. However, we will argue that as Mexican urban narrative develops into the current century, the street will manifest more as what Lefebvre (1996) characterizes as a space of contestation, and it will demand of the *flâneur* and/or *flâneuse* some level of confrontation with patriarchal and monumental gestures.

In this context, two specific urban novels intrigue us: *Los deseos y su sombra* by Ana Clavel (2000), and *Y retiemble en sus centros la tierra* by Gonzalo Celorio (1999). Both novels were given recognition and/or published in 1999, at a point in which Mexico, DF was on the threshold of its 2010 bicentennial of independence, while the *Distrito Federal* approached its shift to CDMX, a process that we will consider toward the end of our study. The city and the memories that both authors present are complicated palimpsests, an interaction of personal biography, consecrated architectural form, and the growing imposition of the megalopolis on the metropolis. Clavel's Soledad García and Celorio's Juan Manuel Barrientos walk among ordered, monumental sites and zones couched within the disorder of heavy traffic, over-industrialization, and disintegrations of traditional social structures, especially that of the nuclear family. As can be expected, Clavel's and Celorio's Mexico City protagonists display two different kinds of *flânerie* based on their gender, age, profession, previous urban experience, crisis of identity. These *flâneurs* are not the carefree strollers that they might project themselves to be. Their respective historical readings and interpretations of urban signifiers interplay with their particular construction of their personal family history, thereby resulting in a largely conflicted urban actor. Like their minds, their bodies are put to task in the pursuit of *flânerie*, which, as Solnit (2000) would have it in *Wanderlust*, is a practice that requires an embodied presence on the street.[2] Both Soledad and Juan Manuel will have to resolve the challenges of maintaining their presence and their bodies from being ravaged by the potentially disordering contingencies of the street. The endings of both novels will lead to analogies of how legible and available Mexico City truly is to its resident.

Since both protagonists engage the city's monumentality, and at times practice an anti-monumental regard of the city's expansive cultural patrimony, we consider the mapping of the sites visited by Soledad and Juan Manuel a worthy companion endeavor. *Flâneurs*—as well as the authors that portray them—utilize navigational techniques, or mental maps, to recreate subjectively a specific zone within the totality of the city. This is what Fredric Jameson (1991) calls "cognitive cartography," which "in the narrower framework of daily life in the physical city [. . .] enable[s] a situational representation on the part of the individual subject to that vaster and properly unrepresentable totality which is the ensemble of society's structures as a whole" (51). While cognitive mapping may empower urban subjects to make an imposed monumentality their own, implied in the endeavor of relating oneself to a "vaster and properly unrepresentable totality" is a desire to bring some order to that vastness. Jameson cites his cognitive cartography as an enhancement of a mere diagram of a neighborhood, or "itinerary" as Kevin Lynch (1960) calls it. We perceive in these novels the moment when that itinerary becomes a cognitive map, when architectural and historical sites become part of the *flâneur's* integrated vision of the self and the city, in which ordering and disordering gestures confront each other, or, as Rama would have it, when the lettered (imagined) city confronts the empirical city, that is, the contingency of the street that the *flâneur* purportedly seeks.

MAPPING GONZALO CELORIO'S BROKEN *FLÂNEUR*

For his second novel, *Y retiemble en sus centros la tierra,* Gonzalo Celorio (1991) draws from his own architectural knowledge of Mexico City's Centro Histórico, about which he has written extensively in journalistic *crónicas*, the more frequent generic form of literary *flânerie*. A descendent of the sixteenth century conquest narratives that marveled over Tenochtitlán and speculated on how to claim it for the crown, the urban *crónica* flourished after México's Independence from Spain in 1821, particularly in the guise of *cuadros costumbristas*, nationalistic vignettes of idealized city life. Salvador Novo was the first official chronicler after the Revolution of 1910–1916, a period which often continued the nostalgic *cuadro* as escapism from the armed conflict and imminent social change brought on by the Revolution. Novo's accounts of roaring, elegant cars riding on boulevards modeled after Parisian streets and beautiful art nouveau and art deco buildings are recollected in his 1946 *Nueva Grandeza Mexicana* (Gallo 2009, ix). Fifty years later, the grandeur and majesty of that bygone era is weathered and at odds with the megalopolis.

Throughout his essays and novels, Celorio obstinately returns to urban history in order to explore it closely, in an attempt to revise and recover his own story (1996, 115). In 1997, during his inaugural address to the Mexican Academy of Letters, he recognized the paradoxical relationship of authors who write from the city and about the city, and in which they try to capture in Ramanian *letrado* fashion the ebullient, mesmerizing urban form. However, according to Celorio (1997), it becomes instantly a "city of paper." And, as if pictures in a book, the representation of that city is always already past. Thus these authors' city is never truly the present, empirical city before them. In an ironic comment on the first *crónica* of Tenochtiltán, Celorio argues that an attempt to "capture" a city is a failed attempt from the beginning. "It is the city lost by antonomasia, but found by a literature that constructs it day after day, restores it, cares for it, challenges it"[3] (Celerio 1997, 49).

In *Y retiemble*, Celorio recasts his own scholarship as part of the *flâneur's* conflicted engagement of the city. *Y retiemble* narrates the last living days of Juan Manuel Barrientos, a newly retired professor of Baroque Literature. At the beginning of the novel, during his retirement dinner party, his students ask him to lead, for one last time, his well-known tour of the Centro Histórico, what he calls a *práctica de ciudad*, or "city practicum," in which the professor guides the students through the downtown area, teaching them how to recognize and read the city's transformations and re-orderings. Because Juan Manuel thinks of himself as a cosmopolitan *bon vivant*, the tour also includes tasting stops through some of his favorite bars and restaurants, some more monumental than others. In the midst of the euphoria of his retirement festivities, Barrientos agrees to the farewell tour. However, the next morning, fighting a hangover and his own melancholy, the professor regretfully and reluctantly prepares himself to lead the students on his last *práctica de la ciudad*. When they don't show up, Juan Manuel feels betrayed and abandoned. Soothing his soul through more than one hair of the dog, he decides to stay out on the street, and he resolves to carry on with the tour, all the while imagining his group of admiring students following him. Through his erudite gaze, Barrientos tries to replace his sense of sorrow (what Baudelaire calls *spleen*) with a sense of fulfillment at this crucial moment of the end of his professional career. In the pursuit of his life crux, Barrientos will lose himself to the city.

Juan Manuel's final practicum becomes increasingly more contingent and personalized as he persists in mimicking the tour with his imagined (but not imaginary) students. As an example of *flâneur* ordering that will later be jeopardized, he has specific rules with regard to consuming food and drink in the bars, restaurants, and cantinas, which for him are as emblematic as the churches, temples, colonial palaces, and cathedrals that ostensibly bring him and his students there. While his rules and his careful structuring of route and trajectory might contradict the *flâneur's* desire for the solitary, haphazard promenade, Barrientos believes that his years of experience, inside and outside the classroom, make him the ideal instructor to initiate anyone into the art of walking. Critics like María de Alva (2004) and Martín Camps (2005) have pointed to the intimate relationship of the professor with the city and have concluded that Barrientos himself is, in fact, the city. That is to say that the city has molded Barrientos' identity, his memory and knowledge through his years as an academic and as a conscientious pedestrian. In like manner, both critics associate the infrastructural decay of the urban core with the decrepit Barrientos' physical and emotional state of decay. The *flâneur's* dilemma of at once desiring to engage the city at street level and find within that syntagmatic layer a privileged vantage point is embodied in Juan Manuel, whose well-scripted "paper city" is being rewritten by the immediacy of his personal crisis. His insistence on continuing with the tour, then, initiates the aforementioned struggle implicit in cognitive mapping, and Rama's "lettered" (represented) and "empirical" (lived) city.

The first stop on this self-guided tour is the Methodist Temple, whose façade is not of particular architectural notoriety. The Temple formed part of the old monastery of San Francisco established in 1525. Since the Temple was established in 1873, many have walked by it without realizing its ubiquitous presence. Barrientos is interested in this building for its strategic location and inviting interior architecture. As various religious orders founded their monasteries and convents in the city's Centro Histórico, these locales would serve as national evangelization headquarters, and for that reason one can still find a dense cluster of churches within a ten-acre grid. In 1856, with the Reform Laws of President Benito Juárez, all church properties were expropriated and sold to individuals. The street created in front of the Temple was originally called *Independencia*, but the name later changed to commemorate Fray Pedro de Gante, one of the first Franciscan missionaries to arrive in Mexico. Barrientos uses this Temple as an example of the process of destruction, modification, renovation (re-ordering), and repurposing that the structures of the city have undergone for many centuries.

Once inside the Temple, the professor begins his lecture and uses his umbrella to point out for his imagined students the Baroque ornamental details found throughout a church intended, as he explained, to "colmar el horror al vacío" (Celerio 1999, 38). Far from "warding off the fear of the void," the architectural ornament triggers the first of many painful memories surrounding the death of his father, his difficult coming of age, and his estrangement from his own family many years later. From here on, each stop on this tour will prompt the emergence of a repressed memory. It is clear from the emotional toll of these memories that, in true *flâneur* fashion, Barrientos would like to disregard his personal memories in favor of the city facts he would only disclose for his practicum students: "he knew the streets and plazas of the Centro Histórico, its civic and religious buildings, its history of displacements, superimpositions, aberrant alterations, and inconceivable destruction . . ."[4] (30). However, in his last tour, the city is no longer just spectacle under Juan Manuel's gaze, it metamorphoses into a Memory Palace, as described by Frances Yates (1966), and as he walks through it he cannot help but to retrieve memories by the architectonic and/or environmental prompts found throughout the downtown area. Therefore, the city he walks in this tour is the trace of a past city, the city of his youth and early adulthood. In this manner, Juan Manuel's very identity takes on the palimpsestic qualities of the city center's architecture, thus reflecting the *flâneur's* fusion of self and city.

At key moments, it would seem that Juan Manuel's city tour is too predetermined to fulfill the contingency requirement of *flânerie*, even in his increasingly inebriated state. Now several drinks in, he leaves his preferred luncheon spot, the Bar Alfonso, and passes by a well-known stationery store, *Papelería Miguel Ángel*. The sight of the store, with its wide variety of fine pens and papers, leads him to wonder: "And his strides around the city's center, weren't they the stammering or drunken calligraphy that someone was writing without him having anything to do with it?"[5] (Celerio 1999, 80). The fatality that Juan Manuel perceives here is fortified by one of the novel's major motifs. The perceived abandonment of his students and the steady road to his demise at the flagpole after he is robbed, beaten, and naked describes a contemporary parody of the biblical reference to the Passion. However, while Juan Manuel's thoughts allude to the predictable journey through his *vía crucis*, his dedication to the street as the primary space of contemplation positions him as *flâneur*, a "sovereign spectator going about the city in order to find the things which occupy his gaze and thus complete his otherwise incomplete identity; satisfy his otherwise dissatisfied existence; replace the sense of bereavement with a sense of life" (Tester 1994, 7). Even though Barrientos is going through with his city practicum in search of fulfillment in order to replace his sense of sorrow, his life's losses—his father, his friends, his lover, his relationship with his children—catch up to him in apparitions, digging deeply in his psyche and weakening his "sovereign gaze." By the end, Juan Manuel's solitude takes on a more monumental form as his own alienation fuses with that of an alienated cultural patrimony.

It is through this reflective engagement and privileged view on a monumental cityscape that Juan Manuel's *práctica de la ciudad* can be linked to the excursions of Charles Baudelaire in nineteenth-century Paris, or more directly to the nineteenth-century *cronista* Francisco Zarco. In his essay "*Los transeuntes*," Zarco (1968), who appropriates the verb *flâner* to his excursions, identifies and observes social strata by assigning them to individuals passing him by in the plaza. On an intertextual plane, we must ask how a more contemporary *flâneur* like Juan Manuel fares in the same city center about which Zarco wrote his chronicles. In many regards, Juan Manuel's attempt to practice *flânerie* is well intentioned at first, awkward throughout, and disastrous in the end. His drunkenness and clumsiness, as well as his lack of complete awareness of his surroundings, that is, the loss of his "sovereign gaze," mark him as a broken *flâneur*.

Y retiemble abounds in references to a tense interplay between emulation of the *flâneur* and indications that the model handed down by Baudelaire is deteriorating. For example, there is the loss of Juan Manuel's umbrella, a common walking aide for the traditional *flâneur*, and one that is consecrated as emblematic to *flânerie* in Gustave Caillebote's famous painting from 1877, *Rue de Paris, temps de pluie (Paris Street; Rainy Day)*. At the beginning of the tour, Juan Manuel often uses the umbrella to point to architectural details and to dazzle his imagined students with his knowledgeable short lectures. When, in his stupor, he leaves the umbrella behind, he also leaves behind a "sovereign" or authoritative part of his gaze on the city. These and other moments of disconnect between Juan Manuel and what would be the ideal zone for the *flâneur*—the Centro Histórico with its palimpsestic layers of historical architecture, and the re-orderings of the city they imply—also allude to contemporary writer Valeria Luiselli's[6] (2012) current estimation that the act of walking itself is no longer a viable means for practicing *flânerie* in Mexico City:

> It is not possible to extract any comprehensive idea of Mexico City just by walking [in] it. Rosseau's solitary walks, Baudelaire's wanderings, Kracauer's *Bildergänge* o image-walks, and Benjamin's *flânerie* were one way of understanding and portraying the new structure of modern cities. But neither the miniature nor the bird's eye view is conceded to Mexico City residents because both lack any point of reference. The notion of the center, of an articulating axis was lost at some point in time.[7] (33)

The loss of center to which Luiselli refers finds its illustration in Juan Manuel's relationship to the Centro Histórico. It certainly stands as a dense repository of cultural patrimony and as a nexus of the power shifts for which, according to Rama, the letrado is always ready to attend. But for Juan Manuel to engage it as such, he must leave his domestic surroundings in the city's southern zone, which houses the National Autonomous University, and negotiate heavy traffic in order to engage in what was once the most accessible and relevant part of the city. Juan Manuel's relief when he parks his car in the *Palacio de Bellas Artes* lot describes an escapist gesture, far from the direct engagement of the city in real time that Zarco (1968) constructs in his original tour of the plaza.

In addition to the awkwardness of his corporeality on the street, *Y retiemble* foregrounds Juan Manuel's inability to strike the *flâneur's* delicate balance of consuming visually without consuming monetarily, the ideal that placed the *flâneur* above the common pedestrian. Juan Manuel's excessive drinking and almost immediate violation of his one-drink-per-cantina rule precipitates a loss of control, a disorder of the *flâneur's* ordering presence, wherein his body gradually deteriorates as his mind brings up painful repressed memories. This speaks to the side effect of *flânerie* considered by the Walter Benjamin ([1982] 1999) of *The Arcades Project*. Simon Parker (2004) explains, "The sudden remembrance of a once forgotten experience can lead to intoxication but it is a transient sensation that the *flâneur* always seeks to repeat" (18). In a testament to the difficult updating of the *flâneur* in the late twentieth century, it is now intoxication that brings on the remembrance. Juan Manuel has strayed far from the "profane illumination" for which Benjamin strove in his later *flânerie*, or as Andy Merrifield (2002) describes it, the "sober telepathy" that demanded of the *flâneur* an alertness unaltered by narcotic consumption, perhaps only slightly enhanced by wine (60–61). It is also important to underscore here that Juan Manuel often confuses his present experience in a bar with past memories of personal loss. As it has been described above, the phantasms of his personal memory that briefly accompany him form palimpsestic fragments that he gradually adds to his erudite walk around the Centro Histórico in an attempt to form a cognitive map that might at least anchor him in his increasingly disordered *flânerie*.

At *Bar Las Sirenas*, for instance, overwhelmed with the excesses of a two-for-one martini offer, Barrientos vividly hallucinates an encounter with his ex-lover at a hotel in New York. As Juan Manuel fuses his present with his past, his positionality reveals an important feature of the Mexico City *flâneur*. Bar Las Sirenas is coded in the novel to speak to the city's emulation of other cosmopolitan urban cultures (Manhattan in this case), yet is it surrounded by colonial baroque buildings and it overlooks the *Templo Mayor*, underlining the vestiges of the pre-Colombian Aztec capital, Tenochtitlán. This panoramic vista—one of the few that Juan Manuel enjoys above street level—is layered further by Juan Manuel's fantasies of sophistication, framed within a desire to make the city less of a sphere of inquiry and more of a site of privileged consumption.

The *flâneur's* capacity to see and not be seen is also compromised in *Y retiemble*. In the early offing, Juan Manuel is a quiet and careful observer of his surroundings. While it is disappointing to him that his students did not arrive to join him, and he often tells himself that he should just go home, he practices the measured clandestine gazes and musings of a nineteenth-century *flâneur* in the initial chapters and sites of encounter. As Juan Manuel recedes further into his memory, and as he augments his alcohol intake, he becomes more spectacle that spectator, an inversion that culminates in his confused meanderings in an *antro*, or urban dive, where he is summarily robbed of the gentlemanly accoutrements one would associate with a more composed *flâneur*: "They took away your pens, and with them, the fastidious responsibility of writing, of spending hours upon hours before a page disinclined to your penetration"[8] (Celerio, 1999, 181). As a street persona, the traditional *flâneur* is bolstered by a certain economic privilege and high-class masculinity (a characteristic that should be very apparent in the above passage, and which will be explored further with Clavel), and bound by a lettered obligation. In her book, Solnit (2000) traces a developed "language of introspection" from Thomas De Quincey to Charles Dickens to Virginia Woolf that links city writing to the solitude of the *flâneur* (167). According to Solnit, the *flâneur* as a literary figure is rarely identified by an author as such (198), but depictions of the practice of *flânerie* propel the internalized narratives of a city made strange to its inhabitant. By the end of *Y retiemble*, whatever cronista's ease possessed by Juan Manuel has buckled in the unconsecrated zones of the Centro Histórico, which eventually deposit him back in the zócalo, where he will die. As Parkhust-Ferguson (1994) explains, "[o]nce *flânerie* ceases to celebrate urban enchantments, the *flâneur* serves to expose the uncertainty that attends life in the modern city and, more especially, the failure that threatens the creative enterprise. . . . Against the *flâneur* confidently marking possession of the city, the city now takes possession of the *flâneur*" (37–38).

In a foreshadowing scene of *Y retiemble*, Juan Manuel observes the cathedral at midday as he passes by it. He regards it as a mirror image of his progressively disintegrating self. Weilding his umbrella, he begins to mimic his own tour guide register. Celerio's (1999) description has him teetering between elegance and clumsiness as he engages in his confused self-satire:

> You unsheathe your umbrella and with its help you reproduce the twist of one of the jutting corbels, which instead of providing support creates a protrusion. You have to look at this Cathedral upside down, you proclaim out loud before the stares of those passing by who observe your ridiculous contortions with a sarcasm of which you are unaware, because you turn your back on the tower to demonstrate your assertion and you bend over as much as you can, with fragile balance, without bending your knees, in order to bring your head between your

own legs, turned into a triumphal arch, and from there you see the Cathedral's tower upside down and imagine that the sky is the ground and the tower's plinth emerges from the heavily adorned corbels. You return to your normal position so as to continue with your explanation [. . .].[9] (102–103)

The "ridiculous contortions" of Juan Manuel's body, and the images of inversion and imbalance, allude to the tenuous foundations of the cathedral itself, which nonetheless dominates one wing of the city's central plaza as a form of fixed monumentality. As a bearer of historical memory, Juan Manuel himself becomes an odd spectacle to the surrounding public. Foregrounded in this awkward exercise in history and memory, and the articulation thereof, is the conflict between deep knowledge of the city versus the interest of the passerby, the constant dilemma of the *flâneur*.

Steeped in various references to the passion of Christ, Juan Manuel's death scene also places him before the cathedral in a parody of crucifixion. He imagines the cathedral breaking down with him as he bemoans what he deems a wasted lifelong accumulation of reading, knowledge, and historical engagement of the city: "And what is more, who the hell cares about the styles, the damned columns and their capitals! Who the hell cares about everything you learned and taught when you're dying!"[10] (Celerio 1999, 194). This wholesale dismissal contrasts his fantasy of the collapse in stages of the cathedral that follows. Architecture remains in the foreground in spite of Juan Manuel's abandonment of his intellectual passion, and suggests a dilemma with regard to knowledge of the city: is it to be experienced with scholarly depth or not? Is there value in regarding the many layers of the city palimpsest, or does that unraveling lead to a zero sum? The problematic continues after Juan Manuel's death, as Fernando and Jimena, the students who have supposedly absented themselves, arrive at the Centro Histórico the following morning to participate in the architectural tour. The reader discovers that there has been a miscommunication of the day set for the encounter. The final section of the novel describes Fernando and Jimena enjoying each other, their youth and their sexuality (both of which have long since escaped Juan Manuel), in the once again pleasant backdrop of the Centro Histórico.

This array of contradictions of presence and absence begs the question of access to the city and what it means to live (in) it. If, as Harvey (2008) argues, the "freedom to make and remake ourselves and our cities is [. . .] one of the most precious yet most neglected of our human rights," (23) the reader can observe in *Y retiemble* the disastrous consequences of the non-fulfillment of that right. Harvey indicates clearly that the "right to the city" is a fundamentally collective one, and certainly Juan Manuel's isolated regard of it contributes to his downfall. However, it should be remembered that on the day described in the novel, he couldn't find a willing participant in his "city practicum," a longstanding didactic endeavor caricatured by his attempt to give the city tour to himself. The result is the transformation of Juan Manuel from scholar to drunkard to ghost. In fact, in the last lines of the novel he is described spectrally sitting down with a beer in a bar as Fernando and Jimena wake up in a hotel next to the cathedral. As with his inability to share his isolated erudition, his ongoing fantasies about Jimena contrast with the final depiction of the urban Adam and Eve, young and alive visitors of the Centro Histórico, and make of Juan Manuel a sad anachronism of the *flâneur* he perceives in himself.

ANA CLAVEL'S *FLÂNERIE* OF CONTESTATION

Los deseos y su sombra, Ana Clavel's (2000) first novel, tells the story of Soledad, a young woman who one day wakes up in the middle of Avenida Reforma only to realize she is not visible to other people. Unable to remember her last memory and unable to decipher her condition, she decides to recall her entire life in the search of clues to help her understand her current and apparently immaterial state. As with the classical *flâneur*, Soledad embodies a triple alienation: within herself, between herself and her world, and between herself and other people, as she refuses to speak to let her presence be known. The sensation of void, that is, Baudelaire's *spleen*, will be filled through her walks and her gaze with a fresh and eager disposition, unlike the experience of Juan Manuel, who was a seasoned connoisseur or "practioner" of the city. In an analogy of the *flâneur's* predilection for wanting to see (*scopophilia*) without being seen (*scopophobia*), Soledad's invisibility allows her to interact concretely with the city's structures and inhabitants without necessarily being identified herself.[11] During her clandestine excursions, Soledad confronts policemen and security personnel, speaks with monumental figures who complain about being frozen in the form of a statue, and eventually finds solidarity among a group of street children and their blind father-figure, that is, city residents on the margins who experience their own kind of invisibility.

The story is divided into four sections: childhood, youth, early adulthood, and the narrative present. We mostly focus here on the last segment because it is where Soledad is conscientiously trying to define herself—in fact, re-embody herself—as she walks from Chapultepec Park to the Centro Histórico through Avenida Reforma, all the while musing on the city and its history. As it were, her invisibility is the result of her extreme sense of alienation from place and society. Throughout her life, Soledad is always looking for ways to belong, "to feel that, at last, she had a place in the world" ("sentir que por fín tenía un lugar en el mundo") (Clavel 2000, 159). After the death of her father, with whom she identified for his aesthetic inclinations and his storytelling finesse, Soledad remains under the strict domestic tutelage of her mother who names Soledad's older brother, *el hombre de la casa* (the man of the house). Between her mother and her brother, and the extensions of patriarchy they have constructed around her, Soledad finds it impossible to assert her own autonomy and identity. Even her name reminds her of her loneliness. The street, then, provides freedom from her mother's surveillance, but soon she finds out that "(t)he outside space, which is to say the city-text that lies beyond the kingdom of the domestic, is controlled by the marauding bodies of homo-social masculinity" (Venkatesh 2015, 162). Hence, the forces that create and shape street dynamics are male-centered macrocosms of her home life, wherein the city presents to women structural and cultural impediments to fully developing a comfortable relationship with the city space and a sense of belonging on the street. In other words, for Soledad, the venture of cognitive mapping is already compromised.

Although her connection to the city has been identified as part of her search of self, critical sources have yet to relate her wandering and gaze to that of a flâneuse. Through her spectral *flânerie*, Soledad challenges the initiator of the gaze, in this case domestic patriarchy extended to the street, and the meaning (or the lack thereof) of existence, while she develops a sense of belonging in the modern urban spaces of the city. In strolling the streets without male accompaniment, Soledad as flâneuse articulates the text's reconstruction of "an alternative conceptualization of national identity" (Lavery 2015, 35), a *heteroglossia* that creates and adds her own neglected story into the collective city-text. As she wanders through the city and remembers her own story, she will unravel for herself the nation's history as embodied by monuments as well as stories from a marginalized population forgotten by the city (à la Buñuel's [1950] *Los olvidados*, see Rogers in this volume). With this in mind, we'll consider official history as the primary ordering narrative. The Avenida Reforma is a monument gallery out in the open, while the stories of the poor and marginalized, who live in the shadows of the system, are as inconspicuous as Soledad is invisible. As Luzma Becerra (2002) describes broadly, Soledad transits between light and shadows, literally and figuratively, thereby analogizing the at once visible and invisible poverty and marginality to be found in even the most privileged and monumental zones of the city.

In *Los deseos y su sombra*, monumental history is not recited in the monological utterances that we heard from Juan Manuel Barrientos. Rather, it emerges from Soledad's own experiences and reflections as well as from casual street conversations with three men who, in their own marginalized positions, provide germane comments on city and society. Even so, Soledad exercises her *flânerie* from a position of invisibility as well as anonymity; her accessibility to the city is contingent to her non-being, which points to the negation of urban space for women and the role of men in mediating it for them. In order to become visible again she needs to find a way to insert herself back into society, to attain Benjamin's condition of "of" the crowd as much as "in" the crowd. The end of the novel articulates this process of claiming agency and culminates in a series of events and interactions in which Soledad's disembodiment ("her body does not contain her," [Clavel 2000, 307]) enacts from the margins a contestation of the lettered city and its official history.

A closer look at Soledad's personal story and the cityscape that informs it will better articulate how she achieves the *dérive* (drifting), the disordering, haphazard urban journey, so lauded by Guy DeBord (1958). The first parts of the novel signal that Soledad's childhood home is located in Colonia San Rafael. However, in her self-seeking journey, Soledad breaks away from the ordered monotony of her geographical comfort zone to instead venture into a new psychogeographical area that would reorganize her cognitive cartography. That she opts for Avenida Reforma indicates her desire to view herself within the nation's historical framework. Her initial wanderings occur along the Reforma-Chapultepec axis punctuated by monuments and sculptures that gesticulate the political evolution of the country, that is, the various orderings and re-orderings to which Rama's lettered city attends. In her walks through Reforma, Soledad integrates these monuments and their political-historical discourse into her own positioning within the bigger scheme of society, city, and nation. While Juan Manuel Barrientos prefers the predictable closed system of the city's Centro Histórico and the reiteration of a trajectory that he has largely repeated many times over, Soledad allows for the intervention of traffic, agglomeration of people, and supposed vagrants in her historical review.

As she pauses to reflect on herself as a product of her sociohistorical circumstances, it is no coincidence that she starts her journey on Avenida Reforma, since it projects a complex interplay between monument and spectacle, architecture and ideology. In the nineteenth century, Avenida Reforma served a dual purpose: to embellish the city with an appropriate promenade for its aristocrats, and to educate the masses on the historic past of the nation. It was created by Emperor Maximilian of Austria, who cut diagonally across plots of land to open a boulevard that would shorten his commute from his mansion in Chapultepec to his office in the National Palace. *El Paseo de la Emperatriz*, as it was first called, was modeled after Paris's *Les Champs-Élysées*. Culminating in the leisure site of *Parque Alameda,* it was the promenade to see and be seen—thus making it Mexico City's ideal site for *flânerie*, as well as an outdoors gallery that incorporated the symbols of identity and the representations of national heroes. In his short three years in power (1864–1867), Maximilian commissioned the construction of 400 sculptures of the heroes of Independence, specifically Hidalgo, Morelos, and Iturbide, to which Guerrero was added later (Martínez Assad 2002, 27). After the emperor's death, Mexican politicians did not want to be excluded from the project of honoring the memory of national heroes. A monument to Columbus appeared on Avenida Reforma, as well as a monument to Cuauhtémoc in recognition of the city's pre-Columbian past. This open gallery, which presented a collection of heroes and founding artifacts, points to an early reliance on image literacy in a highly illiterate society. The monuments occupied a public space ostensibly made available to everyone, and thus anyone strolling on Avenida Reforma presumably would be reminded of the heroes who made monarchical independence possible.

At the beginning of the twentieth century, the effigies flanking Avenida Reforma were often vandalized and disfigured as targets of discontent. Graffiti tags or residual vandalism signify the physical imprint of contestation; they suggest an interpretation of visual elements within a system of hegemonic signs and, as signifiers of power, they become scapegoats onto which the population projects its anxiety and anger (Boym 2001, 89). As historical manifestations, national monuments reflect the aesthetic and political conception of their time and they are a "metonymy for both the power and ideals of the state" (Banks 2002, 38). However, by mid-century they were being dwarfed by modern skyscrapers, and then mostly forgotten by the end of the century, as noted by the protagonist: "These statues were doomed to go unnoticed. Soledad felt compassion: after all, they were as invisible as she was"[12] (Clavel 2000, 198). When Soledad is wandering through Avenida Reforma, these monuments served mainly as topographical landmarks; over the years, their representational and ordering value gave way to their recognition as prominent points of reunion. For Robert Musil ([1957] 1987), monuments are supposed to "conjure up a remembrance or grab hold of our attention and give us a pious bent to our feelings for this, it is assumed, is what we more or less need; it is in this, their prime purpose, that monuments always fall short" (62). The vulnerability of monuments over time and altered circumstance in the city, in this case the shift from metropolis to megalopolis, makes possible Soledad's contestation of national history and development of Lavery's "alternative conceptualization of national identity," that is, the dialogic engagement that Soledad will practice with monumentality, examples of which follow.

Another factor to be considered when trying to explain the indifference or hostility to which statues are subjected is an increased literacy rate, which competes with the value of images and other visual representations. This reasoning takes us to the heart of the argument of whether reading/writing as memory tool has affected our capacity and efficiency for collective memory. A final contributing factor, referenced in Fuentes's (1958) *La región más transparente*, is that the rapidly changing socioeconomic make-up of the population in Mexico (due to the demographic explosion) together with the transformation of its spaces (through the industrialization of the city during the decades of the "Mexican Miracle") created an illegible, disordered space for almost everyone. Fuentes' narrative plot echoes the observations made by Georg Simmel in his essay, "The Metropolis and Mental Life" ([1903] 1950), in which he noted that overstimulation of urban life led to a "blunting of discrimination" and the development of a *blasé* attitude which keeps the residents of a metropolis from empathizing with each other or sustaining interest in their surroundings. In *The City in Literature* (1998) Richard Lehan corroborates both Fuentes' and Simmel's previous observations and asserts that as cities become more complex as physical structures, ways of seeing them become more difficult and individuals become more passive in their relationship to them. It is precisely under such alienating conditions that the act of *flânerie* presents the occasion of a more active engagement of the city. The *flâneur's* requirement of critical inquiry, which takes place in the public spaces and streetscapes through a clandestine but intense integration among those more passive city dwellers, serves as contestation to this alienated condition.

It may well be, as Rama (1984) asserts, that the lettered city encompasses both official and contestatory discourse (53), but in Soledad a new kind of letrada emerges, one who fuses the contingency of street with the static monumentality of the city. In her attempt to recuperate herself, Soledad takes residence in Chapultepec Castle. It is a significant occupation of patrimonial space; this is the medium by which the personal and private come together with the formal and official in order to interlink them and create wider associations to self and nation. However, even though museums are said to be places where people encounter artifacts that make them contemplate the past within the present, this specific function of museums is extremely limited by the range of lived human experiences permitted within the museum space itself (Kavanagh 2000, 2). In general, a museum, like a monument, is considered material memory by virtue of its architecture. It is supposed to facilitate remembering of all sorts despite the fact that it only houses artifacts that reinforce a very specific version of hegemonic discourse. While the Castle is not usually considered geographically central, in this story it represents the hegemonic center due to its officiality, historicity, and function as the National History Museum. As museum-monument, Chapultepec Castle represents a place of recognition and confirmation of national (and personal) identity, wherein the fight against the dissolution of memory takes place. If individual memory is not supported by subjective memories as much as by social frameworks and external prostheses that, according to Remo Bodei (1995) sustain and perpetuate it as a palimpsestic *lieu de mémoire* (imperial mansion, presidential palace, military school, and museum), it is expected that in the castle the articulation between the nation's tradition, heritage, national culture, and memory would consolidate smoothly to enable national visitors to appropriate those memories.

When Soledad comes to reside here, she presumes that it will serve as a model for personal reconstruction of individual memory. However, that doesn't happen because "(t)hose caught in the spatial net of monumentality have their existence reduced to a predetermined set of signs that represent the abstract desires of the state" (Critical Art Ensemble 1996, 26). The narrative discloses one of the issues that museums and curators have to confront, namely, how to preserve an object and present it in such a way that it does not appear to be frozen in the past and without any relation to the present. Soledad, who intended to occupy Chapultepec Castle (to make it her own), ends up differentiating herself from the visitors, crossing the other side of the rail, and adding herself to the museum's inventory of artifacts fixed in the past, thus failing to establish the connection between the city's past and her present in an affirmation of identity.

As discussed earlier, Clavel's novel suggests there is a breakdown in the dialectical process that allows the monument to represent meaning and makes the receptor "conjure up a remembrance" of their own humanity. This is distinctly exemplified when Soledad meets General Leandro Valle, the historical figure from the Independence war, who happens to reside in his own effigy. In a way, Valle is also invisible because although he speaks, nobody seems to hear him, and although he's visible, nobody pays attention to him, as if his statue form weren't there at all. Nonetheless, and unlike Soledad, Valle remembers his life and death and waking up trapped in his statue. All pomp aside, he turns out to be a very interesting and engaging character who, from his pedestal on Avenida Reforma, has been a witness to the changes of the city, its politics, and its people. He expresses displeasure with what he has seen. From his historical (static) positionality he can't comprehend how is it that the public doesn't know the nation's history and doesn't appreciate all the signifiers mounted to aid their memories. By his logic, if the monuments and statues were placed along Avenida Reforma as memorial remnants, and since the monuments and statues are still carrying on when the people don't remember, it's the people who are at fault, not the monuments. The same argument can be made for the museum artifacts, thus calling for an active mode of observation and exploration while walking through the city, which is what Juan Manuel Barrientos asks of his students (and readers) to little avail.

Once Leandro Valle finds someone who listens, he shares a mixed set of stories about the Independence war: on the one hand, he explains military practices, such as the difference between a saber and a sword, how to load a rifle, when to send in grenadiers on foot and when on horse, and the obligations of trenchers, artillerymen, and lancers. On the other hand, he refutes the information made official on Guadalupe Victoria's plaque which explains that Guadalupe Victoria is a name made up for political reasons, and he tells Soledad that historiography does not always present events accurately. In her conversations with Valle, Soledad gets information that is both pertinent and irrelevant to her quest for self-definition. Valle reveals that all the historical figures on Avenida Reforma inhabited their effigy at one point, but they left one by one when they realized people stopped paying attention to them. So, in an embodiment of shifting attitudes toward monuments of Reforma, their memory/substance has vacated them. Valle's annoyance with his own immobility, and with the indifference of the public, speaks to an immobility of discourse and the intransigence of official hegemonic discourse to connect with new generations.

Unknowingly, Leandro Valle—who complains that everyone forgets history—sends Soledad on a futile pursuit to a neighborhood behind the (historical) Downtown area where she will find herself in a poor area where people and their lifestyles present a different dynamic than the one appreciated up to now. Her walks, up to this point, had subscribed to an established official discourse and a forgotten past. Valle intended to send Soledad to Republic of Guatemala street for a remedy to cure her of her invisibility, and what she found inversely was a zone of illegal activities, *fayuqueros*, drug addicts, and pimps. These are also forgotten city dwellers, not by inertia but by choice and circumstance, participating in an active attempt at not-remembering, as Elizabeth Jelin (2003) calls it. Although part of the city's center, his neighborhood represents the historic periphery. This is the outer rim of official discourse, a heterotopia that stands in contestation to the Centro Histórico's monumental gestures.

In such a periphery, Soledad finds the only statue of a female insurgent from the Independence war; like the rest of the residents here, Josefa Ortiz de Domínguez, known as *La Corregidora*, doesn't have a place in any of the main Avenues of the city. Unlike her male counterparts, who stand dignified, she is portrayed in a passive sitting position. Soledad demands that she speak and help her, but there is no reply. It is one more empty monument. Instead, don Matías, who used to be a librarian at the National Library before his blindness disabled him, answers her call. His sightlessness and friendliness puts Soledad at ease—because he doesn't place any ordering expectations on her—and they are able to spend many nights talking and wandering the city. He becomes a model in the process of symbolic elaboration of meaning (historical, individual, and spatial) in order to actively engage with it. Like a lyrical poet, don Matías enjoys telling stories to whoever likes to hear them, and in contrast to Juan Manuel, he doesn't require a consecrated tour or practicum to do so. His sense, understanding, and assimilation of the city will serve Soledad as an example for her own creative interpretation on the urban palimpsest. In one of their nocturnal strolls through the city, Matías stresses that the "labor of (creating) memory," a term coined by Jelin (2003), is a very subjective process: "I can assure you that the city that you walk upon every day is not the same as my city nor anybody else's. Your city is called Soledad as mine can only be named Matías"[13] (Clavel 2000, 252). He epitomizes what it means to be a living archive, to accumulate spatial-historical information and to contextualize it in order to make sense of the present. He does so by storytelling. For instance, he explains a union dispute in Palacio de Bellas Artes, the Fine Arts National Center, by a fairy tale titled "The Musicians Who Refused to Play for the Emperor" (254). He also inserts those around him, namely the street children known as *los niños de la noche*, in his stories about the city and its landmarks. The children, a group of young petty thieves, operate outside of the hegemonic discourse but Matías finds ways to create for them an "alternative conceptualization of national identity" to help them understand their surroundings and their connection to them.

Through don Matías, Soledad meets the children and Jorge, who works on the street as a pantomiming living statue. Jorge reiterates Leandro Valle's complaints that the public doesn't realize how hard it is to be a representation of meaning, that is to say to be a statue, and how very few people let themselves be moved by the presence of one. "On these days I don't make a lot. People see at me as if I were a window mannequin: they don't notice what I do and I don't seem to connect with them. . . . It's sad and unbearably wearying"[14] (Clavel 2000, 260). He contemplates quitting but reconsiders when he remembers his calling for it and the reaction of the people who do respond effectively to his performance. This signals to the ebb and flow of the residents' interest in their surrounding.

A central monument that seems to function in a different paradigm and never lose signifying value is the cathedral. Although few people appreciate its architectural complexity and its historicity as Juan Manuel Barrientos does, many frequent it on a regular basis. The juxtaposition of individual versus collective engagement of this monumental form occurs in both novels, and, just as it does for Barrientos, for Soledad the cathedral, and its towers as focal point, will represent a turning point in her story. The towers of any church are said to have three functions: (1) direct the viewer's eye vertically up to heaven; (2) to serve as the highest point of the building it serves as an easy landmark to locate; and (3) the bell on the towers have a way of communicating a celebration as well as warn of a danger. As Soledad goes up the bell tower stairs, she likens the cathedral to a magnificent ship by which she can sail through her own overwhelming sense of the concrete city-lake (Clavel 2000, 266). From the highest balcony of the west tower, Soledad has a sweeping view of the metropolis and realizes she was a drop in the overflow of lonesome people. As an initiated *flânuese*, that thought consoles her as she observes the city and understands she is to structure it, from within, according to her needs and passions. Although don Matías had hinted at a way of being together and by one's self, it is from this all-encompassing perspective that she understands what it means to be "of the crowd" and not just "in the crowd." Henceforth, the cathedral towers become her own citadel, the fortified center of her Self.

> At that moment, the bells of the Cathedral tolled. The world was reborn, the city got going. . . . Things like this happened all the time in Soledad's city, but people refused to see them: with blindfolded eyes and souls they gulped down the miracle of a new day like a cheap drink, winged feet made them seek sanctuary in their motorized houses, or rush into mini-busses and the metro, amidst that dirty air of stenches and bad vibes that glazed over their sight, that allowed them to lose themselves anywhere under their own skin, anywhere but in the downtown area.[15] (Clavel 2000, 299)

While most people hurry through life in the city or distract themselves in order not to see it, Soledad makes the Cathedral towers her home, her perspective compass. She also learns to be like the bells, as they are not easily visible but, with their voices, make their presence known.

Paradoxically, Soledad's new self-assurance comes from her understanding and acceptance of the uncertainty that attends life, freeing her of her fear to carve her own story in the realm of the national and/or the collective. The panoramic view the cathedral towers provides Soledad not only a bird's-eye view on the city but also a height and distance from which Soledad is able to put herself above and everything else into perspective. "Although the city that unfolded around her was not infinite, it satisfied her to see it and know it there, ebullient, elusive but for a few seconds. She recognized herself alone, but instead of petrifying her, for the first time it comforted her"[16] (Clavel 2000, 267). At street level, the city seemed to be made up of disconnected parts, and Soledad struggled to interpret their continuity, and how to understand herself within that story. The sight from the towers reveals to her a complex but fluid urban tableau in which she sees that she does not have to carve her own story within a single hegemonic story. This outcome contests the experience of Manuel Barrientos, who in a similar opportunity to view the city from above in the Bar Las Sirenas, imposes the memory of a more favorable city (New York) from a more favorable time. Soledad's panoramic gaze is autochthonous by comparison. Its proximity to a socially marginalized zone turns the monumental cathedral into the ideal fortress from which Soledad can face future contingencies. The city as a whole may still not feel like home, but the cathedral does.

The last place Soledad visits in *Los deseos y su sombra* is the castle in Chapultepec, thus closing the circuit from her search began. With new friends on her side and under happier circumstances, her return shows that remembrance of the past is not confined to a place: it is a continuous labor of codifying and de-codifying stories for the self and the community. On this Sunday outing with don Matías and the children, her perspective on the city is refreshed:

> Soledad contemplated it as if she at last possessed it. Well, it wasn't a complete possession but rather that she felt she was part of the city and that she loved it like her own body, with the face of a poor sooty girl who bathed in dew every now and then, with its imperfect but flexible and vigorous form, with bad breath and unforeseeable entrails, with outbursts that made her touch the sky and with its efforts to resist destruction.[17] (Clavel 2000, 305)

Soledad senses the city as a lovable, physical extension of her body; her fear of marauding male bodies controlling urban space is countered. However, even though Soledad learns to use alternative means to help her mediate through her musings and excursions, the city as a patriarchal space persists. This is most noticeable in one scene of the novel in which Soledad is spotted by an anti-riot police officer during a demonstration, thus ending her ability to confront similar authority figures without being seen or reprimanded. In the end, as Lavery (2015) points out, Soledad's unknowable truth becomes a comment on the juncture of historic reality, "symbolically illustrating that what we might perceive as reality or 'truth' is ultimately an imaginative construct" (36). Moreover, the real and symbolic elements of this construct serve to maintain and perpetuate a repressing patriarchal order within the urban space.

THE *FLÂNEUR* BEFORE THE CATHEDRAL

Flâneurs as gendered figures in a gendered city inevitably form intertextual relationships with each other as they do with their city-referent. In the case of the novels discussed here, the omnipresence of monumental architectural structures, and their presence as sites of memory as well as sites of encounter, immediately offers rich focal points that bring to bear the limits and transformations of *flânerie*. The *flâneur* experiences in *Y retiemble* and *Los deseos* intersect more than once, but here we focus on the two protagonists' regard of the Metropolitan Cathedral in the Centro Histórico, even when neither protagonist takes a stroll inside.

As in the case of the ruins of the Templo Mayor, a historically marked structure in that zone of the city, the Cathedral operates palimpsestically, as much within itself as with its surroundings that represent multiple possessions by multiple ordering entities. The first phase of the structure coincided with the conquest of Tenochtitlán as an imposition of the new order, literally over the rubble of the Templo Mayor, upon which Cortés erects an emulation of the Andalusian *mudejar* style, which in turn synchretizes Moorish architecture. A form of topographical resistance emerged in that the original plan could not be brought to fruition due to the instability of the firmament: the structure required 20 years of foundational work. After 40 years, the existing walls were only half completed. In a broader arc, the cathedral's construction and resulting variance of style spanned a total of 300 years. Different architects took charge of walls, the domes, vaults, towers, and the façade. The result is a conglomeration of aesthetics and power plays that encapsulates similar varied transformations in the city itself.

Though monumental and historically charged, the Cathedral seems to be ruled by a value system that makes it an iconic structure in the Zócalo area, one that often eclipses the National Palace, the site of the Presidential offices. Barrientos does not even mention the National Palace, and Soledad spends a few hours inside, but it is not crucial to her identity definition as the Cathedral towers will be. The Cathedral seems to fulfill Musil's ([1957] 1987) described function of grabbing hold of people's attention and giving them "a pious bent to their feelings." In the construction and obstacles of building this monumental church, we can trace the history of growth of the city. If "the city is an onion" (Celorio 1999, 101), as Juan Manuel Barrientos stated, then the Cathedral is the core of that onion, as it bears centrifugal layers that embody its urban development. As a spiritual center, its legibility remains firm, even in the midst of increased Protestantism in Mexico and many other layers of architectural spirituality like the ones visited during Juan Manuel's city practicum. In Soledad's case, the "peripheral" condition attributed to the Cathedral and its northern neighborhood, Santo Domingo, means they were precluded from the modernization process that took place alongside Avenida Reforma. The exclusion suggests that people living within the national imaginary are influenced by traditional values around religion and family ties, as we see in one of the last scenes of *Los deseos* when both the living and the dead come to the Cathedral to visit each other during the Day of the Dead mass celebration. National identity and its legibility, then, operate on a continuum of personal relationships, family ties, and ritual.

However, and as we have seen, at the end of the twentieth century, the determiners of the city's legibility are fragile, and they are subject to const-estation. The *flânerie* of both our protagonists represents a recuperative act in which the cultural patrimony available to them serves as a backdrop for their exercise of memory and identity construction. On the one hand, the solitary professor, the presumed heir to the *flâneur* tradition, holds the key to dispelling prejudices about the Centro Histórico in order to unravel the stories contained there. However, his consumerism—the thirst that propels his steps—sets him astray. In the end, he is overtaken by the city before he can formally pass the baton to his teaching assistant, Antonio, who takes possession of the lettered city without Juan Manuel's consecration. Conversely, Soledad, a young adult female who only went out to the street to carry on respectable everyday practices—school, work, shopping—realizes she is invisible and her invisibility allows her to wander the streets freely, to be a secret spectator of the city, and to create a narrative space for herself. As Solnit (2000) would describe it, Soledad thus achieves the ideal of city walking, "the mingling of the errand and the epiphany" (178). In the end, she joins a group of kindred city dwellers who understand that they don't require a homogeneous experience of the city in order to form a community of stories, capable of enacting Harvey's (2008) transformative agency. In both narratives, monuments are signs without signification; it is difficult not to equate them to the empty hegemonic discourse from the official political party, which fell briefly out of power in 2000, a year after the publication and recognition of the novels discussed here.

A few years later, the extensive renovation of the Historic Center, and the main roads leading to it, optimized its cultural consumption potential to coincide with the Centennial and Bicentennial celebrations of 2010. However, instead of strengthening the historic memory of the area, it sought to suppress the small, local businesses and to steer human behavior toward a globalized commercialization. In expanding its economic capabilities, the downtown has become a modern, but quaint, retail quarter that incites constant foot traffic and a steady demand of goods; this is what Rama might have called *la ciudad marcada*, the branded city. Any possible self-affirmations expressed within this space only reaffirm the Mexican citizen as part of the global economy. At the beginning of the new millennium, the capital city becomes city of capital. Celorio's and Clavel's novelizations serve as anxious precursors to that shift. What such narratives might reveal about the current guise of CDMX remains to be seen.

NOTES

1. To this list we could add Carmen Boullosa, José Emilio Pacheco, Elena Poniatowska, María Luisa Puga, and Luis Zapata.

2. While *flânerie* as an embodied practice might seem self-evident, some contributors to Tester (1994) such as Bauman and Morawski argue for mediated and virtual *flâneurs* who don't necessarily take to the street.

3. *Es la ciudad perdida por antonomasia pero encontrada por la literatura que la construye día a día, que la restaura, que la revela, que la cuida, que la reta.*

4. *Conocía las calles y las plazas del centro de la ciudad, sus edificios civiles y religiosos, su historia de dezplazamientos, de superposiciones, de alteraciones aberrantes, de destrucción inconcebible.*

5. *Y sus pasos, ésos que daba por el centro de la ciudad, ¿no eran la caligrafía tartamuda—o ebria—que alguien iba escribiendo sin que él tuviera nada que ver en el asunto?*

6. For more on Luiselli's take on *flânerie* in Mexico City, see O'Connor in this volume.

7. *No es posible extraer ninguna idea comprehensiva de la ciudad de México con sólo caminarla. Los paseos solitarios de Rousseau, los vagabundeos de Walser o Baudelaire, las Bildergänge o las caminatas-imagen de Kracauer y las flâneries de Benjamin fueron una manera de entender y retratar la nueva estructura de las ciudades modernas. Pero a los habitantes de la ciudad de México no les está concedido el punto de vista de la miniatura ni el del pájaro porque carecen de todo punto de referencia. Se perdió, en algún momento, la noción del centro, de un eje articulador.*

8. *Te quitaron tus plumas, y con ellas, la fastidiosa responsibilidad de escribir, de pasarte horas y horas ante una página renuente a tu penetración.*

9. *Esgrimes tu paraguas y reproduces con su ayuda el giro de unas ménsulas inusitadas que en lugar de soportar un cuerpo saliente sostienen un cuerpo remetido. A esta Catedral hay que mirarla de cabeza, sentencias en voz alta, ante las miradas de quienes por ahí circulan y observan, con una sorna de la que tú no te percatas, tus ridículas contorsiones porque le das las espaldas a la torre para demostrar tu aserto y te agachas tanto cuanto puedes, con frágil equilibrio, sin flexionar las rodillas, para asomar la cabeza por entre tus propias piernas convertidas en arco triunfal y desde ahí ver, al revés, la torre de la Catedral e imaginar que el cielo es el suelo y que el basamento sobresale de las gargoladas ménsulas. Vuelves a tu posición normal un tanto mareado y tambaleante, pero suficientemente lúcido como para seguir tu explicación.*

10. *Y además, qué carajos importan los estilos, las pinches columnas y sus capiteles. ¡Qué carajos importa todo lo que aprendiste y enseñaste si te estás muriendo!*

11. See O'Connor in this volume for more on women's invisibility in the city.

12. *Estas estatuas estaban condenadas a pasar inadvertidas. Soledad sintió compasión: a fin de cuentas eran tan invisibles como ella.*

13. *Puedo asegurarte que la ciudad que tú recorres todos los días no es mi ciudad ni la de otros. Tu ciudad es Soledad como la mía sólo puede llamarse Matías.*

14. *En estos días sale poco dinero y la gente me ve como un maniquí de aparador: ni reparan en mí ni yo tampoco les transmito nada . . . Es triste y tremendamente cansado.*

15. *En ese momento, las campanas de Catedral tocaron a rebato. El mundo renacía, la ciudad tomaba su curso. . . . Cosas como éstas pasaban de común en la ciudad de Soledad, pero la gente se negaba a verlas: vendados los ojos y el alma apuraban el milagro como un mal trago, los pies alados la hacían buscar el refugio de sus casas con ruedas, precipitarse en peceras y el metro, en ese aire turbio de olores y malsabores que les vidriaban la mirada y les permitían perderse en cualquier rincón debajo de su piel, menos en el centro.*

16. *Aunque aquella ciudad que se desplegaba a su alrededor no era infinita, verla y saberla ahí, bullente, inasible salvo por algunos segundos, la colmaba. Se reconoció sola, pero eso en vez de asustarla, por primera vez, la reconfortó.*
17. *Soledad la contempló como si por fin la poseyera. Bueno, no era una posesión completa sino más bien que se sentía parte de la ciudad y que la amaba como a un cuerpo propio, con su cara de niña pobre hollinada y de vez en cuando lavada de rocío, con su cuerpo imperfecto pero flexible y vigoroso, con su mal aliento y sus entrañas insospechables, con sus raptos que la hacían tocar el cielo y sus esfuerzos por resistir la destrucción.*

WORKS CITED

Banks, Miranda. 2002. "Monumental Fictions: National Monuments as a Science Fiction Space." *Journal of Popular Film and Television* 30 (3): 136–145.

Becerra, Luzma. 2002. "Otra forma de estar en el mundo o la ciudad subterránea en *Los deseos y su sombra* de Ana Clavel." *Iztapalapa* 23 (52): 245–259.

Benjamin, Walter. (1982) 1999. *The Arcades Project.* Translated by Howard Eilin and Kevin McLaughlin. Prepared on the basis of the German text by Rolf Teidemann. Cambridge, MA: Belknap Press of Harvard University.

Benjamin, Walter. 2006. *The Writer of Modern Life.* Edited by Michael W. Jennings. Translated by Howard Eiland, et al. Cambridge: Harvard University Press.

Bodei, Remo. 1995. "Memoria histórica, olvido e identidad colectiva." In *La tenacidad de la política*, compiled by Nora Rabotnikof, Ambrosio Velasco, and Corina Yturbe, 81–101. México: Universidad Nacional Autónoma de México.

Boym, Stevlana. 2001. *The Future of Nostalgia.* New York: Basic Books.

Brushwood, John S. 1981. "Sobre el referente y la transformación narrativa en las novelas de Carlos Fuentes y Gustavo Sáinz." *Revista iberoamericana* 47 (116): 49–61.

Buñuel, Luis, director. 1950. *Los olvidados.* Ultramar Films.

Camps, Martín. 2005. "*Palimpsesto urbano: Amor propio y Y retiemble en los centros su tierra de Gonzalo Celorio.*" *Con-Textos* 17 (35) (Julio-diciembre): 64–71.

Celorio, Gonzalo. 1996. "*Amor propio* con amor propio." *Revista de Literatura Mexicana Contemporánea* 1 (3): 115–116.

———. 1997. *Ciudad de papel.* México: Universidad Nacional Autónoma de México.

———. 1999. *Y retiemble en sus centros la tierra.* México: Tusquets.

Clavel, Ana. 2000. *Los deseos y su sombra.* México: Editorial Alfaguara.

Critical Art Ensemble. 1996. "Nine Thesis Against Monuments." In *Random Access 2: Ambient Fears*, edited by Pavel Büchler and Nikos Papastergiadis, 22–30. London: Rivers Oram Press.

De Alva, María, and José Martí. 2004. "Memoria y ciudad. *Y retiemble en sus centros la tierra* de Gonzalo Celorio." *Revista de Literatura Mexicana Contemporánea* 10 (24) (Septiembre-Diciembre): v–ix.

DeBord, Guy. 1958. "Theory of the Dérive." *Internationale Situationiste #2* (December): 62–66.

90   *Alejandro Puga and Carmen Patricia Tovar*

Fuentes, Carlos. 1958. *La región más transparente*. México: Editorial Alfaguara.

Gallo, Rubén. 2009. Foreword to *And Let The Earth Tremble at Its Centers*, by Gonzalo Celorio, translated by Dick Gerders, ix–xx. Austin: University of Texas Press.

Harvey, David. 2008. "The Right to the City." *New Left Review* 53 (September–October): 23–40.

Jameson, Frederic. 1991. *Postmodernism, or, the Cultural Logic of Late Capitalism*. Durham, NC: Duke University Press.

Jelin, Elizabeth. 2003. *State Repression and the Labors of Memory*. Translated by Judy Rein and Marcial Godoy-Anativia. Minnesota: University of Minnesota Press.

Kandell, Jonathan. 1988. *La Capital: The Biography of México City*. New York: Random House.

Kavanagh, Gaynor. 2000. *Dream Spaces, Memory and the Museum*. London and New York: Leicester University Press.

Lavery, Jane Elizabeth. 2015. *The Art of Ana Clavel: Ghosts, Urinals, Dolls, Shadows and Outlaw Desires*. London: Legenda.

Lefebvre, Henri. (1974) 1991. *The Production of Space*. Translated by Donald Nicholson-Smith. Cambridge, MA: Blackwell.

Lehan, Richard. 1998. *The City in Literature: An Intellectual and Cultural History*. Berkeley: University of California Press.

Luiselli, Valeria. 2012. *Papeles falsos*. México: Editorial Sexto Piso.

Lynch, Kevin. 1960. *The Image of the City*. Cambridge, MA: MIT Press, 1960.

Martínez Assad, Carlos. 2002. *La patria por la Avenida Reforma*. México: Fondo de Cultura Económica.

Merrifield, Andy. 2002. *Metromarxism: A Marxist Tale of the City*. New York: Routledge.

Musil, Robert. (1957) 1987. *Posthumous Papers of a Living Author*. Translated by Peter Wortsman. Colorado: Eridanos Press.

Parker, Simon. 2004. *Urban Theory and Urban Experience: Encountering the City*. New York: Routledge.

Parkhurst-Ferguson, Priscilla. 1994. "The flâneur on and off the streets of Paris." In *The Flâneur*, edited by Keith Tester, 22–42. New York: Routledge.

Puga, Alejandro. 2012. *La ciudad novelada a fines del siglo XX: Estructura, retórica y figuración*. México: Universidad Autónoma Metropolitana.

Rama, Ángel. 1984. *La ciudad letrada*. Hanover: Ediciones del Norte.

Simmel, Georg. (1903) 1950. "The Metropolis and Mental Life." In *The Sociology of Georg Simmel*, edited and translated by Kurt H. Wolff, 409–426. New York: Free Press.

Solnit, Rebecca. 2000. *Wanderlust: A History of Walking*. New York: Penguin Books.

Tester, Keith, editor. 1994. *The Flâneur*. New York: Routledge.

Venkatesh, Vinod. 2015. "The Ends of Masculinity in Urban Space in Ana Clavel's *Los deseos y su sombra*." *Letras Hispánicas* 11: 158–170.

Yates, Frances A. 1966. *The Art of Memory*. Chicago: University of Chicago Press.

Zarco, Francisco. 1968. *Escritos literarios*. México, DF: Porrúa.

Chapter 5

Securing the City in Santa Fe

Privatization and Preservation

Shannan Mattiace and Jennifer L. Johnson

The financial district of Santa Fe, which, for the purposes of this essay we call "new Santa Fe," is located in the extreme western fringe of Mexico City proper, and is the newest and wealthiest residential and commercial district of the city. Whereas wealthy neighborhoods such as *Lomas de Chapultepec*, which is located just north of Santa Fe and closer to the city center, was modeled after the Garden City utopia of North American urban planners of the 1920s and was zoned as strictly residential, new Santa Fe was built for the express purpose of enshrining consumer capitalism for the nouveau riche, who live surrounded by easy and exclusive access to a range of services. The property that embodies this wealth—in the form of shopping malls, corporate headquarters, and gated communities—is heavily guarded by private security guards. Moving around this district is virtually impossible as a pedestrian, in stark contrast to the other neighborhoods we study here. In the shadow of new Santa Fe, is the historic Pueblo Santa Fe, which, for the purposes of this essay, we call "old Santa Fe." Old Santa Fe, founded in the sixteenth century, is a working-class neighborhood known for its marginality and crime. The two Santa Fes exist side by side and represent worlds of extreme contrasts. The story of Santa Fe we tell here is the story of these contrasts.

VIGNETTE

Vasco de Quiroga Street, part of the *Camino Real*, or "Royal Road" in colonial times, continues to be the main thoroughfare through old Santa Fe. Collective buses leaving the Tacubaya and Observatorio Metro stations lumber up the steep hills of western Mexico City via Vasco de Quiroga. No subway line extends to Santa Fe, marking the area as being on the edge, or at the boundary, of city limits. During the daylight hours, the streets are persistently congested; the bright green collective buses, or *colectivos*, are visible to all as they make their way up and down the hill, hour after hour. Most of the passengers live and work in the many working class and poorer *colonias*, or "neighborhoods" that comprise the greater Santa Fe area: *colonias* called *La Mexicana, La Pólvora, Pueblo Nuevo, Pueblo Santa Fe*, and *Tecolalco*. Some passengers, however, continue their journey, passing the roundabout that divides the older sections of Santa Fe from the new, commercial Santa Fe.

On a sunny and hot June day, we walk through some of the older sections of Santa Fe with two community activists and long-time residents, who offered to take us on a walking tour of the area. Both women serve as volunteer representatives of their neighborhood in a program run by Álvaro Obregón borough. One of our guides is also a salaried employee in the *delegación*, or "borough" offices and is deeply involved in party politics, as a member of the left-of-center party that has dominated electoral politics in the borough for years, the Party of the Democratic Revolution (PRD). The other guide works with a community food program funded by the Mexico City government and organizes a network of women's organizations in old Santa Fe.[1]

Tuesdays are the days for *tianguis*, or "open-air market-bazaars," in old Santa Fe, and on those days, hundreds of people buy their weekly groceries and relax for a moment to sample the many snacks and meals prepared by vendors—fruit salads with chile, corn cobs slathered with mayo and chile powder or fresh cheese, pastries filled with blackberry custard, and enchiladas smothered in hot green sauce. Old and used clothing is also for sale, as are school supplies, musical instruments, and plants, among many other items. Old Santa Fe teems with people: pedestrians pick their way up the fairly narrow sidewalks of Vasco de Quiroga Street amid the exhaust fumes of the hundreds of collective buses, taxis, and private cars that line the central artery, linking the older neighborhoods of Santa Fe with the new, commercial district of Santa Fe and everywhere in between. Presiding over old Santa Fe, and visible from the market, is a smokestack perched high on one of the many hills that ascend from the ravines. Virtually all long-time residents of old Santa Fe are eager to answer our questions about La Pólvora, a gunpowder factory that provided steady jobs to residents for almost one hundred years, before shuttering its doors in 1989, a reminder of more prosperous times.

As we approach the *glorieta*, the traffic circle or "roundabout" that divides the new and old Santa Fe, it is clear that our walking tour has ended. There are no real sidewalks leading pedestrians up the hill. New Santa Fe is a car culture. The *flâneur* experience, described in many of the chapters in this volume, is not easily accessible at this edge of Mexico City proper. New Santa Fe is built on a scale not easily apprehended on foot. Instead of murals, which have been painted on many of old Santa Fe's walls by young artists and former gang members, commercial billboards stud the landscape of new Santa Fe, mainly catering to a moneyed clientele. Quite suddenly, the streets empty of people even as collective buses continue their route toward new Santa Fe: workers, domestic and other, who staff the many commercial and residential establishments need access to public transportation. Students who don't have cars also make the journey by collective bus. On one edge of the *glorieta* is a new car dealership and showroom, which opened in mid-2015. Beyond it are luxury condominiums and multi-family houses, stretching along the built-up hills up across a ravine (see Figure 5.1). On the other, western side, we can see the highway leading to the capital of the State of Mexico, Toluca, that runs parallel to Vasco de Quiroga. Directly ahead of us we see the skyline of new Santa Fe. Since its development in the 1990s, new Santa Fe has become the most important financial and corporate center in Mexico, and one of the most important in all of Latin America. Some of Mexico's most famous architects designed the corporate headquarters of *Televisa*, *Bimbo*, Coca Cola, and IBM, and the many high-rise condos have made the region a highly desirable place for wealthy Mexicans to live (see Figures 5.2). Santa Fe also boasts Latin America's third largest shopping mall, *Centro Comercial Santa Fe*, or "Santa Fe Commercial Center," attracting well-off shoppers from across the city and surrounding areas (see Figure 5.3).

Figure 5.1   Precarious Residences on Ravines, or *Barrancas*, in Pueblo Santa Fe. *Source*: Note the modern, planned housing in the background. Photo: Jennifer L. Johnson.

Figure 5.2 View of Corporate Headquarters in New Santa Fe. *Source*: Photo: Jennifer L. Johnson.

Before heading up the hill, we stop to get a cold drink at a small stand selling a variety of candies, snacks, newspapers, and soft drinks. We ask our two guides about what we were seeing. We were especially curious about a neighborhood that sits high on the hill directly behind the billboards along the *glorieta*, which seems out of place. We were surprised to see that a home had survived all the relocations, dislocations, and development in the area over the last thirty years. Our guides told us that the house belonged to squatters who had refused to negotiate with the government over their removal. As late as the mid-1990s, new Santa Fe was a wasteland. Virtually nothing drew people to the area above the *glorieta* except the Jesuit Iberoamerican University, which opened its doors in 1988. Until the mid-1980s, what is now new Santa Fe had housed Mexico City's second largest garbage dump, employing thousands of people as scavengers and processing several hundred tons of garbage a day. If Mexico City residents thought at all about Santa Fe, they associated it with waste, foul smells, and insalubrious conditions. When the dumps were closed, hundreds of people living on or near the dumps were relocated and forced to find alternative employment. Life in the garbage dumps was extremely difficult, but it was steady employment. The question of housing and its formality and informality is a major issue, perhaps *the* main social issue, in the Santa Fe area. So much of the old Santa Fe is made up of precarious settlements that are in danger of flooding, or worse, during

Figure 5.3 A View of High-Rise Apartments in New Santa Fe from the Parking Lot of Centro Comercial Santa Fe. *Source*: Photo: Jennifer L. Johnson.

rainy season. The built environment has been constructed on top of mines, and the land is inherently unstable. Poorer residents are especially vulnerable, given the makeshift character of residences huddled on the side of the many ravines that characterize the region. Our guides told us that the further from Vasco de Quiroga Street one walks, the more precarious and dangerous it is. We wonder how many of the people living in the ravines of old Santa Fe had once been working in the garbage dumps that used to operate in what is now new Santa Fe. Where are they working now? Had the promise of jobs in the new Santa Fe for working-class people materialized? Many questions remain about the people living in the shadows of the high-rises and skyscrapers of the new Santa Fe.

We continue up the hill to new Santa Fe, to get a sense of the contrasts we'd witnessed. Virtually all observers of new Santa Fe point to its lack of public spaces. There are few sidewalks and public spaces to speak of. Most students at the nearby private universities drive private cars to attend their classes; shoppers arriving at Centro Comercial Santa Fe exit the highway to enter cavernous underground parking garages. In contrast to the narrow and busy streets of old Santa Fe, the Centro Comercial, mid-week, is relatively quiet. On level one, we see a few kids skating on the ice rink, watched by expectant parents and nannies. As we choose a place to sit down and have some lunch, we walk past many familiar U.S. and Mexican chain stores, including *Cielito Lindo*, a Mexican version of Starbucks, Louis Vuitton, and Teavana, a high-end purveyor of fine teas. At the food court, we choose from a variety of international and national selections, served deli-style. While relatively inexpensive by U.S. standards—lunch for two comes to less than $10.00 given the favorable exchange rate—it is still very much out of the range for working-class Mexicans. Not that there were any working-class Mexicans in sight.

This short vignette illustrates the three themes that form the backbone of this essay: the role of elites in envisioning and ordering the built environment and in shaping citizen behavior (which we refer to as "the lettered city"); the role of global capital in shaping each neighborhood; and local citizen responses to insecurity or perceived insecurity.

As you'll see in this essay, the 1980s was a crucial decade for both old and new Santa Fe. The gunpowder factory and the garbage dumps were main sources of employment for residents, in addition to the many commercial establishments lining Vasco de Quiroga as well as other busy streets. Former garbage dump workers, as well as Santa Fe residents in general, were promised jobs in new Santa Fe, which was slated to become Mexico City's premier financial and consumer district. Residents of old Santa Fe today speak of low-paying service jobs and informal employment that have filled the gaps when more steady employment ended. The garbage dumps are gone, but even the rich of new Santa Fe are not immune from the noxious gases that ooze from their remains, along with other significant infrastructural problems in greater Santa Fe—drainage and sewer systems are not adequate to the population base and water treatment stations are inactive or insufficient (Lida 2008, 54).[2] The development of high-end real estate and commercial enterprises in new Santa Fe has generated environmental problems for those who live (literally) downstream. Residents and long-time observers of old Santa Fe note that crime became a big problem in the 1980s, with the rise of youth gangs, or *"chavos banda."* The 1980s was also the beginning of the end of the state corporatist system that practically guaranteed electoral wins for the official (PRI) party for much of the twentieth century. For decades, employees in the garbage dumps were forced into joining PRI-affiliated unions; the unionized employees of the gunpowder factory received subsidized housing, some meals, and social benefits from the state, all supplemental to their salaries. In its place, during the neoliberal era, has been a mix of opposition to party corporatism (when possible) and public-private partnerships to fund neighborhood projects. In this essay, we'll examine these macro shifts—from public to private-sector employment and the decline of state corporatism—from the micro perspective of the two Santa Fe's.

THE LETTERED CITY

In one of the two texts that serve as muse for this project, *The Lettered City* ([1984] 1996) by Ángel Rama, the author reminds us that the principal challenge to the lettered city—where high, literary culture, state power, and urban location come together—emanated from the city of social realities, "its constant and docile companion." While it is unclear whether Rama would have seen new Santa Fe as a contemporary expression of the lettered city, it seems accurate to portray old Santa Fe as part of the city of social realities.[3]

To be sure, this city of social realities was created by a man of letters, and the interaction between the lettered city and the city of social realities can be seen in its early history. Old Santa Fe was founded by the Spanish priest, lawyer, judge (*oidor*), and later Bishop of Michoacán, Vasco de Quiroga, in 1532 in the *Náhuatl* and *Otomí* indigenous settlement of Acaxóchic. In that year, Vasco de Quiroga established a large-scale project of social assistance in what is now the center of old Santa Fe. The complex he founded included an orphanage, a hospital for those in need, and a school for indigenous people where native peoples learned to write, read, sing, and play musical instruments (Ciudad de México 2007, 39). The living spaces were organized— ordered, to use Rama's language—much like a commune; jobs rotated among residents every seven days, in order to give each person an equal stake in the work of the community (Rodríguez López 1994, 8). Vasco de Quiroga sought to create a social utopia that was self-sufficient and autonomous. According to one source, the population grew to number approximately 30,000 inhabitants at its height and lasted until the seventeenth century (Rodríguez López 1994, 9). In front of the seventeenth-century church built on the original site, Our Lady of the Assumption, is a bronze statue of Vasco de Quiroga. The church is located only a few blocks from the eponymous Avenida, which in Colonial times was part of the Camino Real, the principal route connecting Mexico City to Toluca.[4] (see Figure 5.4)

The public murals that adorn the walls of many structures throughout the Santa Fe region (north of the Televisa roundabout) frequently include images of Vasco de Quiroga, suggesting that the Bishop's legacy forms part of the neighborhood's identity and history (see Figure 5.5). In informal conversations with taxi drivers from the surrounding neighborhoods on our trips up Vasco de Quiroga from the Observatorio subway stop, the Bishop's name is invariably invoked when asked about the history of the region. Materials produced by the Iberoamerican University on its social programs in the Santa Fe area describe Vasco de Quiroga as a visionary cleric whose utopian plan for Santa Fe became an inspiration for Bartolomé de las Casas, a young Spanish priest who would later become Bishop of San Cristóbal de las Casas, Chiapas, and one of the most vehement defenders of the New World's indigenous

Figure 5.4   Roman Catholic Church of the Assumption on the Site of Vasco de Quiroga's Original Church and Hospital. *Source*: Photo: Jennifer L. Johnson.

peoples (CORSI n.d., Chapter 1). To be sure, the ordering of space by Spanish colonizers and clergy was interested and consequential: one of the advantages for the Spanish colonizers of founding towns and hospitals in colonial Mexico was to force indigenous peoples to congregate in certain areas, which made evangelization easier as well as facilitating the control of their new subjects.[5] Missionaries were part and parcel of the political elite of New Spain. While progressives and proud town residents today tout Vasco de Quiroga's legacy as a progressive thinker, his utopian ideas involved forced conversion to Roman Catholicism and adherence to the Bishop's ideas of what it meant to be productive and valuable citizens of the regime.

When we think about the person of Vasco de Quiroga, he seems to conform quite well to Rama's description of the lettered elite. Vasco de Quiroga was clearly an educated, lettered man. And while he butted heads with Spanish state officials over the treatment of indigenous peoples, he ordered and organized old Santa Fe in accordance with his utopia and vision. As noble as Vasco de Quiroga's intentions might have been, especially in comparison to the rapacious and self-seeking actions of other clergy/conquistadors during the early Colonial period, he sought to order and rationalize Santa Fe and its residents according to his vision of the 'good society,' which was mostly in keeping with late medieval models of monastic communities but certainly took some progressive approaches to housing and labor. Speaking

Figure 5.5 Street Art (and Graffiti) in Pueblo Santa Fe. *Source*: Photo: Jennifer L. Johnson

of the first years of Spanish colonization in the Americas, Rama notes that the word 'order' appears obsessively in letters from the king to conquistadores. While some conquistadores and clergy were more charitable than others, all were part of Spain's civilizing mission in the New World. As Rama ([1984] 1996) notes, ventriloquizing the perspective of the colonizers, ". . . the cities founded by the Spanish and the Portuguese had to dominate and impose certain norms on their savage surroundings" (12). As we will see, a version of the lettered city's demand for order as a precondition for peace and prosperity was recreated in the twentieth century by means of the post-revolutionary labor unions and then again in the twenty-first century by private capital in the construction of new Santa Fe.

Meanwhile, the social labor of the Catholic Church in old Santa Fe continues with the work of the Iberoamerican University, whose main campus is located in new Santa Fe.[6] The university has worked extensively in the older, poorer neighborhoods of the Santa Fe region, engaging in community service and a variety of outreach programs since it made plans to move the campus to the area in the early 1980s. While some of the old Santa Fe area is solidly working class, particularly the old Santa Fe neighborhood proper, others are much poorer and marginalized, particularly areas of more recent migration and displacement. The old Santa Fe region has been the site of extensive internal migration since the 1940s, as rural Mexicans sought a better life for themselves and their families in Mexico City. Residents of old Santa Fe, who have a strong identity rooted in village traditions and its long history, describe old Santa Fe as having a rural feeling well into the twentieth century. Given the abundance of fresh water, good soil, and clean air in Santa Fe, residents report growing their own food until rampant urbanization and growing population density made it increasingly difficult (Díaz Nava 2005, 36).[7] In the 1940s, migrants populated the colonias of La Mexicana, then extended to Pueblo Nuevo and *Bejero* in western Santa Fe (Díaz Nava 2005, 37). In the 1960s and 1970s, Santa Fe's *barrancas* (deep gullies) were populated with families displaced from the construction of the city's subway system (Díaz Nava 2005, 37). Beginning in the 1950s, the Santa Fe area also attracted thousands of workers to sort garbage in the large, open-air dumps that were among the city's largest. Shortly after the Iberoamerican University made plans to relocate their campus in new Santa Fe, students and staff were active in working with these laborers and their families, advocating for housing separate from the dumps, as well as for social and other services, such as a school, clinic, market, and a chapel (Moreno Carranco 2005; Rodríguez López 1994, 44).[8]

In January 2016, we spent several hours with Javier Sánchez, who is currently the coordinator of the university's cultural programs in old Santa Fe. Sánchez works with residents in the areas of music, video, literature and poetry, and graffiti/street art. While his work isn't exclusively with young people, many of the cultural workshops he leads focus on using art to keep young people away from illicit activities, violence, and bad behavior in general. Sánchez grew up in Santa Fe and was a *chavo banda* (gang member) in the 1980s as a teenager. Today as a musician and poet, he is eager to help young people cultivate and develop a love for the arts as a way of pursuing a positive path forward. Sánchez studied psychology in college, and our conversations with him reflected his interest in using group therapy to help young people addicted to over-the-counter and other drugs. He is a strong proponent of using interactive methodologies in his work and was eager to explain the university's and his own philosophy of listening, and not proposing or preaching, to the people with whom he is working. Sánchez stressed the importance of developing an agenda *with* people and not for them, to guide the subsequent programs and initiatives that arose.

In written materials published by the university, much is made of the horizontal relationships and focus on social justice that it has tried to foster among residents, very much in the style of Paulo Freire, the Brazilian pedagogue and author of *Pedagogy of the Oppressed* ([1968] 2000). Written materials also reference Ernesto Lleras's methodology of "*actuación y acompañamiento,*" or "acting and accompanying." The Iberoamerican University frames its work in Santa Fe as "accompanying" the people with whom it works, and not directing or designing projects for them; it seeks to promote active agents and not passive recipients of aid.

Fundamental to the university's mission is community involvement and grassroot development of projects and leaders. Written materials also emphasize the plethora of grassroots social organizations and the vibrancy of social actors in the community, such as the *Asociación de Vecinos de Santa Fe*, or "[Old] Santa Fe Neighborhood Organization," which has been active since the 1960s in historical restoration and improved access to public services. The university is careful not to take credit for fostering social development in the region; it prefers to frame its role as a promoter of projects that the people themselves design, staff, and manage. Sánchez, in his role as cultural programming coordinator, underscored the importance of working with local leaders, whom he called "active minorities." These leaders might not be the most visible individuals in a neighborhood or association, but are individuals recognized by the community as having leadership potential, and often are people who have been active in their neighborhoods, often informally.

The inauguration of the Casa de Ernesto Meneses (CEM) in October 2011 represented the culmination of the university's work *"en la calle,"* or "on the street" and "with the people" for decades (interview with Lorena Álvarez).[9] Since this time, the university's programs in Santa Fe have been run out of the CEM, located in the heart of Pueblo Santa Fe (1613 Vasco de Quiroga). Consistent with its Jesuit foundation, the Iberoamerican University places a great deal of emphasis on the fostering of a culture of peace and the peaceful resolution of conflicts. Conflict resolution, in the view of those working for the university in Santa Fe, has a societal as well as an individual component. The mission of the CEM as stated on its official web page is "to support community-generated projects that seek to promote the personal, familial, and community development of Santa Fe residents" (Casa Ernesto Meneses, n. d.). In addition to its work in community development and on the strengthening of social capital among neighbors and neighborhoods, the university sponsors programs that involve psychotherapy and that treat individual trauma and behavior.

Many if not most observers of the university's work in Santa Fe would say that it contributes positively to the life of residents. The individuals we met at the CEM and with whom we interacted in the neighborhoods were energetic, eager, and principled. They truly seemed to follow the ideals laid out in the written documents we read about the university's work. There is, however, an ordering process, per Rama, taking place. The university has a psychosocial view of individual and social betterment that it is implementing in Santa Fe, consistent with the progressive, social justice wing of the Catholic Church. This vision can be compared and contrasted with that of two other models/programs visible in old Santa Fe: the city-run Community Program of

Neighborhood Improvement (PCMB) and a political party/corporatist model of local government represented by programs and officials from the Obregón borough. Residents interact with all three programs and actors, taking advantage of the respective benefits on offer.

Since 2008, several neighborhood groups within old Santa Fe have applied for funding from the PCMB, which is run out of the city's Ministry of Social Development (SEDESO). The PCMB sponsors annual competitions and invites organizations to compete for funding based on concrete proposals related to the restoration of public spaces. These funds have been used to improve lighting on streets, construct small "pocket" parks (see Figure 5.6), fund public art, and repave streets for pedestrian use, among other projects. The Iberoamerican University has helped residents with their applications for these funds, as well as working with them to maintain and use these public spaces after the renovations have taken place.

The PCMB is different from other governmental programs in that it appears to be relatively disconnected from the parties' corporatist system and partisan politics. The PCMB is a new program, beginning only in 2007 under Mayor Marcelo Ebrard (2006–2012). According to the founding director of PCMB, Alberto Martínez, program leaders were inspired by Porto Alegre (Brazil)'s experience in the 1990s with participatory budgeting. The PCMB is innovative in that it disperses small amounts of money directly to residents, thus circumventing the borough structure and allowing neighborhood associations and groups to apply for projects of their own design. Martínez told us that governmental officials were initially skeptical about the design of the program, fearing that much of the money would be stolen by participants. That turned out not to be the case, Martínez told us. Several of the projects funded by the PCMB went on to win international prizes for community development, among others the 2010 Deutsche Bank Urban Age Award.

A third key actor in old Santa Fe is the Obregón borough. Since 1997, the Party of the Democratic Revolution (PRD) has been the dominant political party in Obregón borough. In the mid-term elections held on June 7, 2015, the PRD extended its winning streak in Obregón, even as it lost big in Mexico City.[10] The local PRD party has largely replicated the political machine-like tactics used and perfected by the PRI for decades. While corporatism has diminished somewhat in strength at the national level, scholars have noted its persistence at sub-national levels of government. Corporatist systems like Mexico's operate on the basis of reciprocity between voters and elected officials: in exchange for votes, politicians reward voters with preferred access to governmental jobs, contracts, and other favors. Over time, these relationships solidify, making it very difficult for individuals and groups who are not part of the system to gain access to governmental services across a range of policy areas. Unlike the outreach programs of the Iberoamerican University and the

Figure 5.6   A "Pocket" Park in Old Santa Fe. *Source*: Photo: Jennifer L. Johnson.

non-partisan money available from the PCMB, the hierarchical structures one associates with the typical "lettered city" are most visible in the relation between the *delegación Alvaro Obregón* and the residents of Old Santa Fe.

We'll have more to say about each one of these three key organizations visible in Santa Fe—the Iberoamerican University, the PCMB, and the Obregón borough—throughout the rest of the essay. Each has a contemporary version of Rama's *letrados* staffing their interactions with the people of Old Santa Fe, as they help these residents deal with the city of social realities that has overwhelmed the previous attempts to build a lettered city.

The story of the elite who were behind the 'founding' and development of new Santa Fe centers on the figure of Juan Enríquez Cabot. Juan Enríquez hails from an illustrious political family: his father was behind the development of Cancún in the 1970s and his mother is a member of the influential Cabot family of Boston (Pérez Negrete 2007, Chapter 2).[11] Beginning in 1988, Enríquez Cabot served as the director of *Servicios Metropolitanos S.A.* (SERVIMET), a parastatal organization with the authority to acquire and administer land titles and transfers in new Santa Fe. Since 1988, and until its disappearance in 2004, SERVIMET was the chief administrator/governing organization of new Santa Fe. New Santa Fe is unique in that it has never been governed by the two borough authorities to which it belongs, Alvaro Obregón and *Cuajimalpa*. Since 2004, the *Asociación de Colonos Zedec de Santa Fe*, or "Neighborhood Association Zedec of Santa Fe" (ACZSF), took over governing responsibilities from SERVIMET.[12] According to Pérez Negrete (2007), this administrative arrangement is unprecedented in Mexico City. In no other delegación in Mexico City did an essentially for-profit company (SERVIMET) or a neighborhood association serve as chief administrator of an influential area or region of the borough (Pérez Negrete 2007, Chapters 2 and 3).[13]

Virtually all authors writing about Santa Fe emphasize the neoliberal logic that guided its development and growth from the beginning. New Santa Fe was conceived as a place that was deliberately designed to be very different from the rest of Mexico City: a world "city within the city" where well-to-do Mexicans could work, shop, eat, and recreate without having to leave the area or interact with people of different socioeconomic classes.[14] If the rest of Mexico City's neighborhoods and boroughs represented the time period in which they developed and the layers of history acquired over decades and, in some areas, centuries, new Santa Fe was a *tabula rasa*. The *técnicos* (technical experts or technocrats) who developed new Santa Fe imagined the area as Mexico City's showroom for globalization. Since the area had no past (planners conveniently ignored the history of the garbage dump as well as the claims that old Santa Fe residents had on the area as a green space for local recreation), it could showcase the logic of the era in which it was developed and built: the neoliberal era of the 1980s and 1990s. The story of new Santa Fe's lettered elite is intimately tied to our second theme, global capital.

GLOBAL CAPITAL

Nothing shows more clearly the difference between the national ideal of order in the lettered city, and the post-national, global idea of order, than the contrast between the former industrial base of old Santa Fe and the financial and corporate focus of new Santa Fe. Since the colonial period, the Santa Fe region was an area of sand mines.[15] In the late eighteenth century, two other industries drew workers to the area: the *Fábrica de Pólvora,* or Gunpowder Factory, and the *Molino de Belén,* or Bethlehem Water Mill (CORSI n.d., Chapter 1; Pólvora 2015).[16] In 1787, the Gunpowder Factory relocated from the *Chapultepec* area to Santa Fe, due to the region's abundant ravines, water, and forests (used for fuel). In many ways, the history of the Gunpowder Factory is a good illustration of the changing economic profile of Santa Fe and the role of national and global capital over the course of the two hundred years that it remained in operation. The Gunpowder Factory was at the center of formal employment in old Santa Fe and remained so until it closed in 1989. Still today, proud residents of old Santa Fe speak nostalgically about the stability of employment at the factory and the camaraderie among workers. In many cases, these jobs were passed down from generation to generation.[17] While the history of the Gunpowder Factory is closely linked to Mexican national history and security, given the importance of gunpowder to the country's defense, the factory was also a central prop used by the government to showcase the country's "modernity." Much was made of its use of German and French machinery and techniques (*Pólvora* 2015). On September 28, 1910, in one of the last celebrations of the centennial and a few months before he was forced into exile, President Porfirio Díaz came to Santa Fe to inaugurate a new system of smokeless gunpowder, or the "*Fábrica de Pólvora sin Humo.*" At this time, Santa Fe offered abundant land, natural resources, ravines (which were used to dampen the explosions), and a small but willing population of workers. The Gunpowder Factory offered workers stable employment, a military commission (for some), and a pension upon retirement. Testimonies from former workers and family members describe the modern conveniences available at the factory, such as showers with hot water. The factory offered housing at reduced prices in an area known as *La Zona* in old Santa Fe. For more than three decades (1920s–1950s) there were sports teams and an orchestra for the approximately three hundred workers. Old photos show workers celebrating national holidays together over meals at the factory, and there were picnics and excursions to the surrounding forests on weekends. There was a school for adults and a small hospital (*Pólvora* 2015, 127). Employment at the Gunpowder Factory truly was a family affair; relatives exhibited pride almost equal to their loved ones who worked at the factory and recall daily visits to deliver food over lunch breaks. Some former employees are still receiving pensions and many speak of the factory with nostalgia and warm affection (*Pólvora* 2015).

While the Gunpowder Factory was a highly visible governmental employer, at its height it only employed about three hundred workers. The nearby garbage dumps, built on the top of former mines sold to the Mexico City government (then the Federal District Department, or DDF) by private owners, employed thousands of *pepenadores*, or "trash scavengers," from 1950 to the late 1980s. These jobs, however, were not salaried, offered no benefits, and were exceedingly unpleasant and insalubrious. The open-air garbage dump in Santa Fe, created in 1958, was the second largest in the city (until it was closed in 1986), processing some 25.8 percent of all the waste produced in the Federal District (Castillo 1990, 49).[18] At its peak, 2,476 tons of garbage per day were processed in Santa Fe; all day long and every day of the week, trucks lumbered through Santa Fe to the *tiraderos*, or "garbage dumps," and back down the hill (Villanueva 2005, 11). While accurate numbers of *pepenadores* are very difficult to come by, Castillo (1990) estimates that some 500 families belonged to Pablo Téllez Falcón and Julia Muñoz's *Frente*

Único de Pepenadores, located in the upper section of the dump, and that these scavengers comprised 20 percent of the total number of trash pickers in Santa Fe (54). The larger contingent of scavengers (80 percent) worked in the lower section of the dump and were members of the *Unión de Pepenadores de los Tiraderos del DF* under the command of Pedro "Perico" Ruiz. Perico was a *compadre* (godfather) of the city's powerful and notorious "czar of the pepenadores," Rafael Gutiérrez Moreno. Gutiérrez's union was the strongest in the area and was affiliated with the National Confederation of Popular Organizations (CNOP) within the PRI corporatist system (Rodríguez López 1994, Chapter 3). While *pepenadores* are best described as belonging to the informal labor sector, they had institutionalized ties to the political party system in the heyday of Mexican corporatism that, to some degree, blurred the boundaries between formal and informal labor. Today, informal laborers in both old and new Santa Fe have much less access to political party leaders and to the political system more generally.

In the summer of 1987, a Special Zone for the Controlled Development of Santa Fe, or "Zona Especial de Desarrollo Controlado de Santa Fe" (ZEDEC) was formed, consisting of Mexico City officials and private investors.[19] Soon after, SERVIMET, under the direction of Juan Enríquez Cabot, was overseeing land acquisition and sales. David Lida (2008) reports, "Cabot's idea was to fill the dump, get rid of the sand mines, and create a business district for the corporate offices of important industries"(52). By the late 1980s, the majority of the garbage dumps were closed down as the area was repurposed for commercial use.

It was during the *sexenio,* or "six-year presidency," of President Carlos Salinas de Gortari (1988–1994) and Mexico City regent, Manuel Camacho Solís, that the plan for Santa Fe as we know it today—ultramodern with sleek commercial and residential housing—emerged. Salinas and Camacho saw Santa Fe as an opportunity "to create a modern urban center that would push forward economic change in the city and help develop the real estate sector" (Valenzuela 2007, 55). In 1993, the Centro Comercial Santa Fe mall was inaugurated, as well as the new highway linking Mexico City and Toluca. On our walking tour in June 2015 with two guides from Santa Fe, introduced in the opening vignette, we talked about new Santa Fe and its impact on the greater Santa Fe region. Both women described the *colonos,* or "residents" of old Santa Fe as alternatively complacent and passive and as victims of corruption and rapacious developers. They noted that in 1988, land was expropriated to make way for the construction of the shopping mall. During this time, the government established mechanisms through which the government would compensate those displaced. People were promised jobs and, according to these two women, the colonos more or less bought this line. They also were promised, however, an extensive public park, which never materialized, due, they suggested, to some kind of corruption involving *los* técnicos, or "the technocrats."[20] Both pointed out that the jobs people ultimately got were poorly remunerated, such as dishwashers in the many restaurants in new Santa Fe and as custodians (or "*limpieza*"). Several others reiterated this point about the low-skilled jobs available in new Santa Fe—jobs with little possibility of advancement or social mobility.[21]

In 1988, President de la Madrid decreed the closing of the open-air dumps in Santa Fe and the creation of a new *relleno sanitario*, or "landfill," to be located in an area of new Santa Fe called Prados de la Montaña.[22] This decree also mandated the relocation of the pepenadores to a housing complex (*Unidad Habitacional*) called *El Cuervo* (personal interview with María Elena Martínez) in nearby *Colonia Tlayapaca*.[23] Seven hundred and eighty-one families were relocated to Tlayapaca where they continued to work in the landfill and where they lived in homes without access to property titles until 1994 (Moreno Carranco 2005, 44; see also Pérez Negrete 2007, 25). In 1994, the Prados de la Montaña landfill was definitively closed. A pact between the government and the pepenadores was reached to provide homes and property titles to 220 families affiliated with Pablo Tellez's "union" in *Tláhuac* (a borough located in the southeastern region of the city). Approximately 400 families affiliated with José Váldez's "union" were relocated in Iztapalapa (a borough contiguous and to the south of Tláhuac) under a similar agreement.[24] One hundred families refused to move from Tlayapaca, however. In 2002, in the midst of significant protest and tension, the government offered eleven homes to 60 families close to Tlayacapa, directly behind the *Tecnológico de Monterrey*, a branch of the prestigious private university that was in the midst of being constructed.[25] A two-year standoff ensued between the former pepenadores and the Técnológico de Monterrey, delaying the construction process (Moreno Carranco 2005, 46). Eventually, most of these workers were relocated to Iztapalapa (personal interview with María Elena Martínez).[26]

Around the same time as the open-air dumps in Santa Fe were closed, the Gunpowder Factory shut down operations in 1989, also during the *sexenio* of President Carlos Salinas de Gortari. During Salinas' term in office, hundreds of state enterprises were shuttered as the new economic model he championed (in the lead up to the signing of the North American Free Trade Agreement, or NAFTA) was premised on the assumption that the private sector was more efficient than the public in the production of most goods and services.

Today, the world of employment differs greatly from the heyday of the Gunpowder Factory in Santa Fe. If La Pólvora represented Mexican modernity during the Porfiriato, the garbage dumps were the underbelly of Import Substitution Industrialization (ISI), the state-led development model in place from the 1940s to the early 1980s. ISI development generated massive migration from the Mexican countryside to Mexico City.[27] Many of Santa Fe's pepenadores were part of this migration, arriving during the heyday of state corporatism. In the early 1980s, the Mexican government abandoned ISI and adopted a set of neoliberal reforms, in exchange for new loans from the International Monetary Fund (IMF) to cover its massive debt. The development of new Santa Fe coincided with this shift toward neoliberalism. While informal employment has been a significant part of Mexico's economy for many decades, in Mexico's post-industrial economy of today, experts say that it constitutes some 60 percent of the labor market (ILO 2014). One scholar notes that approximately one in five Mexico City workers use public spaces as their primary work site (Duhua 2001, 153).

The occupation of public spaces by informal workers is highly visible in new Santa Fe. A popular lunch for professionals and working-class people alike are sandwiches and prepared food sold directly out of the trunks of vendors' cars and trucks, illegally parked on the sides of the busy roads that transverse new Santa Fe (Moreno Carranco 2008). Moreno tells the story of one woman, Jenny, who sells snacks, sandwiches, medicine, and a variety of other products out of her trunk in front of one of the large corporations headquartered in new Santa Fe. One of the interesting things about Jenny is that she formerly worked as a secretary inside that building, but makes about five times more selling lunches than she did in her previous job. Moreno Carranco (2008) says that the spaces occupied by informal vendors attract a varied clientele, ranging from executives to working-class people, who share the same space for a few moments in time as they eat a quick sandwich before returning to their jobs. Jenny has been working her space and developing her clientele for more than a decade, despite the constant pressure from the neighborhood organization (ACZSF), who sees vendors like Jenny as a source of garbage and traffic congestion. In the built-up area of new Santa Fe, further south from where Jenny parks her lunch truck, working-class women sell tacos to construction workers from makeshift stands while the workers, on break, play pickup soccer or take a nap on one of the green median strips in full view of passersby. Moreno Carranco (2008) sees informal and formal sectors not as separate areas of the economy, but as mutually dependent, interacting spheres that depend on each other.

It is difficult to exaggerate the importance of new Santa Fe as the center of global capital today in Mexico City. Just a decade into its development, new Santa Fe boasted of 170 corporate headquarters, seven primary/secondary schools, over a hundred restaurants, five hotels, a golf course, a shopping center, and three universities (Pérez Negrete 2007, Chapter 3). One author reports 115,000 workers in new Santa Fe, most employed in the corporate sector (Barquín 2005, 76). Virtually all of the most important Mexican, and many Latin American and U.S. corporations have moved their country headquarters to new Santa Fe. Monumental architecture and skyscraper-tall residential buildings dot the skyline. In contrast to older cities where empty spaces (sidewalks, streets, and parks) determined the ordering of the built environment, in Santa Fe buildings are the focus of attention—buildings that tend to be oriented not toward the street but toward internal plazas that are strictly monitored and off limits to outsiders (Pérez Negrete 2007, Chapter 3).[28]

New Santa Fe is the visual and architectural representation of the economic model of globalization; there are almost no traces of the older model of Mexican development in vogue from the 1940s–1970s that privileged state-led and industrial-centered development. Of course, one thing is the utopic vision that planners of the new Santa Fe had for the new city, another is the lived reality of any social space of human interaction. The presence of informal workers serving economical lunches out of their back trunks is only one example of the ways in which people have reworked and reshaped new Santa Fe into an image other than the one imagined by Santa Fe's técnico designers and planners.

RESISTANCE AND RIGHTS: CITIZENS' RIGHT TO THE CITY

In his 2012 book, *Rebel Cities*, David Harvey argues in favor of an urban revolution to restore democratic ideals of citizenship, belonging, and decision-making in cities, where a majority of people now live. This perspective is rooted in his commitment to and focus on urban social movements around the world and on their diverse and varied struggles over "who gets to shape the qualities of daily urban life" (xii). While we did not observe any large-scale urban social movements in Santa Fe, we did see smaller-scale citizen initiatives to improve their own lives and the overall quality of life in their neighborhoods.[29] Given the importance of security as an issue to Santa Fe residents, as well as in Mexico City more broadly, we focus on security-related initiatives and responses in what follows.

Since the 1980s, old Santa Fe has been associated in the public imaginary with crime and insecurity.[30] However, residents and chroniclers since colonial times described it as a close-knit and proud community (see Díaz Nava 2005). Fast forward to the twentieth century: those working in Santa Fe with the Iberoamerican University reported high levels of social interaction and interpersonal trust in Santa Fe neighborhoods through the 1980s.[31] For example, after the displacement of thousands of individuals who had worked at the garbage dumps and lived in its environs, neighbors helped neighbors build new dwellings with raw materials the government provided for the construction of new homes, a kind of urban *faena*, or "communal work" (CORSI n.d., Chapter 1, 30). It is unclear when this social capital began to break down among colonos of Santa Fe, but observers seem to agree that the process began in the 1980s with the emergence of gangs like *Los Panchitos* and the spike in crime and insecurity (Rodríguez López 1994, 19).[32]

Around the same time as displacement and relocation were occurring due to the development of new Santa Fe in the 1980s, crime levels rose and gang activity increased in the greater Santa Fe area.[33] Few residents ventured out in the evenings due to safety concerns and public spaces were abandoned (CORSI n.d., Chapter 1). Gangs emerged to fill the gap (CORSI n.d., Chapter 1, 31).

Lida (2008) reports that Los Panchitos, based in Santa Fe, was one of Mexico City's most dangerous gangs during this period (52). One former gang member said that in his view, the first gangs in Santa Fe were defending themselves from state-sponsored violence (CORSI n.d., Ch. 1, 32). Gangs emerged in the 1980s to defend staked-out territory, victimizing the colonos of Santa Fe as petty theft and drug trafficking became endemic. One author notes that in 1981, approximately 150,000 young people were integrated into 130 gangs in and around Santa Fe (Villanueva 2005, 12). It was during this period of the chavos banda that murals began to appear throughout the area. They started out as hostile forms of aggression, but eventually became more artistic and expressive and less aggressive (CORSI n.d., Chapter 1, 32).

In the photos we took of the murals, some of which are reproduced here, graffiti is often scrawled on top of them. While it is beyond the scope of this essay to analyze the multiple meanings and significance of graffiti in such a dynamic urban landscape, in *The Lettered City,* Rama ([1984] 1996) argues that graffiti "attests to an authorship outside the lettered city" (37). Mexico City has historically been and continues to be a profoundly hierarchical place. As Rama notes, the lettered class has been able to thoroughly monopolize language, thus playing a large role in historically defining who is a subject and a citizen. Graffiti, in Rama's view, poses a challenge to the elitism of the lettered city ". . . because it is written on a wall, because it is frequently anonymous, because its spelling is habitually faulty, and because of the kind of message it transmits" (37).

Today, one of the key projects funded by the Iberoamerican University through their Office of Social Responsibility (*Coordinación de Responsabilidad Social Institucional,* or CORSI) is the recovery of urban spaces; murals have played an important role in recovery and use of public spaces (see André and chapters in this volume). On our walking tour/conversation with Javier Sánchez from the CEM in January 2016, he made an explicit link between the work he does with young people on graffiti and street art and his coordination efforts with residents in the Community Neighborhood Improvement Program (PCMB). During our walking tour with Sánchez, we stopped several times at the homes of residents who have worked to improve public spaces on their block by applying for seed monies from the PCMB to clean up a park, buy a barbeque grill to hold communal, neighborhood meals, purchase supplies to paint murals on nearby walls, or acquire park equipment for the children to play on. Sánchez works with neighborhood associations and dedicated resident activists to maintain and use these newly improved public spaces. One problem we observed (and was called out specifically by Sánchez and neighbors alike) was the importance of keeping the public spaces free of drug users, many of whom are teenagers who hang out and smoke with their friends, thus scaring away families, especially those with young children.

On our June 2015 walking tour through Santa Fe, it was difficult for us to get our two guides to speak specifically about initiatives and programs related to security. We suspect that this silence was because neither of them were directly involved in programs related to crime prevention or other types of security-related initiatives. Our guide, who has worked for years for the borough, told us that the delegación Obregón no longer sponsors security-related projects. Both, however, readily admitted, when asked, that there were grave problems of security in Santa Fe. They mentioned the presence of gangs and emphasized the number of assaults and robberies that occur. They made specific reference to the large number of male teenagers who drop out of school so that they can work.

Like many residents of Mexico City, particularly in more marginalized neighborhoods, our two guides reserved special disdain for the police. Even in the middle of the day, they said, people are getting robbed in front of their homes or in their homes. People don't call the police, they claim, because "they let the guilty go and arrest the innocent" (*dejan a los culpables y llevan a los inocentes*).

The women told us a story of a drunk who leaned against a car that wasn't his and the next thing he knew he was taken to the *Reclusorio* (prison). The colonos, they said, are more afraid of the police than of the young people, an all-too familiar refrain among Mexicans. They did not believe that police behavior had improved, despite the steady stream of reforms by Mexican executive-level officials that have become virtually obligatory and rarely endure for more than the 'reformer's' term in office. Both women told us that there were no programs that they were aware of that attempted to forge bonds between police and residents.

In the area of security, the Iberoamerican University's work in old Santa Fe is organized around the idea that security is a problem that must be tackled holistically. The assumption is that if residents do not feel comfortable going out into the streets and do not use public spaces, the streets will be less safe for all. If there is not proper lighting on the street, for example, people feel less safe. If public spaces are ugly and dirty, people are less likely to utilize them. If young people do not have jobs and activities to fill their time, they will turn to destructive habits, such as drugs and gangs. If neighbors do not see one another regularly, if they never share a meal, if they do not cooperate in projects of mutual interest, they will not trust one another, thus making the neighborhood and its residents more vulnerable to crime and violence.

The neighborhoods in Santa Fe that have the most problems with security are the colonias furthest away from the main artery, Avenida Vasco de Quiroga (CORSI n.d.; interview with Álvarez). Several individuals told us that the closer residences are to the ravines, particularly the area near the *Becerra* River, the higher the level of poverty and violence. The university reports much more participation and visibility of the police in old Santa Fe than in these areas closer to the river and to the ravines (e.g., *Colonias Talud, Tlapechico, Cuevitas* and *La Cañada*) (CORSI n.d., Chapter 2, 28).[34]

In conversations with Sánchez and Álvarez of the CEM, and in the university's written documents, there appears to be a consensus that since the 1980s violence has become "normalized" for many residents of Santa Fe. Normalization of violence often results in the under-reporting of crimes because people do not see violence as something out of the ordinary, making it difficult to get a handle on the problems and possible solutions. Yet, the university's written materials make it clear that many young people may also not be reporting violence because of fear or coercion.[35] Many of the Iberoamerican University's programs in old Santa Fe are focused on channeling young people into positive activities, and helping them develop resilience against destructive social behavior, such as gangs and drugs.

During the heyday of Mexico's state corporatist system (1940s–1980s), most all financing of community projects was funneled through the state's system of interest representation. As the corporatist system has significantly weakened in the neoliberal era, residents of Santa Fe have sought monies from several sources—both public and private—to fund neighborhood projects. In addition to applying for funding from the Community Program for Neighborhood Improvement (PCMB), some old Santa Fe residents have worked with the Televisa Foundation and the Obregón borough to clean up and rehabilitate the *Sendero Buenavista*, or "Buenavista path." This path runs from the Church of the Assumption to a historic pilgrimage site called "*La Ermita*," or "The Shrine," past some historic mineral springs (now the property of the National Water Agency) and the Tacubaya River. Before the work started in 2006, the Buenavista path was an area filled with garbage, rocks and dirt (Rodríguez López 1994, 12–3). The idea behind the project was to restore a historic area of old Santa Fe, a place where residents picnicked with their families and made trips to the mineral waters and the shrine at the top of the hill. Residents speak of a time when the waters of the river ran clear and the many trees provided shelter from the sun. The Televisa Foundation, whose corporate headquarters are located in new Santa Fe, provides funds for developing and implementing a range of community-focused projects and programs throughout Mexico. The Foundation's representative on the Buenavista path project, Cecilia Barraza, told us that a focus of her work in old Santa Fe was on the recovery of historical memory and identity among residents. She found that in order to restore the physical infrastructure of the Buenavista path, residents wanted to know and understand the history of their town—in effect, reconstructing an identity and restoring pride in the history of old Santa Fe. While some of Barraza's energy was directed toward the infrastructure, most of her time was spent on this historical recovery project, which culminated in the publication of *Pólvora: Retratos y murmullos de la Fábrica de Pólvora en Santa Fe* in 2015. The compilation of the book included the search for photos of the Gunpowder Factory and the people who worked there from 1910–1989. In 2012, the Foundation, working closely with the Iberoamerican University and the National Institute of Anthropology and History, helped curate an exhibit of some of these photos and testimonials in the Ermita of Santa Fe, which later found their way into the book.

The Obregón borough contributed funds for the Buenavista path project, including cement for the path itself, the construction of several small, "pocket" parks, and the lampposts that light the length of the path. We got some sense of the borough's work as we observed one of our guides on our June 2015 walking tour of old Santa Fe who has served for years as a PRD politician and as an administrator in the borough. As we walked through old Santa Fe, our guide exchanged greetings and news of the recent mid-term legislative elections that took place just days before, on June 7. The PRD lost several boroughs in the city to the new Morena party, but managed to hold on to Obregón. Our guide asked many of the people we passed about the voting at neighborhood polling places; it was clear that she was a seasoned political operator. While party political machines are not nearly as strong as they were during Mexico's corporatist period, working with the PRD in Obregón borough is one path for residents to have their voice heard and acquire funds for neighborhood projects.

Today, philanthropic and not-for-profit organizations and governments alike have shifted their discourse about the relationship they have with their "clients" and constituents. The language used emphasizes empowerment, participation, and partnership. There is an explicit downplaying of organizational hierarchies and unequal power structures, despite the dramatic and persistent socioeconomic differences between funders and their clients/beneficiaries/constituents. We wonder whether the very concept of the lettered city, per Rama, continues to be relevant in this contemporary context. One of the hallmarks of the lettered city was its focus on writing. Elites mastered the world of letters and controlled and ordered the urban population through the manipulation of architectural plans and administrative forms and permits. Today, in the PCMB program, for example, we noted that community members themselves are responsible for crafting a proposal for neighborhood projects for which they are applying for funds, which include architectural sketches of proposed plans, proof of land ownership based on governmental records, and a narrative description of the proposed project, among other items. The *Pólvora* book project seems to be another example of this appropriation of writing by residents, who are largely working-class people in old Santa Fe. Their memories and their photos are the centerpiece of the book, which gives voice to people who have been largely marginalized within the urban context. On the other hand, governmental officials (in the case of the PCMB and the Obregón borough) and foundation and academic leaders (in the case of the Buenavista path project), continue to initiate and direct these projects and, most importantly, wield the funds to make them happen.

In our observation, projects to enhance security in old Santa Fe often involve the private sector (e.g., Iberoamerican University, Televisa Foundation); public/private partnerships also appear to be increasingly common (e.g., the Sendero Buenavista and the PCMB projects). What seemed noteworthy to us was the absence of initiatives focused on increasing the presence or performance of city police. These trends are also on display in new Santa Fe, a place whose spatial form resembles Harvey's (2012) description of cities as increasingly consisting of "fortified fragments," "gated communities," and "privatized public spaces kept under constant surveillance" (15). One of the most striking aspects of new Santa Fe is the almost complete reliance on private security for both commercial and residential properties (Pérez Negrete 2007, Chapter 4). While moneyed residents and businesses in other areas of Mexico City also rely heavily on private security, nowhere is this trend more ubiquitous and complete than in new Santa Fe, where police and public safety officers are almost never seen. In most all residences, commercial establishments, and private schools, visitors must pass through security checkpoints before gaining entrance. Admission typically requires an official ID; visitors must submit a photo ID in exchange for a lanyard that visibly identifies the visitor as such.

Gates, *casetas*, or "security booths," surveillance cameras, and mirrors, are ubiquitous elements of new Santa Fe design and architecture. While additional security features on the inside of buildings and residences are not visible to casual observers, individuals living and working in these structures describe additional high-tech measures: bulletproof elevators and doors for families of high-level executives who fear kidnappings and assault.[36] In some neighborhoods, residents have closed off formerly public streets to traffic, literally sealing off one end of the street, and constructing a caseta at the other end to regulate admission and entrance (see Figure 5.7).[37]

The ads for new Santa Fe's residential condominiums and apartments highlight the security features on offer to residents. Given the number of amenities that are provided—salons, gyms, spas, laundry services, restaurants, bars, and entertainment centers—residents may have little need to venture out of doors. These ads draw a sharp demarcation between being inside the complex, which is presented as peaceful, safe, orderly, and comfortable, and outside, which is implicitly understood as violent, chaotic, uncomfortable, and unsafe.[38] One such condominium, Sendero Santa Fe, sells the complex as a new way of living in Mexico City where residents are connected with nature (on the periphery of the city where there are many trees and the air is clear) and security is guaranteed.[39]

Virtually all authors writing about the greater Santa Fe region speak of the tremendous contrasts between rich and poor. While Mexico is one of the most unequal societies in the most unequal region of the world, the gap between rich and poor in new Santa Fe is especially glaring. Shoddily constructed huts cling to the sides of steep hills directly behind tall residential skyscrapers and corporate headquarters designed by so-called "starchitects," such as Ricardo Legorreta and Agustín Hernández. One moment you are driving through a new tunnel to *Interlomas*, one of the most exclusive areas of new Santa Fe, and the next you find yourself on the old route between Interlomas and Cuajimalpa, *Avenida Tecamachalco*, where those living in the surrounding poorer colonias do their shopping and socializing. Suddenly you see streets teeming with pedestrians again. Small commercial establishments selling fruit, construction materials, household items, and tortillas line the street. Residents make the climb up steep concrete stairs from their colonias perched on the hills right below Avenida Tecamachalco.

Rich and poor alike in the Greater Santa Fe region are concerned about safety and security and are taking measures to improve their neighborhoods, as they see fit and as they are able. Gating and withdrawing to private spaces is a pattern we observed in both new and old Santa Fe; at risk in both areas is the quality and utilization of public spaces. As new Santa Fe was originally conceived as a private, enclosed, and gated area, the erosion of public spaces does not appear to be a problem for residents, who can and do purchase security to protect their property and their person.[40] However, residents of old Santa Fe involved in the PCMB and local government lament the loss of public exchange on the neighborhood level and link this exchange to the ongoing safety and quality of life of these neighborhoods. Residents of old Santa Fe cannot make up the gaps in public services and public life by purchasing private goods and rely much more on their neighbors and friends for support and resources.

The erosion of public spaces is of interest to citizens and scholars alike given the negative impact this erosion may have on democracy. Speaking

Figure 5.7   Closed-off Street in New Santa Fe. *Source*: Photo: Shannan Mattiace.

about common-interest developments (CIDs) and gated communities in the United States, Susan Bickford (2000) notes that designers purposely create "'border vacuums' to ensure seclusion and control" (369). John Parkinson (2012) discusses the possible implications of this type of bordering or limited access: "This does not necessarily mean that one cannot get into or out of such exclusive zones; even without private security guards patrolling exclusively upper class neighborhoods, crossing these boundaries requires more conscious effort, a deliberate decision as opposed to relying on chance encounters . . . these patterns mean they [citizens] are much less likely to encounter others, less likely to understand others' needs and desires, and less likely to feel that they are members of a common public" (74). Teresa Caldeira (2000) also worries about the social separation that may result from the design of areas without sidewalks and public spaces: "Streets designed for vehicles only, the absence of sidewalks, enclosure and internalization of shopping areas, and spatial voids isolating sculptural buildings and wealthy residential areas effectively generate and maintain social separation" (307). One wonders if the lifestyle on offer in new Santa Fe is only possible in the absence of public spaces that is so characteristic of the area.[41]

CONCLUDING REMARKS

Harvey's *Rebel Cities* (2012) speaks to the incredible transformation of lifestyles in contemporary world cities. Interestingly, his descriptions of and warnings about the perils of urban life seem more apt for new Santa Fe than for old. His documentation of the lack of public spaces and decline in citizenship and sense of belonging in contemporary cities seems particularly fitting to describe new Santa Fe, although, as we have seen, the preservation of public spaces and the nurturing of a sense of belonging on the community level in old Santa Fe has not been automatic, but the result of hard work and deliberate struggle. Without romanticizing old Santa Fe and underscoring the significant changes that have occurred during the neoliberal era, aspects of "traditional" Mexico persist: Tuesday tianguis are still held, small commercial establishments line the main avenue, and residents continue to plant gardens and lookout for one another's children. We are aware of drawing too stark a contrast between old and new Santa Fe, however, as neoliberal-era policies have affected both areas significantly. In both richer and poorer neighborhoods of Santa Fe, two-income households are now the norm, as women have become more educated and independent and as costs and expenses have risen. Residents of both Santa Fe's are concerned about security and battle traffic congestion, even as the resources they have for dealing with these issues vary significantly. While we have not addressed this issue directly in this essay, environmental contamination from noxious gases that seep from the former garbage dumps continues to be an ongoing problem for residents of both Fe's, as well as contamination of the two rivers that flow through the region, the Becerra and the Tacubaya.[42]

Harvey (2012) calls for an urban revolution with the city being at the center of struggle, not just serving as a site where class conflicts are played out, as traditional Marxism suggests. Harvey's vision is one of a revitalized and reconstructed urban setting that upends the dominant class structure. While he seems to be calling for large-scale macro change within cities, he is opposed to top-down leadership, calling for popular democratic assemblies at the local level. Interestingly, he views neighborhood organizations as having great potential as vehicles for emancipation and the local level as the site where important decisions are made about distributing the surplus value produced by the city. The case of new Santa Fe may be instructive here. As we mentioned, since 2004 new Santa Fe has been governed, not by borough authorities, but by a neighborhood organization, ACZSF, that also functions legally as a Zedec, a Zone of Controlled Development. Rather than serve as a democratic instrument of popular control, however, ACZSF Zedec has tended to promote developers' interests over average citizens' and has almost continually sought to remove ambulatory vendors seeking to sell their products in the area. Certainly, Harvey was not imagining ACZSF Zedec when he put forward neighborhood organizations/assemblies as a solution to top-down city governance! However, it is difficult to imagine an urban social movement, of the type that Harvey describes in his book, capable of challenging the current political structure/arrangement in new Santa Fe. An urban social movement in old Santa Fe, however, is easier to imagine, given the history of protest and the prior existence of social demands in the region. Nonetheless, the historic social and socioeconomic divisions within old Santa Fe are significant; paradoxically, the pride and identity expressed by residents of old Santa Fe proper may be one of the chief obstacles to building such a movement: residents of old Santa Fe seem to feel superior to those much poorer residents living in the many ravines that line the area, seeing them as interlopers who have brought crime, low-class activities, and insecurity to the region. They see themselves as the 'true' denizens of Santa Fe, preservers of local identity and purveyors of the area's rich history. It is difficult to imagine residents of old Santa Fe overcoming these divisions to unite forces.

A look at the transportation issue is a good case study for thinking about the potential for sustained collective action in the region. As anyone who has spent any time in greater Santa Fe knows, traffic congestion is endemic. Car owners speak of the hours of standstill traffic in new Santa Fe during peak hours. Traffic is slow-moving and congested on Vasco de Quiroga at virtually all hours of the day and some of the night, affecting both private cars and collective transportation alike. Larger, more structured transportation, such as the Metro, Metrobús, and rapid train does not currently extend to either old or new Santa Fe.[43] Government solutions to traffic congestion in the two Santa Fe's have differed significantly. In new Santa Fe, the city government has invested millions of *pesos* in new roads and tunnels to accommodate the thousands of private cars that pass through the area daily. Solutions to improve traffic flow in old Santa Fe have typically involved widening Vasco de Quiroga Street, which have been met by strong and sustained resistance from residents of old Santa Fe. The most recent city transportation proposal involves a highspeed interurban train that connects Mexico City to Toluca, running through Santa Fe via Vasco de Quiroga. Slated to open in 2018, the proposed train route would connect the Observatorio metro station on the western end of Mexico City with Zinacantepec in the Valle de Toluca (CNN México 2014). Residents of old Santa Fe have been strongly opposed to passing of the train through Vasco de Quiroga Street. These protests have not coalesced into an urban social movement in the way Harvey described. But they have drawn on longer-standing demands by residents of old Santa Fe regarding the displacement of residences and commercial establishments along Vasco de Quiroga. These recent protests against the highspeed train route prompted project planners to move the route through the surrounding ravines rather than along the main thoroughfare (Rodríguez and Martínez 2015, 1).[44]

While traffic congestion is an endemic problem in both new and old Santa Fe, residents see very different solutions to the problem. These different visions are largely due to car ownership and the use (or not) of public transportation, which are issues of class. Harvey's (2012) vision for the transformation of urban life includes the reallocation of surplus value production toward the less fortunate. Yet, Mexico City monies, even under left-of-center city governments, have gone toward improving highway and tunnel systems in new Santa Fe, which is not of use to most residents of old Santa Fe. And while protests over the highspeed rail line and the widening of Vasco de Quiroga in old Santa Fe were sustained and ultimately successful in shifting the proposed route, these protests did not result in alternative projects to improve access to public transportation. Even more important for the long-term, these protests did not coalesce into a social movement proper, as social movements go beyond the mere oppositional and suggest long-standing, coherent and consistent leadership, and durability.

NOTES

1. Fieldwork for this project took place over two weeks in June 2015, a week in January 2016, and two weeks in June 2016. We want to especially thank our two student collaborators, Leopoldo Burguete (DePauw University) and Paul Cancilla (Allegheny College) for their help on this project. We also want to thank our two community guides to old Santa Fe, as well Javier Sánchez, from the Iberoamerican University. We are indebted to María Elena Martínez who helped get this project off the ground and has been a tremendous support throughout the project. Special thanks also to María de Jesús Díaz, Alberto Martínez, and Cecilia Barraza who all spoke to us about their work in old Santa Fe. Warm thanks to Ricardo García for the architectural driving tour of new Santa Fe and to all those who spoke to us informally (often *en la calle!*) about their neighborhoods.

2. The garbage dumps that operated in Santa Fe from the 1950s–1988 were open-air dumps. When these were closed in 1988, a new landfill (*relleno sanitario*) was created, also in Santa Fe, called *Prados de la Montaña* (closed in 1994). Numerous studies and reports have underscored serious problems associated with the closing of the open-air dumps, namely that toxic fumes continue to seep into the air and contaminate the area (See Castillo Bertheir 1990; Moreno Carranco 2005).

3. Rama seems to be suggesting that ordering and disordering are mutually constitutive, a point underscored by many of the authors in this volume.

4. Until the federal highway was finished in 1961, Avenida Vasco de Quiroga was the main road to Toluca.

5. State control of subject/citizen bodies is a theme developed by Marta Sierra in her chapter in this volume.

6. Obviously, we are jumping forward through history quite dramatically here. The Jesuits' work in the Americas shifted significantly from colonial times to the present. Notably, as Rama ([1984] 1996) points out, during colonial times the Jesuits were charged with the education of the criollo (Mexican-born Spanish) elite (20). In the latter quarter of the twentieth and into the twenty-first century, some Jesuits began to work extensively with poor and marginalized communities, allying themselves with the social justice wing of the Catholic Church. The degree to which this happens depended on many factors, among them the leadership of the national Jesuit order.

7. On our walking tours through old Santa Fe, several residents proudly showed off their backyard gardens, some filled with herbs and medicinal plants, in addition to vegetables and flowers.

8. In the early 1980s, the Iberoamerican University began constructing a new campus in Santa Fe on land donated by the federal government after a 1979 earthquake damaged buildings on their previous campus in the south of the city (*Campestre Churubusco, San Ángel*). Santa Fe was attractive to university officials not only because the land was given to the university by the government, but because, according to one author, it was close to the original settlement/hospital of Catholic Bishop Vasco de Quiroga (Barquín 2005, 83).

9. Interview with the director of CORSI, Lorena Álvarez, by research assistant Leopoldo Burguete, July 7, 2015. The Casa Ernesto Meneses in Santa Fe is named for a former rector of the Iberoamerican University, Ernesto Meneses. Meneses, Jesuit theologian, professor of psychology and of education, held many administrative and educational capacities at the university over 45 years of service.

10. Prior to the elections in June 2015, the PRD controlled 14 of Mexico City's 16 delegations. After the elections, they held on to only four. Their biggest losses were to a rival left-of-center party led by former PRD presidential candidate and mayor of Mexico City Andrés Manuel López Obrador, who split from the PRD in 2012 to form a new political party/organization, *MORENA (Movimiento de Renovación Nacional)*.

11. The Cabot family's most important political figure was Henry Cabot Lodge Sr., who served as Republican U.S. Senator from Massachusetts from 1893–1924. He is best known for opposing Woodrow Wilson on the League of Nations' vote in the wake of World War I. His grandson, Henry Cabot Lodge Jr. also served as U.S. Senator from Massachusetts from 1947–1953.

12. Barquín (2005, 73) describes the ACZSF as a Zedec, that is, a *Zona Especial de Desarrollo Controlado* (Special Zone of Controlled Development). It is important to note that ACZSF of new Santa Fe is a very different organization than the Asociación de Vecinos de Santa Fe; the latter is active in old Santa Fe. These differences will be discussed further in what follows.

13. Pérez Negrete (2007) argues that while SERVIMET was legally a parastatal, its logic of operation was essentially that of a for-profit company.

14. For an example of the type of residences developed in new Santa Fe, see video on the condominium Sendero SF at https://www.youtube.com/watch?v=9nLt6Tet35w, accessed June 20, 2017.

15. The earliest written materials on Santa Fe describe the region's abundance of natural resources, including forests, fertile soil, natural springs, and clean air. Jesuits

arriving to New Spain in the sixteenth century were sent to Santa Fe to recover and recuperate from their long journey (Villanueva Avilez 2005, 10). As Mexico City grew exponentially in the 1930s and 1940s, natural sand deposits from Santa Fe were used for building construction, resulting in subsequent depletion of fertile topsoil formerly used for agriculture (Villanueva 2005, 11).

16. The Molino de Belén operated until the War of Independence. The Gunpowder Factory remained open until 1989. Today, the remains of this factory have become part of the *Campo Militar No.1*, located on a hill above old Santa Fe (Ciudad de México 2007, 29).

17. In 2015, the Iberoamerican University, in conjunction with the National Institute of Anthropology and History (INAH), published a glossy, coffee table book of essays and photos about the history of the factory, told through the stories of workers and their families: *Pólvora: Retratos y murmullos de la Fábrica de Pólvora en Santa Fe (Gunpowder: Portraits and Murmurs from the Gunpowder Factory in Santa Fe)*.

18. The city's largest garbage dump (also open air) was *Santa Cruz Meyehualco* located in *Iztapalapa*, which processed 66.6 percent of the city's trash. In addition to Santa Cruz Meyehualco and Santa Fe, there were several much smaller dumps that processed the remaining five percent: *Cerro de la Estrella* (1.9 percent), *Tarango, San Mateo Nopala*, and *Milpa Alta* (5.7 percent) (Castillo 1990, 71).

19. Announcement of the creation of the ZEDEC in Santa Fe was first mentioned in the *Diario Oficial de la Federación* on July 16, 1987. http://dof.gob.mx/nota_detalle.php?codigo=4666718&fecha=16/07/1987

20. The two women may have been referring to a class of political leaders, *los técnicos*, who were ascendant within the PRI beginning in the late 1980s. Los técnicos were very different from the *políticos* (or "politicians"), who had dominated the party for decades. The técnicos, often U.S.-educated, typically garnered their political experience within the federal bureaucracy, rather than in local electoral positions, and were largely responsible for the neoliberal, free market turn in Mexican politics in the 1990s. President Salinas de Gortari, for example, was considered a técnico.

21. In an in-depth interview with Enríquez Cabot in 2005 in Wellesley, MA with Margarita Pérez Negrete, Enríquez claimed that local residents were given preference for job openings in new Santa Fe: jobs were opened to local residents three days prior to postings for the general public and much effort was made to encourage local residents to apply. Pérez Negrete argues, however, that in practice these ideals never became a reality and that integration of local residents into new Santa Fe has been poor (Pérez Negrete 2007, Chapter 2).

22. Castillo (1990, 163) notes that Prados de la Montaña was located very close to the open-air dumps: about 1.5 kilometers.

23. The relocation of the *pepenadores* became a thorny, drawn-out ordeal for the government, largely because the scavengers' ties with the PRI, through the corporatist system, meant that moving them became a political issue that lasted more than a decade (Moreno Carranco 2005, 44). Some *pepenadores* strongly opposed the government's plans to relocate them, which also made the struggle a protracted and difficult one. Castillo (1990) describes the homes offered to the pepenadores in Tlayacapa as thin-walled constructions (*de tabique*) with tin roofs (163).

María Elena Martínez, who has worked on social and development projects in Santa Fe for many years, helped us understand the history of garbage dump displacements that is described here.

24. Four hundred is my estimate based on reading between the lines of Moreno Carranco (2005) and Pérez Negrete's (2007) work. Moreno Carranco does not note the exact number.

25. Barquín (2005, 68–9) notes that there were numerous accusations of irregularities against SERVIMET regarding the purchase of land on which the Técnológico de Monterrey eventually built its campus.

26. The struggle over housing for the former pepenadores is only one of the many protests that have emerged over land and housing in the last twenty-five years in Santa Fe. Many of these protests involve the now-defunct SERVIMET. Accounts of the disputes over land administered by SERVIMET are difficult to sort out, given the level of byzantine bureaucratic intrigue involved. Some of these protests have involved unilateral shifts in zoning and land use permits in *Colonia La Mexicana*, for example, without prior consult of local residents (Barquín 2005, 70–71). Some residents have simply refused to be relocated, like the 61 families who live in *Colonia Carlos Madrazo*, an irregular settlement high on a hill above the Televisa glorieta (Pérez Negrete 2007, Chapter 3).

27. ISI-generated growth brought migrants from rural Mexico to all of Mexico City's peripheral regions from the 1950s through the 1970s. See Johnson and Mattiace and Blair chapters in this volume.

28. As Kuecker notes in his chapter on Plaza Carso in this volume, there are few public spaces or traditional plazas in newly constructed residential and shopping developments in Mexico City.

29. Interestingly, residents in the old Santa Fe area were not active participants in the important waves of urban social movement activity that swept Mexico City in 1968 and 1985.

30. As a student at the Iberoamerican University in 1990–91, I was warned daily by my landlady about the harm that could befall me on the bus ride from Observatorio metro station to the university's campus in new Santa Fe. Fortunately, her warnings were not prophetic.

31. By social capital we are referring to non-monetary resources available to individuals based on their membership in networks of friends and associates. While individuals of all socioeconomic classes use social capital, it is particularly crucial for individuals with low levels of material capital.

32. While gangs are seen by many as creating disorder, they can also be read as a kind of order, clearly not lettered, but stable and deliberately drawn. The young teenage males who join gangs may reasonably view gangs as their own kind of resistant counter-order, very different from the order and vision put forward by borough authorities, the corporatist unions, and the Iberoamerican University. While many see gangs as an expression of declining social capital, they can also be understood as a form of networking for young people, mostly young men, that extends their social contacts and connections. (We are indebted to Glen Kuecker and Patrick O'Connor for these observations.)

33. While it is difficult to establish a causal arrow between the emergence of gangs in Santa Fe and the displacement of people, it is true that there was and is a high degree of resentment over the way that Santa Fe developed and the dislocations that occurred in order to make way for that development. A long-time resident of Santa Fe told us in January 2016 that in the 1980s, settlers from the neighboring Tacubaya region built homes in and on the ravines surrounding old Santa Fe.

34. Lorena Álvarez noted in her interview with Burguete (written documents also attest to this) that when security conditions improve in neighborhoods and authorities see the rise in organization and grassroot participation, they begin to seek out residents for meetings with *Seguridad Pública* (CORSI n.d., Chapter 4, 9). The Iberoamerican University materials also note that one of the challenges faced by local residents is that local police are always on the look-out for emerging leaders to co-opt into their own networks and for their own interests.

35. It is interesting to note that old Santa Fe is one of the neighborhoods where demand for the university's programs and services is highest. Old Santa Fe is not the most vulnerable or poor of Santa Fe's neighborhoods (CORSI n.d., Chapter 4, 85). Lorena Álvarez made an interesting observation that the places where the most crimes are reported in Santa Fe are not the most dangerous places.

36. Personal communication from architect Ricardo García, July 2016.

37. Even more modest, middle-class neighborhoods in new Santa Fe often have small security checkpoints. This phenomenon of closing off formerly public streets is not unique to new Santa Fe. Stephen Graham and Simon Marvin note (2001, 281) that in Johannesburg, South Africa, residents often simply close off their own roads and destroy their systems of sidewalks in the process of enclosing, or gating, a neighborhood. This often happens, they note, without the permission of municipal authorities.

38. This view of the traditional street as a place of crime, disorder, poverty, and danger is replicated across the globe today as more and more citizens with money elect to distance themselves from the wider urban fabric (Graham and Marvin 2001, 259). Graham and Marvin call this practice "urban secession" (268). As gated communities/complexes on the periphery of cities proliferate, there are fewer and fewer sidewalks, which were so crucial for urban life in a previous era (see Jane Jacobs 1961).

39. Tellingly, in her chapter in this volume, several of Charlotte Blair's informants from Colonia Santo Domingo spoke to her about their desire to move from the neighborhood to a gated community.

40. Interestingly, the architectural guidebook *Guía de arquitectura Ciudad de México* (Arquine/CDMX 2015) contrasts the different utopic visions at play in the creation of old and new Santa Fe. In remarks introducing the most notable buildings in new Santa Fe (nothing in old Santa Fe is highlighted), the authors note, "while old Santa Fe was imagined by Vasco de Quiroga as the materialization of Erasmus's utopia, new Santa Fe was an unrealistic version of La Défense in Paris" (191).

41. We are grateful to Paul Cancilla, who brought the work of these scholars to our attention.

42. Our two guides in June 2015 pointed out garbage in the Tacubaya River we passed on the way to Pueblo Santa Fe's *ermita*. Both women attributed the source of the sewage and the filth of the river to new Santa Fe, more precisely, the Centro Comercial. The contamination of the Becerra and the Tacubaya have been amply documented in many studies, reports, and chronicles of Santa Fe (see Rodríguez López 1994; Tellechea 2010).

43. Vásquez notes that only eight percent of daily trips in public transportation in Mexico City are made via the larger, more structured forms of transit such as the Metro, Metrobús, and rapid train while sixty percent of daily trips are made via microbus, combis, and other forms of low capacity transportation (Vázquez 2016, 4).

44. Although construction on this part of the route has not yet begun, it will most certainly result in displacement of residents living in the ravines. As we have noted, these more marginalized residents have been subject to discrimination by residents of old Santa Fe for years.

WORKS CITED

Barquín, Julián. 2005. "Santa Fe o la dualidad conciliable." In *Santa Fe: Crónica de una comunidad. Catálogo de exposición,* edited by María de Jesús Díaz Nava, Gilberto Prado Galán and Carlos Villanueva Avilez, 51–84. Ciudad de México: Universidad Iberoamericana.

Bickford, Susan. 2000. "Constructing Inequality: City Spaces and the Architecture of Citizenship." *Political Theory* 28 (3) (June): 355–376.

Caldeira, Teresa. 2000. *City of Walls: Crime, Segregation, and Citizenship in São Paulo.* Berkeley: University of California Press.

Casa Ernesto Meneses. N.d. "Espacio de encuentro para la comunidad de Santa Fe." Accessed July 1, 2018. http://www.dis.uia.mx/grupos/2014p/dw_a/victormaximo/html_final/index.html

Castillo Berthier, Héctor. 1990. *La sociedad de la basura: Caciquismo urbano en la ciudad de México.* México: Universidad Nacional Autónoma de México, Instituto de Investigaciones Sociales.

Ciudad de México: Crónica de sus delegaciones. 2007. Mexico City: Gobierno del Distrito Federal.

CNN México. 2014. "Seis datos que debes saber sobre el tren de pasajeros México-Toluca." *CNN México.* Cable News Network-Turner Broadcasting, Inc. July 8. Accessed June 20, 2017. http://expansion.mx/nacional/2014/07/08/seis-datos-que-debes-conocer-sobre-el-tren-mexico-toluca

Coordinación de Responsabilidad Social Institucional (CORSI), Iberoamerican University. N.d. "La Casa Ernesto Meneses: Las huellas de un acompañamiento en las Colonias de Santa Fe." Four chapters.

Díaz Nava, María de Jesús. 2005. "Santa Fe." In *Santa Fe: Crónica de una comunidad. Catálogo de exposición,* edited by Díaz Nava, María de Jesús, Gilberto Prado Galán, and Carlos Villanueva Avilez, 15–40. Ciudad de México: Universidad Iberoamericana.

Duhua, Emilio. 2001. "La megaciudad en el siglo XXI: de la modernidad inconclusa a la crisis del espacio público." *Papeles de Población* 7 (30) (octubre-diciembre): 131–161.

Freire, Paulo. (1968) 2000. *Pedagogy of the Oppressed.* Translated by Mirya Bergman Ramos. New York: Continuum Books.

Graham, Stephen and Simon Marvin. 2001. *Splintering Urbanism: Networked Infrastructures, Technological Mobilities and the Urban Condition.* New York: Routledge.

Guía de arquitectura Ciudad de México. 2015. Mexico City: Arquine/Gobierno de la Ciudad de México.

Harvey, David. 2012. *Rebel Cities: From the Right to the City to the Urban Revolution.* New York: Verso.

International Labour Organization (ILO), Regional Office for Latin America and the Caribbean. 2014. "Notes on Formalization: Informal Employment in Mexico: Current Situation, Policies and Challenges." Accessed June 20, 2017. http://webcache.googleusercontent.com/search?q=cache:dgAxlryVviEJ:www.ilo.org/wcmsp5/groups/public/--americas/--rolima/documents/publication/wcms_245889.pdf+&cd=1&hl=en&ct=clnk&gl=gt

Jacobs, Jane. 1961. *The Death and Life of Great American Cities.* New York: Random House.

Lida, David. 2008. *First Stop in the New World: Mexico City, The Capital of the 21st Century.* New York: Riverhead Books.

Moreno Carranco, María. 2008. "La producción espacial de lo global: lo público y lo privado en Santa Fe, Ciudad de México." *Alteridades* 18 (36): 75–86.

———. 2005. "Transformaciones urbanas: de basura a edificios corporativos. In *Santa Fe: Crónica de una comunidad. Catálogo de exposición*, edited by Díaz Nava, María de Jesús, Gilberto Prado Galán, and Carlos Villanueva Avilez, 42–49. Ciudad de México: Universidad Iberoamericana.

Parkinson, John. 2012. *Democracy and Public Space: The Physical Sites of Democratic Performance.* Oxford: Oxford University Press.

Pérez Negrete, Margarita. 2007. "Santa Fe: Ciudad, espacio y globalización." Ph.D. diss. Universidad Iberoamericana.

Pólvora: Retratos y murmullos de la Fábrica de Pólvora en Santa Fe. 2015. Ciudad de México: Universidad Iberoamericana.

Programa delegacional de Desarrollo Urbano de Alvaro Obregón. Diario Oficial de la Federación. DOF: 14/04/1997. Accessed June 20, 2017. http://www.dof.gob.mx/nota_detalle.php?codigo=4875377&fecha=14/04/1997

Rama, Ángel. (1984) 1996. *The Lettered City.* Translated by John Charles Chasteen. Austin: University of Texas Press.

Rodríguez, Darinka and Everado Martínez. 2015. "Cambian trazo del tren México-Toluca por inconformidad de vecinos." *El Financiero*, Octubre 6.

Rodríguez López, Yolanda. 1994. *Participación de la UIA en la comunidad de Santa Fe: Sistematización de la experiencia con el Consejo Popular Juvenil Ricardo Flores Magón.* México D.F.: Universidad Iberoamericana.

"Sendero Santa Fe: Condominios en Altura." Accessed June 20, 2017. https://www.youtube.com/watch?v=9nLt6Tet35w

Tellechea, Samuel. 2010. "East of the Roundabout: Activating Space in the Town of Santa Fe, Mexico City." Capstone Project, Pratt Institute. Graduate Center for Planning and the Environment.

Valenzuela, Alfonso. 2007. "Santa Fe (México): Megaproyectos para una ciudad dividida." *Cuadernos Geográficos* 40 (1): 53–66.

Vázquez, Norberto. 2016. "Todos ponen su parte." *Vértigo Político*, May 16. Accessed June 5, 2016. http://Vértigopolítico.com

Villanueva Avilez, Carlos. 2005. "Introducción." In *Santa Fe: Crónica de una comunidad. Catálogo de exposición*, edited by Díaz Nava, María de Jesús, Gilberto Prado Galán, and Carlos Villanueva Avilez, 9–13. Ciudad de México: Universidad Iberoamericana.

Chapter 6

Muralism, Graffiti, and Urban Art
Visual Politics in Contemporary Mexico City

María Claudia André

Mexico City's patrimonial order rests largely on an array of more than 90 private and public museums and a preponderance of art galleries. A twenty-first-century *flâneur*,[1] in a single day, may view the treasures of pre-Columbian civilizations at the National Museum of Anthropology and History, marvel at the sumptuous architecture of the Palace of Fine Arts, and delight in the eclectic art collection of the postmodern Soumaya Museum. Of the extensive cultural and historical sites that the city has to offer, the mural artwork by *los tres grandes*, the consecrated triumvirate of Diego Rivera, Clemente Orozco, and David Alfaro Siqueiros, still remains the most popular attraction for locals and tourists not only for their creative genius and their striking representation of Mexican culture and society, but also for their imprint on the political and artistic landscape of the country.

As a sociocultural expression, mural art still remains a vivid reminder of the values and ideals of the Mexican Revolution, inspiring younger generations of artists to make out of Mexico City's walls a canvas on which to express their political engagements as well as their own "dream of an order" (Rama [1984] 1996, 17). Displayed like colorful tattoos over the cityscape, contemporary urban art (graffiti, tagging, and street murals) conveys a myriad of symbols, letters, and icons to be deciphered (or not) by the casual passer-by. Defiant and unapologetic in nature, this controversial art form establishes a powerful dialogue between the country's past and present, challenging the way art functions in society as well as traditional forms of art, culture, and aesthetics.

Endorsing Néstor García Canclini's opinion that postmodern movements in Latin America are highly relevant as "they prepare the ground for a rethinking of the links between tradition, modernity and postmodernity" (1996, 22), the first half of this essay focuses on the role of muralism and museum building in Mexico City as instrumental "ordering" devices set in place by the state and the elites to modernize the country, consolidate the ideals of the revolution, and broaden the cultural market through the legitimization and assimilation of indigenous traditions into the long-term process of nation construction. The second half explores the significant role of urban artwork and graffiti as "disordering" counter-culture strategies that redefine monolithic constructs of *mexicanidad* (Mexican identity) in visual arts, promote social agency and mobility, and revitalize art as a tool of contestation and resistance.

As this essay contends, the muralist movement, infused by the systematic modernization of the state, aimed to erase social and racial divisions by fusing European aesthetics with vernacular Mexican arts and crafts; nonetheless, the dominance of politics over art as well as the emphasis on dogmatic realism hindered the movement's dynamism, and dissolved its original objectives. Challenging the progressive mindset of modernism, contemporary graffiti and urban artists seek to reformulate stagnant social metaphors conceptualized under the muralist movement, through the implementation of ingenious cultural practices centered on the construction of collective identities. Within the frame of the Mexican megalopolis, these artists are taking the streets to reach vast audiences beyond the constraints of museum or art gallery walls.[2] The spatial frame that the city offers, allows them to produce experimental artwork that expresses a strong aesthetic values without sacrificing its underlying social or political message.

REORDERING THE POST-REVOLUTIONARY STATE

The aftermath of the Mexican Revolution (1910–1920) laid fertile ground in which to implement many of the social and cultural changes brought along by modernity and technological advances. After a ten-year bloody civil war, however, the country was still reeling from shifting power struggles, regional instability, and a weakened economy. Former revolutionary general and newly appointed head of state, President Álvaro Obregón (1920–24) faced the dual challenge of asserting effective civilian control and implementing the comprehensive restructuration promised by the revolution. Charged with the task of stabilizing and modernizing the nation, Obregón made land reform and education the focal points of his government. The development on the latter hinged on a consecrated national image that would emerge from the capital.

Fulfilling the third article of the Mexican Constitution of 1917, which prioritized the value of education, Obregón created the Ministry of Public

Education as a tool to promote and preserve the revolutionary principles of equality and democracy. Under the direction of writer and philosopher José Vasconcelos,[3] the Ministry of Education "became one of the most dynamic branches of government, not only through the control of the educational system of Mexico and its Bellas Artes program, but also because it undertook *the most* ambitious construction program in Mexico from 1920 to 1952" (Méndez-Vigatá 1997, 64).

As a representative of the lettered elite who was influenced by avant-garde European aesthetics, Vasconcelos sought to rewrite the national narrative through the revitalization of Mexico's mythical past. In this new light, artists, writers, and intellectuals were charged with the task of reformulating an ideal and utopian society in which cultural and artistic production would take a center stage. Vasconcelos as well as some of the other participants of the muralist movement were of the opinion that a controlled fusion of the country's diverse artistic expressions would produce a unifying aesthetic vision, which in time would favor the ordered practices and perceived good taste of European art in contrast to the disordered practices and unrefined style of folk art. French artist Jean Charlot, one of muralism's founding members, shared this view, stating: "When native and middle class share one criterion where art is concerned, we shall be culturally redeemed, and national art, one of the solid bases of national consciousness, will have become a fact" (quoted in Dawn Ades 1989, 153).[4]

Like other intellectuals of his time,[5] Vasconcelos promoted the concept of the *mestizo* as an idealized race forged by four centuries of the mixture of European and Amerindian blood. In *La raza cósmica*, published in 1925, he proposes that through aesthetic eugenics this fifth hybrid race would "take ownership of the axis of the future world, then airplanes and armies will travel all over the planet educating the people for their entry into wisdom" (1979, 65). Racial miscegenation, as a transcendent eugenic principle, would promote the inclusion of indigenous peoples into the fabric of modern Mexican society, while art, placed at the service of building a new and equitable society, would heal the divisions that had not been resolved by politics. The muralists painted this "dream of an order" on walls throughout key locations in the nation's capital, which constituted a post-revolutionary articulation of Mexico City's monumental spaces that give deeper, semiotic meaning to *lo mexicano*, what it means to be Mexican. The post-revolutionary state did not commission the civics lesson haphazardly in just any city. It had to be Mexico City as it manifested the "dream of an order" promoted by Vasconcelos's cosmic race.[6]

The recasting of the capital city was crucial to the installation of *Vasconcelismo* on a national level. The walls of public institutions, such as banks, schools, museums, and other government buildings became the privileged

loci of the political program of the newly created PRI (Partido Revolucionario Institucional), serving the double purpose of openly exposing the tyranny
and decadence of the old regime, and transforming the population into a
useful resource for the state. Mexico City, as the axis of cultural renovation illustrative of the state-led transformative policies, once again stood as
a referent of the privileges and positivistic values of Western civilization.
Interpreted under the focus of a Saussurian (1974, 65–67) lens, the Mexican metropolis constituted a mechanism of order and a sign of the complex
network of power relations and distinctions mediated by the state. Mexico
City's museums–perhaps even more so than any other public institution–,
became ordering instruments of governmental control where culture could
be codified, historical citizenship defined, and *mexicanness*, as a mestizo
identity, could be (re)configured and (re)presented under a positive light.
Mary Coffey (2012) departs from Foucault's claim that each society derives
its discourses, which it then accepts and implements as true; she contends
that in post-revolutionary Mexico, through the institutional apparatus of the
museum, "mural art became a technique of didactic museology and, as such,
a technique of exercising power" (20).

The reordering of the nation's ethnic and cultural heritage was not an
unprecedented governmental initiative. In 1825, shortly after independence
but several decades prior to the Mexican Revolution, President Guadalupe
Victoria had already issued a decree to regulate and subsidize most national
patrimony, such as archaeological sites as well as any objects of historical value. As Luis Gerardo Morales-Moreno (1996, 177) argues, the first
National History Museum, inaugurated in 1790 to commemorate the ascent
of King Charles IV to the Spanish throne, and originally located at the heart
of Mexico City's historical center, would be the first to legitimize the practice of successive Mexican governments to gather and preserve all objects
considered of "use and national glory." Such strategic planning by the state
continued under Porfirio Díaz's regime (1876–1911), which supported an
established and increasing budget for museum and archaeological explorations. According Morales-Moreno (1996, 185), the National Museum not
only produced the first elite group of professional historians, archaeologists,
and museographers in modern Mexico, but also participated directly in the
labors of reinventing and rewriting national Mexican history through the
transmission of images, symbols, and myths, many of which belonged to
civic rituals and traditions envisioned by ordering state agents or which were
the product of popular culture that purportedly revived the past.[7]

With the calamity of the Mexican Revolution, however, the nineteenth century "dream of an order," and especially its Positivist Porfirian version of the
modern narrative, fell from respectability. Unwilling to abandon modernity,
the post-revolutionary elite, led by visionaries like Vasconcelos, recast the

modernist "dream of an order." This recasting required a new national narrative, and left-wing artists like Diego Rivera and José Clemente Orozco were instrumental in the creation of the new myths that legitimized state sponsored political culture. While the Mexican intelligentsia of the 1920s approved of such institutional alliances, subsequent critics found the idea of placing art at the service of the government's agenda highly problematic. Octavio Paz, for example, argues that, "while art was an important tool to legitimize the authoritarian state, artists' desire to obtain federal patronage was fatal as power and capitalism distorted the popular nationalism inspired by the revolution" (quoted in Coffey 2012, 3). Ricardo Pérez Montfort (1999), sharing Paz's concern, also acknowledges that many renowned artists, in order to accommodate the government's objectives, erased local and traditional popular expressions in favor of a homogeneous representation of Mexican history. Such emphasis on popular iconography as a means to articulate a new social memory constituted an illusory identity that led to the stereotyping of Mexican culture: "Zapata's agrarianism, enchiladas and tequila, indigenous, proletarian and peasant modes of dress built a post-revolutionary state and society" (205).

While residing in Europe in 1920, Diego Rivera was summoned by Vasconcelos and granted the privilege of redirecting the country's conventions of art, culture, history, and identity through an aesthetic influenced by Mexican folklore but refined through a study of European Renaissance practices. In January 1921, Rivera, joined by Ramón Alva de la Canal, Fermín Revueltas, Fernando Leal, José Clemente Orozco, David Alfaro Siqueiros, and Jean Charlot, started a collective work at the *Antiguo Colegio de San Ildefonso* (formerly Escuela Nacional Preparatoria, a colonial structure built in 1749). The majority of the artists were responsible for the mural design in the interior courtyards, while Rivera singlehandedly undertook the challenge of painting the thousand square-foot back wall of the Bolívar Amphitheater.

Considered Rivera's first government-commissioned mural, *Creation* is an allegorical composition based on Vasconcelos' views on miscegenation and the positive attributes of *mestizo* as the cosmic race. Focusing on the idea of the union of humanity and the divine principle of creation through art and religion, the experimental fresco depicts the Holy Trinity with blessing hands over the nine muses, the four cardinal virtues (Justice, Prudence, Fortitude, and Continence) as well as the three theological virtues (Faith, Hope, and Charity). *Creation*, however, received contradictory reviews. It was praised by many of Rivera's fellow artists as a masterpiece, but likewise severely scorned by fellow left-wing artists, like José Clemente Orozco, who referred to it as "worth a peanut." David Alfaro Siqueiros deemed it "a tremendous letdown" (both quoted in Flores 2013, 71) for having an overly Westernized imagery and technique. Ades (1989, 152) explains that while the aesthetic principle and the nature of beauty as represented in Western Classical art and promoted by the state played a significant role in the forging of a new modernist consciousness and identity, left-wing muralists questioned the dominance of European art as a uniform aesthetic paradigm, demanding the eradication of bourgeois art in favor of the native pre-Hispanic themes and techniques as their model for the socialist ideal.

By 1923, Vasconcelos launched a new government-sponsored project at the *Secretaría de Educación Pública* (Secretariat of Public Education), the institution responsible for implementing and regulating national education policy and school standards across the nation. Like many others in the Centro Histórico, this old colonial building (built in 1530) was remodeled and redesigned with the sole purpose of standing as a legacy of Vasconcelos's "dream of an order," especially his vision of democracy and European liberalism. To pursue the task of reinventing and ordering Mexico's history, its landscapes, its heroes, and its people through the lens of the spirit of modernity, and to center this reordering in the city's most monumental places, Vasconcelos once again hired an entourage of painters and artists whose work would be overseen by Rivera.

Inspired by *corridos* (post-revolutionary agrarian peasant ballads), Rivera's murals on the top floor of the Secretariat of Public Education building— *Corrido of the Agrarian Revolution* (completed in 1926) and *Corrido of the Proletarian Revolution* (completed in 1928)—depict the glory of the revolution and the struggle of the working class matched against the exploits and abuses of the conquerors, aristocrats, and capitalists.[8] The bottom floor images recreate European categorizations of arts and sciences coupled with traditional Mexican customs and traditions.

In her analysis of mural art, cultural policy, and the development of citizenship-making institutions, Coffey (2012, 14) sustains that muralism reached its apogee of receiving steady federal support between the 1920s and 1930s; nonetheless, the implementation of state-funded historical sites and museums remained very much alive between the 1940s and 1950s. As she explains, the end of Lázaro Cárdenas's six-year term (1934–1940) does not mark "the end of mural art's revolutionary ambitions but rather a shift in the locus of this struggle from municipal, regional, and corporate locales back to the capital city and its burgeoning infrastructure of public museums" (14). In fact, for Coffey (17), mural projects that took place after the 1930s were not only just as implicated in the formation of a national myth as they had been in the immediate post-revolutionary years, but they were even more effective at conveying and asserting the state's rhetorical ordering of Mexico. The federally subsidized and administered system of public museums and government buildings was a crucial ordering mechanism for the instrumentalization and development of mural art. One of the most significant institutional infrastructures for the promotion and dissemination of national culture, for example was the 1934 completion of the remodeling of the magnificent *Palacio de Bellas Artes* (Palace of Fine Arts), whose history reflects the narrative reordering of Mexican modernity. It was originally inaugurated in 1844 as the Santa Anna Theater, demolished 1901 by the Porfirians who commissioned it for a rebuild in 1904 as Mexico's national theater by Italian architect Adamo Boari. The revolution, however, disrupted construction, which did not re-start until the early 1930s.

Once again, a government founded on the institutionalization of revolutionary practice—this time under President Plutarco Elías Calles (1924–28)—summoned the triumvirate of Rivera, Siqueiros, and Orozco along with Rufino Tamayo, Jorge González Camarena, Roberto Montenegro, and Manuel Rodríguez Lozano as "ordering" agents to place their artistic talent toward the task of reformulating an imagined community in which cultural and artistic production would take a center stage. The frescos, according to the Minister of Housing and Public Credit Alberto J. Pani, would hopefully educate a "public whose ignorance in matters of the plastic arts is frequently manifested in a mixture of incomprehension and under appreciation of the pictorial work of our days" (quoted in Coffey 2012, 28).

For Mexico as well as most of Latin American countries with large percentages of indigenous populations, the dream of a modern order—in the eyes of many intellectuals and members of the upper class–, seemed unattainable since they thought both indigenous and other rural folk cultures were beyond the reach of modernity. The challenge of refashioning and ordering the nation's cultural identity to fit the trends of the modern avant-gardes was further complicated by the shifting socio-economic and political conditions during World War II as well as the new advances in industrialization and technology, which threatend to destabilize and disorder their modernizing agenda. The murals of the Palace of Fine Arts depict the artists' concern with some of these complex issues as well as the threat of fascism. Whereas Rivera's controversial *Man, Controller of the Universe* (1934)[9] may be interpreted as a tribute to the ordering of modern technology in its metaphoric depiction of the laborers' bodies forging a future through modern machine energy, Orozco's *Katharsis* (1934)[10] and Siqueiros's *The New Democracy, Victims of War* and *Victims of Fascism* (1944–45) deploy forceful eschatological images of disorder, especially the decadent and destructive aspects of warfare machinery and the perils of fascism.

The primary interest for these artists, according to Coffey (2012, 45), was to emphasize the relevance of mural art, both at home and abroad, by placing it within the wartime context of their times. Concurrently, their art also grappled with the problematic relationship between early PRI-era Mexico the United States: many artists enthusiastically supported American visions of industrial and scientific progress, but also condemned its paternalism and economic exploitation. In a similar fashion, the theme of *mestizaje* (mestizo identity) and the plight of Mexico's indigenous population was addressed a few years later by Siqueiros in *The Torture of Cuauhtémoc* and *The Resurrection of Cuauhtémoc* (1951), a diptych representing the episode of the torture of the Aztec ruler of Tenochtitlán and the subsequent resurrection of his spirit as an avenger for his demise and the enslavement of his people.

The focus on order as a governmental strategy and practice was also the driving force of Lázaro Cárdenas' presidency (1934–40). Following the steps of his predecessors, Cárdenas also sought to leave his own architectural imprint on the City of Mexico. In 1939, he inaugurated the *Instituto Nacional de Antropología e Historia* (National Institute of Anthropology, INAH) a state agency dedicated to the preservation and restoration of archaeological, artistic, and historic patrimony, and turned the *Palacio de Chapultepec* (Chapultepec Castle) into the National History Museum. Coffey (2012) quotes a reporter from *El Universal Gráfico,* who in 1953 enthusiastically writes: "Chapultepec is the sanctuary for the Patria, and its altar is the museum. . . . Here, the civic conscience of the people lives and grows" (78). As in previous decades, murals served as an essential didactic tool to educate citizens and instill a love for the motherland. Orozco, Siqueiros, and González Camarena, joined by Juan O'Gorman, worked between 1948 and 1969 in their striking representation of the country's most significant historical events. In this joint effort, Siqueiros led the group in undertaking the formidable task of painting *From Porfirianism to Revolution* (1957–1965)[11] see Figure 6.3), a 3,875 square-foot visually stunning account of the Porfirian dictatorship and the revolution. O'Gorman's panoramic fresco *Mural of Independence* (1960–1961), while considerably smaller than Siqueiros's, is equally arresting. The vast iconography of historical figures, meticulously spread over the 700 square feet of a concave wall, depicts a visual allegory of the emergence of a forward-looking nation forged by the egalitarian alliance of its people. Painted a year before his death, Orozco's *Juárez and the Reform* (1948) reinterprets Juárez's victory over the opposing political forces of Emperor Maximilian (1864–1867) through the representation of the disembodied visage of this iconic figure encircled by allies and enemies. The mural, as the centerpiece of the gallery, serves the double purpose of glorifying the triumph of the Mexican army over the French intervention (1861–1867) and casting Juárez as a heroic figure and an emblematic leader for the indigenous sectors of the population.

To better understand the "dream of an order" behind the nation-making process that took place in Mexico during the first decades of the twentieth century, we may refer to Benedict Anderson's ([1983] 1996, 6–7) definition of "imagined communities." For Anderson, the nation is an imagined political community, which is socially constructed by community members who share a common discourse. A nation is imagined because, its citizenry can maintain shared values and experience while alienating its sectors: "Regardless of the actual inequality and exploitation that may prevail in each, the nation is always conceived as a deep, horizontal comradeship" (6–7). Nations and nationalism, according to Anderson, are products of modernity and have been created to satisfy political and economic governmental agendas of the different constituencies and institutions that conform it. In Mexico, the pressures of industrial capitalism, the need for foreign investment as well as the advances in technology brought on by modernization required post-revolutionary regimes to reorganize and revamp the country's archaic infrastructures. The remodeling and reordering of the country's sociopolitical image was a precondition for future economic growth. Muralism, as such, not only became an institutionalized tool to bridge the contrasts and differences between the disparate sectors of the population, but also a powerful means to rescript the possibilities of mechanization and industry in accordance with the socio-economic "dream of an order" envisioned by the state.

As the political scenario continued to evolve and change in the years after the revolution, so did the government's agenda. From the 1930s to the 1960s, Mexico experienced the so-called "Milagro Mexicano" (Mexican Miracle), a period of economic growth, solidly grounded in the advancements in education, high import tariffs, and public investment in energy, agriculture, and transportation. These decades of relative prosperity, however, came to an end partly as a result of the PRI's financial mismanagement and internal corruption. The political unrest of the 1960s—which culminated with the Tlatelolco massacre in 1968—and the economic crises that swept the nation between 1976 and 1982, paved the road for a new order defined by neoliberalism's pro-privatization policies which, since then, have mostly focused on concentrating economic and political power in the hands of the few, doing little for the development and preservation of the nation's cultural capital.

The neoliberal state's lack of efficient and comprehensive acquisition planning, as García Canclini (2006, 83) notes, has had a negative impact on the safeguarding of the country's art collections and archaeological sites, which have become valuable works of art to be sold abroad. According to García Canclini (2006, 83) there is no place in Mexico where local people may acquire a balanced overview of Mexican art after muralism and geometrism.[12] Such a void, he argues, has forced the stereotyping of Mexican culture, reducing it to nothing more than "pyramids, muralism, and Frida Kahlo." In addition to raising the question of ownership and representation of both art and cultural artifacts, García Canclini's assessment of neoliberalism's impact on the nation's cultural patrimony additionally brings forth the question of space in which such objects are exhibited for public viewing.

Public space, as a locus for social governance, is highly relevant for David Harvey. In *Rebel Cities: From the Right to the City to the Urban Revolution,* Harvey (2012) argues in favor of the "right to the city," as a basic human right, implying that citizens should not only have access to the city's urban resources and cultural patrimony, but they should also have the freedom to remake the city to their own desire. According to Harvey the question of what kind of city we want—the popular as against elite "dream of an order"-- has a direct correlation with "the kind of social ties, relationship to nature, lifestyles, technologies and aesthetic values we desire." Stephen Luis Vilaseca (2012), concurring with Harvey, argues that the notion that public space always belongs to the state instead of the citizens is highly problematic since it deepens the social divide that is tenuously mediated by the myth of the nation as an "imagined community," in this case through the networks of post-revolutionary imagery that reside in the consecrated "dream of an order" embedded in the foundational and monumental sites throughout the capital city. In Vilaseca's assessment, "When public space is increasingly regulated by the State, an unscripted way of living based on sharing and social interaction becomes problematic if not impossible" (9).

Since the beginning of the twenty-first century, the neoliberal reordering of urban space has consistently become the battleground for the struggle of visibility and representation as most of the city's real estate, resources, and cultural patrimony continue to be appropriated by private or semi-private interests, which as Harvey has pointed out, profit from the commercialization and commodification of its capital surplus. In the past few decades, museums worldwide intensified their commodification as tourist attractions as well as profitable sources of income since, in addition to their itinerant and permanent exhibits, they house bookstores, restaurants, auditoriums, and provide a wide range of services and events, such as workshops, concerts, films, and lectures. Contemporary museums, their contents and their exhibits, are no longer content in creating and sustaining a national sense of pride, identity, and vision—"the dream of an order"—but instead, just like any lucrative enterprise, they are subjected to the demands and whims of affluent consumers who are seeking some form of entertainment and are able to cover the expense of the entry ticket. Two perfect examples are the Museo Soumaya and the Museo/Galería Jumex, both located in Plaza Carso, a mixed-use development in the up-scale *Nuevo Polanco* area. The first one, owned by the mega-rich businessman, Carlos Slim, hosts a personal art collection that diverts from Mexico's national narrative; the second, belongs to artist and entrepreneur Eugenio López Alonso, and offers exhibits that cater to international taste that is not specific to Mexico either.[13] Contemporary sociocultural configurations, fueled by a series of marketing strategies, have placed an emphasis on multiple identities, which are no longer defined by the state, but instead by the fluctuating trends of consumer markets and commodities. Whereas marketing and advertising have significantly altered the urban landscape, consumerism—along with the evolution of capitalism in Mexico-- has transformed traditional forms and modes of signification originally intended to build a sense of community and national pride.

URBAN ART AND GRAFFITI COUNTERCULTURES AT WORK

In the neoliberal kaleidoscope of semiotic and communicative exchange, urban art and graffiti have emerged as new markers of identity, protest, and remembrance. Detached from the ordering mechanisms of state-sponsorship and commercial restrictions, and fueled by a desire for recognition of its transgressive power, the work of graffiti and street artists in peripheral neighborhoods of Mexico City disorders normative discourse of the private sector and state institutions by inscribing, both legally and illegally, demands and grievances on the walls of the city's streets (see Figure 6.1). Disillusion and disapproval of governmental policies are some of the leading motivators that inspire young graffiti writers to leave their mark over previous attempts at ordering urban space. A second motivation is the artists' thrill that comes with the challenge of inscribing their names atop bridges, tall buildings, and highways even at the risk of their own lives.[14]

Born from deeply rooted barrio and ghetto social and racial issues—discrimination, oppression, and economic inequality—the graffiti movement emerged in the 1960s, rapidly spreading throughout low-income peripheral neighborhoods and cities along the border of Mexico and the United States, finally finding its place in the *DF* (*Distrito Federal* or Federal District) by the 1990s via the relocation of Tijuana-based artists in the metropolis.

Three factors that distinguish contemporary street artists from their post-revolutionary muralist counterparts are: (1) their desire to remain anonymous—yet eager to gain visibility and recognition among their peers, (2) the ephemeral and unpretentious nature of their art, and (3) their different levels of talent and expertise as well as a variety of art mediums, types, and techniques. The most basic types are: "tagging," the artist's signature in a single color; "throw ups," a signature with more than one color creating a more intricate design; a "piece" or a "masterpiece," a more elaborate signature; "stencils," a print made out of a template; and most recently, digital graffiti, which uses animation and projection to showcase original artwork. While some artists may have basic to advanced art instruction—mostly from the field of graphic design–, others are limited to basic graffiti and tagging techniques picked up from fellow crew-members. Territoriality and socio-cultural identity are additional elements that provide cohesion to the different graffiti types and styles

Figure 6.1   Various Artists. Colonia Roma (May 2016). *Source:* Author's photo.

as well as the different gangs or groups. As an example, José Manuel Valenzuela Arce (2012) notes that while *Cholos* and taggers tend to be a product of similar cross-cultural dynamics, the Cholo remains entrenched to the intimate routines of the barrio, while the tagger "roams like a flâneur, signifying the city as a whole" (8).[15] Inspired by the long-standing tradition of Mexican muralism, Cholo murals, in particular, serve as neighborhood identity signifiers for community members and, as such, they must be protected from vandalism by other crews. Their pictorial vocabulary, in addition to representing social issues and historical figures, also includes fantastic figures, futuristic images, graffiti calligraphy, urban scenes, and Mexican symbols and iconography such as the Mexican flag, the Virgin of Guadalupe, Emiliano Zapata, Frida Kahlo, Sub-Comandante Marcos, pre-Hispanic images, etc. (see Figure 6.2).

   While the semiotics of graffiti and urban art serve to order the barrio, they have also respectively emerged as disordering strategies, allowing artists to reposition themselves in terms of identity, race, and class with respect to the state's official ideologies and their "dream of an order." As visual tools for anarchy and rebellion, they stand as signifiers of a disordering process set in motion to deconstruct monolithic interpretations of culture, society, and community. According to Spanish graffiti artist Escif, an interesting aspect to consider is the fact that graffiti's power resides in the use of closed codes only understood by those in the graffiti community. As a visceral protest that emerges from the heart of city, it is not tied to any political discourse, "there

Figure 6.2 Artist Unknown. Historic City Center (January 2017). *Source*: Author's photo.

is no manipulation possible because there is no construction of such discourse, and that can't be controlled. This is more bothersome than any other construction" (quoted in Vilaseca 2012, 12).

Likewise, the order of the names listed in a tag is a sign of hierarchy, power, and recognition as much as a means to mark territorial lines, warn adversaries, and honor their deceased. As Valenzuela Arce (2012) posits, "Graffiti entails circuits of communication involved in the signification of the city and imply enthusiasm for transgression, a bold claim for recognition, identity codes, group references, an ideal of vanity, slices of fame scattered all over the walls, and folk art" (14).

Taggers and graffiti writers, unlike Cholos, are not confined by neighborhood boundaries, as their main purpose is to defy ordering groups such as police and property owners, and through a contestation of assigned space leave an imprint on Mexico City's façade. Theirs is a symbolic dispute for the urban space, and tags and graffiti are means of dialogue through which the different crews settle rivalries and challenges. Talking about his first impressions as a graffiti artist, Vicente Israel Elizondo de la Cruz (Shente), recalls joining HEM (*Hecho en México*/Made in Mexico) because, as an artist, he wanted to paint freely all over the city instead of remaining tied to a specific barrio. "Graffiti is all about doing something 'all city,'" he claims, "being a graffiti artist all over the city and not having anything to do with barrios; you are not just defending a street corner" (quoted from Valenzuela Arce 2012, 178). For Ricardo Buil Ríos (2005), this type of artistic intervention reflects the tension between cultural identity and modernity, clearly conveying the fact that in Mexico City, more than anywhere else in the country, identity is constantly being reinvented through the advancement of new technologies, globalization, and neoliberal policies. Such dynamics bring disorder to official discourse, since they "deform and distort local and national cultures, fostering tribalization and fundamentalism" (16). It is precisely the anonymity, the capacity of moving freely and fluidly throughout the cityscape, and the multiplicity of techniques, styles, and skills, that allow artists to acquire agency and serve as mediators of identity in the globalization process; for identity, as Stuart Hall (1989) posits, emerges from a cycle of construction, deconstruction, and reconstruction, not as accomplished historical fact, but a "production which is never complete, always in process, and always constituted within, not outside, representation" (68).

In Buil Ríos' (2005) opinion, another issue that must be taken into consideration when analyzing the social impact of street art in Mexico City's communities is the lack of cohesion between formal education provided at school and the realities of living in a postmodern society. Whereas the school system still remains a mechanism of "order" that promotes traditional values (patriotism, democracy, family values.), external social factors can promote inequality, consumerism, and lack of democracy. In Mexico City, as in many globalized urban forms, the clash between these social and political discourses has sparked the proliferation of new subcultures emergent from different strata of society in addition to alternative forms of community organization (see chapters by Blair, Johnson and Mattiace in this volume), that both counterbalance the negative aspects of globalization and provide a certain level of autonomy from state policies and economic capitalism.

The delirious urban disorder that is Mexico City, with its innumerable socio-cultural and identity markers, makes the city itself an omnipresent sign in most of the street art, even when the art piece offers no direct reference to it. Buil Ríos (2005) interprets Mexico City as the embodiment of a postmodern megalopolis: "it is multifaceted, polymorphic and in constant and daily mutation. The city is *de facto* impossible to apprehend; it moves faster than us. We live in a mirage" (133). Street art challenges spatial conventions by disordering public space and accomplishing an immediate effect within a community through the demarcation of territory, the re-articulation of identity, and the reversal and resistance to the acculturation process. In this daily mutation, the walls, the murals, and the fences provide the much-needed reflection and experience of those who are ignored by institutional policies, unacknowledged by the official discourse. The setting and the framework that the city offers allows for countless possibilities of expression, since each element present in the field, both the artists and the consuming public, collaborate in the signifying process. This collaboration suggests the mutually constitutive relationship between order and disorder in the urban form.

Neighborhood graffiti and urban art have mostly remained outside of the consumer market as the work itself cannot be neither bought nor sold, although they can be factors in gentrification's increase in property values. In this capacity, these artists are able to question the aesthetic principle of art as a sublime experience, alien to political and social issues, and only accessible to the cultural elites. As postmodern *flâneurs*, street artists challenge the ordering barriers between the public and the private and reaffirm a social identity through the personal story they inscribe within Mexico City's urban landscape. As Claudia Kozak (2004) indicates, "doing graffiti implies a sort of experimenting in the urban space from the body outside of the norms established by the rest of the population" (70). These analytical points about graffiti art reveal, on one hand, the ways in which the intricate network of private and public power relations affect a particular community of individuals; and on the other, how the different constituencies contest such power relations through their own personal interpretation and appropriation of the city space. Appropriation as a disordering strategy for identity construction is a social, material, and symbolic practice that extends beyond the production of a particular art piece, as it also involves the appropriation of a specific location. Parks, corners, abandoned lots, and the city streets are some of the

Figure 6.3   Artist Unknown. Historic City Center (January 2017). *Source:* Author's photo.

many sites used for their artistic production. With each *"pinta"* (act of painting), street artists claim their right to the city that Harvey speaks of, and along with this appropriation, the public space recovers its ordering significance within the community. Beyond its effect on a specific site or zone of the city, this layer of signification ultimately questions the stagnancy of the more institutionalized and consecrated revolutionary art of the post-revolutionary enterprise of nation construction (see Figure 6.3).

In recent years, the appeal of urban and graffiti art has gained the recognition of private and public entities, many which are now investing in these controversial art forms for marketing purposes and promotional campaigns, aspiring to reach younger consumers and marginal sectors of the population. With this in mind, and seeking to make Mexico City, now branded as "CDMX," one of the hip artistic capitals of the world (see this volume's Conclusion for discussion of CDMX as a "world" city), city councils and local communities have started to pass municipal ordinances granting graffiti and urban artists the use of the much cherished wall space in some of new gentrified metropolitan areas close to the Centro Histórico. Street art, according to Winifred Curran (quoted in Arlandis 2013), is an efficient way to bring "cultural assets to a neighborhood that didn't have any"; nonetheless, the arrival of affluent consumers skyrockets the cost of rent causing the poorest residents to leave. A few blocks away from the *Zócalo,* Regina Street, for example, has become an trendy part of town, full of bars and coffee shops, where pedestrians may catch a glimpse of this striking, ephemeral artwork. In a similar fashion to Buenos Aires, Santiago, and Río de Janeiro, Mexico City periodically hosts international graffiti and urban art competitions, attracting hundreds of talented artists who flock to town seeking fame and recognition among their peers and the casual pedestrians.

No longer commissioned by the revolutionary state to define a national and aesthetic identity, these nonconformist artists are drawn to the transformative potential of art to engage a postmodern society that has replaced the social ethos by making the consumer market the ultimate marker of success. Beyond the trends and the traditional forms of exhibition, nonetheless, the artistic discourse continues to stand as contestation of utopias and ideals, a challenge to the *status quo*, and a powerful force to counterbalance the skepticism that renders a complacency in the ordering process.

NOTES

1. Made popular in the poetry of Charles Baudelaire, the term *"flâneur"* refers to the casual street wanderer and observer of everyday life of a modern city. Walter Benjamin envisions the flâneur as the modern urban observer, participant, and witness

of postmodern urban life. For further references to the flâneur or flânerie, see the chapters by O'Connor as well as Puga and Tovar in this volume.

2. See Puga and Tovar's chapter in this volume for more on the politics of museum attendance.

3. The philosopher, writer, and politician José Vasconcelos (1882–1959) was exiled in Europe from 1916–1920. Upon his return he was appointed the Director of the *Universidad Nacional de México* in 1920, and minister of education.

4. The distinction between painting and folk art was also shared by José Clemente Orozco in whose opinion "'painting in its higher form and painting as a minor folk art differ essentially in this: the former has invariable universal traditions from which no one can escape himself . . . the latter has purely local traditions. He abjured "painting Indian sandals and dirty cotton pants, and naturally I wish with all my heart that those who use them will discard them and become civilized" (quoted in Ades 1989, 168).

5. See: José Carlos Mariátegui, *Siete ensayos de interpretacion de la realidad peruana* (Seven Interpretative essays of Peruvian Reality), (1927) 1979; José Martí, *Nuestra América* (Our America), (1891) 2005; *Mi raza* (My Race), 1893 (2003); Jose Enrique Rodó, *Ariel*, (1900) 1988; and Vasconcelos, *La raza cósmica* (Cosmic Race) (1925) 1979.

6. According to Marta Sierra, a significant endeavor of Porfirio Díaz's regime—and one continued by Obregón—was to systematically achieve control over public space and prevent the spread of disorder and chaos. Through the implementation of a city planning aimed at bringing stability after decades of conflict, the government sought to establish a natural order that justified the power of the ruling class over the lower classes and other disenfranchised sectors of the population. See Sierra's chapter in this volume.

7. John Mraz (2009, 26) argues that photography under the *Porfiriato* presented a particular problem for the training and depiction of social order inside and outside the Mexican borders, both in its capacity for mechanical reproduction as well as in its explicit portrayal of poverty stricken neighborhoods surrounding Mexico City. To curtail any undesired publicity that would scare off foreign investments, Mexico's rulers, as early as 1866, began to pass laws against "obscene and indecent" images, in order to prevent pictures of poverty from circulating.

8. Images of this work can be found online in "The Arsenal, 1928, by Diego Rivera," *Diego Rivera: Paintings, Biography, Quotes*, accessed August 29, 2017, https://www.diegorivera.org/the-arsenal.jsp#prettyPhoto[image1]/0/

9. *Man at the Crossroads* was a new version of his infamous Rockefeller mural (1932–1934), originally commissioned, and later destroyed, by Nelson Rockefeller for its depiction of Vladimir Lenin, the Russian communist leader.

10. An image of this work can be found online in "Mexico City's 7 Most Beautiful Murals," *MXCITY: Guía Insider*, accessed August 29, 2017, http://en.mxcity.mx/2016/09/7-most-beautiful-murals/

11. An image of this work can be found in "The Agrarian Revolution of Emiliano Zapata. From Porfirianism to the Revoltuion," *SCALA Image Archive*, accessed August 29, 2017, http://www.scalarchives.com/web/dettaglio_immagine.asp?idImmagine=A133593&posizione=2&inCarrello=False&numImmagini=22&

12. Derived from Abstract Expressionism, geometrism is an artistic expression characterized by clearly defined geometric forms as well as colors, with an effect that makes them look like low relief. Geometrism, in Mexican art, was one of the different international trends that emerged as a reaction against muralism and figurative art.

13. For further information on Plaza Carso and the museums it houses, see chapters by Kuecker and O'Connor in this volume.

14. For further information on the development of graffiti and urban art, see Steven Hager (1984); Fiona McDonald (2013); and Alison Young (2013).

15. Cholo (lower class Mexican migrant) culture became a significant presence in the 1960s in Mexican and Chicano neighborhoods; it is a phenomenon linked to the *pachucos* of the 1930s to 1950s. The term "pachuco" refers to Mexican-Americans usually associated with neighborhood or street gangs with a taste for flashy clothing.

WORKS CITED

Ades, Dawn. 1989. *Art in Latin America.* New Haven and London: Yale University Press.

Anderson, Benedict. (1983) 1996. *Imagined Communities: Reflections on the Origin and Spread of Nationalism.* London: Verso.

Arlandis, Fanny. 2013. "The Perverse Effect of Street Art on Neighborhood Gentrification." *Le Monde*, April 4. Accessed June 28, 2017. https://www.worldcrunch.com/culture-society/the-perverse-effect-of-street-art-on-neighborhood-gentrification/graffiti-banksy-urbanism-suburbs-urban/c3s10800

Buil Ríos, Ricardo. 2005. *Graffiti, arte urbano (educación, cultura e identidad en la modernidad).* Tlalpan: Universidad Pedagógica Nacional.

Coffey, Mary. 2012. *How a Revolutionary Art Became Official Culture: Murals, Museums, and the Mexican State.* Durham, NC: Duke University Press.

Flores, Tatiana. 2013. *Mexico's Revolutionary Avant-Gardes: From Estridentismo to ¡30-30!* New Haven, CT: Yale University Press.

García Canclini, Néstor. 1996. "Modernity after Postmodernity." In *Beyond the Fantastic: Contemporary Art Criticism from Latin America*, edited by Gerardo Mosquera, 20–51. Cambridge, MA: The MIT Press.

———. 2006. "A City that Improvises Its Globalization." In *Cultural Agency in the Americas*, edited by Doris Sommer, 82–92. Durham, NC: Duke University Press.

Hager, Steven. 1984. *Hip Hop: The Illustrated History of Break Dancing, Rap Music, and Graffiti.* New York: St. Martin's Press.

Hall, Stuart. 1989. "Cultural identity and Cinematic Representation." *Framework* 36: 68–71.

Harvey, David. 2012. *Rebel Cities: From the Right to the City to the Urban Revolution.* New York: Verso.

Kozak, Claudia. 2004. *Contra la pared: sobre graffitis, pintadas y otras intervenciones urbanas.* Buenos Aires: Universidad de Buenos Aires.

Mariátegui, José Carlos. (1927) 1979. *Siete ensayos de interpretación de la realidad peruana.* Serie popular Era 67. Mexico: Ediciones Era.

Martí, José. (1891) 2005. *Nuestra América*. Caracas: Biblioteca Ayacucho.
————. (1893) 2003. *Mi raza*. Accessed July 5, 2017. Biblioteca Virtual Universal. http://www.biblioteca.org.ar/libros/656489.pdf
McDonald, Fiona. 2013. *The Popular History of Graffiti: From the Ancient World to the Present*. New York: Skyhorse Publishing.
Méndez-Vigatá, Antonio E. 1997. "Politics and Architectural Language: Post-Revolutionary Regimes in Mexico and Their Influence on Mexican Public Architecture, 1920-1952." In *Modernity and the Architecture of Mexico*, edited by Edward R. Burian, 127–151. Austin: University of Texas Press.
"Mexico City's 7 Most Beautiful Murals," *MXCITY: Guía Insider*, accessed August 29, 2017, http://en.mxcity.mx/2016/09/7-most-beautiful-murals/
Morales-Moreno, Luis Gerardo. 1996. "History and Patriotism in the National Museum of Mexico." In *Museums and the Making of "Ourselves:" The Role of Objects in National Identity*, edited by Flora E. Kaplan, 171–191. London and New York: Leicester University Press.
Mraz, John. 2009. *Looking for Mexico: Modern Visual Culture and National Identity*. Durham, NC: Duke University Press.
Pérez Montfort, Ricardo. 1999. "Muralismo y nacionalismo popular 1920-1930." In *Memoria Congreso Internacional de Muralismo. San Idelfonso, cuna del muralismo mexicano, reflexiones historiográficas y artísticas*, edited by Antiguo Colegio de San Ildefonso, 173–206. Ciudad de México: Antiguo Colegio de San Ildefonso.
Rama, Ángel. (1984) 1996. *The Lettered City. Post-Contemporary Interventions*. Translated by John Charles Chasteen. Durham, NC: Duke University Press.
Rodó, José Enrique. (1900) 1988. *Ariel*. 1st ed. Austin: University of Texas Press.
Saussure, Ferdinand de. 1974. *Course in General Linguistics*. London: Fontana.
"The Agrarian Revolution of Emiliano Zapata. From Porfirianism to the Revoltuion," *SCALA Image Archive*, accessed August 29, 2017, http://www.scalarchives.com/web/dettaglio_immagine.asp?idImmagine=A133593&posizione=2&inCarrello=False&numImmagini=22&
"The Arsenal, 1928, by Diego Rivera," *Diego Rivera: Paintings, Biography, Quotes*, accessed August 29, 2017, https://www.diegorivera.org/the-arsenal.jsp#prettyPhoto[image1]/0/
Valenzuela Arce, José Manuel. 2012. "I Have Seen the Writing on the Wall." In *Welcome amigos to Tijuana. Graffiti en la frontera*, edited by José Manuel Valenzuela Arce, 10–23. Mexico: CONACULTA.
Vasconcelos, José. (1925) 1979. *The Cosmic Race/La raza cósmica*. Translated by Didier T. Jaén. Baltimore, MD: Johns Hopkins University Press.
Vilaseca, Stephen Luis. 2012. "From Graffiti to Street Art: How Urban Artists are Democratizing Spanish City Centers and Streets." *Navigating through the Spanish Urban Space in the Twentieth and Twenty-First Centuries. Transitions: Journal of Franco-Iberian Studies* 8 (Fall): 9–34.
Young, Alison. 2013. *Street Art, Public City: Law, Crime and the Urban Imagination*. New York: Routledge.

Chapter 7

Securing the City in La Polvorilla

The Spatial Logic of Self-Sufficiency

Jennifer L. Johnson and Shannan Mattiace

The borough of Iztapalapa is located on the fringe of Mexico City proper and constitutes the most populated, young, and one of the poorest and highest-crime areas in the City. The *La Polvorilla* neighborhood is situated on the southeastern boundary of this borough, and was a destination for migrants who came to Mexico City beginning in the 1970s and who fled the city center following the mass destruction of the 1985 earthquake. Flat, sprawling, semi-industrial, and low-lying, this area exudes a sense of social anomie. *Los Panchos*, a leftist housing cooperative in La Polvorilla, has responded to this sense of alienation and insecurity in its environs by enclosing itself behind walls, seeking self-sufficiency and a certain autonomy from both the state and the capitalist economy.

Like our *Santa Fe* chapter in this volume, this chapter originated as an attempt to map the responses of *capitalinos* (those from Mexico City) in distinct neighborhoods to the dramatic increases in criminal violence that have affected megacities in Latin America since the 1990s. Compared to its regional counterparts, levels of violence in Mexico City (measured, for instance, by homicide rates) are relatively low, and the drug wars that have devastated smaller cities and large swathes of the Mexican countryside and secondary cities have not yet manifest fully in the megalopolis (Kruijt and Koonings 2015). The literature on insecurity in Mexico City, however, suggests that residents live in fear of victimization and have very little faith in the ability of authorities to keep them safe, leading one source to characterize violence and insecurity there as "a 'phantom' that walks the metropolis" (Pansters and Castillo Berthier 2007, 36). How do urban denizens cope with this fear? How do their responses, in the aggregate, reorganize space in the City?

One well-documented response theorized by Teresa Caldeira (2000) is the privatization of public space through the "walling" of the City. Examining the case of São Paulo, Caldeira argues that the fear of crime disrupts and disorders. In response to these fears, citizens with the economic means to do so retreat into self-contained, gated communities in the suburbs. These "fortresses" disconnect residents from the public life of cities by literally closing their doors to the socioeconomic and racial/ethnic mix of people who comprise cities as a whole, but also by their increasing reliance on private services (e.g., policing/security) and infrastructure (e.g., transportation and telecommunication). This is a prime example of what Stephen Graham and Simon Marvin (2001) call splintering urbanism, and is evident in Mexico City, in places like new Santa Fe (see Mattiace and Johnson, this volume) or *Nuevo Polanco*'s *Plaza Carso* (see Kuecker, this volume). In Mexico City, the upper classes have a long history of self-segregating spatially by moving westward out of the city into new (in the 1940s) developments like *Lomas de Chapultepec*, so the gated community phenomenon is a continuation of a historical trend rather than a break with the past (Sheinbaum 2008).

Another form of privatization of space that plays upon fear of crime is the urban renewal of Mexico City's historic center. In addition to renovating housing stock that displaces low-income residents, investors and public officials make public space less accessible to the urban poor through securitization, that is, increased surveillance and zero tolerance policing that criminalizes the use of streets for certain activities like street vending (Davis 2013; Becker and Müller 2013). Both trends—gating in the suburbs and securitization in the City Center—provide the means by which wealthier residents can allay their fears of crime and insecurity. Both trends also have clear links to global capital.

But how do poor residents cope? We examine Los Panchos' experiment in urban community-building for what it can tell us about how the working poor shape the built environment in ways that both mimic and resist these trends prevalent in wealthier parts of the City. We begin with a vignette that introduces Los Panchos through a thick description of the place as we, the researchers, encountered it during fieldwork in the summer of 2015. We then analyze how their experiment is embedded in alternative urban imaginaries and global flows of capital, and with what consequences for the quality of public life and urban space. The three thousand residents who live within the settlement's walls are a small drop in Mexico City's ocean of 20 to 25 million urban denizens, yet their existence begs the question of whether the enclosure of public space always works to diminish the urban commons or whether other outcomes are possible. Could it be, in fact, that this type of experiment is precisely what David Harvey (2012) had in mind when he called for city dwellers to reclaim their right to the city?

VIGNETTE

At first blush, the housing settlement built by the organization nicknamed Los Panchos in *La Polvorilla* neighborhood might seem like any one of the many gated communities that have transformed the sprawling peripheries of Latin American cities. Enter the development by car and you will need to make the mandatory stop at the main gate secured by guards who are stationed in a gatehouse built of thick concrete walls. Surveying incoming traffic through darkened glass, the guards on duty sort residents—nearly 600 families, some 3,000 individuals—from strangers. Flood lights mounted on the gatehouse ensure effective surveillance 24/7. In this part of the city where violent crime is endemic, trust in police is very low, and nearly 40 percent of population lives at or below the poverty line (SEDESOL n.d.), this controlled access enclave provides a rare sense of security.

Look more closely, though, and you will notice that the vehicle exiting as you enter is not a sleek luxury sedan or an SUV of the newest make and model but a well-used Volkswagen bug. The guard who opens the gate does so manually—there are no automatic gate openers here or, for that matter, other state-of-the-art technology—and he is wearing a sleeveless T-shirt, work pants and tire-tread sandals instead of the professional-looking uniforms typical of privately contracted security services. In fact, he is not a private security guard at all, but rather a resident taking his turn in the daily rotation of volunteers charged by the community's "vigilance committee" with monitoring this entrance. Sidewalks run parallel to the vehicular lanes, welcoming rather than discouraging pedestrians who seek to enter through a secondary door. You might also notice that the imposing 15-foot metal gate that physically separates this community from the rest of the world is emblazoned with an enormous red star (See Figure 7.1). This is clearly a gated community of a different sort.

Inscribed in La Polvorilla's built environment, these details reflect the rich history of Mexico City's urban popular movement and its decades-long struggle to claim the right to adequate housing for all Mexican citizens, but especially the working poor and landless. They also hint at the unique role that the socialist *Frente Popular Francisco Villa* (FPFV) (Francisco Villa Popular Front) played in this movement by spearheading a series of militant land invasions dating back to the 1980s. Today, these have become an archipelago of self-help housing developments that stretch across the southeastern quadrant of the city. The settlement named *Acapatzingo* that is located in the La Polvorilla neighborhood is the island at the very tip of this archipelago, ensconced in the most far-flung and marginalized of all Iztapalapa neighborhoods where the FPFV has established a presence (CIJ 2013, Cuadro 5). Built by the *Frente Popular Francisco Villa Independiente* (FPFV-I) (Independent

Figure 7.1   La Polvorilla, Community Guard Booth and Gate. *Source*: Photo: Jennifer L. Johnson.

Francisco Villa Popular Front), or "Los Panchos," which is a faction that split from the main FPFV branch in the late 1990s to maintain independence from left-leaning political parties, Acapatzingo is one of the most radical experiments in urban resistance and autonomy to grow out of the FPFV (Zibechi 2014). It is also one of the few that is walled. Its red-starred gate, its communally organized guards, and its unmistakably proletarian aura are all testaments to this distinctive lineage.

Search for La Polvorilla on an otherwise detailed street map of Mexico City boroughs, though, and you will discover that this neighborhood is quite literally off the map. A full fifth of Mexico City's population lives in Iztapalapa and a large portion of the borough *does* appear on standard maps like the *Plano de la Ciudad de México Ed. 2015* (Mexico City Plan, 2015 edition), but the frontier zone where La Polvorilla is located has been conveniently hived off. This is an apt metaphor for the utter neglect that this and other poor, peri-urban settlements ringing the metropolis have experienced at the hands of municipal authorities. Population has grown so rapidly in these areas that it has more than offset population declines in the center city since the 1970s, yet government officials have turned a blind eye to the need for planning, regulation and service provision here (Aguilar 2008; Connolly 2009). The upshot is the proliferation of neighborhoods like La Polvorilla—chronically underserved and only tenuously integrated into the fabric of the city as a whole—where inhabitants turn regularly to self-help to fill the vacuum created by the state.

Try to get to La Polvorilla from the city center without a private vehicle, and these deficiencies become evident in the gradual decline in the quality of and ultimately discontinuation of public transportation. In June 2015, our research team traveled to La Polvorilla in the company of Elisa Benavides, an FPFV-I ally who lives closer to the city center.[1] A few blocks from her home, we catch the ultramodern *Metrobús* that whisks us eastbound. A world-acclaimed green initiative inaugurated in 2005, the Metrobús is the epitome of progressive urban planning and sustainability, and we arrive at our destination quickly and in First World comfort. From here we head southeast by subway on the Green Line. The Golden Line would have gotten us much further had it not been closed down for months due to design faults. Four hundred and fifty thousand commuters, most in the Iztapalapa and *Tláhuac* boroughs, have been stranded by the Golden Line stoppage, but no one can say when it will be back in service (Malkin 2014).[2] We disembark at the last stop on the Green Line and crowd into an economy-class taxi for the final leg of our itinerary. For the better part of half an hour, our driver deftly navigates the streets of Iztapalapa as they narrow noticeably and begin to wind by low-lying, graffiti-marked dwellings until the road turns to *terracería* or unmade, gravel road. We have arrived at the *Comunidad Habitacional Acapatzingo* (Housing Community of Acapatzingo).

We meet Alejandro, the member of Los Panchos who will be our guide today, at their headquarters in a single story building situated well beyond the main gate. Its interior is painted with brightly colored murals depicting Che Guevara, Emiliano Zapata and, of course, Francisco Villa. In Spanish, "Pancho" is a shortened version of Francisco and, in this case, the "Francisco" in question is Francisco Villa, a general in the Mexican Revolution whose betrayal by those in power made him a hero among Mexican popular movements fighting against entrenched interests. We learn from Alejandro that the residents here—many of whom work in *maquilas* or in-bond assembly plants scattered throughout the City—have come up with their own solution to the transportation deficit we have just witnessed: they drive themselves. We leave headquarters and stroll along the double-wide streets of one of the rectangular housing blocs that make up this settlement. Compact cars in various states of repair and disrepair, including the occasional off-duty taxi, are parked along sidewalks that stretch in front of rows of modest two story town houses each painted the same color green (See Figure 7.2). Alejandro says that unlike surrounding neighborhoods that have grown up without any thought or planning whatsoever, here a representative community assembly decides how every inch of space is allocated, right down to the width of streets to accommodate much-needed parking.[3]

Inaccessibility to public transportation is only one gap in municipal services that residents confront, and at every turn of our walking tour we

Figure 7.2   Skyline of La Polvorilla Viewed from Inside the Comunidad Habitacional Acapatzingo. *Source*: Photo: Jennifer L. Johnson.

see signs of Los Panchos' search for self-sufficiency coming into physical being. Alejandro points out the solar streetlamps recently installed to replace conventional streetlamps. The latter had long been inoperable because the community could not afford to connect them to the municipal power lines. Near the basketball court, we stop to chat with a worker digging a drainage ditch to capture rainwater that accumulates on this large, flat surface. The public water supply is notoriously unreliable in the outer rings of Mexico City, and collecting rainwater is part of a much larger project to enable the Comunidad Habitacional Acapatzingo to become independent of this supply. And untreated, it is also unfit for human consumption so residents buy bottled water instead. Alejandro says Los Panchos hopes to help residents break this cycle (*"romper con esa lógica"*) by building their own water treatment plant, and points out the vacant lot with a gaping hole where construction has begun. We pass by an empty lot with a pile of bricks where Alejandro indicates a health clinic will be built, and another earmarked for a school.

Behind the site of the future health clinic, the concrete walls that enclose the Acapatzingo settlement turn to wire mesh and a narrow side street that dead-ends as the mesh comes into view. The street is lined with half and haphazardly built bare concrete block houses packed tightly together and littered with hubcaps, trash cans and buckets, and discarded construction materials (See Figure 7.3). The crowded and chaotic nature of this scene contrasts starkly with the sense of spaciousness and orderliness that pervades our side. Alejandro attributes this to the "every man for himself" individualism and

Figure 7.3 A Neighborhood Abutting the Comunidad Habitacional Acapatzingo.
Source: Photo: Jennifer L. Johnson.

opportunism that political parties breed among the poor and that taint other ways of doing self-help in Iztapalapa. The neighborhood we survey through the mesh used to belong to Los Panchos, but split off in 1997 when the left-leaning *Partido de la Revolución Democrática* (PRD) (Democratic Party of the Revolution) promised government-subsidized financing for housing to residents in exchange for votes. Los Panchos jealously guards its autonomy from parties and protects the collective spirit or *"compañerismo"* (camaraderie) that governs in the Comunidad Habitacional Acapatzingo from the corrupting influence of clientelism. In fact, residents of Acapatzingo do not even vote in state-sponsored elections.

This profound disillusionment with electoral democracy becomes clearer at the end of the day when we stop in at the community's radio station installations where the many posters on the walls around us declare as much. *"Votes o no votes, no te representan"*—"whether you vote or not, they don't represent you"—reads one. Another displays a ballot with multi-colored party logos and facetiously urges voters to check the box for their favorite color. We continue our conversation about Los Panchos' vision here. At the core is the drive to construct a society grounded in mutual aid through *autogestión* and *autonomía* (roughly "self-governance" and "autonomy"). This vision takes inspiration from the Zapatista movement. Indeed, in many ways, Los Panchos are an urban version of the Zapatistas: both strive *for* autonomy and *against* capitalist and party ideology. Both are led by idealistic leaders and populated by dedicated followers—you need both to move against the current as they are doing. As we depart La Polvorilla that afternoon, we register the dignity and pride residents take in the self-sufficiency they have achieved thus far, and how their experiment in walled resistance has transformed the urban landscape of a small corner of Mexico City in the process.

A LETTERED CITY OF A DIFFERENT STRIPE? ORDERING MEXICO CITY'S PERIPHERY

As the vignette above intimates, Los Panchos have altered the built environment in La Polvorilla to reflect a utopian vision of society understood as a radical alternative to the status quo. Crucial to this vision is the ideal and process of ordering their community internally as they see fit and in contrast with the City at large, which they view as dangerously disorderly. In *The Lettered City* ([1984] 1996), literary critic Ángel Rama traces the efforts of educated or "lettered" elites to order Latin American cities dating back to the European conquest, and contends that the alleged *tabula rasa* quality of the New World provided a unique opportunity for these elite aspirations of ordering. "The ideal of the city as the embodiment of order," he notes, "corresponded to a moment in the development of Western civilization as a whole, but only the lands of the new continent afforded a propitious place for the dream of the 'ordered city' to become a reality" (1).

In this section of our essay we explore how the sparsely inhabited and undeveloped fringes of southeastern Mexico City provided a similar opportunity for a late twentieth-century lettered class to make their particular dream of an ordered city a reality. These leaders emerged from the student movement of the late 1960s and joined hands with the working poor in the 1980s and 1990s to carve out physical spaces like La Polvorilla where social activists and residents could quite literally build social justice from the ground up. The blueprint for this project originated in the Line of Masses variant of Maoist and Marxist-Leninist thought that inspired a cadre of student leaders in the 1970s to break from more mainstream efforts to make the authoritarian regime democratically accountable to the masses. Instead, it exhorted middle class university-educated youth to cultivate relationships directly with the masses—workers, peasants, indigenous peoples, among others—and to instill in them the desire and capacity for "self-management" (*autogestión*).[4] Student leaders dedicated to these principles—transforming society by rejecting the state as the architect of human affairs and embracing self-management as the key for reordering human community—founded the FPFV in 1989 in solidarity with squatters in Mexico City. Their unique vision of social change persisted through the 1990s when violent government repression and opportunities to become part of cutting edge progressive electoral campaigns split the FPFV into partisan (FPFV) and independent (FPFV-I) factions in 1997.

La Comunidad Habitacional Acapatzingo in La Polvorilla owes its existence to this leadership and vision. To understand how this legacy shapes residents' outlooks and collective life even today requires a closer examination of the history of Mexico's student movement and the evolution of its relationship with the landless working classes.

When historians write about Mexico's student movement, they usually mean either the mobilizations that culminated in the 1968 Tlatelolco massacre in the Plaza de Tres Culturas (Plaza of Three Cultures) in Mexico City or those organized by the Consejo Estudiantil Universitario (CEU) at the National Autonomous University of Mexico (*Universidad Nacional Autónoma de México* or UNAM) in 1986. In both cases, the issues that motivated young people to protest extended far beyond those of immediate concern to students alone, such as tuition hikes or the protection of university campuses from police raids, though these concerns were at play as well. Indeed, during both phases of organization, students demanded redress to state abuses that affected a broad swathe of Mexican society. In the 1960s, students rallied to free railway union members jailed a decade earlier for their activism, to remove from office Mexico City police officials who condoned blatant human rights violations, and, more generally, to pressure for greater transparency in the exercise of political power in their country. In 1986, they opposed top-down reforms to the university system that would reduce access for young people of limited means. In defense of the right of all Mexicans to a publicly funded college education, they took to the streets shouting slogans like "*La educación primero/al hijo del obrero; La educación después al hijo del burgués*" (Education first for the children of workers, education later for the children of the bourgeoisie" (Monsiváis 1987, 292). These mobilizations helped build the cross-class solidarity between students and popular sectors beyond the university gates that would become the fabric from which the FPFV would be cut in 1989.

The repression of student protests at Tlatelolco in 1968 and Corpus Christi in 1971, however, disabused an entire generation of students of the notion that Mexico's authoritarian and corrupt political system could be reformed through peaceful, democratic means. Many who escaped death or imprisonment during the government crackdown went underground or moved to more peripheral areas of the country—like Guerrero's rural hinterland or the shantytowns ringing the cities of Durango, Monterrey, and Mexico City—in search of opportunities to live out the radical ideals they had forged in the movement (Bennett 1992; Bruhn 2008; Haber 2006; Zugman Dellacioppa 2009). These events coincided with the tail end of a period of intense population growth in Mexico City, on the order of 5 percent per year until the 1970s (Aguilar 2008, 135) that created an extensive pool of workers whose demands for housing fell largely on deaf ears in the halls of government. In September

1985, an 8.1 magnitude earthquake exacerbated this crisis by destroying whole neighborhoods in the city center, sending residents in search of refuge to other parts of the metropolis. Expansive informal settlements materialized on the outskirts of the city as a result of these combined developments. These settlements provided fertile ground for disaffected student leaders, especially those influenced by the Line of Masses philosophy, who endeavored to create communities that mirrored its ideals of collectivism and autonomy in contrast to the corporatist system of intermediation. And, when the need to establish additional settlements arose, they worked with squatters to claim new, unoccupied tracts of land through invasions, sometimes massive, like the one in Santo Domingo discussed by Charlotte Blair's chapter in this volume.

The relationship between students and the working poor strengthened further in the aftermath of the earthquake thanks to the active role that students took to compensate for the slow-moving and largely incompetent government response to the vast devastation that had occurred. Political scientist Kathleen Bruhn (2008) notes that CEU leaders in particular formed brigades to rescue victims trapped in the rubble and prevented the military from demolishing collapsed buildings prematurely in the hopes of locating additional survivors. These acts, she contends, made students into heroes in the eyes of the organizations that had comprised Mexico's urban popular movement (*"movimiento urbano popular"* or MUP) since the 1970s (125).

This confluence of forces set the stage for the birth of the FPFV which began informally when CEU-affiliated students on UNAM's campus in the south of Mexico City offered shelter to the close to 3,000 squatter families dislodged from a nearby property in university buildings that the students had taken over to protest tuition hikes. Formalized in 1989, the FPFV was not the only or even the biggest organization to join the ranks of the MUP during this period but it was, according to some scholars, one of the most militant. In contrast to their counterparts, FPFV leaders understood that obtaining land for the urban poor was not as an end in itself but rather a means for building an alternative, socialist society, and that achieving *this* goal warranted the use of force if necessary (Bruhn 2008; Zugman Dellacioppa 2009). Employing what Bruhn calls aggressive protest tactics like militant squats, by 1995, the FPFV had secured a presence in nine boroughs across the City. One of these properties, taken in 1994, was the parcel that would become the site of La Comunidad Habitacional Acapatzingo.

Two decades later, La Comunidad Habitacional Acapatzingo's physical landscape bears witness to this fierce resolve to build a socialist society, block by block, and the impetus that a lettered leadership with roots in the student movement has given it. We get our first glimpse of the process by which the empty lot that Los Panchos occupied in La Polvorilla acquired the features it possesses today when Alejandro shows us the full-sized architectural drawings of the community that hang in Los Panchos' headquarters. Drafted with the assistance of students at the UNAM years ago and yellowing with age, these drawings map out every detail of the eight hectares that comprise the settlement, including the designated location and names of streets, pedestrian walkways and public squares or *plazas*. Blocks of housing numbered and laid out in grid-like fashion surround open spaces with names like Unity Square (*Plaza de la Unidad*) and Philosophers Square (*Plaza de los Filósofos*), the former framed by the Socialist Revolution Walkway (*Andador Revolución Socialista*), the Workers Movement Walkway (*Andador Movimiento Obrero*), the Popular Movement Walkway (*Andador Movimiento Popular*) and the Peasant Movement Walkway (*Andador Movimiento Campesino*), and the latter by the Karl Marx Walkway (*Andador Karl Marx*), the Friedrich Engels Walkway (*Andador Federico Engels*), and the General Emiliano Zapata Walkway (*Andador Gen. Emiliano Zapata*). This nomenclature attests to the cooperative's history of and continued solidarity with a broad range of popular sectors but also—with shout-outs to Marx and Engels—to the lettered nature of its leftist origins. Names given to other squares—Poets Square, Painters Square, and International Writers Square (*Plaza de los Poetas, Plaza de los Pintores*, and *Plaza de los Escritores Internacionales*)—suggest an appreciation for "letters" in the more traditional sense of literary culture and the fine arts as well. And the names of the streets that flank *these* squares hint at the cosmopolitan breadth of this literary culture; at one end of International Writers Square, for example, Ernest Hemingway Walkway (*Andador Ernest Hemingway*) intersects with Alejo Carpentier Walkway (*Andador Alejo Carpentier*) and Herman Hesse Walkway (*Andador Herman Hesse*).

We pass a few of these public squares on our walking tour in 2015. Philosophers Square, identified as such by a simple, hand-lettered sign that is easy to overlook, has become a playground with equipment crafted by the residents themselves, including a wooden structure made with the oversize tires of a John Deere tractor for children to climb on and crawl through. We walk by a lot on the opposite end of the settlement where the blueprints indicate Unity Square should be, but Alejandro refers to this space as Senior Citizens Square (*Plaza de la Tercera Edad*) instead. Here, a bocce ball court, a pair of chess tables, and exercise equipment for the elderly dominate. We also discover that International Writers Square is, in actuality, a wide open-air esplanade shaded by a corrugated tin roof where the community holds its monthly assemblies. At other stops along our route, Alejandro mentions public places where community members can likewise congregate and spend time together (*convivir*)—like the open-air amphitheater or the square showcasing a bandstand for community concerts—but we need to use our imaginations to see these because they are still works-in-progress. None of these squares look much like we had imagined them from the blueprints; residents have molded them into spaces that they desire and have made them their own. And they have done so collectively.

In Rama's ([1984] 1996) discussion of the lettered class or "letrados," he notes that their monopoly over the written word and cartographic renderings of places distinguished them from ordinary citizens, and enabled them to first imagine, then erect the city of their dreams. "Only the letrados," he writes, "could envision an urban ideal before its realization as a city of stone and mortar, then maintain that ideal after the construction of the city, preserving their idealized vision in a constant struggle with the material modifications introduced by the daily life of the city's ordinary inhabitants" (28). Los Panchos imagine a city of a different sort, one that is ordered and that privileges public spaces that nurture communication and community; they have given this vision a certain permanency by inscribing it in blueprints that rationalize and name the spaces that comprise La Comunidad Habitacional Acapatzingo. And, if the reality of incongruities like a playground occupying Philosophers Square is any indication, ordinary inhabitants have indeed amended and modified this idealized version to suit their needs. Here, however, the parallels with Rama's analysis begin to break down. Rather than accepting the inevitability of a rigid distinction between elite imperatives to order the inherent disorderliness of ordinary inhabitants, Los Panchos reject this distinction in theory and work to collapse it in practice. Indeed, they understand the masses themselves to be potential agents of order, structuring their environment through the disciplined practices and processes of self-management.

Examples of self-management include the fact that all of the projects that Alejandro shows us—both completed and in-progress—developed from community-wide decisions and fundraising. He also explains to us that the collective decision-making processes and spirit of equality and solidarity so central to self-management are the reason the housing units in the settlement are of uniform height and quality. When families began to qualify for credit to build their homes, the community assembly agreed that no single family would build a second story (even if they could obtain the credit to do so) until *all* residents had completed their first.

That these efforts of "the masses" can *order* as opposed to disorder, however, comes into even clearer focus for us when—months after our initial visit with Los Panchos—we discover Google images that provide an aerial view of the entirety of Iztapalapa. There are no labels affixed to the image where La Polvorilla appears that identifies La Comunidad Habitacional Acapatzingo, but there is no mistaking where this settlement begins and ends. Set apart from its neighbors by its wide avenues, abundance of open space and brightly colored housing laid out in neat rows, the area controlled by Los Panchos is a paragon of orderliness in an otherwise aesthetically drab and haphazard urban landscape.

In the following section, we turn our attention to the political economic context in which Los Panchos managed to mold this swatch of Mexico City in its desired image. Specifically, we examine how changes in Mexico's land rights regime, linked to the workings of global capital, created the opportunity in the late 1990s for Los Panchos to gain legal title to the land they had invaded earlier in the decade. In an ironic twist, the same forces that swept the landless aside to make room for global capital in Santa Fe, (as discussed by Mattiace and Johnson in their chapter in this volume) helped squatters strengthen their claim to land in Iztapalapa.

THE WORKINGS OF GLOBAL CAPITAL: LAND RIGHTS AND NEOLIBERALISM

In contrast to parts of the city like new Santa Fe or Plaza Carso where global capital has converted former industrial sites and garbage dumps into spaces for luxury living, upscale shopping and the business dealings of some of the largest transnational corporations in the country, global capital has marked the course of urbanization in Iztapalapa mostly through its absence. Stand at the center of Los Panchos' compound in La Polvorilla, and it is not the skyscrapers housing the corporate headquarters of IBM and Coca Cola that dominate the skyline. Rather, it is the volcanoes that ring Mexico City that rise to meet your gaze. These brown- and red-streaked slopes press so close to La Comunidad Habitacional Acapatzingo that they appear to be within walking distance (see Figure 7.2).

To the extent that capital investment has had a hand in influencing urbanization on this edge of the city, these sights tell part of the story. Like much of the land upon which Mexico City has expanded since the 1940s, the land on which Los Panchos built La Comunidad Habitacional Acapatzingo had been communally owned and likely used by *campesinos* (farmers or peasants) for small-scale agriculture. The metropolitan construction boom in the 1970s, however, increased the value of this land as a source of sand and gravel, key ingredients for concrete. The slopes that encircle La Polvorilla are streaked brown and red because mining concessions that leased the land—some still operating today—stripped them bare of any foliage in order to extract voluminous quantities of these materials. After 1985, the lower-lying areas also became used as a destination for debris produced by the earthquake. Much of this landfilling activity went unregulated, creating terrain that is mostly unstable for high-rise construction today (Juárez-Galeana 2006).

In the late 1980s, Mexico largely abandoned the import-substitution model that had fueled both homegrown industrialization and urbanization by concentrating industrial growth in cities. The neoliberal model that took its place focused instead on creating favorable conditions for foreign investment with minimal interference from the state. For instance, in 1992, the legislature amended Article 27 of the Mexican Constitution to pave the way for the conversion of communally held land into private property and the consolidation of the many individually owned plots carved out of communally held property into larger tracts more propitious for capital intensive uses. A cornerstone of the Mexican Revolution (1910–1917), Article 27 endeavored not only to redistribute but also to protect in perpetuity peasants' usufruct rights to land by prohibiting the partition, individual titling and sale of property deemed communal. By removing these legal protections in the 1990s, the state relinquished its role as guardian of the commons in rural and peri-urban areas, and ushered in an era of privatization.

In La Polvorilla, the regime's incentive to regularize property—divide, title, and subject it to commercial transaction—unleashed an intense period of political jockeying for ownership over unoccupied land there. Deploying strength in numbers and the threat of violence should state forces attempt to remove them, Los Panchos secured the opportunity to legally purchase the lot they occupied (and the promise of government-issued credit to help them do so) in spite of the disadvantage the organization faced due to its very public distrust of and opposition to political parties of all stripes.[5] A 2009 interview with Enrique Reinoso, one of Los Panchos' leaders who witnessed these events, describes how this was no mean feat given that the political party in power at any given time controlled access to titling and credit administered through Mexico City's Instituto de Vivienda del DF (Federal District Housing Institute or INVI). *"Nos pusieron muchas trabas"*—"they shackled us"— he tells interviewers, referring to the seemingly endless delays, false starts, and bureaucratic red tape that this agency subjected Los Panchos to (but not partisan supporters) in the process of soliciting credit. Nonetheless, Los Panchos of Acapatzingo-La Polvorilla gained official recognition as a Housing Cooperative in 1998 and by 2001 won legal possession of their land and loans to cover part of the price.

To date, there is no visible sign that global capital has or will in the near future target La Polvorilla as a site for real estate development or other forms of large-scale investment (for comparison see the story of real estate development in Santo Domingo as told by Charlotte Blair in her chapter in this volume). One way that this area feeds the global economy largely in the absence of capital and the state, however, is by provisioning the unskilled and semi-skilled labor on which this economy depends.[6] That La Polvorilla and its environs warehouse an overwhelmingly informal work force follows a historical pattern. During the height of ISI-led growth, Mexico City's eastern flank housed industrial workers through the accretion of informal or irregular settlements populated by newcomers to the City. Indeed, Mexico's post-Revolutionary regime never prioritized housing for popular sectors to the same degree as it did other public services like education and health. Instead, it tolerated the illegal takeover and encroachment on communally held land, and the unregulated, self-help construction of housing in these areas. Some scholars discuss this in terms of the absence, inability, or failure of the state to control catch-as-catch-can urbanization. This benefited industry by guaranteeing a labor supply housed through self-help. Today, though radical in its intentions, Los Panchos' determination to build and sustain itself through self-management may unwittingly aid and abet this history of state neglect.

The final section of our essay explores Los Panchos' relationship to the state and the system more broadly through the lens of its response to insecurity, a challenge that all Mexican citizens today must confront in one way or another. At first blush, the residents of the Comunidad Habitacional Acapatzingo endeavor to keep themselves safe much like wealthier residents in the City do: they wall themselves off from the dangers that surround them by erecting physical barriers that exclude. This is part of Los Panchos' story but it is at best a small one. Indeed, focusing solely on this similarity risks obscuring how the lived experience of security within these walls differs fundamentally from the individualized and inward-looking culture of fear that pervades gated communities where security is reduced to a commodity.

Walled Resistance and Insecurity

The Comunidad Habitacional Acapatzingo is not the only settlement that the FPFV has founded in Mexico City. Of those still in existence today, some developed under the auspices of the original FPFV and benefit from ties they have cultivated with the political machines that left-leaning parties like the PRD have built up in recent years. This is the case, for example, of the *Unidad Habitacional Nuevo Aztlán*, also located in Iztapalapa, that successfully taps city programs like the *Programa Comunitario Mejoramiento Barrial* (Community Program of Neighborhood Improvement, PCMB) to fund "pocket parks" and other infrastructure projects for their community, similar to old Santa Fe's neighborhood associations we discuss in our chapter in this volume. Although the degree to which any given FPFV settlement enmeshes itself in local politics varies, Alejandro tells us that virtually all of these settlements are gated.

Urban planners studying Mexico City who focus on urban resilience (that is, the ability of city dwellers to cope with chronic violence) critique these gated experiments in low-income neighborhoods for their insularity. In their analysis of Nuevo Aztlán, for instance, Broid and De la O. (n. d.) acknowledge that this housing cooperative provisions security internally but characterize this success as a "double-edged sword." These "isolating efforts" or "islands of resilience," they assert, keep members safe, but also potentially "hamper the sustainability of the neighborhood's overall resilience" (28). Scholars of the gated community phenomenon among the urban middle and upper classes also posit that walling off and privatizing public space may create the illusion of security for those within, but simultaneously undermines trust, civility, social cohesion, and equality in the broader societies they exist in (c.f. Caldeira 2000; Graham and Marvin 2001). Taken together, these analyses cast doubt on the potential of gating or walling to ever work in the public interest or for the common good. In the language of David Harvey (2012), one of the theorists that inspires the work in this edited volume, we might ask whether one can ever assert the right to the city through the enclosure and privatization of public space. That is, can enclosure—"walling" or "gating" to keep others out—ever foment the kind of progressive, revolutionary change that David Harvey had in mind when he wrote about urban denizens asserting their right to the city?

To address these questions using evidence from our research, we first draw a loose comparison between what we observed to be the lived experience of security and insecurity in other parts of Mexico City and those experiences in the Comunidad Habitacional Acapatzingo. We then explore how walls and walling in this community function to help create what is distinctive about this space and the notions of security and insecurity that circulate within it. Finally, we return to the questions inspired by Harvey's framework: what *can* the Comunidad Habitacional Acapatzingo tell us about the prospects for restoring the commons and reclaiming the right to the city in Mexico City today?

In October 2015, respected *cronista* (journalistic essayist) of modern Mexico City David Lida rebuked city officials for denying the existence of organized crime there by blogging about the torture and murder of three victims of drug cartels in as many days in Iztapalapa, "the most dangerous of the Federal District's *delegaciones* (boroughs)." Below a photo depicting the grisly display of one of these cadavers stripped and hanging from a bridge over a major thoroughfare in Iztapalapa, Lida wrote: "There is plenty of armed robbery, car theft, homicide, and . . . extortion in Mexico City. We don't live in a bubble. Watch your backs" (Lida 2015, n.p.). During our time in Mexico City just three months earlier, residents of high-end neighborhoods like Lomas de Chapultepec echoed these sentiments. They readily shared stories with us that conveyed their fear of falling prey to armed robbery and theft, if not homicide, themselves and they recalled—blow-by-blow—how people they knew (or knew of) had actually been victimized.

In La Polvorilla, however, our conversations about security did not revolve around talk of victimization, despite residents' physical proximity to some of the most violent criminal acts committed in the city and the disproportionately high frequency with which they occur around them. Alejandro, born and raised in Iztapalapa to parents active in FPFV even before it was formally constituted, does not mince words when he told us that organized crime had infiltrated the borough. "It arrived about three years back," he tells us matter-of-factly. He admits that it's dangerous "out there" (*afuera*) but has no lurid tales to tell about violent crime, organized or otherwise. The stories he tells us about insecurity in the place he has lived all of his life are not fraught with anxiety or despair. Rather, he speaks about crime as just one among many opportunities for the people of the Comunidad Habitacional Acapatzingo to create a new, superior way of thinking and being, "*nuestra propia cultura*" (our own culture), in Alejandro's exact words.

Key to this cultural project is rebuilding the social fabric torn by the individualism that perverts human relationships in mainstream society. The problem in a society like that, Alejandro suggests, is that people rely on themselves instead of each other to keep safe. And they don't organize. "You are your own security" (*La seguridad eres tú*), Alejandro states succinctly. In this world of every man, woman, and child for him or herself, you watch what time you go out, you look over your shoulder when you walk the streets, and you barricade yourself behind locks and bars. And since you don't know your neighbor, you don't mess with him. After all, he could be a senator, a councilman or—who knows?—a drug dealer (*narco*). In the Comunidad Habitacional Acapatzingo, at the very least, you know who your neighbors are; everyone is a known quantity and everyone is an equal. This means that on most days, Alejandro asserts, the vigilance committee (*comisión de vigilancia*) can resolve the disputes that arise among neighbors simply by bringing them together to dialogue. The solution, he emphasizes, is to communicate (*la solución es hablar*). This method has been so successful that on occasion even folks in La Polvorilla who do not belong to the Comunidad Habitacional Acapatzingo come to the cooperative seeking help from the committee to iron out conflicts. Alejandro concedes that this model doesn't work in every situation, and that there are cases that the vigilance committee can't handle. For example, when someone from the outside enters and commits a crime or if it is very serious matter, like rape or homicide, then the community calls the police and turns in the perpetrator. "We know that's not the solution," Alejandro explains, referring to their reliance on the state's mode of policing which jails, punishes, and extorts rather than seeks justice. But the cooperative, Alejandro adds, has simply not yet been able to build the kinds of structures they need to resolve these problems in ways that chime with their communitarian and anti-statist values.

As this example illustrates, total autonomy from the state is not yet a present reality for the Comunidad Habitacional Acapatzingo, though it is still a goal they aspire to. And, interestingly, to listen to Alejandro speak, this dependence on the state and the capitalist economy entwined with it poses a far greater source of insecurity to residents than criminals of the flesh and blood kind. Indeed, everything we learned about the Comunidad Habitacional Acapatzingo suggests that what residents fear most is the precariousness that comes from being subject to the market economy and the political system that profits from it and caters to its needs. In this more holistic sense, *in*security means the uncertainty of not knowing whether you will be able to obtain clean water, healthy food, electricity to light your streets at night, education for your children or work for yourself. Conversely, *security* is self-sufficiency.

Everywhere you turn in the Comunidad Habitacional Acapatzingo there is evidence that Los Panchos have chipped away at the root causes of insecurity in this more holistic sense—dependence on the state and the cash nexus—through projects that, little by little, make their community more self-sustaining. As in policing, in education Los Panchos have achieved partial autonomy from the state by starting up a provisional high school with curriculum designed by the community. This is progress despite the fact that only 80 students currently attend, and many schoolchildren still leave the settlement for an education in public schools in the surrounding neighborhood. Alejandro explains that unlike efforts to build autonomous communities in rural areas—like their Zapatista counterparts in southern Mexico—settlements in urban areas still need to have their schools certified by the state so the diplomas they issue can open doors to jobs in the formal economy. In the Comunidad Habitacional Acapatzingo, full-time committee work and infrastructural projects generate some employment, and there is a community garden and solar energy projects that reduce but do not eliminate the need for wages to pay for food and other necessities. Until these enterprises expand and diversify to meet the material needs of all community members, however, the state and state-sanctioned education will retain their importance as a gatekeeper to economic opportunity and security.

Although these lingering ties to mainstream society persist and breach the physical walls that enclose this community, so, too, do ties of solidarity with like-minded organizations and social movements. A case in point is Los Panchos' relationship with the Zapatista movement in Chiapas, the *Ejército Zapatista de Liberación Nacional* (Zapatista Army for National Liberation or EZLN). Like Los Panchos, the EZLN seeks autonomy from state and market forces by building a new way of life practiced in self-contained communities. The seven "servant leadership" principles that guide this movement and shape communal life in Zapatista settlements—serving others rather than oneself, representing rather than superseding, constructing and not destroying, obeying and not dictating, proposing and not imposing, convincing and not vanquishing, and self-abasement rather than putting on airs (Zibechi 2014, 62)—resonate strongly with Los Panchos' own philosophy. For these reasons, Los Panchos have long supported the Zapatista cause. In December of 1997, for example, when paramilitary forces killed 45 members of a civil society organization in Acteal, Chiapas, Los Panchos took to the streets in protest and solidarity, and offered housing in a sister settlement to the Comunidad Habitacional Acapatzingo for a Zapatista delegation that had traveled to Mexico City. And, in 2006, during EZLN sub-commander Marcos' "Campaign" for President, the Comunidad Habitacional Acapatzingo welcomed him into their midst and invited him to broadcast the Zapatista message from their very own, community-run FM radio station.

Other signs of solidarity that transcends settlement boundaries come to light during our walk with Alejandro. Brightly colored murals span the interior of one cinderblock wall dividing the Comunidad Habitacional Acapatzingo from the outside. We stop to admire them, and Alejandro and Elisa tell us that youth from HIJOS Colombia and HIJOS México painted them. The acronym HIJOS spells the Spanish word for "sons and daughters," and stands for Sons and Daughters for Identity and Justice, and against Forgetting and Silence (*Hijos por la Identidad y Justicia, contra el Olvido y Silencio*). The Mexican branch of this international organization represents the children of individuals disappeared or detained, some of them victims of the student massacres during the late 1960s and early 1970s. Later on our tour, on the northeastern edge of the community where blueprints indicate an open-air amphitheater will be built, these walls seemingly dissolve to reveal a sea of gray housing built by squatters who do not belong to the community (see Figure 7.4). Alejandro jokes that these are squatters squatting on squatters' land, then clarifies that the Comunidad Habitacional Acapatzingo will allow these folks to use this land until cooperative members are ready to use it themselves.

These examples call into question the characterization of the Comunidad Habitacional Acapatzingo as hermetically sealed or insular, and reveal the limits to comparisons between Los Panchos' settlements and gated communities for middle- and upper-class Mexicans. Despite initial appearances, walls and gates here do not keep everyone who does not belong out,[7] but this—it turns out—is not their main purpose. Rather, we believe that for Los Panchos, walls work primarily to demarcate the outer bounds of a human community rooted in a geographic place where people know one another and where repairing the social fabric is of utmost importance. In other words, walls function less to exclude than to symbolize and nurture the utopia that is unfolding within.[8]

In point of fact, this utopian community-building project closely resembles what Harvey (2012) calls the process of "commoning" or reclaiming or

Figure 7.4   The Porousness of the Comunidad Habitacional Acapatzingo's Northeastern Boundary. *Source*: Photo: Jennifer L. Johnson.

constructing a commons. The term refers back to the oft lamented loss of the commons brought about historically by the enclosure and privatization of spaces previously accessible to all. Commons, he argues, distinguish themselves from other spaces as "collective" or for mutual benefit and "non-commodified," and urban denizens can reclaim their right to the city by contributing to the creation of such spaces. Describing this generative action, Harvey writes, "At the heart of the practice of commoning lies the principle that the relation between the social group and that aspect of the environment that is being treated as a common shall be both collective and non-commodified—off limits to the logic of market exchange and market valuations" (73). Furthermore, Harvey acknowledges that enclosure through walling is not necessary antithetical to the commons. Indeed, in "a ruthlessly commodifying world," groups seeking alternatives that fly in the face of dominant institutions and norms may very well require barriers—physical or otherwise—to protect and nurture the fledgling values and practices that constitute these alternatives (70).

CONCLUDING REMARKS

Through the theoretical lens that Harvey (2012) provides, La Polvorilla and the work that Los Panchos do within its walls come into focus as a very real—if incomplete and at times contradictory—example of capitalinos staking their claim—their right, even—to a better way of life in Mexico City. As Daniel Rogers' chapter in this volume illustrates, for more than half a century, the urban poor have struggled to make a place for themselves in the City and in Mexican society more generally, over and against the neglect and exploitation of the post-revolutionary regime. For Los Panchos, this impulse to place-make involves more than just securing land, housing and protection from crime, as crucial as these may be; it entails, above all, radically transforming citizens' relationship to state and market, and the built environment that fosters new, more collective forms of human community.

NOTES

1. We would like to express our sincere gratitude to Elisa Benavides for her hospitality, time and the invaluable insights that she has shared with us. We are also indebted to Glen Kuecker for bringing Los Panchos to our attention and opening the doors to our initial visit through his dedicated work with and contacts at the Mexican Solidarity Network. Last but not least, we gratefully acknowledge all of the members of Los Panchos who welcomed us into their community, but especially Alejandro Juárez, head of the organization's Comisión de Cultura and our primary contact during this phase of fieldwork. Our analysis here stems largely though not exclusively from the intense field visit we conducted with Alejandro's guidance in June 2015.

2. The Golden Line originally opened in October 2012, closed for repairs in March 2014, and reopened in November 2015 (http://geo-mexico.com/?p=8202, accessed February 3, 2017).

3. Decisions are made by consensus within community assemblies and all work is done collectively, organized on the basis of brigades. The Unidad Habitacional Acapatzingo consists of 28 brigades, which are made up of 25 families. Each brigade determines the leadership of its commissions, including press, culture, vigilance, and maintenance (Zibechi 2014). The General Council of the Settlement, which consists of representatives from each brigade, meets monthly.

4. Ironically, given the Line of Masses' (or LMs') rejection of politics generally and political parties more specifically, one clear contemporary articulation of the LM philosophy can be found on the Mexican Workers Party (Partido de Trabajo or PT) website. In a statement that highlights how its embrace of LM principles distinguishes the PT from other parties, PT spokespersons note: "Without the fundamental masses—workers, peasants, women, youth, professionals, intellectuals, employees, day laborers, small-scale merchants, small- and medium-sized business owners, indigenous peoples, students and other popular sectors—the transformation of the country cannot be brought about. This means that it is necessary to fully integrate oneself into the masses, learn from their struggles, and systematize and synthesize their experiences. The Line of Masses emphasizes the need to develop the masses' organized and democratic decision-making capacity about how to solve their concrete

problems and how to carry out their social struggles. The Line of Masses is a liberating process since it allows one to learn how to rely on one's own strengths" *(Es a partir de la idea de que sin las masas fundamentales: obreros, campesinos, mujeres, jóvenes, profesionistas, intelectuales, empleados, jornaleros, pequeños comerciantes, empresarios medios y pequeños, indígenas, estudiantes y demás sectores populares, no se puede efectuar la transformación del país. Implica la necesidad de integrarse plenamente a las masas, aprender de sus luchas, y de sistematizar y sintetizar sus experiencias. La Línea de Masas hace hincapié en la necesidad de desarrollar la capacidad de las masas para decidir organizada y democráticamente la solución de sus problemas concretos y la conducción de sus luchas sociales. La Línea de Masas es un proceso liberador, porque permite aprender a basarse en sus propias fuerzas)* (Partido de Trabajo n.d.).

5. With the emergence of electoral competition and party alternatives to the dominant PRI in the late 1980s at sub-national levels, the leadership of many of the organizations that comprised the MUP enter the electoral fray by allying with left-leaning parties. In the case of Los Panchos, soon after the original land occupation, in 1997, the larger FPFV split into an independent faction, FPFV-I, over the question of whether to participate in the mayoral contest to elect leftist Cuauhtémoc Cárdenas. Los Panchos of Acapatzingo-La Polvorilla have maintained their distance from political parties and electoral politics since this time.

6. Our data on this point are preliminary, but anecdotal evidence suggests that residents of the Comunidad Habitacional Acapatzingo work predominantly in the service and maquila sectors, and that very few are employed in the formal sector with the possibility of unionization; rates of unemployment also seem high.

7. The walls do effectively regulate vehicles that wish to enter the area. And, judging from the absence of Google Map street views of the Comunidad Habitacional Acapatzingo on the internet, they have also effectively blocked access to this area from this corporate behemoth that appropriates images of places and circulates them without the express permission of the people who inhabit them.

8. In this respect walls function much like the ski masks that Zapatistas wear to obscure their individual identities and thus signal opposition to individualism and a commitment to collectivity. Thank you to Glen Kuecker for sharing this astute observation with us.

WORKS CITED

Aguilar, Adrian Guillermo. 2008. "Peri-urbanization, Illegal Settlements and Environmental Impact in Mexico City." *Cities* 25: 133–45.

Becker, Anne and Markus-Michael Müller. 2013. "The Securitization of Urban Space and the 'Rescue' of Downtown Mexico City." *Latin American Perspectives* 40: 77–94.

Bennett, Vivienne. 1992. "The Evolution of Urban Popular Movements in Mexico Between 1966 and 1988." In *The Making of Social Movements in Latin America*, edited by Sonia Álvarez and Arturo Escobar, 240–59. Boulder: Westview Press.

Broid, Daniel and Marlene de la O. N. d. "Urban Resilience in Situations of Chronic Violence: Case Study of Mexico City, Mexico." Case study prepared for MIT's Center for International Studies (CIS), for the Urban Resilience in Chronic Violence project co-directed by Diane Davis and John Tirman, and funded by USAID [GRANT # AID-OAA-G-10–00002].

Bruhn, Kathleen. 2008. *Urban Protest in Mexico and Brazil.* New York: Cambridge University Press.

Caldeira, Teresa. 2000. *City of Walls: Crime, Segregation, and Citizenship in São Paulo.* Berkeley: University of California Press.

Centros de Integración Juvenil, A.C. (CIJ). 2013. *Estudio básico de comunidad objetivo: diagnóstico del contexto socio-demográfico del area de influencia del CIJ Iztapalapa oriente.* Accessed June 21, 2017. http://www.cij.gob.mx/ebco2013/centros/9370SD.html

Connolly, Priscilla. 2009. "Observing the Evolution of Irregular Settlements: Mexico City's *colonias populares,* 1990–2005." *International Development Planning Review* 31: 1–35.

Davis, Diane. 2013. "Zero-Tolerance Policing, Stealth Real Estate Development, and the Transformation of Public Space: Evidence from Mexico City." *Latin American Perspectives* 40: 53–76.

Geo-Mexico. "Line 12 of Mexico City's metro (subway) reopens." Accessed February 3, 2017. http://geo-mexico.com/?p=8202.

Graham, Stephen and Simon Marvin. 2001. *Splintering Urbanism: Networked Infrastructures, Technological Mobilities and the Urban Condition.* New York: Routledge.

Haber, Paul Lawrence. 2006. *Power from Experience: Urban Popular Movements in Late Twentieth Century Mexico.* University Park: Pennsylvania State University Press.

Harvey, David. 2012. *Rebel Cities: From the Right to the City to the Urban Revolution.* New York: Verso.

Juárez-Galeana, Luis Gabriel. 2006. "Collaborative Public Open Space Design in Self-help Housing: Minas-Polvorilla, México City." In *Designing Sustainable Cities in the Developing World,* edited by Georgia Butina Watson and Roger Zetter, 179–95. New York: Routledge.

Kruijt, Dirk and Kees Koonings. 2015. "Exclusion, Violence and Resilience in Five Latin American Megacities: A Comparison of Buenos Aires, Lima, Mexico City, Rio de Janeiro and São Paulo." In *Violence and Resilience in Latin American Cities,* edited by Dirk Kruijt and Kees Koonings, 30–52. New York: Zed Books.

Lida, David. 2015. "Blue Monday." October 26. Accessed June 22, 2017. http://davidlida.com/?p=3249

Malkin, Elisabeth. 2014. "Golden Line Adds Tarnish to Sprawling Subway System." *The New York Times,* May 22. Accessed June 21, 2017. http://www.nytimes.com/2014/05/23/world/americas/golden-line-brings-tarnish-to-mexicos-subway-system.html?_r=0

Monsiváis, Carlos. 1987. *Entrada libre: Crónicas de la sociedad que se organiza.* Mexico City: Ediciones Era.

Pansters, Wil and Hector Castillo Berthier. 2007. "Mexico City." In *Fractured Cities: Social Exclusion, Urban Violence and Contested Spaces in Latin America*, edited by Kees Koonings and Dirk Kruijt, 36–56. New York: Zed Books.

Partido del Trabajo. N.d. "Declaración de principios." Accessed June 22, 2017. http://www.partidodeltrabajo.org.mx/2011/principios.html#iii

Rama, Ángel. (1984) 1996. *The Lettered City. Post-Contemporary Interventions*. Translated by John Charles Chasteen. Durham, NC: Duke University Press.

Secretaría de Desarrollo Social (SEDESOL). N.d. "Informe annual sobre la situación de la pobreza y rezago social." n.d. Accessed June 21, 2017. http://www.gob.mx/cms/uploads/attachment/file/32197/Distrito_Federal_007.pdf

Sheinbaum, Diana. 2008. "Gated Communities in Mexico City: An Historical Perspective." *Urban Design International* 13: 241–52.

Zibechi, Raúl. 2014. "Mexico: Challenges and Difficulties of Urban Territories in Resistance." In *Rethinking Latin American Social Movements: Radical Action from Below*, edited by Richard Stahler-Sholk, Harry Vanden, and Marc Becker, 49–65. Lanham, MD: Rowman & Littlefield.

Zugman Dellacioppa, Kara. 2009. *This Bridge Called Zapatismo: Building Alternative Political Cultures in Mexico City, Los Angeles and Beyond*. Lanham, MD: Lexington Books.

Chapter 8

Porous Urbanism

Order and Disorder in Colonia Santo Domingo

Charlotte Blair

After several years of participant-observation research in Mexico City's *Colonia Santo Domingo* anthropologist Matthew Gutmann (2002) tells the story about the "good-sized piece of lava from the volcano Xitle"(248) that he received as a farewell gift from his friends living in the neighborhood. Gutmann relates that the *pedregal*, the Spanish name for the volcanic rock, carries special meaning to many residents of Santo Domingo, because it represents both the "difficulties residents faced in establishing their neighborhood and the actual rock they had to cut through to construct their houses there" (248). The gift-giving episode invites this chapter's consideration of *pedregal* as a metaphor for thinking about the logic of urban order and disorder within Santo Domingo's resistance to elite conceived development projects.

The story begins on September 3, 1971, when practically overnight thousands of squatters "invaded" the sparsely populated plot of land that is now Colonia Santo Domingo. While the Mexican state encouraged the land grab (Gutmann 1996, 33) municipal authorities did not provide Santo Domingo's *originarios*, or original settlers, with services or basic infrastructure until several years after this initial settlement. Instead settlers relied upon their own labor to order their space: they strung telephone wires, negotiated with public officials to install sewage pipes, built Colonia Santo Domingo's first school, and cut through the *pedregal* that overlay their new home.

Describing this land grab, geographer Peter Ward (1978, 39) writes, "lots of 200 square meters in size were allocated by the [political] leaders and to stake their claim squatters erected shacks of *lamina de cartón* (plastic coated cardboard sheets) or any material upon which they could lay their hands." In 1974, three years after the squatters "invaded" Santo Domingo's sparse land, an "agreement was reached whereby residents were given the opportunity to purchase their lots at a price commensurate with their incomes" (40). Over

171

the next few years, Santo Domingo's original settlers organized collective workdays to transform their cardboard and metal shacks into concrete cinder-brick dwellings.

Land titling, itself a form of state-sanctioned spatial ordering, enabled new residents to transform the rural landscape into a densely populated neighborhood of 120,000 inhabitants. Through this act of spatial re-ordering, original settlers paved the way for future capital accumulation in the colonia. Writing of squatter settlements and urban social movements, Manuel Castells (1983) describes this re-ordering process in two stages. In the first stage, land owners and private developers provide squatters with the materials necessary for the construction of their homes. In the second stage, after land values increase due to a stabilized infrastructure, squatters are "expelled from the land they have occupied and forced to start all over again on the frontier of a city which has expanded as a result of their efforts" (191). By giving land titles to Colonia Santo Domingo's original settlers, the state gave squatters the opportunity to begin a process of step-by-step settlement capitalization, reminiscent of Karl Marx's "primitive accumulation," the preliminary stage of capitalist development through which a market economy is established. Original settlers systematically commodified Colonia Santo Domingo by building their homes and businesses; obtaining property rights; and reproducing their labor for surrounding communities in an effort to survive.

By 2015, every inch of Colonia Santo Domingo was put to use—cinder-block dwellings were built atop older, cinder-block dwellings, and window gardens were far more popular than the few anemic trees struggling to grow next to busy streets. This act of primitive accumulation paved the way for the potential displacement of original residents through a process of "accumulation by dispossession," which, as theorized by David Harvey (2008), is the process by which the rich centralize their wealth by dispossessing people and the public of their land and capital. Accumulation by dispossession was a concept familiar to Santo Domingo's *originarios* who were uprooted from their communities prior to the 1971 land grab and the term certainly remained relevant in 2015 when the state-sanctioned housing complex development project, *Quiero Casa*, threatened to displace neighbors.

While cutting through volcanic rock was itself the first act of ordering the land into a capitalist asset, however limited in market value, in 2015 *pedregal* was being used by residents of Colonia Santo Domingo as a metaphor of resistance; a creative and playful counter-ordering to accumulation through dispossession. By investing deep meaning into their neighborhood and its formation, the neighborhood's residents also utilized their history as a self-built community to resist the very process of displacement that their initial settlement sparked. With limited resources, members of Colonia Santo Domingo's informal neighborhood association, *Asamblea General de los*

Pueblos, Barrios, Colonias y Pedregales de Coyoacán, organized political-cultural events and solidarity-building workshops in an attempt to withstand their foreseen displacement.

Order and disorder in Colonia Santo Domingo are mutually constitutive. To create urban order, real estate developers must perceive the community as a disordered space—a space that is, like volcanic rock, full of gaps that need to be filled with profit-producing projects. Likewise, grassroots neighborhood associations require perceived disorder to function; the threat of capitalist development is a stable force that compels neighbors to continue organizing. In this chapter, I analyze the porous relationship between order and disorder in Colonia Santo Domingo and argue that capitalism's logic of accumulation contains the seeds necessary for its ruination.

THE DELIRIOUS AND THE DANGEROUS

There are several ways that people have imagined Colonia Santo Domingo. These orderings are socially constructed perceptions about the neighborhood as a marginalized community. Describing Santo Domingo in 1996, for example, Gutmann writes: "Santo Domingo today is gray. A dull, concrete tone dominates things and social life in the *colonia*, from the masonry walls that shield homes from the foot traffic if not the noise of its streets to the dingy sky above, from the packs of roving dogs underfoot to the rocks boys and girls throw at rats caught in the open" (36).

Images of Santo Domingo as a messy, transient, disordered space stands in contrast to images of the space as delirious; as a place where "reality becomes fantasy and fantasy becomes reality" (Poniatowska 2000). A particular, fantastic order, according to Mexican writer Elena Poniatowska, arises from chaos. The congested streets, the endless construction, and the "click-click-click-click of a car that will not start" (Gutmann 37), seduces Poniatowska and others who attempt to escape an elite-ordered branding of the city. I, too, was drawn by this delirious space while living and doing ethnographic research in the neighborhood from June through December of 2015. During this period, the streets never appeared empty: Children dodged *peseros*, or small buses, while playing soccer in the streets; stray dogs lingered near *tamale* and *tlocyoco* stands; and women could always be found chatting on the street in the early mornings while waiting for the next informal *Zumba* class to begin. As a "city within a city" (Poniatowska 2000), Colonia Santo Domingo was a dynamic space; one that was consistently re-ordered by its diverse inhabitants as a means to fit their needs.

Cities are the product of utopian experiments; of liberation and creativity, yet also the home of "the anonymous alien, the underclass . . . the site of an incomprehensible 'otherness' . . ., the terrain of pollution (moral as well as physical), and of terrible corruptions, the place of the damned that needs to be enclosed and controlled . . ." (Harvey 2000, 158). While some are drawn to the disordered delirium that Santo Domingo's congested space conveys, others imagine the neighborhood to be a hotbed of crime and insecurity. Labeling Santo Domingo as a "squatters community" has allowed many to identify it as a space in which such "anonymous aliens" have settled.

While many living outside of the neighborhood had not heard of Colonia Santo Domingo, others associated the space with the real or imaginary incidents of gang violence, kidnapping, and homicide—rendered especially visible by area journalists and local newscasts.

For example, some time before my arrival in Santo Domingo, rumors about child organ trafficking circulated within the community and were printed in *La Jornada*, an independent, Left-leaning Mexican newspaper (Salgado and Sirvín 2015). After several protests, the incidents were discovered to be a politically inspired rumor initiated by the Morena political party. In an attempt to undermine the legitimacy of PRD (Partido Revolucionario Demócratico or Democratic Revolutionary Party)—the current incumbent party of Santo Domingo—Morena's motivation for planting the rumor was to undermine the PRD's ability to protect the safety and wellbeing of Santo Domingo's children. If residents could not trust PRD representatives to protect neighborhood children they would be more likely to back a political party, such as Morena, that focused on increased security as a political platform.

Other news articles focused less on individual cases of kidnapping and homicide and, instead, generalized neighborhood crime. In 2015, Gerardo Suárez, a journalist working for the centrist Mexican newspaper *El Universal*, wrote that "robberies of cars and stores, along with homicides, are common stories for neighbors [living in Colonia Santo Domingo] who attempt to shake the fear and live in a community tainted with drug activity." Avoiding the neighborhood out of fear, pitying those living within the colonia, or condemning them as pathologically abnormal, was not only perpetuated through the mainstream media, but also through a perception held by those not living in poverty that people living in Santo Domingo were confined within a culture of poverty.

Esteban, a middle-aged businessman who worked for his father's construction company articulated this view during one of our two-hour English conversation classes held at his office in *Colonia Roma*. "The relationship between the poor and dirt is too close," he told me during our conversation about *colonias populares* (working-class neighborhoods). The "dirt" that Esteban related to working-class neighborhoods in Mexico City derived from a culture of bad habits. "Poverty is a culture," he told me, "it began in the home; then after that, of course, in the school. Parents are responsible for that situation, but it's difficult because they don't have education. You learn the things you see, bad habits . . . you don't take care of your things."

Esteban's attitude toward Mexico City's working-class poor is neither new nor uncommon. Oscar Lewis (1963), a major influence on the field of anthropology in the United States as well as Mexico, theorized a culture of poverty based on his fieldwork in Tepito, Mexico City. The poor, a population culturally lumped together by Lewis, are described as pathologically inferior and have developed a "class stratified, highly individuated, capitalist society" (21) as a result. In other words, the harsh culture of individualism makes people helpless, dependent, and unable to ascribe to a healthy way of living. While recognizing the structural restraints that keep poor people poor, Lewis writes that it is "much more difficult to undo the culture of poverty than to cure poverty itself" (25).

Almost sixty years after Lewis published his work ideas around this so-called culture of poverty persist. Stereotypes of the working poor are reflected in the subtle reputations of Santo Domingo and other working-class neighborhoods that circulate within Mexico City. Despite the fact that I had been living in the neighborhood for months, taxi drivers would warn me of the criminals that supposedly flooded the streets at night. Female students from UNAM would refuse to enter my neighborhood without a male escort. I even found myself hesitant to tell Esteban where I was living for fear that he would identify me, too, as dirty. According to neoliberal ideology, dirt and poverty are, as Esteban clearly articulated, "too close." Because of its assigned reputation as a tainted space, the neighborhood became a disorder that many of Mexico's political elite promised to re-order with state-sanctioned development projects.

DEVELOPMENT AND (DIS)ORDER

One way that elite ordering is crafted in cities is through public-private capital investment projects. In 2015, as part of Mexico City's Social Economic Development Zones (ZODES) project, otherwise known as the "City of the Future" initiative, a number of capital-producing megaprojects were underway. While the details regarding this initiative were not always readily available to many living within Santo Domingo, many of my neighbors feared that Simon Levy–Dabbah—the chief executive officer of ProCDMX, the Mexico City Agency for Development and the principle developer spearheading this initiative—would partner with foreign companies in order to construct new shopping malls, parking lots, and offices around the neighborhood. New construction projects, such as the Oasis Shopping Mall, built in 2015, threatened many people living in Colonia Santo Domingo who foresaw the water scarcity and potential gentrification that these projects might produce. Neighborhood anxiety rose to a new high, when in the fall of 2015, brothers Jose Shabot Cherem and Salomon Shabot Cherem of the real estate company, Quiero Casa, began the construction of a thirty-seven story apartment complex in the adjacent neighborhood *Colonia Los Reyes* (Fragoso 2015, 3).

Many of those living in Colonia Santo Domingo and nearby colonias populares feared that the construction of this building would raise the overall cost of living in and around their communities. Emerging as a limb of the "City of the Future" initiative, the apartment complex and subsequent shopping centers were based on a model of land management by which "strategic partnerships between the public sector, the private sector, and the social sector, aimed at improving the quality of life in the city" (Fragoso, 3). According to *Agencia de Gestión Urbana*, Mexico City's Urban Management Agency (2015), this public-private partnership sought to attract foreign investment from companies interested in the promotion of projects that would supposedly "increase the competitiveness and economic growth of the city." Some of Santo Domingo's original settlers and their children feared that this "economic growth" would lead to the economic disempowerment of those living in the neighborhood, and potentially their displacement.

The apprehension that many people felt regarding this project was also due to the fact that neighbors themselves could do little to stop the apartments from being built. Especially worrisome was a change in Article 41 of the Law on Urban Development of the City, which permits alterations in public land use to be made by a technical committee without first consulting with the people living near public areas (Reveles 2015). There was no legal mechanism to encourage developers to consult with local residents before beginning construction on what residents believed to be their land.

In addition to the fear of displacement, many community members contested this particular development project because they believed that Quiero Casa was stealing the neighborhood's water supply and subsequently selling this resource to private stakeholders. According to some community members, Quiero Casa began pumping out potable drinking water from the neighborhood's aquifer, located directly below the construction site. Word spread that this water was being privatized: drained, bottled, and then sold in the marketplace.

As a project made to provide housing for those living in the city, the proposed apartment complex was an elite method of urban ordering; the new and exclusive housing complex would stand out like a gem amid the sea of gray described by Gutmann. The appearance of this new corporate-built complex would set-off Harvey's process of accumulation through dispossession by encouraging other speculators to invest in Santo Domingo; making it a safer spot for further experimentation of finance capital. In an attempt to tame an unwieldy space, Quiero Casa's presence caused many of those living in the community to feel paralyzed and without control over their resources, especially their land and water.

Water scarcity in the Pedregales—the communities surrounding Colonia Santo Domingo—has been a major issue since the neighborhood's first settlers arrived in 1971. Throughout my six months living in the neighborhood, before construction of the apartment complex began, some of my neighbors would go days without water. This became a major problem for restaurant workers and other business owners whose daily wages depended on running water. Operating a small, open-air *lavandaria* (laundromat) out of her home, my next-door neighbor Magdalia was compelled to close her business's doors several times a week due to water scarcity in the neighborhood.

Marxist urbanist Andy Merrifield (2002), in his interpretation of David Harvey's analysis of cities, writes that "financial institutions and property capital actively *produce* scarcity, actively structure urban land use and residential patterning through their 'normal' daily functioning, their 'normal' desire to maximize profits" (140). By producing scarcity, investors could more easily expropriate the land of Colonia Santo Domingo's urban poor— the squatters who settled the land in 1971, making it ripe for contemporary capitalist projects such as Quiero Casa. Explaining the capitalist logic behind accumulation by dispossession in urban slums, Mike Davis (2006) writes that, "everywhere the most powerful local interests—big developers, politicians, and military juntas—have positioned themselves to take advantage of peripheral land sales to poor migrants as well as members of the urban salariat" (91). Magdalia, who was just six years old during the land invasion, had lived in the colonia her entire life. She grew up attending primary school in Colonia Santo Domingo, raised her two children within neighborhood boundaries, and, through a process of primitive accumulation, built two homes and one *lavandaria* on Santo Domingo's serpentine streets. As a working-class woman, Magdalia and many others living in Colonia Santo Domingo are particularly vulnerable to being driven out of the community due to large-scale investors such as Quiero Casa.

Like primitive accumulation, accumulation by dispossession requires spatial re-ordering. Anna Tsing's (2005) consideration of "salvage frontier," which explains the re-ordering of frontier spaces as they become further integrated into a messy global capitalist system, is useful for thinking about how Colonia Santo Domingo's settlement by squatters, an act of primitive accumulation, prepared the way for the accumulation by dispossession of urban development. As a frontier that has yet to be fully conquered by capitalist regimes, Colonia Santo Domingo is imagined by some to be a disordered space in need of order through capitalist management and investment. Salvaged by the penetration of capitalist investment, the colonia undergoes the "series of twists" (33) that other frontier spaces experience. The illegality of potable public water extraction, for example, is made legal precisely because neighbors themselves are seen as being illegal. Likewise, community members' houses, under-capitalized according to logic of market economics, sit on productive, resourceful land that, if managed by the "right" people, could flow with profit.

Merrifield (2002) elaborates on what Harvey means by urban development for the "right" people. It is when "Landlords desist from doing repairs, from providing proper services, even resort to arson and tenant intimidation." Merrifield explains, "The idea here is to plunder properties and people until the land is ripe for redevelopment, for potential upscaling, when the 'wrong' people have been supplemented by the 'right' people. Whole blocks are willfully torn down, or renovated, and their scruffy inhabitants displaced, but are absent minded, or ignorant, about the block's dubious past life . . ." (Merrifield 2002, 141; see Harvey 1972, 140).

By depleting Colonia Santo Domingo of its most essential resources, the City of the Future project, especially the construction of the Quiero Casa apartment complex, threatened neighbors who may lose access to such resources: the neighborhood, ironically or intentionally, became worn down by the very capitalist project that was supposed to restore it.

Investors plant gardens of capital over the land that they, themselves, devastate. According to Harvey's accumulation by dispossession analysis, increasingly degraded urban landscapes become ripe for the urban re-ordering carried out by financial institutions. This is a process of creative destruction by which "industrial mutation incessantly revolutionizes the economic structure from within, incessantly destroying the old one, incessantly creating a new one" (Schumpeter [1942] 1994, 82). By extracting the colonia's water supply, Quiero Casa was able to re-order the space into a fantastic utopia for capitalist investors who dream of making profits.

MEMORY, ART, AND PLAY

Despite their precarious historical position as so-called squatters, many of those living in Colonia Santo Domingo were not passively witnessing this particular project as it was planned in real time. Borrowing from their experiences with grassroots community organizing in the 1970s, members of the Asamblea General de los Pueblos, Barrios, Colonias y Pedregales de Coyoacán (hereafter Asamblea) drew from a sense of collective nostalgia in order to circumvent power and become educators of their own design. While attempts to appeal to public officials and those with political agency were not always successful, the community projects and activities that the

Asamblea organized—such as collective workdays, community meetings, neighborhood cultural events, and political demonstrations—required that members build caring relationships with one another; relationships that were based on the notion of mutual trust and the shared interest of neighborhood preservation. The group members were not bound together by occupation nor age, but rather their collective goal of community preservation and a shared sense of belonging. Many living within the community shared a feeling of accomplishment regarding the neighborhood's initial settlement: *they* built their houses, *they* built Santo Domingo's first school, *they* carried large tanks of water home when they were delivered weekly by water trucks. Asamblea members took these memories from the past, re-worked them, and subsequently used them in the present to paint a future of radical democracy.

In the Spring of 2015 Asamblea members collaborated with surrounding communities in order to sponsor a *plantón;* a long-term, tented, sit-in. For over eight months, the community members maintained the plantón as a collective protest against the Quiero Casa apartment complex. Adjacent to the construction site in Colonia Los Reyes, the plantón boasted a makeshift kitchen, a private sleeping space, and a bathroom equipped with a portable toilet—all of which were just steps away from *Avenida Aztecas*, a busy avenue in Southern Mexico City.

Before entering the plantón, bypassers see murals leading up to the large tent. In white-painted capital letters on a makeshift cardboard wall leading up to the plantón, the bypasser would see *"Quiero casa, the Shabot family, in conjunction with the government, dumped more than 1500 million liters of water in one year and now it's contaminated."*[1] The by passer would then see the hole through which onlookers can see a construction site and the pool of water that would have been drained and privatized if not for the plantón and the neighbors who spend every night guarding the development site. The water below is dirty from the now-suspended project; the only living things in this space are the ducks that group together under abandoned cinder blocks. When people pass by, they often stop to marvel at the polluted spectacle, a gray wasteland that is simultaneously preserved and neglected. A wooden cutout of Emiliano Zapata is one of the first things to greet those who step inside the plantón's tented space. He looks staunchly out over the plantón's main area; *"AGUA"* (WATER) in black calligraphy and the red Zapatista National Liberation Army (EZLN) star are painted just below his face. Upon walking further, one comes across a well-adorned table altar made up of volcanic rocks, plants and flowers; all of which sit neatly on a red Zapatista bandana. Neighborhood meetings and other events are sometimes held within the plantón; and, on particular nights, one hears the strum of an acoustic guitar or a collective *signa*—a shout of protest, from those who have convened under the large tent.

In a collaborative report Pedregales resident, Ariana Mendoza Fragoso (2016), describes these signas. These chants, she writes, "are heard in rural villages, by peasants and indigenous peoples; but not by the inhabitants of 'the great city'" (3). Colonia Santo Domingo's residents are muted by those who participate in the trademarking of *Ciudad de México* as "*CDMX*," which is the state-produced emblem of modernity and global capitalism, a topic explored further in this volume's conclusion. As a collective blemish on the self-proclaimed "City of the Future," those living in Colonia Santo Domingo have been systematically quarantined from participating in CDMX's decision-making processes. Arguing that urban segregation is a social war rather than a frozen status quo, Davis (2006) writes that the state intervention in urban land and the redrawing of spatial boundaries is "regularly in the name of 'progress,' 'beautification,' and even 'social justice for the poor'" (98). By redrawing spatial boundaries to re-order the city, developers, investors and elite capitalist entrepreneurs systematically attempt to silence the signas of those who stand in the way of "progress." The silencing is fundamental to the twenty-first century's process of accumulation through dispossession.

The instability brought about by the contestation of urban ordering between Colonia Santo Domingo's original settlers and capitalist developers makes the neighborhood space ripe for revolutionary potential *vis-á-vis* collective organizing. The plantón was just one means of collective organizing. Asamblea members also coordinated neighborhood meetings, political-cultural events, and *faenas*—collective workdays. While organizing different workshops for the demonstrations that were frequently held on Colonia Santo Domingo's streets, Gael, an active member of the Asamblea, gave me the typical list of volunteer options: "Which do you prefer to work," he asked, via Whatsapp, "The chess workshop, the children's workshop, or the food?" Often opting for the children's workshop, I worked alongside many of the group's young mothers who, when attendance was low, would organize games and political-cultural activities with their own children. At one event that Asamblea members organized in conjunction with neighbors in the nearby *Colonia Ajusco*, I spent the day with neighborhood kids coloring pictures of desert landscapes, flowers, and scorpions—all of which represented what the colonia would have looked like when the "great invasion" of settlers arrived in 1971.

After drawing, the children made an altar out of volcanic rock and plastic snakes, birds, and bugs. This altar not only represented the historical topography of the neighborhood, but it also allowed children to practice resistance, hard work, and collective organizing—traits that many members of the neighborhood group hoped to instill and re-instill into Colonia Santo Domingo's youth. Children were made to walk back and forth to a performance stage several times, each time carrying a different, sometimes heavy, item for the altar. Together, after tedious and tiring work, the children accomplished their goal of creating a steady mound of rock where happy plastic snakes, tarantulas, and birds could live. Building up and preserving the Earth and its inhabitants as represented in the altar relates to the ways in which Colonia Santo Domingo was established and should be conserved.

Play became a method to occupy and educate children, as well as adults. According to Mexico City–based geographer, Veronica Crossa (2013), play is "an arena where socially constructed rules and relations can be pushed, expanded, or brought to the surface, facilitating their denaturalization" (841). Many of the neighborhood's tented events functioned as dynamic playful spaces: children not only built altars, but they also often painted political murals and listened to honored originarios as they described the struggles of the neighborhood's initial settlement. Likewise, chess, salsa dancing, good music, and the free taco lunches that were sometimes provided, allowed many adults to join the political festivities and, for many, disrupted mundane daily routines.

Anthropologist Nicole Fabricant (2012), in her work with the Bolivian Worker's Socialist Movement (MST), writes of the ways in which performing music after meals acted as a "vehicle through which MST emotively animated and inspired its bases while reinforcing a particular leftist ideology" (149). Members of the Asamblea, likewise, offered music as one of the main attractions of neighborhood events. In between songs, Doña Fili, one of the neighborhood's most experienced social activists, would often ignite a multitude of chants such as *"Los Pedregales no se venden, se aman y se defienden"*; and *"Los pueblos unidos jamás serán vencidos"*; or *"Fuera Peña!"* (The Pedregales are not for sale, we love them and we defend them; The people, united, will never be defeated; Out with Peña.) Politically charged music, collective shouts, and the salsa dancing that would conclude most political-cultural events, as with their Bolivian counterparts "illustrated a deepening of roots between people and an overcoming or melding of difference" (Fabricant 2012, 150). The festive events also allowed neighbors to learn about the political activities that their fellow neighbors were organizing within the colonia.

To attract a diverse group of neighbors as potential allies, Asamblea members stressed the importance of gluing community members together with nostalgia. To create a sense of unity within the community, group members attempted to appeal to the emotions of other neighbors—tortilla shop owners, local gang members and electricity workers alike were involved in this process. Just as "displacement, migrations, disassembly, and reassembly of life and livelihood link disparate groups in a common struggle to claim territory" among peasants in Bolivia, "framing the present moment as a continuation of an age-old ethnic battle to hold on to historic rights to land, community, and ways of governing . . ." (Fabricant 2012, 51) is apparent in the ways in which

Asamblea members organized and embellished political-cultural events. Large black and white photos of the colonia's first years were strung together and hung by Asamblea members at each *manifestación* (public demonstration) and, on more than one occasion, originarios or their children would, in passing the tented event, stop and comment on the photos, emphatically crying out things like, "Oh look, that's Toñito! He must have been only six or seven in this photo!"

Street art, like the vintage photographs that were displayed at political-cultural events, appealed to a sense of collective nostalgia for the past as well as a creative vision for the future. Painting street murals, in particular, was a significant way that members and allies of the Asamblea re-imagined and re-created visual representations of the past. After returning to Colonia Santo Domingo in August 2016, I was invited to participate in a mass mural making event. The event was inspired by the foreseen water scarcity due to the future construction of the Quiero Casa complex in Colonia Los Reyes. Organized as a collaborative event between Asamblea members and local artists, the theme of each mural was centered on land reclamation and the human right to have access to clean water. The purpose of the event, according to those who made the flyer that was passed out in an attempt to gather muralists, was to publically display the neighborhood's historical relationship to water. After securing permission from a neighborhood church, members of the Asamblea passed out the flyer that announced:

> we need to remember that water is a human right that should be respected, because water is life and life is likewise defended. Our grandparents and parents, they taught us that it was not easy to have basic services like water, light and drainage. Aguantadores [originarios who carried water during the colonia's early years] had to walk across the land carrying buckets of water to their makeshift homes. Today, forty years after exercising this right, we are once again suffering a shortage of water because of the construction of commercial buildings built by large real estate companies that monopolize the water, damage the aquifer, and drain clean water. After hearing this, we cannot help but remember how much our parents and grandparents had to do to make it.

Together, local muralists and Asamblea members convened at the church in order to paint a series of murals that represented water, desolation, and the colonia's unique history of collective workdays and popular struggle. Most artists painted murals by hand, others included phrases that originarios had once said about the neighborhood, and some, in an attempt to attract the participation of non-artists, were stenciled and sprayed. The murals, which were located on a busy avenue, were painted with bright colors to catch the eyes of those passing by. While many of these by passers may not have taken notice of the principal messages that members of the Asamblea were trying to convey, many of those who had no relationship to the community would see the murals and think of the Pedregales as a unified place.

POROSITY AND PEDREGALES

Despite being branded by elites as a space void of proper capitalist development, Colonia Santo Domingo was a fundamental spot for strengthened social relations between neighbors. According to Merrifield (2002), Walter Benjamin saw capitalism and culture—in urbanism and architecture—as porous: making the "economy leaky, subject to subversion, and full of 'unseen constellations'" (58). Like the arcades and shopping malls that Benjamin ([1978] 1986) observes in Paris, there is a particular "porosity" between street spaces and social interactions during political-cultural events: they are sites where "public and private lives get commingled" and ". . . every private attitude or act 'is permeated by streams of communal life'" (Merrifield 2002, 58). The political-cultural events, neighborhood meetings, and demonstrations that Asamblea members orchestrated were located on Colonia Santo Domingo's most densely populated streets and were always open to the public.

Neighborhood solidarity allowed many living in Colonia Santo Domingo to develop their own processes of urban ordering. One Asamblea member communicated this to me after a long day of mural painting: "Pedregales has allowed me to grow up with a sense of friendship and fraternity," she said, "They show us that the hardships can be lessened in communities where solidarity is present—a solidarity [crafted from] the defense of a territory [that was] constructed with our own hands." Solidarity allowed resistance to flourish in Colonia Santo Domingo's un-ordered, or empty, urban fabric.

The playful and deliberately anti-capitalist events that community members organized in Colonia Santo Domingo were orchestrated, likewise, on porous land. Around 200–100 B.C. the volcano, *Xitle*, erupted, and covered the ground with twenty to thirty feet of pedregal. Noting the colonia's landscape, Gutmann (1996) writes, "Because of this solid foundation, the Mexico City earthquake of 1985, which crumpled many central neighborhoods of the capital, did virtually no damage in the Pedregales a few miles to the south. Before the invasion of 1971, the area was a wasteland of volcanic rocks, caves, shrubs, snakes, and scorpions" (34).

Echoing Gutmann's observations, many of my neighbors occasionally talked about the Pedregales as precious, earthquake-proof land that might prove valuable for urban developers seeking to construct skyscrapers on stable terrain. During one neighborhood meeting, Doña Fili described the value of the land and the subsequent anxiety that she and many others felt about gentrification that development could ignite: "The Pedregales are a pirate's gold," she said, "We are a little square, a piece of a sidewalk, that they [the state; big business] are already counting on for millions of, not pesos anymore, but dollars, and that is what our neighborhood is worth, millions of dollars. It is a booty that the capitalists and the bourgeoisie want."

Colonia Santo Domingo's sturdy, igneous landscape was not only an ideal spot for capitalist entrepreneurs who wanted to build on investment-safe spaces, but it was also said to be brimming with the cosmic energy that many of the colonia's original settlers assigned to the neighborhood. My landlady, Renata, for example, once told me stories about the ghosts of those who had lived on the land prior to the 1971 land invasion. "Sometimes I hear the whisper of the originarios, the indígenas—they live underneath us in the rocks," she explained to me one evening. Just as volcanic rocks are "born from fire and originate deep from within the earth" (Taylor 2000, 28), the spirits of the colonia's indigenous inhabitants, according to Renata, continue to dwell within the rocky terrain.

THE MODERNIST ORDERING OF PEDREGAL

Even though they lived and worked within the cash-nexus, many community members were more interested in ordering the neighborhood space as a basis for community building rather than capitalist market exchanges. Acknowledging the ways in which "planned intervention in nature is fundamental to the Western notion of production," anthropologist Tim Ingold (2000, 39) argues that this production-is-progress mentality is not an inherent human attribute. Instead it is socially constructed: through human-made models, scales, and maps, the Earth becomes something to be managed rather than made sacred. Modernity's abstraction of nature is a dualism that "involves the fundamental belief that nature and society are separate realities. Among other things, it provides a cultural rationale for seeing nature in the abstract, an essential step in its classification as a commodity" (Mrozowski 1999, 156). Many of my neighbors did not see themselves as tied to these abstractions because they—or their mothers, fathers, and grandparents—helped to build the colonia with their own hands, a process that forged a lived connection to the colonia's geological and environmental landscape.

Each person in Colonia Santo Domingo, one of my neighbors suggested, "adds a spark to the energy" of the neighborhood. Similar language has been used in literature to describe the colonia's original settlers. Poniatowska (2000) writes, "The thousands of men and women that came to Santo Domingo thought that the waste of space was an injustice when they needed a place to live. For this reason, twenty-nine years ago, in 1971, men, women, and children, raised the colonia over the lava, on inhospitable land where only rocks and vipers lived."[2] According to Poniatowska, Colonia Santo Domingo's *originarios* created their neighborhood over the lava; they worked collectively to transform this disparate "wasteland" into something more. Using pedregal for various purposes over the decades, original settlers transformed the colonia into a space of solidarity and community resistance.

Creating their initial dwellings from pedregal, sheets of scrap metal, tarp, and other salvaged materials, many of Santo Domingo's original settlers—and their respective families—felt a deep connection to their environment. This lived connection, however, gradually entered into the colonia's role within the structures of capitalism's urban reproduction, but did so unevenly as the lived connection to the pedregal underlie the bonds of community. Year after year, the colonia's feeble tented dwellings transformed into cinder-block structures; and today many homes are creative embellishments that reflect the diverse personalities of their occupants. Ingold (2000), writing about dwellings, underscores the so-called building perspective that people share regarding their socially constructed environments. The starting point for such a perspective, he explains, "is an imagined separation between the perceiver and the world, such that the perceiver has to reconstruct the world, in the mind, prior to any meaningful engagement with it" (178). As an abstract ordering of space, socially constructed environments are necessary for the material ordering of space. Nature and humanity, in both spatial order-ings, are distinct—humans dwell on the earth, not within it. The environment, Ingold states, is "given in advance, as a kind of container for life to occupy" (180).

If original settlers perceived the Pedregales to be a "container for life," it was a vessel that they took great care in safeguarding. Many of the colonia's original settlers spent long hours defending their makeshift dwellings after first arriving in the early 1970s. The neighborhood's *originarias*, according to historians Alejandra Massolo (1992) and Fernando Díaz Enciso (2002), protected their homes by throwing pedregal at the *granaderos* (riot police) who attempted to evict them while their husbands were at work during the colonia's early years. Building the community through harsh environmental conditions and with limited resources, *originarios* initially ordered the space that they felt was worth defending. Through this spatial ordering, many of Colonia Santo Domingo's original settlers and their children shared a con-cept of resistance that was rooted in a tension between their being part of the location's geology and environment and the step-by-step capitalization of the neighborhood land.

Settlers who re-ordered Colonia Santo Domingo's volcanic land also helped cultivate the contemporary capital circulation that, in 2015, threatened to displace them. Settlers and their families transformed nature—in this case, *pedregal*—into commodities. The shabby dwellings that settlers built atop volcanic rock in 1971 are now sturdy, alienable properties that can be bought, sold, and rented. Through this process of step-by-step primitive accumulation, land and resources in Mexico City, and other urban and rural spaces worldwide, are exchanged for capital-producing projects. In an unequal transaction, expensive condos and exclusive shopping malls litter cityscapes today, all the while pushing many poor and working-class people to the urban and suburban margins.

Mike Davis (2004, 23), in his *Planet of Slums*, sees informal settlements like Colonia Santo Domingo as geographies of surplus humanity that provide capitalism a cheap source of labor. He takes from the 2003 United Nations Human Settlements Programme (UN Habitat) 2003 Annual Report, entitled *The Challenge of the Slums*: "instead of being a focus for growth and prosperity, the cities have become a dumping ground for a surplus population working in unskilled, unprotected and low-wage informal service industries and trade . . ." (quoted in Davis 2004, 24). Following Davis, we can see that Colonia Santo Domingo, as one of the most densely populated Mexico City neighborhoods, has an important function as providing surrounding neighborhoods and the city at large with surplus labor. Located in the southwestern margin of Mexico City, many of Colonia Santo Domingo's inhabitants find employment as housekeepers, cleaners, or taxi drivers in the nearby wealthy neighborhoods of *San Ángel* or Coyoacán. Colonia Santo Domingo's urban workers, however, are not likely to defend themselves from the very system that devalues their labor-power.

Arguing that "the uprooted rural migrants and informal workers who have been dispossessed" are unlikely to engage in massive social movements because they have "little access to the culture of collective labour or large-scale class struggle," Davis (2004) also questions the revolutionary potential of densely concentrated surplus labor: "But aren't the great slums, as a terrified Victorian bourgeoisie once imagined, volcanoes waiting to erupt?" (28). Again, the metaphor of pedregal is useful for interpreting the possibilities that lie in the aftermath of neoliberal development. The eruption of neoliberal urban development in Mexico City has, in its aftermath left porous, yet durable, volcanic rock.

LOS PEDREGALES: FROM DF TO CDMX

Harvey (2000) writes, "as we collectively produce our cities, so we collectively produce ourselves. Projects concerning what we want our cities to be are, therefore, projects concerning human possibilities, who we want, or, perhaps even more pertinently, who we do not want to become" (159).

Many popular, elite-crafted representations of Santo Domingo—and of working-class neighborhoods more generally—are centered on crime: on the glue-sniffing, organ trafficking, degenerate culture(s) of poverty. These representations conflict with Mexico City's transition from the *Distrito Federal* into the elite branded CDMX. They also incentivize developers to re-order the city's most "underutilized" or "underdeveloped" communities. In short, state officials employ a discourse of development to justify the displacement of Colonia Santo Domingo's original settlers.

"The incessant accumulation of capital across the variegated spaces of the global economy by whatever means" according to Harvey (2003), will end in a moment "full of volatility and uncertainties" but also a moment of "the unexpected and full of potential" (83). To contest accumulation by dispossession, Asamblea members have deployed pedregal as a metaphor of resistance; an imaginative counter-ordering to their own potential displacement. On the eve of my departure, I too ceremoniously received a fist-sized volcanic rock from Doña Fili—the same neighborhood social activist who gave Gutmann this gift fourteen years prior. The value placed on these volcanic rocks differed from the value placed in a commodity system: it was based on "social obligations, connections, and gaps" rather than "things for use and exchange" (Tsing 2013, 22). Volcanic rocks—as pieces of nature that are not ordinarily bought and sold in the marketplace—hold so much more intrinsic value than the venture capitalist, developer, or investor would ever assume. They tie neighbors together under a collective history of struggle and resistance, strengthen existing social relations, and forge new networks of reciprocity with those who become allies or long-lasting compañeros.

Like pedregal, human relationships in Colonia Santo Domingo can also be seen as porous—most neighbors welcomed me into their lives and homes; they absorbed me and others in a large web of ever-expanding social relations. Volcanic rock is made up of gaps, holes, and crevices that allow animals and insects to invade, to burrow, and create their own dwellings. Colonia Santo Domingo, as a dwelling within a dwelling or, to use Poniatowska's (2000) words, "a city within a city," has its own social gaps: gaps between urban investors and neighbors, neighbors and outsiders, and neighbors and other neighbors. The same porous cavities, however, allow some igneous rocks to float in water—they, like the ideal social movement, are solid and unsinkable despite the overwhelming pressure to comply with the top-down, elite driven spatial re-ordering of their neighborhood.

Like pedregal, Colonia Santo Domingo's originarios were imagined by some neighbors to be strong and resilient; unwilling to break under the capitalist projects that were rapidly re-ordering their environment. As ancient, durable forces, pedregales can be moved and displaced, but cannot be destroyed easily. Doña Fili concluded one important neighborhood meeting by pulling out and passing around a fist-sized volcanic rock, one that she brought to nearly every protest and neighborhood event. This rock represented the community symbolically: Santo Domingo, like the pedregal, is resistant and comprised of a powerful cosmic energy. While colonias populares such as Colonia Santo Domingo may be lost to corporate developers and elite business owners, the volcanic rocks and the ghosts of those who dwell within them will remain, steadfast in resistance.

NOTES

1. *QUIERO CASA FAM. SHABOT EN COMPLICIDAD CON EL GOBIERNO TIRARON EN 1 AÑO MAS DE 1500 MILLONES DE LITROS DE AGUA EN EL DRENAJE Y AHORA LA ESTÁN CONTAMINANDO.*

2. *Los miles de hombres y mujeres que llegaron a Santo Domingo pensaron que era injusto el desperdicio del espacio cuando a ellos les urgía un lugar para vivir. Por eso, hace 29 años, en 1971, hombres, mujeres y niños levantaron la colonia sobre la lava, en una tierra inhóspita en la que sólo vivían piedras y víboras.*

WORKS CITED

Agencia de Gestión Urbana. 2015. "GDF atraer inversión extranjera para diversos proyectos." February 4.

Benjamin, Walter. (1978) 1986. *Reflections: Essays, Aphorisms, Autobiographical Writings*, edited and translated by Peter Demetz. New York: Schocken Books.

Castells, Manuel. 1983. *The City and the Grassroots: A Cross-Cultural Theory of Urban Social Movements*. Berkeley: University of California Press.

Crossa, Veronica. 2012. "Play for Protest, Protest for Play: Artisan and Vendors' Resistance to Displacement in Mexico City." *Antipode* 45 (4): 826–43.

Davis, Mike. 2006. *Planet of Slums*. New York: Verso.

Enciso, Fernando Díaz. 2009. *Las mil y una historias del Pedregal De Santo Domingo*. Ciudad de México: Conaculta.

Fabricant, Nicole. 2012. *Mobilizing Bolivia's Displaced: Indigenous Politics and the Struggle over Land*. Chapel Hill: University of North Carolina Press.

Fragoso, Ariana Mendoza. 2016. "Memoria y comunidad frente a la gentrificación." Unpublished manuscript.

Gutmann, Matthew. 1996. *The Meanings of Macho: Being a Man in Mexico City*. Berkeley: University of California Press.

———. 2002. *The Romance of Democracy: Compliant Defiance in Contemporary Mexico*. Berkeley: University of California Press.

Harvey, David. 1972. "Revolutionary and Counter Revolutionary Theory in Geography and the Problem of Ghetto Formation." *Antipode* 4 (2): 1–3.

———. 2000. *Spaces of Hope*. Berkeley: University of California Press.

————. 2003. *The New Imperialism.* New York: Oxford University Press.

Ingold, Tim. 2000. *The Perception of the Environment: Essays on Livelihood, Dwelling and Skill.* London: Routledge.

Lewis, Oscar. 1963. "The Culture of Poverty." *Society* 1 (1): 17–19.

Massolo, Alejandra, ed. 1992. *Mujeres y ciudades: Participación social, vivienda y vida cotidiana.* Mexico City: El Colegio de México.

Merrifield, Andy. 2002. *Metromarxism: A Marxist Tale of the City.* New York: Routledge.

Mrozowski, Stephen. 1999. "Colonization and the Commodification of Nature." *International Journal of Historical Archaeology* 3 (3) (September): 153–166.

Poniatowska, Elena. 2000. "Las invasión del Pedregal De Santo Domingo." *La Jornada, Octubre* 21. Accessed June 22, 2017. http://www.jornada.unam.mx/2000/10/21/05aa1cul.html

Reveles, Karla. 2015. "'La ciudad del futuro' y Las ZODES de Mancera." *De la Izquierda Diario.* Accessed June 23, 2017. http://www.laizquierdadiario.com/spip.php?page=gacetilla-articulo&id_rubrique=2653&id_article=23277

Schumpeter, Joseph A. (1942) 1994. *Capitalism, Socialism and Democracy.* London: Routledge.

Sirvín, Mirna and Agustín Salgado. 2015. "Protestan En Coyoacán por supuesta desaparición de niños." *La Jornada, Abril* 20. Accessed June 22, 2017. http://www.jornada.unam.mx/ultimas/2015/04/20/protestan-en-coayoacan-por-desaparicion-de-ninos-4496.html

Suárez, Gerardo. 2015. "Santo Domingo, Bastión En Punga." *El Universal, Abril* 29.

Taylor, Charles. 2000. *The Kingfisher Science Encyclopedia.* New York: Kingfisher.

Tsing, Anna. 2005. *Friction: An Ethnography of Global Connection.* Princeton, NJ: Princeton University Press.

————. 2013. "Sorting out Commodities: How Capitalist Value is Made Through Gifts." *HAU: Journal of Ethnographic Theory* 3 (1): 21–43.

UN Habitat. 2003. *The Challenge of the Slums: Global Report on Human Settlements 2003.* London: Earthscan.

Ward, Peter. 1978. "Self-Help Housing in Mexico City: Social and Economic Determinants of Success." *Town Planning Review* 49 (1): 38–50.

Chapter 9

Sense-Making in the Megalopolis

Navigating Korean Signs in Pequeño Seúl

Karen Velasquez

This chapter explores the tension between linguistic order and disorder in the megalopolis, through an analysis of Korean business signs in Pequeño Seúl (Koreatown), located in the *Zona Rosa* (Pink Zone, or nightlife district) neighborhood of *Colonia Juárez*, Mexico City. The chapter considers how business signs and the messages they communicate help us to understand how people make sense of spaces they encounter in the megalopolis. It attempts to further understand the ways linguistic landscapes help constitute the urban form.

Amid the apparent disarray of information encountered in the city, there are always recognizable patterns that help people find their way and make sense of their surroundings. As people navigate a megalopolis like Mexico City, they engage in sense-making processes, actively deciphering the familiar and unfamiliar signs that adorn the city's landscapes. Signs inscribed on city streets tell stories about how people make sense of the places the live, work, and play in. Both newcomers and natives are continuously decoding the products and artifacts of linguistic evolution within the signs as they make their way through the city. This process of sense-making is deeply tied to place-making and the deeper structures of urban ordering. By learning to read signs around us, spaces become identifiable as distinct, knowable places. The creative tension between an idealized version of symbolic order and the everyday disorder of the city make the megalopolis come to life, even if in a delirious fashion. In Pequeño Seúl, Korean language and culture becomes a deeper part of Mexico City's identity as business signs become more recognizable to visitors and locals.

In the last decade, linguistic landscaping studies and the field of geosemiotics have emerged as ways of understanding the social and cultural construction of urban spaces through the analysis of linguistic artifacts (see,

191

for example, Backhaus 2007). A linguistic landscape refers to "the visibility and salience of languages on public and commercial signs in a given territory or region" including "public road signs, advertising billboards, street names, place names, commercial shop signs, and public signs on government buildings" that combine to "form the linguistic landscape of a given territory, region, or urban agglomeration" (Landry and Bourhis 1997, 25). According to Blommaert (2013), "The locus where such landscapes are being documented is usually the late-modern globalized city: a densely multilingual environment in which publicly visible written language documents the presence of a wide variety (linguistically identifiable) groups of people" (5). Signs are complex semiotic systems that vary in appearance, function, visibility, and placement, and also convey a great deal of information about a city and its inhabitants. The relationship between sign, signifier, and signified that defines the processes within semiotic systems carries the symbiotic relationship between order and disorder, which provides the link between the symbolic meanings of signs and urban place-making.

In the Mexico City iteration of the megalopolis, there are many markers of cultural and linguistic diversification inscribed on publicly visible signs. Some of these are official markers created by the city government, its agencies, or major companies with a close relationship with the state. Others are more informal processes of forming linguistic landscapes from below as neighborhood residents post signs for a variety of purposes. The main thrust of this chapter's use of linguistic landscapes is their formation from below in Mexico City's Koreatown.

By framing the signs in Pequeño Seúl as a unit, the "linguistic landscape," this chapter imbues an imaginary order and structure to a dynamic, often chaotic neighborhood within Mexico City's Zona Rosa. These signs form a collective ensemble or urban assemblage that make Pequeño Seúl recognizable and identifiable to locals and visitors. There is, however, a constant interplay and destabilizing tension between the production of signs and the way the signs are read and understood. As Korean businesses try to market and sell their goods by creating these signs, they are attempting to instill an order into the megalopolis. While not Ángel Rama's ([1984] 1996) original conception of the "lettered city," their signs are a lettering of the city, in which the signifier makes a sign that attempts to signify an urban space. The signs tell potential customers that they are in Koreatown, and this semiotic place-making is crucial for the business owners to market their products. Not only are business owners interested in making signs that market their products, Koreans are also invested in making their goods appear culturally authentic. Through the production of signs, Korean business owners try to communicate their authenticity in order to draw in customers seeking the true "ethnic" Koreatown experience, and the more authentic, the better.

KOREANS AND PLACE-MAKING IN MEXICO CITY

The most recent wave of Korean migration to Mexico accelerated in the 1990s and 2000s. In 1997, 2,000 Korean immigrants were residing in Mexico, and by 2003, there were 17,000. In 2003, 70 percent of these immigrants worked in various businesses, 10 percent were students, and 9 percent were business owners (Castilla 2009). Not all Koreans in Mexico City work in Zona Rosa or Colonia Juárez; a segment of middle- and upper-class Koreans in Mexico City work for transnational Korean corporations, such as car manufacturing, media, and technology businesses. A working-class and lower middle-class segment of the Korean population run small businesses and vendor stalls in *Tepito,* which is infamous for its black market. Koreans there compete with Mexican merchants and sell electronics, fashion accessories, and apparel. Mexican merchants in Tepito informed me that Mexican and Koreans conduct business in a segregated fashion in the informal market. According to the community leaders who oversee the market, I also learned that there are few instances of overt conflict between the groups. There are also some stories of illegal activities in Tepito that involve Koreans who were caught selling black market items (Cevallos 2003).

Koreans who work and reside in the Zona Rosa primarily arrived during post-1980 migration waves. Castilla (2009) describes the changes in Korean migration over the course of the twentieth century-from their arrival as *henequen* contract workers in the Yucatán at the start of the century to business owners in Colonia Juárez. He argues that areas like Pequeño Seúl represent the transient or floating character (*"el caracter flotante"*) of Korean communities in the city. Castilla asserts that Koreans migrate in search of economic opportunity and their constant movement inhibits them from establishing a permanent presence in Pequeño Seúl. Despite Castillo's assertion that Korean communities of Tepito and Zona Rosa would move on to the next profitable location for their businesses, my field work suggests that they have continued to endure and expand their businesses in these neighborhoods. They are not as transient as one might assume based on Castillo's narrative.

The growth of Mexico City's Korean population should be seen as part of a broader pattern of migration to the megalopolis. In the past few decades, Mexico City's immigrant population has grown, and newcomers are constantly competing with locals for economic opportunities around the city. Internal migrants from Mexico have also traveled to Mexico City in search of a better quality of life for their families. Using statistics from Mexico's *Instituto Nacional de Estadística y Geografía* (National Statistic and Geography Institute) Anna Winiarczyk-Raźniak and Piotr Raźniak (2014) state, "the ethnic minorities of Ciudad de México (Mexico City) are a true conglomerate of languages and cultures. This degree of ethnic diversity remains unmatched anywhere in Mexico" (96). Mexico's national census identifies 70 different ethnic indigenous languages, and 58 of these languages can be found in Mexico City.

As a factor of the globalizing forces that have redefined the country, Mexico's foreign-born population nearly doubled between 2000 and 2010. Mexico has attracted growing numbers of immigrants from the United States, Europe, Asia, and Latin America. Immigrants, according to Damien Cave (2013), are "becoming a larger proportion of the population and a growing part of the economy and culture, opening new restaurants, designing new buildings, financing new cultural offerings and filling a number of schools with their children. . . . Economics has been the primary motivator for members of all classes." Economic opportunity is a major catalyst in bringing international migrants to Mexico City, and Koreans have been part of this diasporic trend. Best estimates show that up to 20,000 Korean immigrants live in Mexico, and approximately 12,000 of them live in Mexico City (Cave 2013).

Indeed, the presence of the Asian diaspora in Mexico City has captured the attention of the international media. *The Economist* (2006), for example, informed its readers: "today, the economic realities of globalisation have displaced political migration as the driving force behind Mexico City's multiculturalism. This has resulted, among other things, in a rich and diverse culinary scene . . . many visitors to what is one of the world's largest capitals will be struck by a visible Asian influence in its bars and restaurants." This cosmopolitan trend in multiculturalism is a key feature in Mexico City's efforts at becoming a "world city," which is a topic explored in this volume's conclusion. Pequeño Seúl is part of this trend, as it is a place where visitors experience a linguistic landscape in which the Korean language lives and thrives on many visible spaces. This presence is a result of the Korean community's effort at communicating and marketing their cultural presence, which inserts Korean culture into Mexico City's established norms and orderings of urban spaces. In Pequeño Seúl, the growing Korean presence both destabilizes local orderings through its cultural insertion, while also adding to the city's multicultural ordering. This tension demonstrates the ways immigrant communities add to the inherent tensions between order and disorder in a megalopolis like Mexico City.

Koreans have worked toward achieving greater solidarity with each other and the surrounding Mexican communities, through their work in cultural and religious organizations, where they offer services translated for Spanish audiences. Their media presence is expanding and more Koreans are seeing the benefit of organizing and growing their customer base.

According to the editor of *Sección Coreana* (*Hanin Sinmun* 2015), a Korean magazine produced and printed in Mexico City, Korean businesses in Zona Rosa are primarily bounded by *Calle Sevilla*, where *Metro Sevilla* is located, and *Calle Genova*, which borders with *Metro Insurgentes*, *Paseo de la Reforma*, and *Avenida Chapultepec*. There are several businesses that exist outside these parameters of course, but the Korean magazine has deliberately drawn these boundaries to show where the majority of businesses exist. The magazine staff is conducting its own Korean business mapping processes to get a sense of where Koreans conduct their business, and who consumes their print material. *Sección Coreana* and the Korean newspaper *Hanin Dario* are sold in shops throughout Zona Rosa, and can be found beside Chinese and Spanish language newspapers.

PEQUEÑO SEÚL AND PLACE-MAKING IN ZONA ROSA

Walking around Zona Rosa, there is a palpable and vibrant energy that fills the streets. As more Korean immigrants have become established in the city, Mexicans and international tourists have been increasingly exposed to Korean language and culture. First and second generation Koreans have experienced a Mexico City that is increasingly diverse and accepting of the plural identities that thrive and flourish in the megalopolis. Part of this diversity comes from Zona Rosa's "red-light" district libertine culture, as well as Mexico City's increasingly liberal posturing. Mexico City's queer and trans-gendered population, for example, found safe space within Zona Rosa during the late 1980s and early 1990s, an opening that by the late 2000s became a vibrant queer space equal to any world city's. Pequeño Seúl has historically developed alongside Mexico City's queer and transgendered spaces in Zona Roza, a development that marks the megalopolis's status as a cosmopolitan, world city.

Koreans formed a popular cultural center that offers language classes of varying difficulty levels. During one weekend visit to the cultural center, I observed Korean language classes with Mexican and Korean teenagers/young adults who had signed up weeks in advance to enroll in the lessons. As a result of the growing popularity of Korean popular culture in the region, Mexican youth have become cultural ambassadors for Korea. Korean pop music, films, and dramas have gained enormous attention and influence in Mexico and many other parts of Latin America, an unexpected surprise for Korean media corporations. In 2015 alone, Latin American viewership on popular Korean drama site DramaFever jumped by 250 percent, and Latin American viewers now account for over 30 percent of DramaFever's viewers (*Latin Post* 2016). Some restaurants in Pequeño Seúl display Korean music videos for customers while they enjoy their meals. When I arrived in Mexico City I was pleasantly surprised to learn it was Korean international movie festival week, and Korean films were playing at major movie theaters all around the city. I watched two Korean films with Spanish subtitles at a movie theater near Zona Rosa, both of which drew large audiences.

On any given day in the neighborhood, one can find Mexicans enjoying Korean food and shopping, or singing *karaoke* in the jovial nightlife ambiance. As a result, Pequeño Seúl has become a center of this pop cultural explosion and "Korean wave" fascination. At the same time, there are many Mexicans who have never been inside a Korean establishment even though they live and work in or near Pequeño Seúl.

Mexico City's government has recognized the Korean community's efforts and abilities to attract visitors. In December 2016, for example, the city government teamed up with the Korean Culture Center to launch the first annual Korean street festival in Pequeño Seúl, with support from the South Korean Foreign Ministry and the Korean Culture and Information Service (Yonhap News Agency 2016). The festival included traditional Korean percussion music, K-pop music performances, Korean food stalls, traditional Korean *hanbok* dress, Korean calligraphy lessons, places to play the Korean board game *baduk*, among other activities. The event successfully introduced many people to Korean food, music, and dance, and fostered greater "cultural exchange" between Mexicans and Koreans.

While the December 2016 street festival exposed more people to the linguistic landscape of Pequeño Seúl, and provides those who return with context for deeper understandings, the festival's ordering of Pequeño Seúl was limited in time and numbers of people reached. After the Korean stalls and vendors that clearly marked the presence of Pequeño Seúl were taken down, the space returned to being one part of Zona Rosa, a part that is a fragmented landscape of Korean symbols scattered along the streets.

PEQUEÑO SEÚL AS A LINGUISTIC LANDSCAPE

Although various efforts have been made by the Korean community to become a noticeable presence in Zona Rosa, the extent to which visitors in the area actually attempt to make sense of Korean symbols and signs is unclear. The point at which signs become meaningful and relevant depends on several factors, especially the individual's familiarity and prior experience with Korean language and culture. These symbols and signs can hold multiple, contested meanings for diverse audiences, and are open for interpretation. The interpretive work of reading a landscape can be a conscious effort or a subtle process.

It is difficult to know precisely how this process unfolds for each individual, but there are clues embedded in linguistic landscapes that suggest possible avenues or reading pathways. No matter how foreign, every linguistic system has "structuration principles"—cues that guide people through ambiguity inherent in making sense of a language. In a linguistic landscape of foreign signs, an individual sign may not hold any particular significance—but collectively experienced, the signs take on greater meaning. From a disordered assemblage, emerges order, and the visitor suddenly finds herself experiencing a piece of Korean culture in a globalized megalopolis.

And that is precisely what I experienced during my fieldwork in Mexico City. I ate at various Korean restaurants and bakeries in Koreatown, observed workplace interactions, and talked with Mexican employees whenever I had the chance. I focused primarily on Korean food businesses because they were abundant and amenable to participant observation, and I spent most of my time documenting linguistic evidence on business signs.

Zona Rosa's Koreatown manifests many of the characteristics of a linguistic landscape. Among them is the flow of linguistic information that balances uneasily for the viewer between noise and information, what Mark Taylor (2001) calls the "moment of chaos," the point when data either emerges from noise and becomes a recognizable order or it shifts from an ordered state of information and becomes disordered and unrecognizable noise. A key concept within the study of linguistic landscapes is understanding this interplay between order and disorder, as clearly presented in the introduction to Elana Shohamy, Eliezer Ben-Rafael, and Monica Barni's *Linguistic Landscape in the City* (2010a). Their consideration of ordering mechanisms within linguistic landscapes invites us to think about how to decipher Koreatown's place within the megalopolis's order and disorder by seeing the "disorder reigning in the linguistic landscape by trying to single out given structuration principles accounting for its moulding—however chaotic it appears on the surface" (xvi). The structuration principles that give order and meaning to linguistic landscapes, however, can be tricky, as they are often "diverse, uncoordinated and possibly incongruent" (Shohamy, Ben-Rafael, and Barni 2010b, 345). The approach is to see beyond the linguistic landscape's "appearance as a jungle of jumbled items, and grasp the intermingling of those structuring principles that makes of LL [linguistic landscapes] a system" (345–346). In this fashion, linguistic landscapes help to find the order within disorder of places like Zona Rosa, an often delirious landscape within the delirious city.

A TYPOLOGY OF SIGNS IN PEQUEÑO SEÚL

To help identify the structuration of the underlying order within the diversity, instability, and chaos of Koreatown's linguistic landscape, we need to look for the emergent properties within the signs posted by Korean storeowners. These properties reveal the articulated patterns of the structures of meaning that help to order the space we know as "Koreatown." Charlotte Blair, who has a chapter in this volume, accompanied me around Zona Rosa, and together we photographed all the non-Spanish language shop signs we could find in the neighborhood. We observed visible public signs—storefronts, awnings, posters, advertisements visible from the street—in order to capture a snapshot of the linguistic landscape. We took pictures of 205 signs in five languages: Korean, English, Chinese, Japanese, and Sanskrit. This section of the chapter seeks to create a typology of the structures from this data. It identifies five distinct types of signs: Mixed language signs, pictures of food, characters and imagery, English on Korean signs, and Romanized Korean Signs. These signs contribute to the construction of the linguistic landscape, and constitute a structured assemblage of meaning for people as they experience this part of the megalopolis.

Mixed Language Signs

In Figure 9.1, a Korean restaurant sign found in Zona Rosa incorporates pictures of Korean dishes (*galbi* on the left, *bibimbap* on the right), Spanish (*restaurante coreano,* meaning "Korean restaurant"), Romanized Korean (*Biwon,* meaning Secret Garden), Chinese characters, and Mexican beer logos. The beer logos may appeal to a Mexican audience who recognize the brand, serving as a relatable, familiar symbol. The Chinese characters on the sign mean "South Korea." The inclusion of Chinese on Korean storefronts might be an attempt to market their food to Chinese speakers by making it easy for them to recognize what kind of food is served at the restaurant. It may also indicate that the storeowner speaks Chinese or is Chinese-Korean.

In the Korean Red Ginseng storefront shown in Figure 9.2, there is a combination of Chinese, English, and Korean language, product logos, and the

Figure 9.1   Mixed Language Sign, Korean Restaurant. *Source:* Author's photo.

Figure 9.2   Mixed Language Sign, Red Ginseng Storefront. *Source*: Author's photo.

business telephone number. Translated into English, the prominent Chinese characters mean "original," possibly an attempt to market a sense of product authenticity to a Chinese-speaking audience. The sign may also be attempting to invoke a sense of prestige and modernity by incorporating English, a language that also carries significant symbolic value in Mexican business advertisements.

There were also instances of informal, typed or handwritten "help wanted" signs posted on several Korean businesses around Zona Rosa. Many of these ads were written in Spanish. Small typed or handwritten signs can be found around Pequeño Seúl, posted outside of Korean businesses (see Figure 9.3). The signs are public notices indicating that the businesses are hiring new employees. Because they are written in Spanish, they appeal to a local Mexican audience. In my fieldwork based in Koreatown, New York City, I found that Mexicans often served as translators and interpreters for Koreans. In this case of Pequeño Seúl in Zona Rosa, it is possible that Koreans rely on their Mexican workers to help recruit new employees and facilitate

Figure 9.3 **"Help Wanted" Signs.** *Source*: Author's photo.

their transition and training. Although the signs were most likely written by Mexican employees, it is also possible that Koreans could have authored the signs themselves, due to several years of interaction and informal language learning at the workplace.

In the signs depicted in Figure 9.3, it is evident that female employees are preferred over males; three of the five signs specify *"empleada"* (female employee). The others advertise positions that are non-gender specific—"lava losa" (dishwasher) or ayudante de cocina (kitchen assistant). On another sign, a person has responded to the ad by using a pen to write in (and then crossing out) the question "fuerte?" (strong?) along with a drawing of a muscular arm, as though asking the creator of the sign to specify whether or not physical strength is a requirement of the position. Koreatown in New York City provides an interesting contrast; men were often hired instead of women for work in the Korean food industry. Unfortunately, Mexican and Korean men in the Korean food industry of New York often assumed that women wouldn't be capable of keeping up with the physical demands of restaurant work. In Koreatown New York City, handwritten/informal signs were not popular ways of recruiting employees; rather, Mexicans were primarily hired through informal networks and Korean employment agencies. The use of typed or handwritten signs as an informal method of recruiting employees demonstrates that Koreans do not rely entirely on their staff to supply new labor through their existing connections. The signs could also indicate that there is a high turnover rate for Mexican employees in Zona Rosa, in the same way that there is a high turnover of Mexican employees in Korean businesses of New York City.

Other handwritten signs were bilingual, intended for both Korean and Spanish literate audiences. Some signs posted outside of Korean businesses in Zona Rosa are written in both Korean and Spanish, indicating that a store is open or closed for business. One sign said "no smoking" in Korean, and in small, almost undetectable handwriting above the Korean words, the Spanish translation (*no fumar por favor* [no smoking please]). Such signs may indicate that some Koreans are responding to employees' demands and expectations by closing their businesses for one day per week. Mexicans in Zona Rosa may exhibit some control over work conditions that many Mexicans in Koreatown New York City could not as a result of their unauthorized legal status. The editor of Korean newspaper I interviewed indicated that Koreans prefer to keep their businesses open 7 days a week, whereas Mexicans refuse to work on Sundays (or at least one day per week). He noted a difference of "work ethic" or "work habits/dispositions" between Koreans and Mexicans.

Pictures of Food

Pictures of food were also prevalent on signs around Pequeño Seúl. Korean restaurants often advertise their food offerings by posting pictures of the restaurant menu on the restaurant facade. Names of Korean dishes, in *Hangul* and Romanized Korean, are often accompanied by corresponding pictures and Spanish translations that help people understand the contents of each dish. Pictures are especially helpful in facilitating communication between Korean speakers and non-Korean speakers. Pictures also appeal to the curiosity of potential customers by offering them images of food served in the restaurant. If a Korean employee is unable to explain the contents of the dish to customers, he or she can always refer to the pictures as a reference.

During one of my dining experiences at a Korean restaurant in Pequeño Seúl, a Mexican pedestrian approached the outside of the restaurant to observe the large picture menu posted outside. He glanced at me as I enjoyed my food and asked whether it was any good; I answered positively and he continued to decipher the picture menu. He was eventually swayed to step inside the restaurant and I heard him ask the Mexican waiter various questions about the dishes. The waiter then pulled out a binder full of menu items with corresponding pictures, then proceeded to explain, in Spanish, what the customer could expect from his dining experience, as the Korean cooks stood on standby waiting for his order. However, despite all of the explanations, the customer was not entirely convinced and decided to leave the restaurant. One issue that Mexicans who are unfamiliar with Korean food may have difficulty justifying are the prices; Korean food, especially BBQ meat, traditionally costs more than most kinds of dishes.

Characters and Imagery

Fun characters, like the Korean girl wearing traditional Korean dress seen in Figure 9.4, draw people into signs with their bright colors and cute appeal. They are commonly found on Korean business signs in the neighborhood. Characters are relatable images that can be understood by people of many different cultural and linguistic backgrounds. They may help bridge a gap in translation by embodying the food served in the restaurant; for example, the pig pictured in Figure 9.4 is holding a pork dish in his hand, and the dumpling character with a face is posted on a dumpling store. In the sign shown in Figure 9.5 for Korean restaurant Min Sok Chon (민속촌), one sees images of

Figure 9.4   Fun Character Signs for Curb Appeal. *Source:* Author's photo.

Figure 9.5   Sign with Image of a Traditional Meal. *Source:* Author's photo.

a traditional Korean meal gathering. These are pictures of village area, with Koreans men, women, and children eating together while seated on the floor of a hut or tent house; a traditional Korean historical scene. They may communicate and advertise an ideal style eating that might be replicated inside the restaurant; an intimate experience with friends gathered around the table sharing big plates and bowls together, a traditional Korean way of eating. In addition to the images, the sign also features Korean, Romanized Korean, and Chinese text. Min Sok Chon alludes to the name of a village in Korea, and is intended to reference Korean history and traditions. This imagery thus evokes a sense of authenticity.

English on Korean Signs

Several Korean business signs also incorporated English into their advertisements. Of all non-Spanish languages featured on business advertisements in Zona Rosa, English was most prominent. English could be found on nearly every street in Zona Rosa; on advertisements for mainstream brands and in catchy business names. Despite their prevalence in the neighborhood, unlike Korean signs, English signs in Pequeño Seúl are not necessarily tied to a particular sociolinguistic community in the same way Korean signs are, but their salience demonstrates the fact that English remains a dominant minority language in this area of the megalopolis. The use of English may serve multiple purposes: to appeal to diverse tourists using English as an "international language"; or to add an element of exclusivity/authenticity to their advertisements, since English in "South Korea . . . is clearly considered a prestige language" (Galloway & Rose 2015, 134). Korean speakers often incorporate many English "loan words" in their speech, and the two languages are becoming increasingly used together as "Konglish" by Korean youth who can code-switch with ease. Some of these businesses are chain restaurants such as Coffine Gurunaru; the business names and signs outside these shops are most likely created and designed in Korea, where English is commonly found on city streets.

Romanized Korean Signs

Romanized Korean can be found as frequently as Korean around Pequeño Seúl (see Figure 9.6), and is a feature of signs around Koreatowns internationally. Romanized Korean is the pronunciation of Korean words using the Roman alphabet. There are some different reasons why business owners decide to spell out the business name with both character sets. It helps non-Korean speakers pronounce Korean words in a familiar alphabet. It may also make the business seem more "familiar" to linguistic outsiders; even if they

Figure 9.6 Romanized Korean Signs. *Source:* Author's photo.

don't know what the words mean, they can recognize and identify the letters. This familiarization process is an important part of place-making in Pequeño Seúl: small signals referencing familiar symbols transform space into place.

As we have seen, Korean business signs in Pequeño Seúl contain a variety of images and multilingual texts that communicate particular messages in a range of different ways. Collectively, these signs assemble to create an order that constitutes an identity, Pequeño Seúl. It is a knowable identity to those who engage this space within Zona Rosa and the delirious megalopolis. As an assemblage, they serve as markers that guide the passer-by looking for Koreatown as they meander out of the metro, exit taxis, or enter the Zona Rosa by foot. While some visitors might find *Hangul* (the Korean alphabet) on signs to suffice, most others need the assemblage to realize they've landed in the right place. The assemblage provides a stabilizing ordering within the noise of the diverse, multilingual, and chaotic linguistic landscape that infuses the megalopolis.

Linguistic Landscapes and the Right to the City in Pequeño Seúl

Koreatown's linguistic landscape demonstrates the tense balance between order and disorder, where the instability and changeability of an urban neighborhood, vulnerable to so many forces of urban transformation, carries the potential for throwing the signs back into a state of disordered noise. Shohamy, Ben-Rafael, and Barni (2010a) view the linguistic landscape as a "jungle," where, "At first glance, this jungle is, as the term indicates, an extreme example of disorder. New LL items sprout incessantly with the inauguration of new institutions and stores, with the launch of new gadgets and products, and changing window displays. Old LL items disappear just as rapidly, when businesses close down or a department store changes hands. This instability is instantly visible in any central area of a transglobal metropolis" (p. xv).

When studying the linguistic landscape of any place, it is important to remember these "transglobal" forces that contributed to its creation, and which continue to order and disorder its existence. Political and economic pressures have historically exerted pressures on people to migrate and find was to survive in new contexts while facing marginalization and oppression in the process of looking for a better life for their families and communities.

Yet Mexico City has been home to diverse languages and cultures for many centuries. More than ever before, it is a globalized, internationalized city where people from around the world pursue their dreams of finding economic and educational opportunities (Cave 2013). It is a place where tens of thousands of rural migrants, international refugees, and foreign-born immigrants (both documented and undocumented) temporarily and permanently reside. Groups ranging from *Nahua* speaking peasants to Korean entrepreneurs introduce their languages, foods, religions, popular culture, and educational practices to the ever-changing Mexico City landscape that drives the delirious nature of the megalopolis. Chinese, Americans, Spaniards, Lebanese, Mixtecs, to name a few, have developed language schools, businesses, religious sites of worship, and cultural centers across the city. They have all claimed their own linguistic landscape, asserted their culture identity, and participated in the continuous re-ordering of Mexico City's urban form. As agents of transformation creating diverse linguistic landscapes, they are examples of Henri Lefebvre ([1968] 2015) and David Harvey's (2008) "right to the city." While they exercise the right to transform the city, they also experience the right to be transformed by the city, which is the fundamental human right to grow, learn, develop, and realize one's human potential. These diverse inhabitants are carving out a place for themselves around the city, while negotiating their position as minorities in Spanish language-dominant and *mestizo*-majority contexts.

Not all Koreans have been equally successful in their Pequeño Seúl businesses within the transglobal processes that make up the Mexico City megalopolis. Despite various strategies such as offering translated signs and menus for the Spanish speaking public, there is still a great gap between Mexicans and Koreans, in the sense that immigrants in the city often go unnoticed. Although the Korean language is increasingly part of the megalopolis's identity, it is not recognized as a minority language of Mexico City. Journalist Cesar Fernando Zapata (2013) has critiqued his fellow Mexicans for forgetting that Mexico is also home to many immigrants: "Who remembers, for example, the immigrants who live in Mexico? We don't even remember that Mexico also has agents of immigration."[1]

COMPARATIVE CONTEXT: PEQUEÑO SEÚL
AND NEW YORK CITY'S KOREATOWN

To better see the relationship between the right to the city and the order and disorder of the linguistic landscape, we can turn to a comparison between Pequeño Seúl and New York City's Koreatown. From 2011 to 2014 I conducted fieldwork with Latin American immigrants employed in food businesses such as supermarkets and restaurants around Koreatown neighborhoods located in Manhattan and Queens, New York City. I analyzed how Latinos (most of whom originated in Mexico) and Koreans communicate and learn languages through their workplace interactions. Although none of the Mexicans in my study had any background knowledge of the Korean language or food before arriving to work in Koreatown, over time workers developed a repertoire of knowledge about Korean words and phrases and most incorporated Korean food into their diets. Over time and through their work interactions, Koreans and Latinos gained an understanding of each others' languages and cultures.

When I first began exploring Koreatown, New York City, I was just as clueless about Koreatown as the Latino immigrants were when they arrived for their first day of work. Walking around the street and observing the facades of various Korean businesses, things seemed indistinguishable and chaotic. The shapes of Hangul characters were completely foreign to me and I struggled to comprehend the logic and order behind the flashy signs. Although I knew they were trying to lure me into their business by advertising pictures of Korean dishes and displaying big bold neon signs, I felt like an outsider for many weeks and months. I needed the help of my Latino informants who explained the lay of the land and guided me through the symbols and layers of meaning around me. Latinos were valuable teachers and translators who imparted insider knowledge about the communities in which they lived and worked. Thus with their help, I ceased to be a complete outsider, and I was able to make sense of the Koreatown linguistic landscape that at one point in time seemed incomprehensible.

I became acquainted with the fundamentals of Korean language by learning what the Mexican workers had learned through their years in Koreatown. I studied restaurant menus like the Mexicans did and joined them for walks around the neighborhood where they taught me to associate certain phrases and signs on storefronts with particular goods and services. I became a student of Korean and found a Korean tutor, a Korean waitress who married her Mexican coworker. I made friends with Korean employers and employees, and enlisted the help of my Korean-American neighbor who continues to be one of my best friends and is also my Korean language translator. I also ate large quantities of Korean food. And suddenly my surroundings started to make sense; although I could not read Korean, even after months of Korean lessons, the signs seemed to hold meaning and no longer appeared as impossible to understand as they had in the beginning of my fieldwork. And then Koreatown gained special meaning for me, as more than just another city space—I had built associations with the city by expanding my repertoires of linguistic and cultural knowledge.

The closer I became with people in the community, the less social distance there was between me and the Koreatown community—the more the linguistic landscape seemed to speak to me. I read without being able to read, and navigated without having a fixed or stable understanding of the semiotic field around me. For me it was a fascinating research topic, but for my informants, their livelihoods depended on this ability to make sense of a foreign language and communicate across linguistic and cultural boundaries. The stakes were high for unauthorized immigrants in Koreatown, who were often subject to exploitation and discrimination as in the United States. Language is a means to find one's place, a sense of belonging, a necessary element of protecting and representing oneself in often precarious situations.

Upon arriving to Pequeño Seúl, I realized its linguistic landscape is like a foreign world to many Mexicans who encounter indecipherable signs written in unfamiliar languages on the city streets. Much like the Mexican workers in New York City's Koreatown who felt like outsiders when they first came into contact with Korean language and culture in New York (and perceived Koreans' methods of communication to be harsh and unrelatable due to their lack of experience with Korean immigrants), Mexicans in Mexico have also expressed hesitation about Koreans and their ways of speaking and expressing themselves. However, by becoming fully immersed and acquainted with Koreans and their methods of communication for up to 12 hours a day, 7 days a week, Mexicans in New York City's Koreatown not only gained an understanding of Koreans but actually adopted their traditions as their own and infused them with their own Mexican ways of seeing and doing things.

CONCLUDING STATEMENT

In Mexico City, Koreans have responded to their Spanish-dominant language environment by making their signs accessible to outsiders, using pictures and Spanish translations. In other cases, Korean signs fail to offer translations and still appear foreign and indecipherable to non-Koreans. It is possible this act of non-translation can lead to a sense of social distance and isolation. This is what inspired me to do a close inspection of signs on urban spaces of Pequeño Seúl: to bring foreign signs into focus, to bring more recognition of the patterns of language and communication that exist in the neighborhood, to hopefully bridge the gap in understanding and ameliorate the social distance that exists between Mexicans and Koreans in Mexico City.

NOTE

1. *¿Quién se acuerda, por ejemplo, de los inmigrantes que viven en México? Ni siquiera nos acordamos que México también tiene agentes de inmigración?*

WORKS CITED

Arvide, Cynthia. 2011. "Corea-México, La Nueva Corea En La Zona Rosa." *Chilango*, 3 January. Accessed July 3, 2017. http://www.chilango.com/general/corea-mexico-la-nueva-corea-en-la-zona-rosa/

Backhaus, Peter. 2007. *Linguistic Landscapes: A Comparative Study of Urban Multilingualism in Tokyo.* Clevedon: Multilingual Matters, 2007.

Blommaert, Jan. 2013. *Ethnography, Superdiversity and Linguistic Landscapes: Chronicles of Complexity.* Toronto: Multilingual Matters.

Castilla, Alfredo Romero. 2009. "Coreanos. Su presencia ayer y hoy." In *La ciudad cosmopolita de los inmigrantes.* Vol. 1, edited by Carlos Martínez Assad and Alicia Gil Lázaro, 283–305. México, DF: Gobierno del Distrito Federal, Secretaría de Desarrollo Rural y Equidad para las Comunidades.

Cave, Damien. 2013. "Mexico's New Arrivals Mix Praise and Criticism." *The New York Times*, 23 September. Accessed July 2, 2017. http://www.nytimes.com/2013/09/24/world/americas/mexicos-expatriates-mix-praise-and-criticism.html

Cevallos, Diego. 2003. "MEXICO: South Koreans a Growing Presence in Capital's Retail District." *Inter Press Service News Agency*, June 20. Accessed July 3, 2017. http://www.ipsnews.net/2003/06/mexico-south-koreans-a-growing-presence-in-capitals-retail-district/

"DramaFever Logs 250 Percent Jump in Latino Viewership." *Latin Post*, January 29, 2016. Accessed July 3, 2017. http://www.latinpost.com/articles/112337/20160129/dramafever-logs-250-percent-jump-latino-viewership.htm

Galloway, Nicola, and Heath Rose. 2015. *Introducing Global Englishes.* New York: Routledge.

Harvey, David. 2008. "Right to the City." *New Left Review* 53 (October): 23–40.

Landry, Rodrigue and Richard Bourhis. 1997. "Linguistic Landscape and Ethnolinguistic Vitality: An Empirical Study." *Journal of Language and Social Psychology* 16 (1): 23–49.

Lefebvre, Henri. (1968) 2015. *Le droit à la ville.* Paris: Ed. Economica.

"Mexico City." *Seccion Coreana*, Septiembre 9, 2015: 12–13.

"Mexico City A Cultural Melting Pot." *The Economist*, May 9 2006. Accessed July 2, 2017. http://www.economist.com/node/6907576

Rama, Ángel. (1984) 1996. *The Lettered City. Post-Contemporary Interventions.* Translated by John Charles Chasteen. Durham, NC: Duke University Press.

Shohamy, Elana, Eliezer Ben-Rafael, and Monica Barni. 2010a. "Introduction: An Approach to an 'Ordered Disorder.'" In *Linguistic Landscape in the City*, edited by Elana Shohamy, Eliezer Ben-Rafael, and Monica Barni, xi–xxvii. Toronto: Multilingual Matters.

———. 2010b. "Epilogue." In *Linguistic Landscape in the City*, edited by Elana Shohamy, Eliezer Ben-Rafael, and Monica Barni, 344–347. Toronto: Multilingual Matters.

Taylor, Mark. 2001. *The Moment of Complexity: Emerging Network Culture.* Chicago: University of Chicago Press.

Winiarczyk-Raźniak, Anna, and Piotr Raźniak. 2014. "Ethnic Minorities in Ciudad de México (Distrito Federal)." *Procedia—Social and Behavioral Sciences* 120 (March): 90–97.

Yonhap News Agency. 2016. "S. Korea to Hold 1st Korean Culture Fete in Mexico City." December 2. Accessed July 3, 2017. http://english.yonhapnews.co.kr/nation al/2016/12/02/42/0301000000AEN20161202003400315F.html

Zapata, César Fernando. 2013. "Los inmigrantes en México: El otro lado de a moneda." *La Crónica*, Febrero 11. Accessed July 4, 2017. http://www.cronica. com.mx/notas/2004/103241.html

Chapter 10

Riding a Tandem Bicycle

Valeria Luiselli Maps the Sidewalks of Mexico City

Patrick O'Connor

PROLOGUE: CHASING A MOVING TARGET

Much of what historians and literary and cultural critics do involves retracing paths, metaphorical but occasionally literal routes: how did England and Germany enter World War I, how did Mexican poets learn about Japanese *haiku*, what route did Don Quixote take through Spain? The advantage of tracing a path from the past is that it is over and finished, and while the past always knows itself in fuller detail than the historian in the present can recreate, in the present we hope that newer interpretive lenses, and even newer technology, may help us know some things about the past which the past itself could not know about itself. Conversely, an academic who studies an object in the present or near-present can know that world in almost the same detail as the object studied, but that text or object may not really be finished yet; besides, the author of that text or object may share the interpretive lenses and the technology by which the academic hopes to get a hold on the object studied, always staying a bicycle length ahead of the critic. Indeed, in this essay I sometimes felt that I was chasing an essayist/ novelist who intuited our own project of *Mapping the Megalopolis*, and gently satirized it. So this reading of three books by Valeria Luiselli, a sort of story about chasing a woman on a bicycle ride, now has three epilogues, one anticipated by the author herself, another provided by the citizens she mostly keeps at bay in her work, and a third by the city that wants to capture and to a certain extent neutralize the energy unleashed by both the author and the crowds missing in the author's text.

211

VALERIA LUISELLI KNOWS HER WAY AROUND THE BLOCK

As a cosmopolitan and international author, young literary phenomenon Luiselli is surprisingly good at being at the right place at the right time. Born in 1983, an infant in the year of the 1985 earthquake that devastated downtown Mexico City, she had barely turned thirty when her second novel was published in Spanish and then almost immediately translated into English, as had her first collection of essays: the essay collection *Papeles falsos* (Counterfeit Papers; English translation, *Sidewalks*), and the novel *Los ingrávidos* (The Weightless Ones; English translation, *Faces in the Crowd*) were published almost simultaneously in Mexico in 2010 and 2011, and *La historia de mis dientes* (*The Story of My Teeth*) in 2013; their English translations published ratatat, 2013, 2014, and 2015. The books in Spanish were published in the small literary press *Sexto Piso*, which has grown in prominence in the years she has been publishing with them; likewise, her books in English were published by Coffee House Press, which has also grown in prominence over these years, in part because it has become competitive for literary awards—and *The Story of My Teeth* was on the short list for the National Book Critics' Circle Award in 2015 and is on the shortlist for the International Dublin Literary Award 2017. It should perhaps be no surprise that Luiselli, among very few Mexican—indeed, Latin American—authors of her generation, has managed to achieve prominence in a second literary landscape beside her native one: the daughter of a diplomat, she spent many years of her childhood and adolescence in South Africa and India, and pursued a doctorate in comparative literature at Columbia University in New York in the years she was writing her first novel. That novel, *Los ingrávidos/Faces in the Crowd*, is set in equal parts in the New York of the 1930s, the New York of roughly the present day, and in a house in present-day Mexico City. Indeed, her 2010 collection of essays, *Papeles falsos/Sidewalks*, although almost entirely centered on Mexico City, begins and ends with essays set in Venice, including the title essay (with the subtitle "La enfermedad de la ciudadanía," the sickness of citizenship; the essay's title in English is "Permanent Residence"). All signs point to Luiselli being a woman of the world.

Curiously, this *savoir-faire* poses something of a theoretical disadvantage for her. While it is expected for a journalist (or an academic) to convey mastery and confidence, the literary essayist is permitted to be at a loss facing her topic. Indeed, Luiselli takes on in *Papeles falsos/ Sidewalks* the task of "writing the city," and invokes the most prestigious theorist of this concept, Walter Benjamin, who brought so much theoretical attention to bear on the nineteenth-century *flâneur*, the man who leisurely strolls the streets of the metropolis (for more on the *flâneur* see this volume's chapters 4 and 6 by Puga and Tovar, and André, respectively.) By the time Luiselli inherits the concept, the *flâneur* is a figure of double consciousness. Not only is he, famously, someone who comes to observe the crowds and commodities as if to consume them but is really there to be consumed by them, to figure out how to offer his insights and poetry to be purchased by them and not by an aristocratic patron: "In the *flâneur*, the intelligentsia sets foot in the marketplace—ostensibly to look around, but in truth to find a buyer" (Benjamin [1982] 1999, 9). But the figure of Benjamin's Baudelaire has also now overlapped with Benjamin himself, whom we think of simultaneously as the amasser of hundreds of index cards and pages about the city of Paris on the one hand and, on the other hand, the brooder or *Grübler* still puzzled by the urban phenomena he sees and who said, just as famously, "Not to find one's way in a city may well be uninteresting and banal. [. . .] But to lose oneself in a city—as one loses oneself in a forest—this calls for quite a different schooling. [. . .] Paris taught me this art of straying" (Benjamin 1999, 598).

To be savvy about the literary marketplace while telling us stories about getting lost in an unknowable megalopolis is the project Luiselli has set herself.

TRACING A ROUTE IN THE UNMAPPABLE MEGALOPOLIS

In the last essay of the *Papeles falsos/ Sidewalks* collection Luiselli will get lost in the streets of Venice; but in Mexico City itself, wittily enough, she will only describe getting lost in a museum that holds the collection of the maps of the city. The essays of the slim volume *Papeles falsos/ Sidewalks* have frequently been retitled in the English version (as has the collection itself), but they are presented to the reader in the same order: bookended by pieces that mostly take place in Venice, the essays set in Mexico City begin with an essay about approaching the city by air, "*Mancha de agua* [water stain]/ Flying Home," which rings variations on the pointlessness of trying to comprehend Mexico City.[1] Seeing the city from the air is one's best chance to see the city whole; if that doesn't succeed, it is in part because the shape of the city is like a water stain, and in part because the natural outlines that rivers and lakes give to a city, which once suggested comparisons to Venice (Luiselli 2014a, 24), have been destroyed by the decision over the centuries to dry up the lakes of the Aztec city of Tenochtitlán and to dry up or drive underground the natural rivers that once fed the city that became Mexico City (each section of the short essay is titled after one of these old rivers, now most of them names of highways):

Perhaps that's why writing about Mexico City is a task doomed to failure. Unaware of this, for a long time I thought that, if I were to succeed in this task, I had to follow the traditional route: convert myself, à la Walter Benjamin, into a connoisseuse of benches, a botanist of the urban flora, an amateur archaeologist of the façades in the city center and the spectacular advertising hoardings of the Periférico (Beltway, 25).

She declares that she once tried "being a petite Baudelaire" on a side street in *Copilco* full of copy stores near the University and came up with nothing, but found it just as impossible to produce insight by walking through *Calle Donceles* in the City Center, a tourist and bibliophile's attraction for its streets full of used book stores. The Nahuatl etymology of Copilco's name, she jokes, is "place of copies," and walking through the bookstores of Donceles only brings her vague memories of reading Carlos Fuentes and Roberto Bolaño; copying Benjamin/Baudelaire in either of these streets does not provide Luiselli with any direct, "uncopied," or comprehensive experience.

The Map Library in the National Meteorological Service building, where one has to make one's way through narrow corridors where maps hang like "perennially damp sheets" (Luiselli 2014a, 20), embodies the problem: "It's difficult to navigate your way around the Map Library and—although the space is limited—it's impossible not to lose track of where you are in relation to the entrance or, if there were one, some precise center" (20). And worse, there are no originary plans of the city, according to the library's curator. Luiselli concludes that "what is now called 'urban planning' is pure nostalgia for the future" (22).

Maps are damp sheets trying to reproduce lines scratched long ago in damp earth in a water stain of a city that has given up on most of its water: in 2010 Luiselli is already throwing some shade on the entire project of any attempt to "map the megalopolis." Curiously, for an author as well-read in the same works that we the *mapistas* of the Mapping the Megalopolis project have read, Luiselli does not cite or even name-drop Ángel Rama's (1984) *La ciudad letrada,* although here she approximates that book's insight that the maps of early New Spain were utopian, often after the fact, and marked more of a desire for order and a center than they were able to create urban spaces that reflected order or possessed a center. The water is no longer objective but subjective: the essay ends as she returns to seeing the city from an airplane; when she sees a small artificial lake near the airport, she inevitably tears up, in part from a sadness that, once she's on the ground, the city will soon be immeasurable for her again, what this volume's Introduction calls the disorder or *desmadre* of the city, but also as her tribute to the water lost from the drying up of the lakes and rivers whose names can be found on the old maps.

SPINNING HER WHEELS

So Luiselli has put us on notice: she is embarked on the same project as those humanists who want to map the megalopolis, and we are all doomed to fail, and the old methods will not work. In *Papeles falsos/ Sidewalks*'s next essay, *"La velocidad à velo"/ "Manifesto à velo,"* skeptical of her ability to imitate the prestigious *flâneurs* of the European literary tradition—her list includes Rousseau, Baudelaire, Benjamin, the Swiss Robert Walser and the German Sigfried Kracauer—and refusing the consolation of the big data-gathering of the social scientists, Luiselli finds a different machine that will aid her:

> The urban walker [*El peatón defeño*] has to march to the rhythm of the city in which he finds himself and demonstrate the same single-minded purpose as other pedestrians. Any modulation of his pace makes him the object of suspicion. [. . .]
> The cyclist, on the other hand, is sufficiently invisible to achieve what the pedestrian cannot: traveling in solitude and abandoning himself to the sweet flow of his thoughts. [. . .] . The cyclist, thus, possesses an extraordinary freedom: he is invisible. (Luiselli 2014a, 33–34)

If Mexico City is a faster city than the cities of the nineteenth and twentieth century, then a bicycle will allow the *flâneur* to think at the right speed.

This is perhaps the first essay in which the variations between the English and the original are noteworthy: the title in English declares it to be a "manifesto," and it certainly has the tone of one. Perhaps to give it the defiant clout of one, the English version has also scrubbed out all specific references to Mexico City: *"la poco caminable y apenas literaria ciudad de México"* (the not very walkable and barely literary Mexico City) of her first paragraph, followed by the *"peatón defeño"* (pedestrian of the Federal District) in the paragraphs quoted above, and four more times in a four-page essay, have all been eliminated.

Luiselli mentions twice in the essay the need for invisibility, in order to pursue one's thoughts properly, and much of the rest of the essay contrasts the amount of privacy a person obtains in various modes of transport (the car, too much; the metro, not enough). She begins the essay citing Robert Walser's ([1917] 2012) *The Walk* (alluded to in the Spanish, quoted directly in the English).[2] If invisibility is the goal of the contemporary *flâneur*, Luiselli has done right in citing Walser rather than Benjamin's haughty pseudo-aristocrats, who in fact were happy to make a scene, notoriously Gerard de Nerval walking a lobster; Walser does indeed aspire to a kind of invisibility in his walks. The invisibility might allow Luiselli to observe better—at the end of the essay, she compares the cyclist's vision to a camera's versus the car driver's telescope and the walker's microscope—, but it also seems more designed for ignoring the world around her than observing it: "when some stray thought afflicts the cyclist and blocks the natural flow of his mind, he has only to find a good steep slope and let gravity and the wind work their redemptive alchemy" (Luiselli 2014a, 35). Not the faces of the crowd (the title in English of her first novel) or the buildings or the city's history spur Luiselli's speeding imagination, but gravity and wind, the least urban elements of Any-City's milieu. The abstractness with which Luiselli (and Christina MacSweeney, her English translator) reflects upon thinking while bicycling is certainly one facet of much of the "writing about thinking about walking" that is a characteristic of a kind of meditation exemplified by *Wanderlust: A History of Walking* (2000), a book by Rebecca Solnit that can be seen as a kind of precursor to the "atlases" that we the *mapistas* of Mexico City have taken as our point of departure: like Luiselli, it too develops a phenomenology of thinking in motion, through a web of quotations; unlike Luiselli (and, we'd like to think, ourselves), it is far more open to narrating the things Solnit sees in the landscapes and cityscapes through which she passes.[3]

GENDER AND VISIBILITY

The argument that a cyclist would be invisible on the streets of Mexico City, even in a bourgeois residential neighborhood like *la Roma Norte*, strikes me (and natives of Mexico City I know) as implausible, so much so that one is tempted to second-guess Luiselli's argument. To continue the quote from Luiselli's "*La velocidad à velo*"/ "*Manifesto à velo*" cited earlier: "Any modulation of his pace makes him the object of suspicion. The person who walks too slowly might be plotting a crime or—even worse—might be a tourist. Except for those who still take their dogs for a walk, children coming home from school, the very old, or itinerant street vendors, no one has the right to slow, aimless walking" (33–34). (The phrase "or—even worse—be a tourist" replaces the Spanish "or be lost" [*o estar perdido*], perhaps in a gesture toward the more typical complaint made by New Yorkers about slow walkers.) What kind of crime involves walking slowly down a street? Well, the Mexican male imagination has a traditional answer for that, when the person walking the street is a woman. As elaborated in books on women and Latin America since at least Jean Franco's (1989) *Plotting Women*, the confining of women to domestic spaces controlled by their fathers or husbands is an entrenched part of the Mexican cultural system, which more recent feminist attitudes have only partially dislodged: the unaccompanied woman in public can only be a "public woman," that is, a prostitute, and can expect stares and *piropos* (catcalls, wolf whistles, and raunchy phrases) as a result of her visibility.[4] In a previous chapter in our collection, a woman's desire to see and walk in the city unperceived was solved through the fantasy of invisibility, according to Patricia Tovar and Alejandro Puga's reading of Ana Clavel's (2000) *Los deseos y su sombra*; in Luiselli's *"Manifesto à Velo"* the solution is to ride a bike, bringing oneself mostly into interaction with car traffic, not foot traffic, and to ignore more easily any stares or *piropos* that one might provoke.

I repeat, Luiselli doesn't say any of this; to the contrary, she and her translator strenuously avoid language that would smack of a feminist analysis, either of the kind one sometimes sees in Latin American theorizing (with a more prominent place for the rights of mothers and a praise of relatedness) or a more recognizably U.S. feminist approach.[5] In the more gendered language of Spanish, but also in the English translation, the pedestrian is the universal male, "the cyclist, thus, possesses an extraordinary freedom: he is invisible" (Luiselli 2014a, 34)—no "he or she," no recasting into the plural to attenuate male pronouns for universal experience.

It is all the more surprising that the manifesto now reads as applying to all cities and any (i.e., the male) gender when Luiselli's first novel makes such a strong distinction between the woman and public space in Mexico City and New York. *Los ingrávidos* (2011)/ *Faces in the Crowd* (2014b) narrates a present in Mexico City, as the protagonist (let's call her Valeria) brings up two young children while trying to turn her past experiences in New York as a single woman into a novel. While she was in New York she worked at a literary magazine, trying to convince her editor to take an interest in the works of the Mexican writer Gilberto Owen of the 1920s—1930s; Gilberto Owen's bemused and unhappy experiences in New York in those years are also imagined in this novel. Knowing her way around the block as she does, Luiselli has taken on a topic that places her in a specific relationship to the current Mexican literary landscape, where in 1996 a group of young literary intellectuals declared they were "the Crack movement" and affiliated themselves to the same group of 1920s—1930s Mexican writers, *"los Contemporáneos,"* or "The Contemporaries," to which Gilberto Owen also belonged.[6] These authors of post-revolutionary Mexico City were not the allies of the Mexican muralists described in María André's chapter in this volume; the *Contemporáneos* poets were considered by Diego Rivera and others to be too cosmopolitan to be really good Mexicans. Still, they are now treated as an important part of the country's literary tradition, and in centering her novel on one of those members, Luiselli is positioning herself in a similar way, the cosmopolitan who is also a good citizen.

All the more reason to be surprised that Mexico City is declared unrepresentable in *Faces in the Crowd* (2014b). The younger Luiselli wanders at will through New York's streets, sidewalks, bars, and suburbs; in extensive flashbacks Gilberto Owen also occupies these same streets and apartment buildings (Valeria sometimes imagines seeing him on subways that pass by stations where she's waiting). In the 1930s he attends mortifying parties thrown by his ex-wife, who has remarried a wealthy man; in the 2000s she attends ludicrous parties thrown by and for Brooklyn trustafarians. At these parties she declares herself incapable of communicating the feel of any of the streets of Mexico City to her American interlocutors. She tries once, as part of a routine she tells at parties in which she lies and says that she took a photo of Gilberto Owen once, on Calle Donceles:

> I was in a Lebanese café in Calle Donceles in the historic district of Mexico City, and Owen walked past under a huge umbrella. There had just been one of those summer rainstorms, the likes of which only fall in Mexico City and Mumbai. The sidewalks were beginning to be filled again with ambulant street vendors, tourists, cockroaches, and the sad peregrinations of public servants hurrying back to their cubicles, suffused with satisfaction and guilt—their shirts wrinkled, their skin glinting with grease—after a short but sweet encounter in one of the pay-by-the-hour hotels in the zone. I told all that to Salvatore and then repented it. Describing Calle Donceles that way to a foreigner has an air of literary imposture I'm now ashamed of. (47)

Luiselli eroticizes this Mexico City street, but in a sordid way; she acknowledges its global status (and invokes her own global experience) through a comparison between tropical rainstorms in legendarily crowded and dirty cities.

However, the real reason Valeria seems incapable of describing Mexico City is because she is a woman there, a married woman who develops agoraphobia. The one time she goes out into the house's patio to breastfeed her infant son she discovers that roofers on a nearby construction project have been watching her. Through a variety of passive-aggressive moves (including writing disparaging comments about her protagonist's future husband into the novel she is writing about her New York years, and then sharing the manuscript with her husband), Luiselli drives her husband out of the house. The novel ends with a moderately strong earthquake in the city: instead of fighting her way out of the house, Luiselli lets rubble pile up against the doors and sits with her two children under a table. As a single woman in New York she was intrepid, sloughing off being drugged at a local bar and having non-consensual sex, and flirting with the Ecuadorian-American policeman who came to take her statement about the experience; conversely, as a mother in Mexico City she is guarded and fearful. Is it the difference in age or in city, in combination with her gender, that shuts Luiselli down from observing the streets around her?

A BICYCLE BUILT FOR TWO: TRANSLATING
LA ROMA NORTE'S *SIDEWALKS*

The essay in *Papeles falsos/Sidewalks* in which one would expect the most overlap with the project of mapping the megalopolis is *"Dos calles y una banqueta/* Alternate Routes." Our narrator leaves her house in the *colonia* of Roma Norte, gets on her bike, stops at a bookstore, and then bicycles around the neighborhood, a left turn here, a right turn there, occasionally getting off to walk the bike through a park or across a street; each small section is titled the block she is on and the left or right, the stop or the straight ahead, that would allow the reader to follow her on a map of the city, perhaps the one in the mammoth *Guía Roji* (2015), whose 200+ maps aspire to cover the entire megalopolis, or Google Maps.[7] But the reader might be, then must be, disappointed if he or she tries to do so.

Luiselli might have taken advantage of the ride to observe the streetscape, which has been the purpose of *flâneurs* since the label was invented, and presumably the justification in her book for the approving quotes from such notable walkers as Rousseau, Benjamin, and Walser. Yet the entire essay passes with only the most minimal description of the neighborhood. She starts by stopping to pick up a copy of a Portuguese dictionary at a bookstore, in order to learn a little more about the concept of *saudade*, a melancholy expression whose Iberian pedigree might indeed allow a Latin American to put herself in relationship to that great melancholic Benjamin. Saudade tends to be free-floating; for a more specific kind of nostalgia about a neighborhood's past, see Blair's chapter in this volume. Indeed, as the essay and its thoughts on melancholy and nostalgia progress, Luiselli makes no reference to the city that passes before her eyes at all, beyond the names of the streets and travel directions in her subtitles. Her reminiscences are all cosmopolitan and literary: a childhood in El Salvador first trying to dig a hole back to Mexico, then burying her own mementos there for some future girl to dig up; a postcard of the *Calle de los Melancólicos* in Madrid; two quotations from Fernando Pessoa's prose and poetry. And the punch line to the essay is that the bike ride has been mental, not actual: she has been sitting on a bench outside the bookstore, thinking these things as she leafs through the Portuguese dictionary.

Of course it's not impossible that the twists and turns of her ride had affected the turns of her thought—until one reads MacSweeney's translation (2014a). The units of the essay are still marked off by legs of the bicycle ride—but the route of the ride has changed, and the order of many of the paragraphs has been radically changed. The English version wards off the image of the lonely bicyclist through the insertion of the figure of "Sara," a character (friend? sister? lover?) who declares that in El Salvador, there is a separate word for nostalgia (in the Spanish, she is merely *alguien*, "someone"). The description of the Paseo de los Melancólicos in the English is introduced by "Sara is doing an oil painting from a snapshot she took years ago, when we lived there together." And while in the Spanish, a meditation on Pessoa begins abruptly, "*Una postal*" (a postcard), MacSweeney's translation, in contrast, has the thoughts inspired by and passages from Pessoa read or remembered not by Luiselli alone but once again with Sara, "Over dinner, we read aloud randomly chosen fragments from *The Book of Disquiet,* which has been lying around the house for more than a month—sometimes in her bedroom, sometimes in mine" (Separate bedrooms: so, friends or sisters, then, after all) (Luiselli 2014a, 51). MacSweeney's friendship with Luiselli drains some of the energy of the text away from saudade and the solitariness of the cyclist.

Before ending, Luiselli (2010) in the original Spanish has a brief paragraph citing some street names before quoting Ludwig Wittgenstein and revealing that, having bought the dictionary in the bookstore and seeing that it would rain, she got on her bike and went back home. The Wittgenstein quote is an aphorism: "Perhaps what is inexpressible [. . .] is the background against which whatever I could express has its meaning" (52), and in both Spanish and English versions Luiselli interprets this the same way: what is inexpressible in the word saudade will have its meaning colored for her by the streets of *Colonia Roma* that she has been bicycling through. More wittily in the English translation, she will claim to find the passage defining saudade, which she wrote in her original Spanish essay, in a dictionary which she *might* buy if she leaves the house to take the bicycle ride we have just read: "Saudade: streets, cracked sidewalks, archipelagos of dog shit, the leprous walls of old buildings, the concrete sadness of a bicycle ride around the Colonia Roma at the violet hour" (53).

It's probably better that the ride was imaginary: riding a two-seat tandem bicycle, to make room for the translator who undercuts Luiselli's loneliness to show her that her ideal reader has been traveling with her throughout, would no doubt have ruined the anonymity and invisibility that, as a female *flâneur*, is hard enough to achieve in Mexico City to begin with.

THE MICROSCOPIC LENS: *RELINGOS*

So *Papeles falsos/ Sidewalks* puts a bicycle *flânerie* to a use other than what its manifesto promises, riding through a neighborhood in order not to see it, but rather to think more clearly one's own thoughts. But the essay collection is actually capable of close observation of the city at a different level.[8] The chapter "Relingos" (with the subtitle in the English version, "The

Cartography of Empty Spaces"), offers crisp insights and aphorisms about people and places.

The essay describes quickly what relingos are: the fragments that occur when urbanists run a street at an angle through a neighborhood mostly built on a grid, leaving triangular and trapezoidal spaces where it would make little or no sense to build. Much of the essay consists of musings elsewhere: on architectural theory, on the Catalan architect Ignasi de Solá-Morales's concept of *terrains vagues,* and on Roland Barthes's ([1964] 1983) essay on the Eiffel Tower. More musings are on writing: Luiselli enters a nearby museum that used to be a library and finds a curator restoring a series of murals giving a history of writing. She notes ironically that the emptiness of the shelves around her should be the subject of a final mural, "The fall of libraries and bookshops" (Luiselli 2014a, 76). She will connect the musings on architecture and on writing at the end of the brief essay. But although the English version calls the relingo in its subtitle an "empty space," Luiselli herself is quite aware that it is not empty:

> [. . .] Coming out from Hidalgo metro station at the exit nearest to San Judas Tadeo church, there's a small triangular plaza, in the middle of which stands a tribute to the work of Mexican journalists: a statue of the nineteenth-century newspaper editor and politician Francisco Zarco surrounded by a large fountain that bubbles and spits out mouthfuls of gray water. The homeless people of the neighborhood go there with their bars of soap and towels to wash their faces and bodies beneath the bronze figure. At certain hours in the afternoon, that same plaza becomes a six-a-side football field, and at middays on Sundays it's transformed again, into the venue for a tertulia for the deaf-mutes coming out from the sign language mass at San Judeo. (72)

Clearly this "empty space" is hardly empty at all. Luiselli has an architect friend who does consider it empty, though, since he has a plan to build a building on it that could serve as a cultural center and theater for the deaf-mute community. Luiselli has no criticism of the plan's favoring of one of these many uses over all the other current ones; while the English version calls it a "brilliantly crazy idea," the Spanish original is more pragmatic and more specific in expecting that if the *relingo* is ever built on it will just be another "nuevo supermercado o una oficina de teléfonos" (new supermarket or telephone office) (Luiselli 2010, 75).

The payoff to "Relingos" would seem to be its gnomic conclusion that writing is not about forging ahead like some Haussmann to connect a known beginning to a known end, or even about imagining projects to fill the empty spaces of a city, but about plowing ahead, yes, but then taking stock of the jagged fragments left behind in the wake of such institutionally sanctioned bulldozering: "A writer is a person who distributes silences and empty

spaces.// Writing: making *relingos"* (Luiselli 2014a, 78). Yet the linked
essays in *Papeles falsos/ Sidewalks* allow her another payoff: the book's
first and last essays, as I said above, take place in Venice, the first one in
the San Michele cemetery for foreigners, and in the last essay she picks up
the theme of identity implicit in the collection's Spanish title (though not its
English title): thanks to some counterfeit papers, Luiselli can now be legally
buried in Venice, "in some relingo, perhaps not far from Joseph Brodsky, in
the commoners' section of the cemetery of San Michele" (110). If that isn't
an appropriate hope for an *escritora mexicana* (female Mexican writer), she
suggests it's not her fault but her destiny. In her adolescence, she says earlier
in the essay, her father told his three daughters that he had worked to turn
a small relingo "at the *Altavista* exit of the *Periférico"* into a pocket park,
and had paid to have three palm trees planted there, which would be named
after the three of them; but when they finally visited one Sunday, "there
weren't three. The smallest palm tree wasn't there [. . .]. If my palm tree
hadn't taken root, I would never put roots down in Mexico City—that vast
asphalt relingo left over or simply missing from the city" (106). Symbolically
déracinée (uprooted), Luiselli would have liked to be rooted in the city, a part
of its order (if perhaps only as an afterthought), but the inexplicable disappearance of "her" tree suggests disorder rather than order. Perhaps Luiselli
didn't distinguish between the plaza near San Judas Tadeo Church as either
an empty relingo or an already occupied relingo because the relingo that is
supposed to include her doesn't. But this declaration of un-rootedness calls
her authority to speak into question: Why should we trust her to help us map
this megalopolis?

CHASING AUTHENTICITY IN THE OUTSKIRTS OF THE CITY

Luiselli seems to have been aware of her tendency to fend off the outside
world and focus microscopically only on the leftover parts of the city that no
one else claims, that she can call her own, and engages in strategies of collaboration as compensation. We have just seen how, as the text moves from
Spanish to English, she opens up the creative process to her translator, giving
MacSweeney a second seat on the text's tandem bicycle. Still, no one could
have predicted Luiselli's change of style between her first and her second
novel. Where *Los ingrávidos/ Faces in the Crowd* is melancholy and agoraphobic, *La historia de mis dientes/ The Story of My Teeth* is jaunty and city-
spanning. Even its bookishness is zany, not aspirational. And although some
of its gestures toward including other collaborators are on closer inspection
less open than they seem at first, the result paid off admirably.

The Story of My Teeth's (2015) picaresque hero is the brash self-confident man of the people Gustavo "Highway" Sánchez Sánchez, born in the center of Mexico City but whose first career begins as the watchman for the *Jumex* juice factory in the northeast outskirts of the megalopolis, the *Colonia Ecatepec de Morelos*; but his true métier, he discovers, is to be an auctioneer. He discovers that people do not just wish to collect objects, they want to collect the story around the object, and in pursuit of his passion for rhetorical embroidery he leaves his wife and young child in order to train at the feet of a great auctioneer, Master Oklahoma, and travels to Missouri, USA. When he returns, he discovers his wife has left him and when she dies he loses custody of his child. He gets rich and buys a house for himself, building a castle on the improbably named street *Calle Disneylandia*; but in his old age his fortunes decline and, for a time, he is at the mercy of his son (named Ratzinger in the Spanish, Siddhartha in the English), who "buys" him in an auction and imprisons him in an art gallery showing an exhibit of enormous screens of sad and impassive circus clowns; when Highway awakes, escapes, and returns home, he finds that his son has stolen all of his many collectibles, including Highway's own teeth. The Spanish novel and the English version diverge at this point, as it does in many other points of the novel, but in both versions Highway bicycles around Ecatepec looking for his son, recoups at least some of his collectibles, recruits a disciple to write up his biography (the text we are now reading), and dies in the bed of a local motel with three pretty bartenders while he does his famed Janis Joplin imitation. It's not the book one expects to follow the story of a sensitive agoraphobic woman recalling her years as a literary agent in Manhattan tracing the footsteps of a Mexican poet of the 1930s.

It also isn't entirely Luiselli's work. Once again, the English translation is significantly altered from the Spanish version—so much so that the last chapter, with a time line that synchronizes Highway Sánchez Sánchez's life with as many of the names that Luiselli drops as it can, is copyrighted separately by MacSweeney. But the collaborative process began much earlier: in an afterword (that is less than one page in the Spanish but almost six pages in the English version), Luiselli (2015) describes how she was invited to write something for the art gallery *Galería Jumex*, but decided to also write something for the juice workers, for whom she wrote the novel in installments, and then used their comments and reactions, which she received as mp3s, to continue the story, before taking the whole first draft and rewriting it. Once the process had begun, she had no direct contact with the workers who read the story together and commented on it: "They never saw me; I never saw them. I heard them, and they read me"; their help "enabled me, virtually at least, to move around and explore the places I was writing about" (193). The afterword also claims that the various rewritings in tandem with MacSweeney of the English version are an extension of this collaborative process, and a new way to recognize the role of a translator in a piece of fiction: "This book began as a collaboration, and I like to think of it as an ongoing one, where every new layer modifies the entire content completely" (195).

This is an exciting position to take in the field of translation theory. And, for the purposes of a project on mapping Mexico City, it acknowledges slyly that a woman whose first essay collection confesses a problem of authenticity in her *mexicanidad* (Mexicanness) needs to rely on the authentic *mexicanidad* of juice factory workers who helped her (not that they share the profits, but literary fiction can't be expected to make profits anyway); paratextually, the afterword is its own version of the value that Highway Sánchez Sánchez adds to the objects he auctions by telling stories about them; just as the extra chapter with separate copyright reassured the reader that this woman is not cycling through English alone, but with someone behind her, and every so often they change seats and MacSweeney does the driving. Without completely abandoning the normal way for an author to declare her authority and authenticity, Luiselli takes and gives credit for portraying the streets of a part of Mexico City that she has scarcely visited.

EPILOGUE 1: SEE FOR YOURSELF, JANUARY 2016

My own days as a *flâneur* are pretty much over, alas: I'm turning sixty soon, and have arthritis in both knees. As a *gringo* over six feet tall and well over 350 pounds, I have my own issues about achieving the invisibility necessary for a certain kind of observational practice. So it was with some reluctance that in my visit to Mexico City of January 2016 as part of the Mapping the Megalopolis project after I first became fascinated by the nonfiction of Luiselli, I decided that merely mapping the bicycle route she takes in "*Dos calles y una banqueta*"/ "Alternative Routes" would not be enough; I wanted to see the Mexico of her essays and novels as well. I kept reading, and realized that the most important destination would have to be Ecapetec, the neighborhood of the Jumex juice factory that used to house the art gallery where Highway Sánchez Sánchez worked as a guard, and chased his son on bicycle through its streets. But it's so far away, I thought, and I hate taxis and Uber, and the museum has already relocated to Plaza Carso (the topic of Glen Kuecker's chapter in this volume). As I continued to read, I thought, wickedly: why don't I just Google Map the neighborhood, following the protagonists that way, and taking the occasional screen shot when necessary?

Imagine my embarrassment when I reached the last section of the Spanish original text (the penultimate section in the English translation), to find that its *"Paseo Circular"* (Circular Stroll) is a section of eighteen photographs, a few stock images but mostly taken expressly for the novel, almost all of whose subjects are images from Ecatepec's streets, keyed to moments narrated in the previous section (subtitled in the Spanish, "Notes for an epigone's stroll"). Included in these eighteen photos are many screen captures of Google Maps sites, in case we wondered if there really is a "Calle Disneylandia" in Ecatepec—the photograph of that street map, the only one also included in the English version's set of nine photographs, is actually from the Guía Roji. Another Google Maps capture has been altered so that the street says, *"Aquí vivo"* (I live here). And the only photograph in the English version not in the Spanish, "4. Highway's House" (Luiselli 2015, 163), which looks like a Disneyland castle, is probably not an actual house on Calle Disneylandia; in the Spanish version a photograph from that street shows a building in severe disrepair. As noted above, Luiselli happily admits that she didn't take any of the Ecatepec photographs herself, but farmed that out to two of the Jumex workers who were also reading and commenting on her novel in installments. Once again I felt like an epigone, someone who comes after, always a step or a bicycle length behind the leader, chasing a novelist who intuited our own project of Mapping the Megalopolis, even some of its least prestigious neighborhoods ("If there is a physical materialization of nothingness in this world, it is Ecatepec de Morelos" [Luiselli 2015, 150], says one of Highway's disciples—at first), and decided to gently satirize our project, two years before we embarked on it.

EPILOGUE 2: GENDER AND VISIBILITY, APRIL 2016

Having returned from Mexico City in January to teach my regular round of Spanish language and literature classes, I occasionally looked online, as one does, for topics that could interest an American student body, and discovered with pleasure in April that a large march for women's rights was occurring in Mexico City. "Vivas Nos Queremos" was the organizing slogan, an angry, heartfelt, and witty variation on the chant shouted since the days of the Mothers of the Plaza de Mayo and also for the 43 teacher's college students disappeared and presumably murdered in 2014, "Vivos los queremos" (We want them back alive) turned into "Vivas nos queremos" (We want to be alive, we love each other alive). The march had as its goals denouncing Mexico's terribly high rates of crimes against women, from groping on the metro to feminicides, and Mexican political culture is as familiar with marching in the streets as it is difficult for women to feel safe on the street alone. Where was the beginning of the march? The neighborhood with the highest reported incidence of crimes against women—Ecatepec, the distant colonia-suburb where the Galería Jumex had been and where Luiselli's male characters chased each other on bicycle in *The Story of My Teeth* (2015). About 1,200 women set out from there to start the march, most of them apparently traveling by bicycle to the beginning of the line of the *Indios Verdes* metro station in *Colonia Gustavo Madero*, where they took the metro en masse to the Monument to the Revolution, joining other marchers there and going on foot to the statue of the Angel of Independence on the *Paseo de la Reforma*, about 6,000 (according to newspaper estimates), enough to block traffic on some of the city's major thoroughfares for the afternoon, and part of coordinated marches in many other cities in Mexico.[9]

Combining bicycles (but not to attain invisibility), the metro (in Mexico City, not in New York), and the obstreperous walking of a protest march in its transit from Ecatepec to the city center, not far from Colonia Roma Norte where Luiselli mapped the streets without taking note(s) of them, the Vivas Nos Queremos march offers a different way for a woman to move about the city, less suited for cosmopolitan and philosophical purposes. But I suspect that, had Luiselli joined that march—and for all I know, she did—she would have used the space made public and safe by solidarity, for a day, in order to take private note on a microscopic level of odd details others had not noticed, essayistic relingos visible to a woman free for a single day to be just one of the faces in the crowd.

EPILOGUE 3: *CDMX'S* ECATEPEC FOR COSMOPOLITANS, DECEMBER 2016

Novelists, their translators, and professors can map a city, but administrators and city planners can change it. I like to think that Luiselli took pleasure in keeping one bike length ahead of the professors who want to map the megalopolis, as she places photographs and screen shots of Google Maps at the end of *The Story of My Teeth* (2015) to make our work in theory redundant. If she didn't know that the neighborhood of her 2013/2015 novel of male protagonists would be the starting point of a 2016 march demanding female protagonism, well, that day has passed and the novel remains, as do the streets of Ecatepec in my 2015 Guía Roji.

First of all, city administrators can change the context of one's gestures. A woman may see herself as an invisible cycling *flâneuse*, but the city sees her as a valued consumer. Whether she acknowledges it or not, Luiselli's two-wheeled presence on the streets of *Ciudad de México* goes hand in glove with attempts by the city since 2007 to rebrand itself as a bicycle-friendly city, with *EcoBici* (CDMX N.d.), the same kind of "city bike" program that has been instituted in London, Paris, New York, and other major capitals. The program contributes to the kind of "yuppification" of the city that marks the shift from "*el DF*" (the Federal District) to "CDMX" (Mexico City), and marks a health-conscious neoliberalism that any good cosmopolitan would recognize, anywhere.

And in any case, the streets do not remain entirely the same. According to an article in the December 28, 2016, *New York Times* (Burnett), a new piece of public transport has been added to the often bewildering mix of Mexico's desperate need to move its millions where they need to go: not just EcoBici; not just the highways, often following the routes of the rivers and causeways from Aztec times; not just the metro system, which opened in 1969, whose most recent extension was opened just in 2012, and which served over 1.5 billion customers in 2015; not just the big urban-to-suburban bus lines whose routes are provided on subway maps and in the Guía Roji; and not just the hundreds of *pesero* or *combi* lines, minivans and minibuses that crisscross the city on routes mysterious to casual visitors and tourists. Besides these transportation options there is now the Mexicable, an airborne system of gondolas suspended from a cable, whose six stops improve the travel options of a distant suburban neighborhood—Ecatepec. The *Times* article describes the ambivalent satisfaction that the locals feel about the cable car floating above their neighborhood and the beautification programs that have accompanied it: "Along the route, the government has painted facades bright pink, green and mauve, and commissioned about 50 huge murals: a gaping shark's mouth on one rooftop; a portrait of Frida Kahlo by the New York graffiti artist Alec Monopoly; an Elmer-like elephant sculpted by the Oaxacan artist Fernando Andriacci" (Burnett 2016).[10] The locals know that the neighborhood had far more pressing needs but, hey, *algo es algo*, it's better than nothing. The residents Burnett interviewed liked the idea that people from other parts of the city—and possibly the world (the idea, after all, had been borrowed from similar attempts to rejuvenate cities such as Medellín, Caracas, La Paz, and Rio)–would come to Ecatepec to ride the gondolas; she does not say how the same could have been said about the Galería Jumex, opened in 2001 until it closed and was moved to the Plaza Carso in 2013. But in any case the cable car wagons, which everyone agrees are safer than the *combis* that run in the streetbound traffic beneath them, currently tend to be under-utilized outside of rush hour. Hence, a writer who likes to think her own thoughts as she passes slightly above the city streets might be able to use the Mexicable to revisit the neighborhood she had only half-visited a few years ago.

But if Luiselli can do so, it will be because a municipality hell-bent on becoming a destination for cosmopolitans has found a way to woo her back to a neighborhood whose art gallery she visited and then didn't return to as she, in tandem with her translator, wrote a book where that neighborhood figures prominently. I'm that kind of cosmopolitan too, for better or worse; now I might make that trip to Ecatepec I sloughed off in January 2016. Burnett ends her *New York Times* piece interviewing a woman who thinks the attention that the Mexicable brings to the neighborhood is a good thing: "'We thought these things were for pretty places with mountains,' she said of the cable car system. 'There are no pretty views here,' she added. 'But now we're on the map.'"

NOTES

1. Nelly Cardoso (2014) suggests that the title "*mancha de agua*" is a twist on Joseph Brodsky's memoir of Venice, *Watermark*. In the first essay of *Papeles falsos/ Sidewalks*, "Joseph Brodsky's Room and a Half," Luiselli quotes from *Watermark*, and ends her visit to the foreigners' section of the Venice cemetery by visiting Brodsky's grave.

2. This is uncharacteristic; in general, Christina MacSweeney (Luiselli's English translator) and Luiselli have eliminated many of the direct quotations, especially of poetry, that are in the Spanish version. One wonders if they worry that Luiselli will come across as too bookish. Walser, though a writer from the 1900 to 1910s, is a relatively new addition to the comparative literature canon: first translated into English only in 1969, Susan Sontag championed his work in the 1980s and 1990s. He lived the last thirty years of his life in various Swiss insane asylums; when asked whether he was still writing while in the asylum, he responded, "I am not here to write, but to be mad." For the great revival of his works in translation in the last decades, see Benjamin Kunkel (2007), whose title, "Still Small Voice," suggests that Luiselli takes Walser as a model of invisibility in the way I pursue in this essay.

3. Solnit (2000) states, "Walking, ideally, is a state in which the mind, the body, *and the world* are aligned, as though they were three characters finally in conversation together" (5, emphasis added). Although she dutifully mentions the bicyclists' rights movement Critical Mass in her chapter on "Citizens of the Streets" (214), Solnit mostly associates bicycles with the suburbs ("obvious things could be said about bicycling here, were this not a book about walking") (259), which like cars are the antithesis of the landscapes and cityscapes that most attract walkers; in 2000 there was nothing for Solnit to say about the urban cyclist. One cycle length ahead of us again, Luiselli found her way into the third and final atlas co-curated by Solnit (2016), *Nonstop Metropolis: A New York City Atlas*, in which once again she confounds the sense of place that an atlas is supposed to provide: in her contribution to a map, "Singing the City," Luiselli says that the song that reminds her of the first year she spent in Manhattan's Morningside Heights, by the Scottish pop group Belle and Sebastian, is

nominally set in Queens's Shea Stadium but is really about the life of baseball players constantly on the road (17–18).

4. That this restriction of the public space to indecent women is class-based almost goes without saying. For some of the range of conflicts over women and public space in Mexico in the decade of the 1920s, with careful attention paid to different categories (shop girls, market vendors, actresses, etc.), see Ageeth Sluis (2016) and Anne Rubenstein (1997). For general reflections about women and the Latin American city, see Anne Lambright and Elisabeth Guerrero (2007).

5. Chapter 14 of Solnit (2000) also looks at women, walking, and cities. For the most recent feminist examination of the woman who walks in public, in an essay that straddles academic literary criticism with the personal essay, see Lauren Elkin's *Flâneuse: Women Walk the City in Paris, New York, Tokyo, Venice, and London* (2017). The chapter about Venice is not about Luiselli's wandering through Venice, narrated in the first and last chapters of *Papeles falsos/ Sidewalks*, but of the conceptual and performance artist Sophie Calle.

6. Although Ignacio Padilla and Jorge Volpi won international literary awards for novels about Nazi Germany, Volpi wrote a short novel about *Contemporáneos* poet Jorge Cuesta, and Pedro Angel Palou a novel about *Contemporáneos* poet Xavier Villaurrutia. This group of writers were unaware that Chilean-Mexican-Spaniard Roberto Bolaño was organizing his now classic *The Savage Detectives* also around a 1930s writer, but the fictional Cesárea Tinajero comes out of the Stridentist Movement, the politically leftist and nationalist movement that, in the culturally factionalized time of the 1930s, stood in opposition to the cosmopolitan *Contemporáneos* of Cuesta, Villaurrutia, and Owen. The *Contemporáneo* most associated with narrating the street life of Mexico City in the 1930s through the 1950s was Salvador Novo, whom Luiselli mentions three times in *Sidewalks*.

7. Or our own project's maps: see http://www.arcgis.com/home/webmap/viewer.html?webmap=81918c1db6e14e659764c62238ea26f2. For an almost fetishistic appreciation of the Guía Roji, see Francisco Goldman's engaging and moving 2015 essay *The Interior Circuit*.

8. I'm not referring to the single paragraph chapter, "Cement," where Luiselli sees that someone has been killed outside her apartment, describes the corpse's face in detail, but broods more on the chalk outline of the corpse that she sees on the cement sidewalk the next day. An entire chapter of urban history, in which Mexico City has been actually safer than the rest of the country during the *sexenio* of Felipe Calderón (2006–2012), is ignored or misunderstood in this one-paragraph gesture. Francisco Goldman 2015 speculates on why this was so.

9. The newspaper estimates are from Ruiz-Palacios (2016). Good visual coverage of the march accompanies the online journal *Animal Político* (2016). The two hashtags for the march, #VivasNosQueremos and #24A (April 24), can lead to plenty of YouTube videos for this march and for the sister marches in other Mexican cities.

10. Murals like the ones described in the *New York Times* article (Burnett 2017) have very little to do with either the Mexican muralist movement or the local graffiti artists described in Maria Andre's chapter in this volume. It's no surprise that a portrait of Frida Kahlo would be pressed into service for a cosmopolitan's idea of

mexicanidad; see Margaret Lindauer's *Devouring Frida* (1999) on the misappropriations and faulty uses of the Mexican artist.

WORKS CITED

Animal Político. 2016. "La marcha Vivas Nos Queremos contra las violencia machista en fotos y videos." *Animal Politico* (April 24). Accessed June 24, 2017. http://www.animalpolitico.com/2016/04/desde-ecatepec-hasta-el-angel-asi-va-la-marcha-vivas-nos-queremos-contra-la-violencia-machista/
Barthes, Roland. (1964) 1983. "The Eiffel Tower." In *A Barthes Reader*, edited by Susan Sontag, 236–250. New York: Hill and Wang.
Benjamin, Walter. (1982) 1999. *The Arcades Project*. Translated by Howard Eilin and Kevin McLaughlin. Prepared on the basis of the German text by Rolf Teidemann. Cambridge, MA: Belknap Press of Harvard University.
———. 1999. "A Berlin Chronicle." In *Walter Benjamin: Selected Writings: Vol.2, 1927–1934*. Translated by Rodney Livingstone and others. Edited by Michael W. Jennings, Howard Eiland, and Gary Smith, 595–637. Cambridge, MA: Belknap Press of Harvard University.
Burnett, Victoria. 2017. "Near Mexico City, Cable Cars Let Commuters Glide Over Traffic," *New York Times*, December, 28. Accessed June 25, 2017. https://www.nytimes.com/2016/12/28/world/americas/mexico-city-mexicable.html
Cardoso, Nelly. 2014. "Fantasmas y sosias en *Los ingrávidos* de Valeria Luiselli." *Romance Notes* 54: 77–84.
"CDMX: Mejor en bici." N.d. Accessed June 25, 2017. http://www.cdmx.gob.mx/vive-cdmx/post/mejor-en-bici
Clavel, Ana. 2000. *Los deseos y su sombra*. México: Editorial Alfaguara.
Elkin, Lauren. 2017. *Flâneuse: Women Walk the City in Paris, New York, Tokyo, Venice, and London*. New York: Farrar, Straus, Giroux.
Franco, Jean. 1989. *Plotting Women: Gender and Representation in Mexico*. New York: Columbia University Press.
Goldman, Francisco. 2015. *The Interior Circuit: A Mexico City Chronicle*. New York: Grove Press.
Guía Roji. 2015. *Formato Ciudad de México. Area metropolitana y alrededores. 2015. 16a Edición*. México, DF: Guía Roji, S.A. de C.V.
Kunkel, Benjamin. 2017. "Still Small Voice: The Fictions of Robert Walser." *The New Yorker*, August 6, 2007. Accessed June 24, 2017. http://www.newyorker.com/magazine/2007/08/06/still-small-voice
Lambright, Anne, and Elisabeth Guerrero, eds. 2007. *Unfolding the City: Women Write the City in Latin America*. Minneapolis: University of Minnesota Press.
Lindauer, Margaret. 1999. *Devouring Frida: The Art History and Popular Celebrity of Frida Kahlo*. Hanover, NH: Wesleyan University Press.
Luiselli, Valeria. 2010. *Papeles falsos*. México, DF: Ed. Sexto Piso.
———. 2011. *Los ingrávidos*. México, DF: Ed. Sexto Piso.
———. 2013. *La historia de mis dientes*, México, DF: Ed. Sexto Piso.

————. 2014a. *Sidewalks.* Translated by Christina MacSweeney. Minneapolis: Coffee House Press.

————. 2014b. *Faces in the Crowd.* Translated by Christina MacSweeney. Minneapolis: Coffee House Press.

————. 2015. *The Story of My Teeth.* Translated by Christina MacSweeney. Minneapolis: Coffee House Press.

Rama, Ángel. 1984. *La ciudad letrada.* Hanover, NH: Eds. del Norte.

Rubenstein, Anne. 1997. *Bad Language, Naked Ladies, and Other Threats to the Nation: A Political History of Comic Books in Mexico.* Durham, NC: Duke University Press.

Ruiz-Palacios, Fanny. 2016. "Mujeres exigen un México seguro." *El Universal,* April 25. Accessed June 24, 2017. http://www.eluniversal.com.mx/articulo/metropoli/cdmx/2016/04/25/mujeres-exigen-frenar-violencia-de-genero#imagen-1

Sluis, Ageeth. 2016. *Deco City, Deco Body: Female Spectacle and Modernity in Mexico City, 1900–1939.* Lincoln: The University of Nebraska Press.

Solnit, Rebecca. 2000. *Wanderlust: A History of Walking.* New York: Penguin Books.

Solnit, Rebecca and Joshua Jelly-Schapiro, eds. 2016. *Nonstop Metropolis: A New York City Atlas.* Berkeley: The University of California Press.

Walser, Robert. (1917) 2012. *The Walk.* Translated by Susan Bernofsky. New York: New Directions.

Conclusion

From DF to CDMX: The (Dis)order
of Becoming a World City

Alejandro Puga and Glen David Kuecker

The chapters in *Mapping the Megalopolis* bring literary studies and social science thinking into a conversation about one of the world's great cities. We have engaged the reader in this conversation as a way to participate in an effort advanced by a long line of other writers and scholars to comprehend the city that defies comprehension. Our common ground has been the positioning of two significant propositions, the lettered city and the right to the city, as the volume's central analytical frame. We have used two mutually constitutive parts of urban experience—order and disorder—as the volume's thematic thread. Within this larger framework, the chapters have explored urban mobilities, memory, and nostalgia, urban imaginaries both asserted and contested, and the ways urban dwellers have made sense of their city. This analysis brings us to perceive Mexico City as overrun with elite projects to order the city, while it also recognizes the city as a fluid terrain of contestation originating from rejections of the elite projects and their alternative urban imaginaries. The dialogical relationship between order and disorder presents Mexico City as constantly shifting in meaning, as the "dream of an order" (Rama [1984] 1996, 17) intersecting with lived experience constantly makes the city a contingent reality. The city that can't be imagined thrives on its impossibility of closure.

In January 2016, while this volume was in its early stages of drafting, the world learned that Mexico City officials had changed its dream of an order by changing the city's name. The *Distrito Federal* (DF) became *Ciudad de Mexico* (CDMX). The name change stems from the drafting of a new city constitution, also in 2016. It allows for the selection of its own attorney general and chief of police, and greater agency in the city's boroughs with regard to budgeting and leadership. The semantic move also reflects a change in the city's administrative jurisdiction from a federal district to the equivalent of

a state within the republic (Scruggs 2017). The gesture represents a desta-
bilization in the constructed understandings of the city that give measure to
the uncertainties of Mexico City's twenty-first century contingency. In this
conclusion, we invite the reader to join us in unpacking the elite's CDMX
re-ordering of the megalopolis.

We begin with a delirious ordering proposition advanced by a Puerto
Rican novelist, professor, and former *New York Times* editor that appeared
in the travel section of the December 28, 2016 issue of the *New York Times*.
The author, Luisita López Torregoza, relates a nostalgic travel story with
a lamenting premise of the loss of "my city," Mexico City, to the remak-
ing of a city that is now "everyone's." López Torregoza ventures a contrast
between the quaintly ordered Mexico City of her upbringing—rather, three
years of an upbringing that appears to have mainly taken place in the *Centro
Histórico* and *Colonia Roma*—with her experience of a newly ordered, more
globalized, cosmopolis. López Torregoza alludes briefly to reforms such as
the legalization of gay marriage and non-compliance with President Felipe
Calderon's (2006–2012) "all-out-military-style war on the drug cartels" as
the catalyst for the transformation, but the majority of her wonder is directed
at a touristic, and especially gastronomic renaissance that is a direct result of
the shift from DF to CDMX. López Torregoza doesn't explicitly invoke the
new acronym, nor does she mention the immense physical presence of those
letters around the cities' emblematic sites. However, the narrative of gastro
stops consecrates the "symbolic but highly visible result" (Scruggs 2017) of
the CDMX shift, one that doesn't necessarily count on the history of political
maneuvers, especially the city's direct election of its mayor in 1996—previously mayors were appointed by the president—and the 2013 negotiation
of a city constitution that gradually contributed to the conceptualization of
Mexico City as an autonomously functioning urban form. Just as the massive CDMX acronym suddenly appeared on a life-size scale at symbolic sites
around the city, López Torregoza's account of "her" Mexico City, which,
again, is now "everyone's Mexico City," appears to have required little more
than consumer engagement in restaurants whose vibrant color schemes yield
the cosmopolitan appeal she deems be "so Mexico."

For those of us who are literary scholars with an interest in prose narrative from Mexico City—be it fiction or *crónica* of the city, or a combination
thereof—the loss of the DF designation implies a loss in its adjective form
defeño, a term which does not limit itself to describing a resident of the
metropolitan zone, and one which avoids resorting to the sometimes pejora-
tive *chilango*, which, concurrent to the aesthetic transformations that López
Torregosa describes, has evolved into a badge of honor, as in *Chilango*, one
of the city's premier scenester publications. In the study of the Mexican
urban novel, defeño as a literary category emerged as a means of recognizing

that studies of Mexican urban literature could no longer limit themselves to themes of the capital city (Puga 2012). The emergence of the border city as a locus for the examination of immigration, femicide, and narco-state, for example, signals a mandate to retire assumptions that Mexico City is the beginning and end of the city in Mexico. For those who have committed their attention to the inexhaustible exploration of Mexico City, *narrativa defeña* serves as both a concession and a venue for continued study. But, it remains to be determined who or what will constitute *la novela sedemequis*.

Dropping DF in favor of CDMX may well free the city of the "whims of [...] national governments on many local matters" (Scruggs 2017), but it also means losing "*El Defe*," the contestatory informalization of the term's more stolid, nationalistic projections. It would be difficult to reimagine Dylanesque Rockdrigo González's evocative 1982 album *Aventuras en el DeFe* as *Aventuras en Sedemequis*. Certainly this latter term practices the same phonetization of an acronym that makes DeFe so delightful, but what does not continue as readily is DeFe's contestation of the nation-state's ordering of Mexico City implicit in a "Federal District." Indeed, the content of González's emblematic song would seem to contradict through its disorder and contingency the kinds of quaintly accessible and digestible imagery and associations that CDMX seeks:

Around the corner a stinky cloud trapped me
it was a smog cloud that turned into a hateful creature
I was knocked out of my senses, trembling and very confused.[1]

González's lyrics, and the contestatory DeFe, speak to the fallacy of an organizing centrality in the lived experience of Mexico City. *Sedemequis* might do so as well, as the first two syllables enunciate "*sede*," that is, the seat or headquarters. However, we are still not certain where CDMX is, and where its center and contestations are to be located. Still, we offer some views on CDMX, so that *sedemequis* might have a chance at differentiating itself from the ordering of DF and the subtle disordering of DeFe while still offering more to its citizens and the world than restaurants and life-size acronyms.

In some regards, the contemporary exponents of the novela *defeña* discussed in this volume foreshadow the DF to CDMX shift. Influenced by the observations of their social sciences counterparts, chapters in this volume by María André (chapter 6), Patrick O'Connor (chapter 10), Alejandro Puga and Patricia Tovar (chapter 4), Daniel Rogers (Chapter 3), and Marta Sierra (chapter 1), speak to the apparently inevitable private consumerism that happens within spaces of national affirmation, spaces cast as inherently public by their architects. Celorio's Juan Manuel Barrientos's deep architectural knowledge, for example, doesn't require a purchase, but it does require several

drinks and elaborately orchestrated meals. The implicit requirement of purchasing power in the Centro Histórico is observable in Juan Manuel's loss of
life shortly after he is relieved of his wallet. Although they are not novelistic
protagonists, the graffiti artists in chapter 6 (André's chapter) contest an
association with individual boroughs, and seek to branch out in the city, while
their work becomes an object of consumption to be paired with the gastro
scene. O'Connor finds in Valeria Luiselli vestiges of Walter Benjamin's *flâneur*, that contradictory entity who shuns consumerism and yet is on the market as an artist. For that matter, author Ricardo Lugo Viñas has offered a tour
of the cantinas that Juan Manuel Barrientos visited in Celorio's novel, a tour
whose architectural dimension was reduced to establishing the Cathedral as
the meeting place (Perez 2014). If there is not yet a novela *sedemequis*, there
is certainly a *sedemequis* reading of it, one that problematizes the citizen-as-
consumer and her or his centrality to the city's modern ordering.

In fact, within the trajectory and study of the novela *defeña*, there have
been the beginnings of such a reading, one that takes note of the national
imaginary's often conflicted engagement with private investment. An early
example is José Emilio Pacheco's ([1981] 2014) iconic *Las batallas en el
desierto*, in which President Miguel Alemán's (1946–1952) PRI intermingles
with the United States's popular culture and business interests, resulting in a
gradual replacement of provincially born patriarchy with a new ordering on
micro- and macrocosmic scales. The protagonist, Carlos, recalls the substitution of evening tequila with highballs, but he also remembers how his father
redefined himself through engagement with an unnamed soap company,
most likely a reference to the fledgling presence of Colgate-Palmolive.[2] More
recent fiction describes a Mexico City ordered less by a nationalistic *mythos*
than it is by the accumulation of capital. Roberto Mendoza (2012) describes
Juan Villoro's (1997) *Materia dispuesta* and Roberto Bolaño's (1998) *Los
detectives salvajes* as novels of Mexico City that depart from their precursors
in that they emerge from the city's first steps toward what is now a CDMX
designation, namely by the 1997 mayoral election. Ever the companion to the
novela *defeña*, the *crónica* of Mexico City from the latter half of the twentieth
century to the present has tracked the curious privatizations of public spaces
and the often discordant emulations of shopping malls, suburbs, and other
imported orderings. Carlos Monsiváis, José Joaquín Blanco, Elena Poniatowska, and many others have through their crónicas provided important
framings for a *narrativa sedemequis*.[3]

While we posit a shift in the meanings of literature about Mexico City
in the transition from DF to CDMX, we also ponder the implications of the
renaming for social science approaches to the city and its literature. Many
questions come to the forefront, but near the top, we wonder if CDMX constitutes a rupture in the narrative of Mexico City, a significant if not radical

departure in the city's urban form that constitutes the need for the elite project of renaming. This line of analysis suggests CDMX is more than the city's first attempt at giving meaning to its twenty-first century form, although that semiotic enterprise is entirely significant. It is a departure from the problematic, both lived and analytical, of the city's experience with neoliberal globalization, a theme that has dominated social science thinking for over thirty years, and appears in this volume through the chapters by Shannan Mattiace and Jennifer Johnson (chapters 5 and 7), Glen Kuecker (chapter 2), Karen Velasquez (chapter 9), and Charlotte Blair (chapter 8). As the outcome of the city's neoliberal transformation, CDMX gives meaning to a new social, political, economic, and cultural reality for the city. If this social science–defined rupture is valid, we ponder if the novela *sedemequis* is to be interpreted as one of its cultural articulations.

As an attempt at giving semiotic meaning to the urban experience, the CDMX urban imaginary is most visible by a branding that reveals the lettered city's attempt to order the city as a world city. The world city proposition within urban studies emerged from the limitations of reductionist attempts at theorizing the meanings of neoliberal globalization. The world city responds to narrow definitions of the global city as a particular expression of global capitalism. By Saskia Sassen's ([1991] 2001) formulation only three urban forms merited the distinction of "global city": New York, London, and Tokyo. This closure suggested the limitations of globalization studies approaches to urban analysis, while also provoking a critique of the deeply Western-centric framing of the urban experience. The global city approach did not serve urban theory well in understanding the emergence of major urban centers in Asia, Africa, and Latin America, which led theorists to propose the world city concept.

Ananya Roy and Aihwa Ong's (2011) contribution to the world city concept is to offer us the interesting verb form, "worlding," to describe the ways cities like Mexico City strive to become cosmopolitan urban forms that circulate within an elite class of cities throughout the world. They see a worlding city as "a milieu of intervention, a source of ambitious visions, and of speculative experiments that have different possibilities of success and failure." Most provocative in Roy and Ong's argument is the agency implied in their description of "worlding practices." Where urban subjects were once "globalized" in the passive voice, urban dwellers now become actors in the phenomenological landscape through practices such as updated *flânerie* and contestatory acts in monumental spaces, as described in many essays in this volume. They also become actors through branding, which we maintain is a twenty-first century expression of the lettered city. CDMX, from this interpretation, is the worlding of Mexico City. Roy and Ong further describe "the art of being global" as "[i]nherently unstable, inevitably subject to intense

contestation, and always incomplete" (xv), which is an analytical line that
resonates with our notion of the delirious city, a *ciudad inabarcable*. Our
process in this volume serves as a testament to the importance of this agency
that stems from having embraced the perpetually incomplete city, as play-
fully illustrated in chapter 10 (O'Connor's chapter). Our pursuit of Solnit's
definition of an atlas as "a collection of versions of a place" led us to an
encounter of problematically discrete academic disciplines, and an inter-
change of critical apparatus as an acceptance that our *ciudad inabarcable*
defied the inquiry of a single discipline. More importantly, our collaboration
has positioned us, and we hope, the reader, to avoid acts of encapsulation
and closure that lead us to become "globalized" and to seek rather the more
uncertain proposition of a worlding practice. This twenty-first century opening as a rupture from the closed orderings of twentieth-century modernism
suggests endless possibilities for literary and social science pursuits of the
ciudad inabarcable.

The incompleteness of Mexico City suggested by the world city perspective resonates with this volume's exploration of the symbiotic relationship
between urban order and disorder. The incompleteness points toward thinking about Mexico City from the perspective of critical urbanism's use of
assemblage theory, which is derived from Gilles Deleuze and Felix Guattari's
(1987) embrace of non-linearity, which they articulate through the rhizome,
the creeping underground roots that symbolize horizontal networks of disordered, fluid, and diverse social and cultural reality. These horizontal networks
become ordered through a process of assemblage, which itself exists in an
unstable state far from being the fixed order of a closed system. Assemblage thinking about urban order and disorder has provoked debate within
critical urbanism that centers on the proper place for "assemblage urbanism"
within critical urbanism, especially the strong postmodern currents of works
like Deleuze and Guattari's (1987) *A Thousand Plateaus* as well as Bruno
Latour's (2005) actor-network theory. The debate within critical urbanism
questions whether assemblage urbanism is too grand of a distraction from
the work of political economy and the revolutionary potential of the city, a
position taken by Neil Brenner (2011), or whether assemblage urbanism, as
Colin McFarlane (2011) argues, should provide a fundamental rethinking
of critical urban theory. As we collaboratively worked on the Mapping the
Megalopolis grant project for three years, the team nervously attempted to
bring the right to the city into conversation with the lettered city, a mish-mash
that embraced the delirious city that is the *ciudad inabarcable*. The resulting
chapters in this volume provide ample evidence for both sides of the debate
over urban assemblage: we embrace the open, fluid, unstable, and disordered
city while recognizing the critical importance of the right to the city and its
revolutionary potential.

That the chapters in this volume point to the openness of the urban form as key for thinking about twenty-first century Mexico City should not come as a surprise as the volume reflects important trends in how significant urban thinkers are conceptualizing the twenty-first century urban form. Consider, for example, a two-hour presentation made by Richard Sennett (professor of sociology at New York University and London School of Economics), Saskia Sassen (professor of sociology at Colombia University), Richard Burdett (director of London School of Economics Cities program), and Joan Clos (UN Habitat's Executive Director and former mayor of Barcelona) at the closing of the World Urban Forum, which took place in another Latin American capital city, Quito, Ecuador, in October 2016. The forum featured the launching of UN Habitat III's "New Urban Agenda," which is the UN's 20-year agenda for promoting sustainable and inclusive urbanism in the twenty-first century (habitat3.org). In what they are calling the "Quito Papers," these thinkers put forward a stringent critique of the Charter of Athens, an urban planning vision intellectually authored by Le Corbusier, the driving force behind the twentieth century's high modernist architecture and urban planning (Scott 1998). In contrast to the closed urbanism of the high modernists, the Quito Papers advocate an open urban ordering. Clos stated, "All of the ideas," emanating from the Charter of Athens's vision for the urbanism "of the 20th century are in crisis." Sassen added, "we have entered a new epoch, no doubt. . . . The Quito Papers are a first step to recognize the necessity of a *ciudad de variables* [the varied city]. The city is a complex but incomplete system" (Clos and Sassen quotes from Scruggs 2016).

Habitat III's "New Urban Agenda" responds to the mounting crises facing the world's cities, including climate change, energy transition, food and water scarcity, public health, ecological degradation, political instabilities, warfare, and economic stress. These crises are already well known to twenty-first century Mexico City, and add elements of tension, some new and some old, to the relationship between order and disorder. They also challenge our understandings of rupture and the theoretical problem of how humanity will eventually depart from modernity, if we have not already. Assuming modernity will not endlessly reproduce itself in perfect closure, we need to ask if it will evolve through a willful transition into a new epistemic, or will it commit some form of an ecocide driven catastrophic collapse? If CDMX is an elite ordering of Mexico City in the form of worlding, then the city, its literary form, and its social justice struggles are joining the ranks of the cosmopolitan megalopolis at a time when the modern order is most likely giving way to a profound disordering. Perhaps this is the central plot to the novela *sedemequis*.

As we look to the potential for a great disordering in the twenty-first century, Mexico City, the *ciudad inabarcable*, obviously faces an uncertain future, but the chapters in this volume suggest it does so from a familiar, delirious position. How well will theoretical and literary formulas once reliable for understanding the modern city serve us in understanding the *ciudad inabarcable* in the great disordering? How will the *flâneur*, either on foot or on bicycle, help us to map a megalopolis in the perfect storm of climate change, energy transition, and ecological degradation? Where will the *flâneur* get her or his water in a city already facing extreme water crisis? Carlos Slim's *Plaza Carso* or the *Naftalandia* (Naftaland) office complex in Santa Fe are not well suited for extreme disorder, while the *colonias populares* tested by years of resilience to the many-fold crises of extreme marginalization have the tenacity, skills, and knowledge to weather the perfect storm. How these stories play out will define the next epoch in this city's centuries-long history.

NOTES

1. *A la vuelta de la esquina una nube apestosa me atrapó/ era una nube de smog que en un ser odioso se convirtió,/ yo estaba sacado de onda, tembloroso y bien confuso.*

2. See Cynthia Steele (1992) for a thorough analysis of this power shift in Pacheco's *Las batallas en el desierto* and *El principio del placer.*

3. For an overview of how these *cronistas* engage the city in its many contradictions, see Anadeli Bencomo (2002).

WORKS CITED

Bencomo, Anadeli. 2002. *Voces y voceros de la megalópolis: la crónica periodístico-literaria en México*. Madrid: Iberoamericana.

Bolaño, Roberto. 1998. *Los detectives salvajes*. Barcelona: Anagrama.

Brenner, Neil, David J. Madden, and David Wachsmuth. 2011. "Assemblage Urbanism and the Challenges of Critical Urban Theory." *City* 15 (2): 225–40.

Deleuze, Gilles and Félix Guattari. 1987. *A Thousand Plateaus: Capitalism and Schizophrenia*. Translated by Brian Massumi. Minneapolis: University of Minnesota Press.

González, Rodrigo. 1989. *Aventuras en el DeFe*. Performed by Rodrigo González. México, DF: Pentagrama. LP.

Latour, Bruno. 2005. *Reassembling the Social: An Introduction to Actor-Network-Theory*. New York: Oxford University Press.

López Torregrosa, Luisita. 2016. "My Mexico City is Now Everyone's." *New York Times*, December 28. Accessed June 28, 2017. https://www.nytimes.com/2016/12/28/travel/mexico-city-culture-childhood-new-awakening.html

McFarlane, Colin. 2011. "Assemblage and Critical Urbanism." *City* 15 (2): 204–24.

Mendoza, Roberto. 2012. "El vértigo horizontal. La novela urbana de la Ciudad de México de los últimos 20 años." PhD diss. University of Arizona.

Pacheco, José Emilio (1981) 2014. *Las batallas en el desierto*. México, DF: Ediciones Era.

Pérez, Fernanda. 2014. "Recorrido por las cantinas del Centro Histórico." *Masaryk.tv,* Octubre 10. Accessed June 28, 2017. https://masaryk.tv/80532/recorrido-por-las-cantinas-del-centro-historico

Puga, Alejandro. 2012. *La ciudad novelada a fines del siglo XX: Estructura, retórica y figuración*. México, D.F: Universidad Autónoma Metropolitana.

Rama, Ángel. (1984) 1996. *The Lettered City. Post-Contemporary Interventions*. Durham, NC: Duke University Press.

Roy, Ananya, and Aihwa Ong, eds. 2011. *Worlding Cities: Asian Experiments and the Art of Being Global*. Malden, MA: Wiley-Blackwell.

Sassen, Saskia. (1991) 2001. *The Global City: New York, London, Tokyo*. Princeton, N.J: Princeton University Press.

Scott, James C. 1998. *Seeing Like a State: How Certain Schemes to Improve the Human Condition Have Failed*. New Haven: Yale University Press.

Scruggs, Gregory. 2017. "The People Power Behind Mexico City's New Constitution." *Citiscope*, February 3. Accessed June 28, 2017. https://www.citylab.com/politics/2017/02/the-people-power-behind-mexico-citys-new-constitution/515637/

———. 2016. "The Quito Papers: An intellectual counterpoint to the New Urban Agenda." *Citiscope*, October 20. Accessed June 28, 2017. http://citiscope.org/habitatIII/news/2016/10/quito-papers-intellectual-counterpoint-new-urban-agenda

Steele, Cynthia. 1992. *Politics, Gender, and the Mexican Novel, 1968–1988: Beyond the Pyramid*. Austin: University of Texas Press.

UN Habitat. "New Urban Agenda." Accessed June 28, 2017. Habitat3.org

Villoro, Juan. 1997. *Materia dispuesta*. México D.F.: Alfaguara.

Bibliography

Acevedo-Muñoz, Ernesto. 2003. *Buñuel and Mexico: The Crisis of National Cinema*. Berkeley: University of California Press.

Ades, Dawn. 1989. *Art in Latin America*. New Haven and London: Yale University Press.

Adler, David. 2015. "Do We Have a Right to the City?" *Jacobin Magazine,* October 6. Accessed June 25, 2016. https://www.jacobinmag.com/2015/10/mexico-city-df-right-to-the-city-harvey-gentrification-real-estate-corruption/

Agencia de Gestión Urbana. 2015. "GDF atraer inversión extranjera para diversos proyectos." February 4.

Aguilar, Adrian Guillermo. 2008. "Peri-urbanization, Illegal Settlements and Environmental Impact in Mexico City." *Cities* 25 (13): 3–45.

Álvarez, Ana, and Förderverein Deutsches Architektur Zentrum, eds. 2008. *Citámbulos Mexico City: Journey to the Mexican Megalopolis = Viaje a La Megalópolis Mexicana = Reise in Die Mexikanische Magalopole*. Berlin: Jovis.

Anderson, Benedict. (1983) 1991. *Imagined Communities: Reflections on the Origin and Spread of Nationalism*. London: Verso.

Animal Político. 2016. "La marcha Vivas Nos Queremos contra las violencia machista en fotos y videos." *Animal Político*, Abril 24. Accessed June 24, 2017. http://www.animalpolitico.com/2016/04/desde-ecatepec-hasta-el-angel-asi-va-la-marcha-vivas-nos-queremos-contra-la-violencia-machista/

Anonymous. 1918. "Review of *Criminology* by Marurice Parmelee." *Journal of the American Medical Association* 71 (3): 218–219.

Arlandis, Fanny. 2013. "The Perverse Effect of Street Art on Neighborhood Gentrification." *Le Monde*, April 4. Accessed June 28, 2017. https://www.worldcrunch.com/culture-society/the-perverse-effect-of-street-art-on-neighborhood-gentrification/graffiti-banksy-urbanism-suburbs-urban/c3s10800

Arvide, Cynthia. 2011. "Corea-México, La Nueva Corea En La Zona Rosa." *Chilango*, January 3. Accessed July 3, 2017. http://www.chilango.com/general/corea-mexico-la-nueva-corea-en-la-zona-rosa/

Backhaus, Peter. 2007. *Linguistic Landscapes: A Comparative Study of Urban Multilingualism in Tokyo*. Clevedon: Multilingual Matters, 2007.

Banks, Miranda. 2002. "Monumental Fictions: National Monuments as a Science Fiction Space." *Journal of Popular Film and Television* 30 (3): 136–145.

Barquín, Julián. 2005. "Santa Fe o la dualidad conciliable." In *Santa Fe: Crónica de una comunidad. Catálogo de exposición*, edited by María de Jesús Díaz Nava, Gilberto Prado Galán and Carlos Villanueva Avilez, 51–84. Ciudad de México: Universidad Iberoamericana.

Barthes, Roland. (1964) 1983. "The Eiffel Tower." In *A Barthes Reader*, edited by Susan Sontag, 236–250. New York: Hill and Wang.

Bassols Ricardez, Mario. 2011. "México: la marca de sus ciudades." In *Ciudades mexicanas: desafíos en concierto*, edited by Enrique Cabrero Mendoza, 19–64. México, DF: Fondo de Cultura Económica.

Becerra, Luzma. 2002. "Otra forma de estar en el mundo o la ciudad subterránea en *Los deseos y su sombra* de Ana Clavel." *Iztapalapa* 23 (52): 245–259.

Becker, Anne and Markus-Michael Muller. 2013. "The Securitization of Urban Space and the 'Rescue of Downtown Mexico City." *Latin American Perspectives* 40: 77–94.

Beezley, William. 1987. *Judas at the Jockey Club and Other Episodes of Porfirian Mexico*. Lincoln: University of Nebraska Press.

Bencomo, Anadeli. 2002. *Voces y voceros de la megalópolis: la crónica periodístico-literaria en México*. Madrid: Iberoamericana.

Benjamin, Walter. (1978) 1986. *Reflections: Essays, Aphorisms, Autobiographical Writings*, edited and translated by Peter Demetz. New York: Schocken Books.

———. (1982) 1999. *The Arcades Project*. Translated by Howard Eilin and Kevin McLaughlin. Prepared on the basis of the German text by Rolf Teidemann. Cambridge, MA: Belknap Press of Harvard University.

———. 1999. "A Berlin Chronicle." In *Walter Benjamin: Selected Writings: Vol.2, 1927–1934*. Translated by Rodney Livingstone and others. Edited by Michael W. Jennings, Howard Eiland, and Gary Smith, 595–637. Cambridge, MA: Belknap Press of Harvard University.

———. 2006. *The Writer of Modern Life*. Edited by Michael W. Jennings. Translated by Howard Eiland, et al. Cambridge: Harvard University Press.

Bennett, Vivienne. 1992. "The Evolution of Urban Popular Movements in Mexico Between 1966 and 1988." In *The Making of Social Movements in Latin America*, edited by Sonia Álvarez and Arturo Escobar, 240–259. Boulder: Westview Press.

Berman, Marshall. 1988. *All That Is Solid Melts into Air: The Experience of Modernity*. New York: Viking Penguin.

Bickford, Susan. 2000. "Constructing Inequality: City Spaces and the Architecture of Citizenship." *Political Theory* 28 (3) (June): 355–376.

Bird Pico, Maria. 2011. "How Antara Polanco Revived a Corner of Mexico City." February 1. Accessed June 16, 2017. http://www.thecenterofshopping.com/blog/how-antara-polanco-revived-a-corner-of-mexico-city

Bliss, Katherine. 2010. *Compromised Positions: Prostitution, Public Health, and Gender Politics in Revolutionary Mexico*. University Park, PA: Penn State University Press.

Blommaert, Jan. 2013. *Ethnography, Superdiversity and Linguistic Landscapes: Chronicles of Complexity*. Toronto: Multilingual Matters.

Bodei, Remo. 1995. "Memoria histórica, olvido e identidad colectiva." In *La tenacidad de la política*, compiled by Nora Rabotnikof, Ambrosio Velasco, and Corina Yturbe, 81–101. México: Universidad Nacional Autónoma de México.

Bolaño, Roberto. 1998. *Los detectives salvajes*. Barcelona: Anagrama.

Bonfil Batalla, Guillermo, and Philip Adams Dennis. (1987) 1996. *México Profundo: Reclaiming a Civilization*. Translated by Philip A. Dennis. Austin: University of Texas Press.

Boym, Stevlana. 2001. *The Future of Nostalgia*. New York: Basic Books.

Brenner, Neil, David J. Madden, and David Wachsmuth. 2011. "Assemblage Urbanism and the Challenges of Critical Urban Theory." *City* 15 (2): 225–240.

Broid, Daniel and Marlene de la O. N. d. "Urban Resilience in Situations of Chronic Violence: Case Study of Mexico City, Mexico." Case study prepared for MIT's Center for International Studies (CIS), for the Urban Resilience in Chronic Violence project co-directed by Diane Davis and John Tirman, and funded by USAID [GRANT # AID-OAA-G-10–00002].

Bruhn, Kathleen. 2008. *Urban Protest in Mexico and Brazil*. New York: Cambridge University Press.

Brushwood, John S. 1981. "Sobre el referente y la transformación narrativa en las novelas de Carlos Fuentes y Gustavo Sainz." *Revista iberoamericana* 47 (116): 49–61.

Buil Ríos, Ricardo. 2005. *Graffiti, arte urbano (educación, cultura e identidad en la modernidad)*. Tlalpan: Universidad Pedagógica Nacional.

Bunker, Steven. 2014. *Creating Mexican Consumer Culture in the Age of Porfirio Díaz*. Albuquerque: University of New Mexico Press.

Buñuel, Luis, director. 1950. *Los olvidados*. Ultramar Films.

———. 1953. *La ilusión viaja en tranvía*. Clasa Films Mundiales.

———. 1982. *Mi último suspiro*. Barcelona: Plaza & Janes.

Burnett, Victoria. 2017. "Near Mexico City, Cable Cars Let Commuters Glide Over Traffic." *New York Times*, December 28. Accessed June 25, 2017. https://www.nytimes.com/2016/12/28/world/americas/mexico-city-mexicable.html

Butler, Andy. 2010. "Soumaya Museum by Fernando Romero Architects." October 8. Accessed June 16, 2017. http://www.designboom.com/architecture/soumaya-museum-by-fernando-romero-architects/

Cabrero Mendoza, Enrique. 2011. "Introducción." In *Ciudades mexicanas: desafíos en concierto*, edited by Enrique Cabrero Mendoza, 9–18. México, DF: Fondo de Cultura Económica.

Caldeira, Teresa. 2000. *City of Walls: Crime, Segregation, and Citizenship in São Paulo*. Berkeley: University of California Press.

Calvino, Italo. 1978. *Invisible Cities*. Translated by William Weaver. New York: Harcourt Brace Jovanovich.

Camps, Martín. 2005. "Palimpsesto urbano: Amor propio y Y retiemble en los centros su tierra de Gonzalo Celorio." *Con-Textos* 17 (35) (Julio-diciembre): 64–71.

Cardoso, Nelly. 2014. "Fantasmas y sosias en *Los ingrávidos* de Valeria Luiselli." *Romance Notes* 54: 77–84.

Casa Ernesto Meneses. N. d. "Espacio de encuentro para la comunidad de Santa Fe." Accessed July 1, 2018. http://www.dis.uia.mx/grupos/2014p/dw_a/victormaximo/html_final/index.html

Casey, Nicholas. 2011. "Emperor's New Museum." *The Wall Street Journal*, March 3. Accessed June 16, 2017. http://www.wsj.com/articles/SB10001424052748703300904576178381398949942

Castells, Manuel. 1983. *The City and the Grassroots: A Cross-Cultural Theory of Urban Social Movements.* Berkeley: University of California Press.

Castilla, Alfredo Romero. 2009. "Coreanos. Su presencia ayer y hoy." In *La ciudad cosmopolita de los inmigrantes. Vol. 1*, edited by Carlos Martínez Assad and Alicia Gil Lázaro, 283–305. México, DF: Gobierno del Distrito Federal, Secretaría de Desarrollo Rural y Equidad para las Comunidades.

Castillo Berthier, Héctor. 1990. *La sociedad de la basura: Caciquismo urbano en la ciudad de México.* México: Universidad Nacional Autónoma de México, Instituto de Investigaciones Sociales.

Castillo, Debra. 1998. *Easy Women: Sex and Gender in Modern Mexican Fiction.* Minneapolis: University of Minnesota Press.

Cave, Damien. 2013. "Mexico's New Arrivals Mix Praise and Criticism." *The New York Times*, September 23. Accessed July 2, 2017. http://www.nytimes.com/2013/09/24/world/americas/mexicos-expatriates-mix-praise-and-criticism.html

"CDMX: Mejor en bici." N.d. Accessed June 25, 2017. http://www.cdmx.gob.mx/vive-cdmx/post/mejor-en-bici

Celorio, Gonzalo. 1996. "*Amor propio* con amor propio." *Revista de literatura Mexicana contemporánea* 1 (3): 115–116.

———. 1997. *Ciudad de papel.* México: Universidad Nacional Autónoma de México.

———. 1999. *Y retiemble en sus centros la tierra.* México: Tusquets.

Centros de Integración Juvenil, A.C. (CIJ). 2013. *Estudio básico de comunidad objetivo: diagnóstico del contexto socio-demográfico del area de influencia del CIJ Iztapalapa oriente.* Accessed June 21, 2017. http://www.cij.gob.mx/ebco2013/centros/9370SD.html

Cevallos, Diego. 2003. "MEXICO: South Koreans a Growing Presence in Capital's Retail District." *Inter Press Service News Agency*, June 20. Accessed July 3, 2017. http://www.ipsnews.net/2003/06/mexico-south-koreans-a-growing-presence-in-capitals-retail-district/

Ciudad de México: Crónica de sus delegaciones. 2007. Mexico City: Gobierno del Distrito Federal.

Clark, Robert. 2002. *Global Awareness: Thinking Systematically about the World.* Lanham, MD: Rowman & Littlefield Publishers.

Clavel, Ana. 2000. *Los deseos y su sombra.* México: Editorial Alfaguara.

CNN México. 2014. "Seis datos que debes saber sobre el tren de pasajeros México-Toluca." *CNN México.* Cable News Network-Turner Broadcasting, Inc. July 8. Accessed June 20, 2017. http://expansion.mx/nacional/2014/07/08/seis-datos-que-debes-conocer-sobre-el-tren-mexico-toluca

Coffey, Mary. 2012. *How a Revolutionary Art Became Official Culture: Murals, Museums, and the Mexican State.* Durham, NC: Duke University Press.

Columbia University. 2014. *The Urban Imaginary Project, Barcelona's Moveable Feast: A Post-Crash Urban Imaginary.* Columbia University GSAPP, Advance Studio. Accessed June 16, 2017. http://www.columbia.edu/cu/arch/courses/syllabi/20143/A4105_008_2014_3_Goberna.pdf

Connolly, Priscilla. 2009. "Observing the Evolution of Irregular Settlements: Mexico City's *colonias populares*, 1990–2005." *International Development Planning Review* 31: 1–35.

Coordinación de Responsabilidad Social Institucional (CORSI), Iberoamerican University. N.d. "La Casa Ernesto Meneses: Las huellas de un acompañamiento en las Colonias de Santa Fe." Four chapters.

Correa, Felipe, and Carlos Garciavelez Alfaro. 2014. *Mexico City: Between Geography and Geometry.* San Francisco: Applied Research + Design Publ.

Critical Art Ensemble. 1996. "Nine Theses Against Monuments." In *Random Access 2: Ambient Fears*, edited by Pavel Büchler and Nikos Papastergiadis, 22–30. London: Rivers Oram Press.

Crossa, Veronica. 2012. "Play for Protest, Protest for Play: Artisan and Vendors' Resistance to Displacement in Mexico City." *Antipode* 45 (4): 826–843.

Curcio-Nagy, Linda Ann. 2004. *The Great Festivals of Colonial Mexico City: Performing Power and Identity.* Albuquerque: University of New Mexico Press.

Davis, Diane. 1994. *Urban Leviathan: Mexico City in the Twentieth Century.* Philadelphia: Temple University Press.

———. 2013. "Zero-Tolerance Policing, Stealth Real Estate Development, and the Transformation of Public Space: Evidence from Mexico City." *Latin American Perspectives* 40: 53–76.

Davis, Mike. 2006. *Planet of Slums.* New York: Verso.

de Alva, María, and José Martí. 2004. "Memoria y ciudad. *Y retiemble en sus centros la tierra* de Gonzalo Celorio." *Revista de Literatura Mexicana Contemporánea* 10 (24) (Septiembre-Diciembre): v–ix.

DeBord, Guy. 1958. "Theory of the Dérive." *Internationale Situationniste #2* (December): 62–66.

De Certeau, Michelle. 1988. *The Practice of Everyday Life.* Translated by Steven Randall. Berkeley: University of California Press.

de Fuentes, Fernando. 1936. *Allá en el Rancho Grande.* Lombrado Films.

Deleuze, Gilles and Félix Guattari. 1987. *A Thousand Plateaus: Capitalism and Schizophrenia.* Translated by Brian Massumi. Minneapolis: University of Minnesota Press.

Díaz Nava, María de Jesús. 2005. "Santa Fe." In *Santa Fe: Crónica de una comunidad. Catálogo de exposición*, edited by Díaz Nava, María de Jesús, Gilberto Prado Galán, and Carlos Villanueva Avilez, 15–40. Ciudad de México: Universidad Iberoamericana.

"DramaFever Logs 250 Percent Jump in Latino Viewership." *Latin Post*, January 29, 2016. Accessed July 3, 2017. http://www.latinpost.com/articles/112337/20160129/dramafever-logs-250-percent-jump-latino-viewership.htm

Duhua, Emilio. 2001. "La megaciudad en el siglo XXI: de la modernidad inconclusa a la crisis del espacio público." *Papeles de Población* 7 (30) (octubre-diciembre): 131–161.

Elkin, Lauren. 2017. *Flâneuse: Women Walk the City in Paris, New York, Tokyo, Venice, and London.* New York: Farrar, Straus, Giroux.

Enciso, Fernando Díaz. 2009. *Las mil y una historias del Pedregal De Santo Domingo.* Ciudad de México: Conaculta.

Evans, Peter William. 1995. *The Films of Luis Buñuel.* Oxford: Clarendon Press.

Fabricant, Nicole. 2012. *Mobilizing Bolivia's Displaced: Indigenous Politics and the Struggle over Land.* Chapel Hill: University of North Carolina Press.

Fernández, Emilio. 1944. *María Candelaria.* Films Mundiales.

Flores, Tatiana. 2013. *Mexico's Revolutionary Avant-Gardes: From Estridentismo to ¡30–30!* New Haven, CT: Yale University Press.

Foucault, Michel. (1963) 1973. *The Birth of the Clinic.* Translated by A. M. Sheridan. New York: Routledge.

———. 1984. "Of Other Spaces: Utopias and Heterotopias." Translated by Jay Miskowiec. *Architecture/Mouvement/Continité.* October: 1–9.

Franco, Jean. 1989. *Plotting Women: Gender and Representation in Mexico.* New York: Columbia University Press.

Fragoso, Ariana Mendoza. 2016. "Memoria y comunidad frente a la gentrificación." Unpublished manuscript.

Freire, Paulo. (1968) 2000. *Pedagogy of the Oppressed.* Translated by Mirya Bergman Ramos. New York: Continuum Books.

Fuentes, Carlos. 1958. *La región más transparente.* México: Editorial Alfaguara.

———. (1992) 1999. *The Buried Mirror: Reflections on Spain and the New World.* New York: Houghton Mifflin.

Gallo, Rubén. 2004. "Delirious Mexico City." In *The Mexico City Reader*, edited by Rubén Gallo and Lorna Scott Fox, 3–29. Madison: University of Wisconsin Press.

———. 2009. Foreword to *And Let The Earth Tremble at Its Centers*, by Gonzalo Celorio, translated by Dick Gerders, ix–xx. Austin: University of Texas Press.

Gallo, Rubén, and Lorna Scott Fox, eds. 2004. *The Mexico City Reader.* Madison: University of Wisconsin Press.

Galloway, Nicola, and Heath Rose. 2015. *Introducing Global Englishes.* New York: Routledge.

Gamboa, Federico. (1903) 2013. *Santa.* Madrid: Drácena.

García Canclini, Néstor. 1996. "Modernity after Postmodernity." In *Beyond the Fantastic: Contemporary Art Criticism from Latin America*, edited by Gerardo Mosquera, 20–51. Cambridge, MA: The MIT Press.

———. (1996) 2005. *Hybrid Cultures: Strategies for Entering and Leaving Modernity.* Translated by Christopher L. Chiappari and Silvia L. Lopez. Minneapolis: University of Minnesota Press.

———. 2006. "A City that Improvises Its Globalization." In *Cultural Agency in the Americas*, edited by Doris Sommer, 82–92. Durham, NC: Duke University Press.

García Riera, Emilio. 1970. *Historia documental del cine mexicano: Época Sonora tomo 2.* México: Era.

Garrocho, Carlos. 2011. "Pobreza urbana en asentamientos irregulares: La trampa de la localización periférica." In *Ciudades mexicanas: Desafíos en concierto*, edited by Enrique Cabrero Mendoza, 159–209. Mexico City: Fondo de Cultura Económica.

Garza, James. 2007. *The Imagined Underworld: Sex, Crime, and Vice in Porfirian Mexico City*. Lincoln: University of Nebraska Press.

Geo-Mexico. "Line 12 of Mexico City's metro (subway) reopens." Accessed February 3, 2017. http://geo-mexico.com/?p=8202

Glantz, Margo. 1983. *La lengua en la mano*. México City: Premiá.

Goldman, Francisco. 2015. *The Interior Circuit: A Mexico City Chronicle*. New York: Grove Press.

González Iñárritu, Alejandro, director. 2000. *Amores Perros*. Alta Vista Films.

González, Rodrigo. 1989. *Aventuras en el DeFe*. Performed by Rodrigo González. México, DF: Pentagrama. LP.

Graham, Stephen, and Simon Marvin. 2001. *Splintering Urbanism: Networked Infrastructures, Techno- logical Mobilities and the Urban Condition*. London: Routledge.

Gregory, Derek. 1994. *Geographical Imaginations*. Cambridge, MA: Blackwell.

Guía de arquitectura Ciudad de México. 2015. Mexico City: Arquine/Gobierno de la Ciudad de México.

Guía Roji. 2015. *Formato Ciudad de México. Area metropolitana y alrededores. 2015. 16a Edición*. México, DF: Guía Roji, S.A. de C.V.

Gunderson, Lance H., and C. S. Holling, eds. 2002. *Panarchy: Understanding Transformations in Human and Natural Systems*. Washington, DC: Island Press.

Gutmann, Matthew. 1996. *The Meanings of Macho: Being a Man in Mexico City*. Berkeley: University of California Press.

———. 2002. *The Romance of Democracy: Compliant Defiance in Contemporary Mexico*. Berkeley, CA: University of California Press.

Haber, Paul Lawrence. 2006. *Power from Experience: Urban Popular Movements in Late Twentieth Century Mexico*. University Park: Pennsylvania State University Press.

Hager, Steven. 1984. *Hip Hop: The Illustrated History of Break Dancing, Rap Music, and Graffiti*. New York: St. Martin's Press.

Hägerstrand, Torsten. 1975. "Space, Time and Human Conditions." In *Dynamic Allocation of Urban Space*, edited by A. Karlqvist, 3–14. Farnborough: Saxon House.

Haggett, Peter. 1965. *Locational Analysis in Human Geography*. London: Edward Arnold.

Hall, Stuart. 1989. "Cultural Identity and Cinematic Representation." *Framework* 36: 68–71.

Harley, J. B. 1989. "Deconstructing the Map." *Cartographica* 26 (2): 1–20.

Harvey, David. 1972. "Revolutionary and Counter Revolutionary Theory in Geography and the Problem of Ghetto Formation." *Antipode* 4 (2): 1–3.

———. 2000. *Spaces of Hope*. Berkeley: University of California Press.

———. 2004. "The New Imperialism: Accumulation by Dispossession." *Socialist Register* 40. Accessed June 16, 2017. http://socialistregister.com/index.php/srv/article/view/5811/2707#.V0YKgVcVbts

———. 2008. "Right to the City." *New Left Review* 53 (October): 23–40.

———. 2012. *Rebel Cities: From the Right to the City to the Urban Revolution.* New York: Verso.

Hernandez, Daniel. 2011. *Down and Delirious in Mexico City: The Aztec Metropolis in the Twenty-First Century.* New York: Scribner.

Hooks, bell. 2000. "Choosing the Margin as a Space of Radical Openness." In *Gender, Space, Architecture. An Interdisciplinary Introduction*, edited by Jane Rendell, Barbara Penner, Iain Borden, 203–309. New York: Routledge.

"Human Energy Consumption Moves Beyond 500 Exajoules." 2012. *Business Insider*, February 17. Accessed June 16, 2017. http://www.businessinsider.com/human-energy-consumption-moves-beyond-500-exajoules-2012–2?utm_source=readme

Ingold, Tim. 2000. *The Perception of the Environment: Essays on Livelihood, Dwelling and Skill.* London: Routledge.

International Labour Organization (ILO), Regional Office for Latin America and the Caribbean. 2014. "Notes on Formalization: Informal Employment in Mexico: Current Situation, Policies and Challenges." Accessed June 20, 2017. http://webcache. googleusercontent.com/search?q=cache:dgAxlryVviEJ:www.ilo.org/wcmsp5/ groups/public/---americas/---rolima/documents/publication/wcms_245889. pdf+&cd=1&hl=en&ct=clnk&gl=gt

Jacobs, Jane. 1961. *The Death and Life of Great American Cities.* New York: Random House.

Jameson, Frederic. 1991. *Postmodernism, or, the Cultural Logic of Late Capitalism.* Durham, NC: Duke University Press.

Jelin, Elizabeth. 2003. *State Repression and the Labors of Memory.* Translated by Judy Rein and Marcial Godoy-Anativia. Minneapolis: University of Minnesota Press.

Jiménez-López, Erandi, Ana Cecilia Rodríguez De Romo, and Gabriela Castañeda-López. 2014. "La Historia del Instituto Nacional de Neurología y Neurocirugía a Través de un Documento." *Archivos de Neurociencias* 19 (1): 67–70.

Johns, Michael. 1997. *The City of Mexico in the Age of Díaz.* Austin: University of Texas Press.

Jones, Julie. 2005. "Interpreting Reality: *Los Olvidados* and the Documentary Mode." *Journal of Film and Video* 57 (4): 18–31.

Juárez-Galeana, Luis Gabriel. 2006. "Collaborative Public Open Space Design in Self-help Housing: Minas-Polvorilla, Mexico City." In *Designing Sustainable Cities in the Developing World*, edited by Georgia Butina Watson and Roger Zetter, 179–95. New York: Routledge.

Kandell, Jonathan. 1988. *La Capital: The Biography of México City.* New York: Random House.

Kanost, Laura M. 2008. "Pasillos sin luz: Reading the Asylum in *Nadie me verá llorar.*" *Hispanic Review* 76 (3): 299–316.

Kavanagh, Gaynor. 2000. *Dream Spaces, Memory and the Museum.* London and New York: Leicester University Press.

Keen, Benjamin. 1990. *The Aztec Image in Western Thought.* New Brunswick, NJ: Rutgers University Press.

Kirkpatrick, Susan. 1978. "The Ideology of Costumbrismo." *Ideologies and Literature: A Journal of Hispanic and Luso-Brazilian Studies* 2 (7): 28–44.

Korten, David C. 2001. *When Corporations Rule the World*. San Francisco, CA; Bloomfield, Conn: Berrett-Koehler Publishers; Kumarian Press.

Kozak, Claudia. 2004. *Contra la pared: sobre graffitis, pintadas y otras intervenciones urbanas*. Buenos Aires: Universidad de Buenos Aires.

Krauss, Rosalind E. 1996. *The Originality of the Avant-Garde and Other Modernist Myths*. Cambridge, MA: MIT Press.

Kruijt, Dirk and Kees Koonings. 2015. "Exclusion, Violence and Resilience in Five Latin American Megacities: A Comparison of Buenos Aires, Lima, Mexico City, Rio de Janeiro and Sao Paulo." In *Violence and Resilience in Latin American Cities*, edited by Dirk Kruijt and Kees Koonings, 30–52. New York: Zed Books.

Kuecker, Glen David. 2011. "Book Review Essay: Understanding Latin America in the Era Of Globalization." Review of *Latin America and Global Capitalism: A Critical Globalization Perspective*, by William Robinson. *Journal of World-Systems Research* 17 (1): 236–243. Accessed June 16, 2017. http://www.jwsr.org/wp-content/uploads/2013/02/Kuecker-vol17n1.pdf

———. 2013. "South Korea's New Songdo City: From Neo-liberal Globalisation to the Twenty-first Century Green Economy." *Papers of the British Association for Korean Studies* 15: 20–36.

———. 2015. "New Songdo City: A Case Study in Complexity Thinking and Ubiquitous Urban Design." In *Complexity And Digitalisation Of Cities - Challenges For Urban Planning And Design*, edited by Jenni Partanen, 188–226.

Kunkel, Benjamin. 2017. "Still Small Voice: The Fictions of Robert Walser." *The New Yorker*, August 6, 2007. Accessed June 24, 2017. http://www.newyorker.com/magazine/2007/08/06/still-small-voice

Kunstler, James Howard. 1994. *The Geography of Nowhere: The Rise and Decline of America's Man-Made Landscape*. New York: Simon & Schuster.

Lambright, Anne, and Elisabeth Guerrero, eds. 2007. *Unfolding the City: Women Write the City in Latin America*. Minneapolis: University of Minnesota Press.

Landry, Rodrigue and Richard Bourhis. 1997. "Linguistic Landscape and Ethnolinguistic Vitality: An Empirical Study." *Journal of Language and Social Psychology* 16 (1): 23–49.

Latour, Bruno. 2005. *Reassembling the Social: An Introduction to Actor-Network-Theory*. New York: Oxford University Press.

Lavery, Jane Elizabeth. 2015. *The Art of Ana Clavel: Ghosts, Urinals, Dolls, Shadows and Outlaw Desires*. London: Legenda.

Lefebvre, Henri. (1968) 2015. *Le droit à la ville*. Paris: Ed. Economica.

———. (1970) 2003. *The Urban Revolution*. Translated by Robert Bononno. Minneapolis: University of Minnesota Press.

———. (1974) 1991. *The Production of Space*. Translated by Donald Nicholson-Smith. Cambridge, MA: Blackwell.

Lehan, Richard. 1998. *The City in Literature: An intellectual and cultural history*. Berkeley: University of California Press.

León y Gama, Antonio de. [1792] 2006. *Descripción Histórica Y Cronológica De Las Dos Piedras Que Con Ocasión Del Nuevo Empedrado Que Se Está Formando En La Plaza Principal De México, Se Hallaron En Ella El Año De 1790: Explícase El Sistema De Los Calendarios De Los Indios . . . Noticia . . . A Que Se Añaden*

Otras Curiosas . . . Sobre La Mitología De Los Mexicanos, Sobre Su Astronomía, Y Sobre Los Ritos Y Ceremonias . . . En Tiempo De Su Gentilidad. México: Impr. de Don F. de Zuñiga y Ontiveros, 1792. Alicante, España: Biblioteca Virtual Miguel de Cervantes. Accessed June 30, 2017. http://www.cervantesvirtual.com/nd/ark:/59851/bmc1n7z8

López Torregrosa, Luisita. 2016. "My Mexico City is Now Everyone's." *New York Times*, December 28. Accessed June 28, 2017. https://www.nytimes.com/2016/12/28/travel/mexico-city-culture-childhood-new-awakening.html

Lewis, Oscar. 1963. "The Culture of Poverty." *Society* 1 (1): 17–19.

Lida, David. 2008. *First Stop in the New World: Mexico City, The Capital of the 21st Century.* New York: Riverhead Books.

———. 2015. "Blue Monday." October 26. Accessed June 22, 2017. http://davidlida.com/?p=3249

Lindauer, Margaret. 1999. *Devouring Frida: The Art History and Popular Celebrity of Frida Kahlo.* Hanover, NH: Wesleyan University Press.

Luiselli, Valeria. 2010. *Papeles falsos.* México, DF: Ed. Sexto Piso.

———. 2011. *Los ingrávidos.* México D.F., México: Editorial Sexto Piso.

———. 2012. *La historia de mis dientes.* México D.F., México: Editorial Sexto Piso.

———. 2012. *Papeles falsos.* México: Editorial Sexto Piso.

———. 2014. *Sidewalks.* Translated by Christina MacSweeney. Minneapolis: Coffee House Press.

———. 2014. *Faces in the Crowd.* Translated by Christina MacSweeney. Minneapolis: Coffee House Press.

———. 2015. *The Story of My Teeth.* Translated by Christina MacSweeney. Minneapolis: Coffee House Press.

Lukács, György. 1971. *History and Class Consciousness; Studies in Marxist Dialectics.* Cambridge, MA: MIT Press.

Lynch, Kevin. 1960. *The Image of the City.* Cambridge, MA: MIT Press.

Malkin, Elisabeth. 2014. "Golden Line Adds Tarnish to Sprawling Subway System." *The New York Times*, May 22. Accessed June 21, 2017. http://www.nytimes.com/2014/05/23/world/americas/golden-line-brings-tarnish-to-mexicos-subway-system.html?_r=0

Mariátegui, José Carlos. (1927) 1979. *Siete ensayos de interpretación de la realidad peruana.* Serie popular Era 67. Mexico: Ediciones Era.

Martínez Assad, Carlos. 2004. "La ciudad de México en el cine." *Chasqui* 33 (2): 27–40.

Martí, José. (1893) 2003. *Mi raza.* Accessed July 5, 2017. Biblioteca Virtual Universal. http://www.biblioteca.org.ar/libros/656489.pdf

Martí, José. (1891) 2005. *Nuestra América.* Caracas: Biblioteca Ayacucho.

Martínez Assad, Carlos. 2002. *La patria por la Avenida Reforma.* México: Fondo de Cultura Económica.

Massolo, Alejandra, ed. 1992. *Mujeres y ciudades: Participación social, vivienda y vida cotidiana.* Mexico City: El Colegio de México.

McDonald, Fiona. 2013. *The Popular History of Graffiti: From the Ancient World to the Present.* New York: Skyhorse Publishing.

McFarlane, Colin. 2011. "Assemblage and Critical Urbanism." *City* 15 (2): 204–224.

Méndez-Vigatá, Antonio E. 1997. "Politics and Architectural Language: Post-Revolutionary Regimes in Mexico and Their Influence on Mexican Public Architecture, 1920–1952." In *Modernity and the Architecture of Mexico*, edited by Edward R. Burian, 127–151. Austin: University of Texas Press.

Mendoza, Roberto. 2012. "El vértigo horizontal. La novela urbana de la Ciudad de México los últimos 20 años." PhD diss. University of Arizona.

Merrifield, Andy. 2002. *Metromarxism: A Marxist Tale of the City.* New York: Routledge.

"Mexico City." *Sección Coreana,* Septiembre 9, 2015: 12–13.

"Mexico City A Cultural Melting Pot." *The Economist*, May 9 2006. Accessed July 2, 2017. http://www.economist.com/node/6907576

Monsiváis, Carlos. 1987. *Entrada libre: Crónicas de la sociedad que se organiza.* Mexico City: Ediciones Era.

Morales-Moreno, Luis Gerardo. 1996. "History and Patriotism in the National Museum of Mexico." In *Museums and the Making of "Ourselves:" The Role of Objects in National Identity,* edited by Flora E. Kaplan, 171–191. London and New York: Leicester University Press.

Moreno, Antonio, director. 1932. *Santa.* Compañía Nacional Productora de Películas.

Moreno Carranco, María. 2008. "La producción espacial de lo global: lo público y lo privado en Santa Fe, Ciudad de México." *Alteridades* 18 (36): 75–86.

———. 2005. "Transformaciones urbanas: de basura a edificios corporativos." In *Santa Fe: Crónica de una comunidad. Catálogo de exposición*, edited by Díaz Nava, María de Jesús, Gilberto Prado Galán, and Carlos Villanueva Avilez, 42–49. Ciudad de México: Universidad Iberoamericana.

Merrifield, Andy. 2002. *Metromarxism: A Marxist Tale of the City.* New York: Routledge.

Mraz, John. 2009. *Looking for Mexico: Modern Visual Culture and National Identity.* Durham, NC: Duke University Press.

Mrozowski, Stephen. 1999. "Colonization and the Commodification of Nature." *International Journal of Historical Archaeology* 3 (3) (September): 153–166.

Mundy, Barbara E. 2014. "Place-Names in Mexico-Tenochtitlan." *Ethnohistory* 61 (2): 329–355.

Musil, Robert. (1957) 1987. *Posthumous Papers of a Living Author.* Translated by Peter Wortsman. Colorado: Eridanos Press.

Pacheco, José Emilio. 1981. *Las batallas en el desierto.* México: Ediciones Era.

Pansters, Wil and Hector Castillo Berthier. 2007. "Mexico City." In *Fractured Cities: Social Exclusion, Urban Violence and Contested Spaces in Latin America*, edited by Kees Koonings and Dirk Kruijt, 36–56. New York: Zed Books.

Parker, Simon. 2004. *Urban Theory and Urban Experience: Encountering the City.* New York: Routledge.

Parkhurst-Ferguson, Priscilla. 1994. "The flâneur On and Off the Streets of Paris." In *The Flâneur*, edited by Keith Tester, 22–42. New York: Routledge.

Parkinson, John. 2012. *Democracy and Public Space: The Physical Sites of Democratic Performance.* Oxford: Oxford University Press.

Paz, Octavio. 2000. *Luis Buñuel: el doble arco de la belleza y de la rebeldía*. Barcelona: Galaxia Gutenberg/Círculo de Lectores.

Partido del Trabajo. N.d. "Declaración de principios." Accessed June 22, 2017. http://www.partidodeltrabajo.org.mx/2011/principios.html#iii

Pérez, Fernanda. 2014. "Recorrido por las cantinas del Centro Histórico." *Masaryk.tv,* Octubre 10. Accessed June 28, 2017. https://masaryk.tv/80532/recorrido-por-las-cantinas-del-centro-historico

Pérez Montfort, Ricardo. 1999. "Muralismo y nacionalismo popular 1920–1930." In *Memoria Congreso Internacional de Muralismo. San Idelfonso, cuna del muralismo mexicano, reflexiones historiográficas y artísticas*, edited by Antiguo Colegio de San Ildefonso, 173–206. Ciudad de México: Antiguo Colegio de San Ildefonso.

Pérez Negrete, Margarita. 2007. "Santa Fe: Ciudad, espacio y globalización." Ph.D. diss. Universidad Iberoamericana Pile, Steve. 1996. *The Body and the City: Psychoanalysis, Space and Subjectivity*. New York: Routledge.

Piore, Adam. 2010. "Carlos Slim's Bulging Portfolio." *The Read Deal*, October 1. Accessed July 1, 2017. https://therealdeal.com/2010/10/01/carlos-slim-s-bulging-portfolio-1/

Plaza Carso. N.d. Accessed June 16, 2017. http://www.plazacarso.com.mx

Pólvora: Retratos y murmullos de la Fábrica de Pólvora en Santa Fe. 2015. Ciudad de México: Universidad Iberoamericana.

Poniatowska, Elena. 2000. "Las invasión del Pedregal De Santo Domingo." *La Jornada*, Octubre 21. Accessed June 22, 2017. http://www.jornada.unam.mx/2000/10/21/05aa1cul.html

Programa delegacional de Desarrollo Urbano de Alvaro Obregón. Diario Oficial de la Federación. DOF: 14/04/1997. Accessed June 20, 2017. http://www.dof.gob.mx/nota_detalle.php?codigo=4875377&fecha=14/04/1997

Puga, Alejandro. 2012. *La ciudad novelada a fines del siglo XX: Estructura, retórica y figuración*. México: Universidad Autónoma Metropolitana.

Quirarte, Xavier. 2014. "Resumen la estética nacionalista de Gabriel Figueroa." *Milenio*, Noviembre 5. Accessed June 30, 2017. http://www.milenio.com/cultura/Resumen-estetica-nacionalista-Gabriel-Figueroa_0_296970340.html

Rama, Ángel. 1984. *La ciudad letrada*. Hanover: Ediciones del Norte.

———. (1984) 1996. *The Lettered City. Post-Contemporary Interventions*. Translated by John Charles Chasteen. Durham, NC: Duke University Press.

Reforma. 2002. "Alberga cultura la Casa Frissac." *Reforma*, Febrero 25, 9.

Reveles, Karla. 2015. "'La ciudad del futuro' y Las ZODES de Mancera." *De la Izquierda Diario*. Accessed June 23, 2017. http://www.laizquierdadiario.com/spip.php?page=gacetilla-articulo&id_rubrique=2653&id_article=23277

Rifkin, Jeremy. 1980. *Entropy: A New World View*. New York: Viking Press.

Rivera Garza, Cristina. (1999) 2014. *Nadie me verá llorar*. Barcelona: Tusquets. 4a edición.

———. 2014. *La Castañeda. Narrativas dolientes desde el Manicomio General*. México: Maxi-Tusquets. 4a edición.

Robinson, William. 2008. *Latin America and Global Capitalism: A Critical Globalization Perspective*. Baltimore: Johns Hopkins University Press.

Rodríguez, Darinka and Everado Martínez. 2015. "Cambian trazo del tren México-Toluca por inconformidad de vecinos." *El Financiero*, Octubre 6.

Rodríguez De Romo, Ana Cecilia, and Gabriela Castañeda-López. 2013. "El Hospital Granja y La Escuela Granja Bernardino Álvarez: Antecedentes del Instituto Nacional de Neurología y Neurocirugía." *Revista de Investigación Clínica* 65 (6): 524–536.

Rodríguez, Ismael, director. 1947. *Nosotros los pobres*. Producciones Rodríguez Hermanos.

Rodríguez López, Yolanda. 1994. *Participación de la UIA en la comunidad de Santa Fe: Sistematización de la experiencia con el Consejo Popular Juvenil Ricardo Flores Magón*. México D.F.: Universidad Iberoamericana.

Rodó, José Enrique. (1900) 1988. *Ariel*. 1st ed. Austin: University of Texas Press.

Romero, Fernando, and Pablo León de la Barra. 2000. *ZMVM*. México, D.F.: LCM/Fernando Romero.

Rose, Gillian. 1993. *Feminism and Geography. The Limits of Geographical Knowledge*. Minneapolis, MN: University of Minnesota Press.

Roy, Ananya, and Aihwa Ong, eds. 2011. *Worlding Cities: Asian Experiments and the Art of Being Global*. Malden, MA: Wiley-Blackwell.

Rubenstein, Anne. 1997. *Bad Language, Naked Ladies, and Other Threats to the Nation: A Political History of Comic Books in Mexico*. Durham, NC: Duke University Press.

Ruiz-Palacios, Fanny. 2016. "Mujeres exigen un México seguro." *El Universal*, Abril 25. Accessed June 24, 2017. http://www.eluniversal.com.mx/articulo/metropoli/cdmx/2016/04/25/mujeres-exigen-frenar-violencia-de-genero#imagen-1

Sartre, Jean-Paul. 1940. *L'Imaginaire: Psychologie Phénoménologique de l'Imagination*, Paris: Gallimard.

Sassen, Saskia. (1991) 2001. *The Global City: New York, London, Tokyo*. Princeton, NJ: Princeton University Press.

Saussure, Ferdinand de. 1974. *Course in General Linguistics*. London: Fontana.

Schumpeter, Joseph. (1942) 1994. *Capitalism, Socialism and Democracy*. New York: Routledge.

Scott, James C. 1998. *Seeing Like a State: How Certain Schemes to Improve the Human Condition Have Failed*. New Haven: Yale University Press.

Scruggs, Gregory. 2017. "The People Power Behind Mexico City's New Constitution." *Citiscope*, February 3. Accessed June 28, 2017. https://www.citylab.com/politics/2017/02/the-people-power-behind-mexico-citys-new-constitution/515637/

———. 2016. "The Quito Papers: An intellectual counterpoint to the New Urban Agenda." *Citiscope,* October 20. Accessed June 28, 2017. http://citiscope.org/habitatIII/news/2016/10/quito-papers-intellectual-counterpoint-new-urban-agenda

Secretaría de Desarrollo Social (SEDESOL). N.d. "Informe annual sobre la situación de la pobreza y rezago social." n.d. Accessed June 21, 2017. http://www.gob.mx/cms/uploads/attachment/file/32197/Distrito_Federal_007.pdf

"Sendero Santa Fe: Condominios en altura." Accessed June 20, 2017. https://www.youtube.com/watch?v=9nLt6Tet35w

Sheinbaum, Diana. 2008. "Gated Communities in Mexico City: An Historical Perspective." *Urban Design International* 13: 241–52.

Shohamy, Elana, Eliezer Ben-Rafael, and Monica Barni. 2010a. "Introduction: An Approach to an 'Ordered Disorder.'" In *Linguistic Landscape in the City*, edited by Elana Shohamy, Eliezer Ben-Rafael, and Monica Barni, xi–xxvii. Toronto: Multilingual Matters.

———. 2010b. "Epilogue." In *Linguistic Landscape in the City*, edited by Elana Shohamy, Eliezer Ben-Rafael, and Monica Barni, 344–347. Toronto: Multilingual Matters.

Simmel, Georg. (1903) 1950. "The Metropolis and Mental Life." In *The Sociology of Georg Simmel*, edited and translated by Kurt H. Wolff, 409–426. New York: Free Press.

Sirvín, Mirna and Agustín Salgado. 2015. "Protestan En Coyoacán por supuesta desaparición de niños." *La Jornada*, Abril 20. Accessed June 22, 2017. http://www.jornada.unam.mx/ultimas/2015/04/20/protestan-en-coayoacan-por-desaparicion-de-ninos-4496.html

Sluis, Ageeth. 2016. *Deco City, Deco Body: Female Spectacle and Modernity in Mexico City, 1900–1939*. Lincoln: The University of Nebraska Press.

Soja, Edward. 1999. "Thirdspace: Expanding the Scope of the Geographical Imagination." In *Human Geography Today*, edited by Doreen Massey, John Allen and Philip Sarre, 260–278. Cambridge: Polity Press.

———. 2010. *Seeking Spatial Justice*. Minneapolis: University of Minnesota Press.

———. 2010. *Postmodern Geographies: The Reassertion of Space in Critical Social Theory*. New York: Verso.

Solnit, Rebecca. 2001. *Wanderlust: A History of Walking*. New York: Penguin Books.

———. 2010. *Infinite City: A San Francisco Atlas*. Berkeley: University of California Press.

Solnit, Rebecca and Joshua Jelly-Schapiro, eds. 2016. *Nonstop Metropolis: A New York City Atlas*. Berkeley: The University of California Press.

Steele, Cynthia. 1992. *Politics, Gender, and the Mexican Novel, 1968–1988: Beyond the Pyramid*. Austin: University of Texas Press.

Suárez, Gerardo. 2015. "Santo Domingo, Bastión En Punga." *El Universal, Abril* 29.

Swilling, Mark. 2013. "Contesting Inclusive Urbanism in a Divided City: The Limits to the Neoliberalisation of Cape Town's Energy System." *Urban Studies* 51 (15) (September): 3180–3197.

Tagg, John. 1988. *The Burden of Representation*. Amherst: University of Massachusetts Press.

———. 2000. *The Kingfisher Science Encyclopedia*. New York: Kingfisher.

Taylor, Charles. 2004. *Modern Social Imaginaries*. Durham: Duke University Press.

Taylor, Mark. 2001. *The Moment of Complexity: Emerging Network Culture*. Chicago: University of Chicago Press.

Tellechea, Samuel. 2010. "East of the Roundabout: Activating Space in the Town of Santa Fe, Mexico City." *Capstone Project*, Pratt Institute. Graduate Center for Planning and the Environment.

Tenorio-Trillo, Mauricio. 1996. "1910 Mexico City: Space and Nation in the City of the Centenario." *Journal of Latin American Studies* 28 (1): 75–104.

Tester, Keith, ed. 1994. *The Flâneur*. New York: Routledge.

Tsing, Anna. 2005. *Friction: An Ethnography of Global Connection*. Princeton, NJ: Princeton University Press.

———. 2013. "Sorting out Commodities: How Capitalist Value is Made Through Gifts." *HAU: Journal of Ethnographic Theory* 3 (1): 21–43.

UN Habitat. 2003. *The Challenge of the Slums: Global Report on Human Settlements 2003*. London: Earthscan.

———. 2016. "New Urban Agenda." Accessed June 28, 2017. Habitat3.org

Unruh, Vicky. 2006. *Performing Women and Modern Literary Culture in Latin America*. Austin: University of Texas Press.

Valenzuela, Alfonso. 2007. "Santa Fe (México): Megaproyectos para una ciudad dividida." *Cuadernos Geográficos* 40 (1): 53–66.

Valenzuela Arce, José Manuel. 2012. "I Have Seen the Writing on the Wall." In *Welcome amigos to Tijuana. Graffiti en la frontera*, edited by José Manuel Valenzuela Arce, 10–23. Mexico: CONACULTA.

Vasconcelos, José. (1925) 1979. *The Cosmic Race/La raza cósmica*. Translated by Didier T. Jaén. Baltimore, MD: Johns Hopkins University Press.

Vázquez, Noberto. 2016. "Todos ponen su pate." *Vértigo Político*, May 16. Accessed June 5, 2016. http://Vértigopolítico.com

Venkatesh, Vinod. 2015. "The Ends of Masculinity in Urban Space in Ana Clavel's *Los deseos y su sombra*." *Letras Hispánicas* 11: 158–170.

Vilaseca, Stephen Luis. 2012. "From Graffiti to Street Art: How Urban Artists are Democratizing Spanish City Centers and Streets." *Navigating through the Spanish Urban Space in the Twentieth and Twenty-First Centuries. Transitions: Journal of Franco-Iberian Studies* 8 (Fall): 9–34.

Villanueva, Carlos Avilez. 2005. "Introducción." In *Santa Fe: Crónica de una comunidad. Catálogo de exposición*, edited by Díaz Nava, María de Jesús, Gilberto Prado Galán, and Carlos Villanueva Avilez, 9–13. Ciudad de México: Universidad Iberoamericana.

Villoro, Juan. 1997. *Materia dispuesta*. México D.F.: Alfaguara.

Wakild, Emily. 2007. "Naturalizing Modernity: Urban Parks, Public Gardens and Drainage Projects in Porfirian Mexico City." *Mexican Studies/Estudios Mexicanos* 23 (1): 101–123.

Walser, Robert. (1917) 2012. *The Walk*. Translated by Susan Bernofsky. New York: New Directions.

Ward, Peter. 1978. "Self-Help Housing in Mexico City: Social and Economic Determinants of Success." *Town Planning Review* 49 (1): 38–50.

Whelan, Robbie. 2014. "Tony Mexico City Neighborhood Becomes a Cautionary Tale." *The Wall Street Journal*, June 3. Accessed June 16, 2017. http://www.wsj.com/articles/tony-mexico-city-neighborhood-becomes-a-cautionary-tale-1401838409

Williams, Raymond. 1977. *Marxism and Literature*. Oxford: Oxford University Press.

Winiarczyk-Raźniak, Anna, and Piotr Raźniak. 2014. "Ethnic Minorities in Ciudad de México (Distrito Federal)." *Procedia - Social and Behavioral Sciences* 120 (March): 90–97.

Woods, William K. 1971. "American Eye: Cities of Mexico: Old, New, and Dreamt of." *The North American Review* 256 (2): 2–6.

Yates, Frances A. 1966. *The Art of Memory*. Chicago: University of Chicago Press.

Yergin, Daniel. 2008. *The Prize: The Epic Quest for Oil, Money & Power*. New York: Free Press.

Yonhap News Agency. 2016. "S. Korea to Hold 1st Korean Culture Fete in Mexico City." December 2. Accessed July 3, 2017. http://english.yonhapnews.co.kr/nation al/2016/12/02/42/0301000000AEN20161202003400315F.html

Young, Alison. 2013. *Street Art, Public City: Law, Crime and the Urban Imagination* New York: Routledge.

Zarco, Francisco. 1968. *Escritos literarios*. México, DF: Porrúa.

Zibechi, Raúl. 2014. "Mexico: Challenges and Difficulties of Urban Territories in Resistance." In *Rethinking Latin American Social Movements: Radical Action from Below*, edited by Richard Stahler-Sholk, Harry Vanden, and Marc Becker, 49–65. Lanham, MD: Rowman & Littlefield.

Zapata, César Fernando. 2013. "Los inmigrantes en México: El otro lado de a moneda." *La Crónica*, Febrero 11. Accessed July 4, 2017. http://www.cronica. com.mx/notas/2004/103241.html

Zolov, Eric. 1999. *Refried Elvis: The Rise of the Mexican Counterculture*. Berkeley: University of California Press.

Zugman Dellacioppa, Kara. 2009. *This Bridge Called Zapatismo: Building Alternative Political Cultures in Mexico City, Los Angeles and Beyond*. Lanham, MD: Lexington Books.

Index

259

About the Editors and Contributors

EDITORS

Glen David Kuecker is a professor of history at DePauw University. He is coeditor of *Latin American Social Movements in the Twenty-first Century: Resistance, Power, and Democracy*. His current work explores the role of cities within the perfect storm of twenty-first century crises. More importantly, Kuecker is a die-hard supporter of the Chicago White Sox.

Alejandro Puga is an associate professor and the Laurel H. Turk professor of modern languages, and chair of modern languages at DePauw University. He is the author of *La ciudad novelada: estructura, retórica, y figuración*. He is co-editor of *María Luisa Puga y el espacio de la reconstrucción* with Carmen Patricia Tovar and Amanda L. Petersen. In his spare time, he consoles Glen Kuecker during the lesser moments of the Chicago White Sox.

CONTRIBUTORS

María Claudia André is a professor at Hope College, Holland, Michigan. She has published extensively on gender and Latin American studies. Her many publications include *Encyclopedia of Latin American Women Writers*, *The Woman in Latin American and Spanish Literature: Essays on Iconic Characters* and *Dramaturgas argentinas de los años 20*.

Charlotte Blair is a student in PhD program in anthropology at American University. Her current research interests include unplanned communities in

Latin America, the Caribbean, and the US Southwest, community organizing, and state development projects.

Jennifer L. Johnson is an associate professor of sociology at Kenyon College. Her research examines extralegal policing, informal justice administration and changing understandings of citizenship in Mexico and at the US-Mexico border. She is the author of multiple articles, book chapters and papers on social movements in the state of Guerrero, Mexico, and is coeditor of a book on social change in southern Mexico. She is currently working on an ethnography of the gender dynamics of the extralegal border patrol movement at the US-Mexico border.

Glen David Kuecker is a professor of history at DePauw University. He is coeditor of *Latin American Social Movements in the Twenty-first Century: Resistance, Power, and Democracy*. His current work explores the role of cities within the perfect storm of twenty-first century crises. More importantly, Kuecker is a die-hard supporter of the Chicago White Sox.

Shannan Mattiace is a professor of political science and international studies at Allegheny College. She is author of *To See With Two Eyes: Peasant Activism and Indian Autonomy in Chiapas, Mexico*, co-editor of *Mayan Lives, Mayan Utopias*, and continuing editor of the Mexican politics section of the *Handbook of Latin American Studies*.

Patrick O'Connor is an associate professor of Hispanic studies and comparative literature at Oberlin College. He is the author of *Latin American Literature and the Narratives of the Perverse* (Palgrave Macmillan 2004) and co-editor of *Latin American Icons* (Vanderbilt University Press, 2014). His current research is on the posthumous oeuvre and reputation of Julio Cortázar and Roberto Bolaño.

Alejandro Puga is an associate professor and the Laurel H. Turk Professor of modern languages, and chair of modern languages at DePauw University. He is the author of *La ciudad novelada: estructura, retórica, y figuración*. He is coeditor of *María Luisa Puga y el espacio de la reconstrucción* with Carmen Patricia Tovar and Amanda L. Petersen. In his spare time, he consoles Glen Kuecker during the lesser moments of the Chicago White Sox.

V. Daniel Rogers is a professor of Spanish and hispanic studies at Wabash College, where he also chairs the Division of Humanities and Fine Arts. With particular interests in contemporary Latin American literature and culture, Rogers has published extensively on Ecuadorian and literature. In this chapter, he turns to a new interest in mid-twentieth century Mexican film and culture.

Marta Sierra is a professor of Spanish at Kenyon College. Her areas of research include geocriticism, urban studies, women's studies and postcolonial studies. She has published on the intersections between literature and geography, *Gender Spaces in Argentinean Women's Literature* (Palgrave-Mcmillan, 2011) and *Geografías imaginarias: espacios de resistencia y crisis en América Latina* (Cuarto Propio 2014). She is currently working on a book project on the intersections between artistic maps and literature in Latin America.

Carmen Patricia Tovar is an affiliated scholar at Oberlin College. Her research focuses on historical spaces as symbolic places of intersection of collective memory and subjectivity in contemporary Mexican urban novels. She is coeditor, with Alejandro Puga and Amanda Petersen, of *María Luisa Puga y el espacio de la reconstrucción.*

Karen Velasquez is director of experiential learning and an anthropologist of education at the University of Dayton. She is interested in how people learn and educate each other in school, work, and other social contexts. She is also interested in cultural/linguistic diversity, and the experiences of Latin American and Asian immigrants in the United States and Latin America. In her current position, she develops communities of practice around experiential learning and studies the ways students integrate, synthesize, and make meaning of their educational experiences both inside and beyond the classroom.